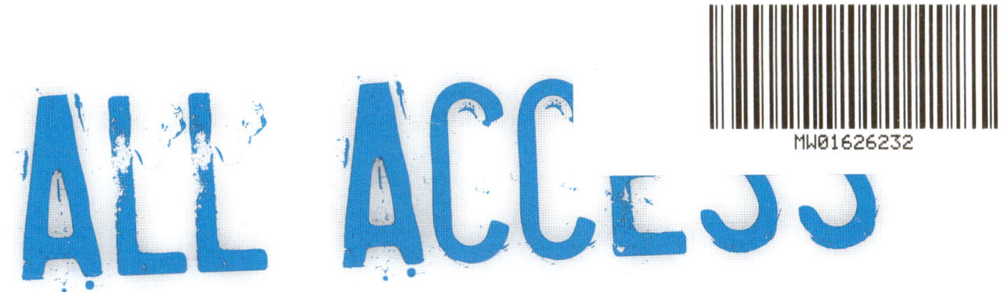

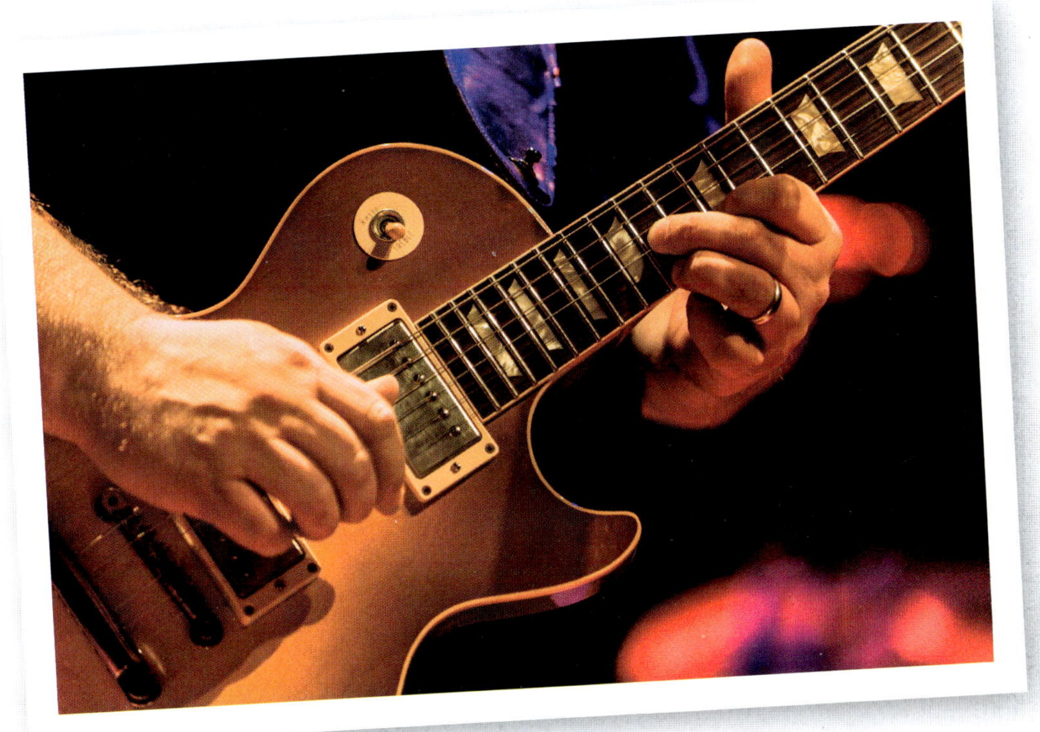

YOUR BACKSTAGE PASS TO CONCERT PHOTOGRAPHY

Alan Hess

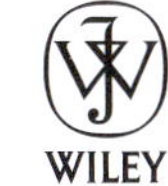

John Wiley & Sons, Inc.

All Access: Your Backstage Pass to Concert Photography

Published by
John Wiley & Sons, Inc.
10475 Crosspoint Boulevard
Indianapolis, IN 46256

Published simultaneously in Canada

ISBN: 978-1-118-17290-2

Manufactured in the United States of America

10 9 8 7 6 5 4 3 2 1

For general information on our other products and services or to obtain technical support, please contact our Customer Care Department within the U.S. at (877) 762-2974, outside the U.S. at (317) 572-3993 or fax (317) 572-4002.

Wiley also publishes its books in a variety of electronic formats and by print-on-demand. Some content that appears in standard print versions of this book may not be available in other formats. For more information about Wiley products, visit us at www.wiley.com.

Library of Congress Control Number: 2011945000

ABOUT THE AUTHOR

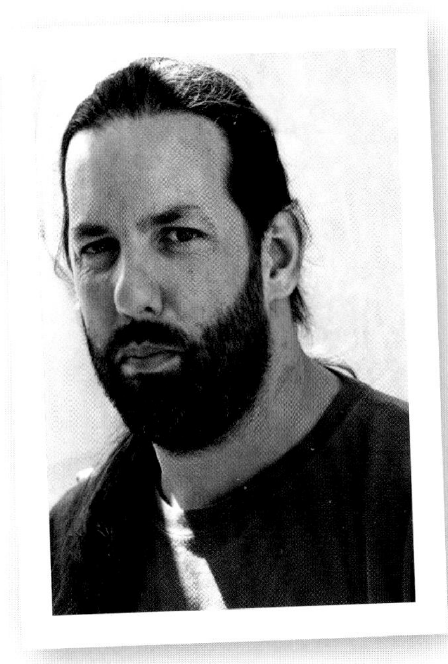

Alan Hess is a concert and event photographer based in San Diego, California, where he lives with his wife and two rescued boxers. He has photographed a huge variety of acts, including some of the biggest names in music.

Alan is the author of seven other books, including the *Exposure Digital Field Guide* and the *Composition Digital Field Guide*, the *Night and Low Light Photography Photo Workshop* and the *iPad Fully Loaded* series. He has been a contributor to *Photoshop User Magazine*, writing articles on Photoshop and Concert Photography.

Alan has been a part of the Photoshop World Instructor Dream Team since 2009 for which he has taught Concert and Event Photography and the Basics of Exposure and Composition.

You can follow Alan at his website www.alanhessphotography.com, where he writes a semi-regular blog, or on Twitter, where he goes by ShotLivePhoto. You can also find Alan on Google+ at http://goo.gl/RmLyw.

CREDITS

Acquisitions Editor
Courtney Allen

Project Editor
Jenny Larner Brown

Technical Editor
Allen Ross Thomas

Copy Editor
Jenny Larner Brown

Editorial Director
Robyn Siesky

Business Manager
Amy Knies

Senior Marketing Manager
Sandy Smith

Vice President and Executive Group Publisher
Richard Swadley

Vice President and Executive Publisher
Barry Pruett

Book Designer
Erik Powers

ACKNOWLEDGMENTS

This book was not an easy undertaking, and there are a lot of different people I need to thank.

First, I need to thank my parents for taking me to my first concert. Thank you for your love and support all these years.

Then there are the bands I hung out with during my college years—guys who remain my friends to this day: Ron Hansen, Jeff Mandolfo, and the rest of guys in BN who rocked out every weekend. Some of my first bar concert shots are of these guys.

Matt, Rob, Gary, Andrews (both of them), Peter, and Chris—the Cardiff Reefers. I still remember photographing you guys on the stage of the Belly Up Tavern way back when. You gave me a real education of what it was like to be a band on the road.

Rich, tour manager and straight shooter, thank you for treating me as a professional. In return, I make sure never to disappoint you by acting like anything else. If only there were more like you.

This book would not have been possible without the great folks at Wiley, including my acquisitions editor Courtney, who fought for this book for years. Thank you for giving me the opportunity to write it. To Jenny, who tries to keep me on track; I know how hard this is to do. Thank you for the late nights and hard work. A big thanks to Erik for the amazing design work and long hours getting it just right. This book needed to have a technical editor, and I got one of the best concert photographers I know to cover my ass. Allen Ross Thomas functioned as the technical editor, and I got him to contribute a Pro Tip as well. Thank you, Allen.

That brings me to the other Pro Tip contributors—photographers, photo editors, publicists, managers, lighting directors, and even musicians themselves. I can't thank you all enough: Billy, Dennis, Heidi, Allen, Maile, Scott, Drew, Hali, Bob, Susana, Groove, Charles, Chelsea, Jay, Brad, and Mark. You made this book so much better with your contributions.

To all the band members, crew, and management staff that have allowed me access over the years, THANK YOU!

Thanks to Brian Ross and Ashley Anton for the access they've provided me to shoot some of the coolest shows and events ever.

To Scott Kelby, who gave me the opportunity to bring my concert photography knowledge to the attendees at Photoshop World, and to the Kelby training subscribers, thank you. It means the world to me.

To my wife, who puts up with the crazy hours and weird schedule, I love you and couldn't do what I do without you.

For Nadra

TABLE OF CONTENTS

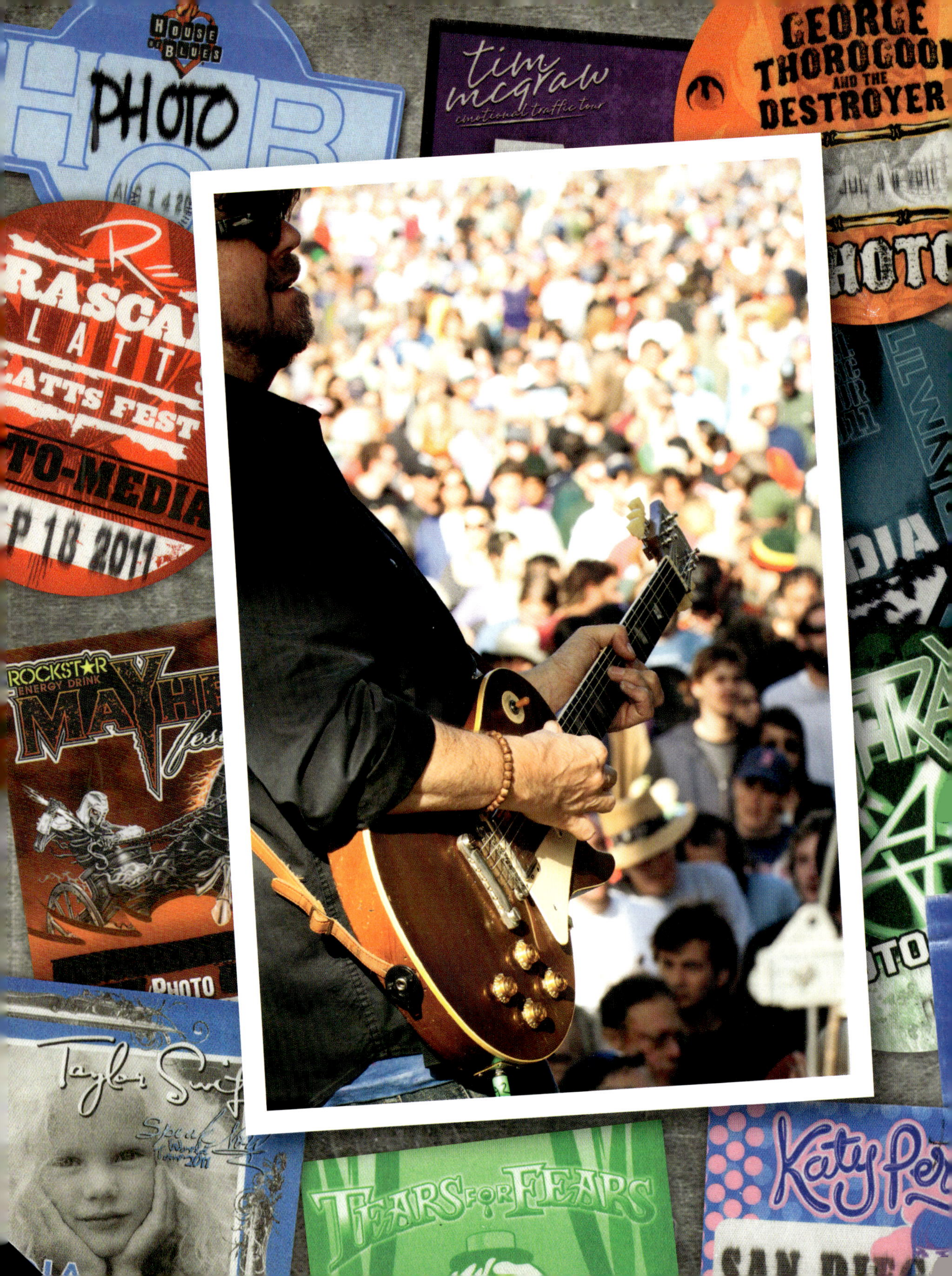
HOUSE OF BLUES
PHOTO
tim mcgraw
emotional traffic tour
GEORGE
AND THE
DESTROYER
ROCKSTAR
ENERGY DRINK
PHOTO
TEARS FOR FEARS

INTRODUCTION

The research for this book was the most fun I've ever had. That's because instead of coming up with an idea for a book and then executing it, I've been living this information and advice by photographing concerts since the late 1980s.

While it started out as a fun thing to do on weekends, concert photography has become my full-time job. And I couldn't be happier about it.

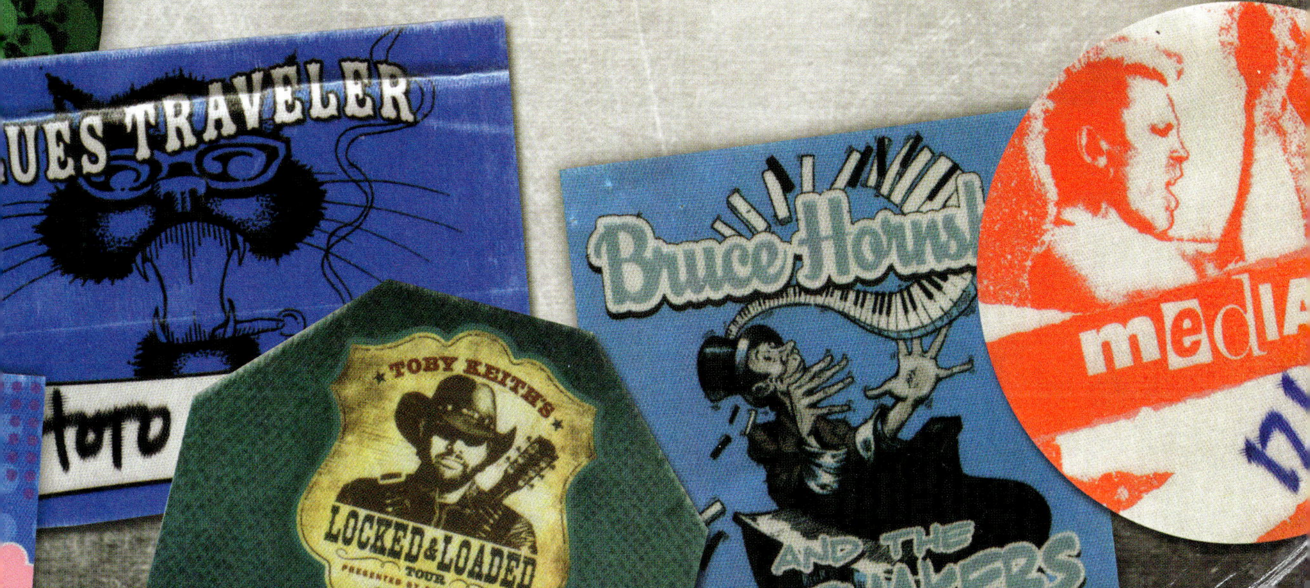

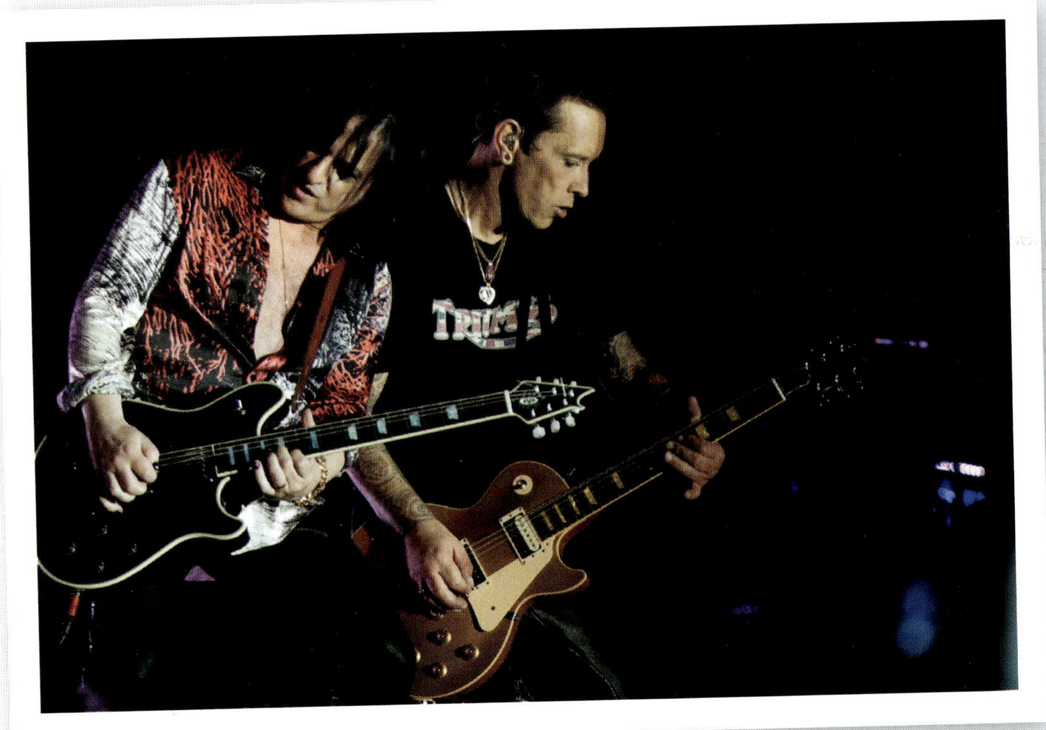

Guitarists Steve Stevens and Billy Morrison photographed in late 2011while on tour with Billy Idol.
Taken at 1/400 second, f/2.8, and ISO 1600

I've spent many, many nights photographing in bars and shooting in clubs; countless hours crouched in front of stages at performance halls and large concert venues; and I've walked hundreds of miles at all-day festivals.

And I've loved every minute of it. Seriously. There's just something really special about this genre of photography. Even at its worst—when it gets frustrating or stressful or crowded or whatever—it's still pretty awesome. Concert photographers get to do what most people only wish they could. It's a great job.

Even now, with hundreds of thousands of concert images generated over the last twenty years or so—from photographing my friends' bands in local bars, covering festivals for local promoters, and shooting big shows for venues—I still love the feeling I get when the house lights go down and the band takes the stage.

The book you're holding in your hands is something I've wanted to write for a long time. It covers a wide variety of topics, including the most common concert photography questions I get, which are basically variations of how to get a photo pass, what's the best camera/ lenses, and what settings to use in different types of venues.

This book also offers specific tips and insight for shooting in bars, clubs, halls, and even major arenas, where the big rock and roll shows happen. There are even chapters that can help you shoot backstage and on the stage and deal with different types of music. Post production techniques and step-by-step information on how to copyright your images are here, too.

As a bonus, since the concert photography business is so complex, I reached out to people in the business and got their take on certain aspects of concert photography. A great variety of folks took time out of their busy schedules to answer my questions and contribute to this book, making it not just a single point of view but a complete guide to succeeding at concert photography. I hope you'll find value in the insight that these tested professionals have provided.

The Pro Tips start in Chapter 1 with insight from guitarist (and a subject of many of my shoots), Billy Morrison. Pro Tips continue in Chapter 2, where publicists Dennis McNally and Heidi Ellen Robinson-Fitzgerald give their unique perspectives on photo credentials.

Chapter 3 covers working as a pro photographer—what to do and what not to do. Atlanta-based concert photographer Allen Ross Thomas weighs in here with his concert shooting tips, and band manager/tour manager Maile Hatfield offers some advice as well.

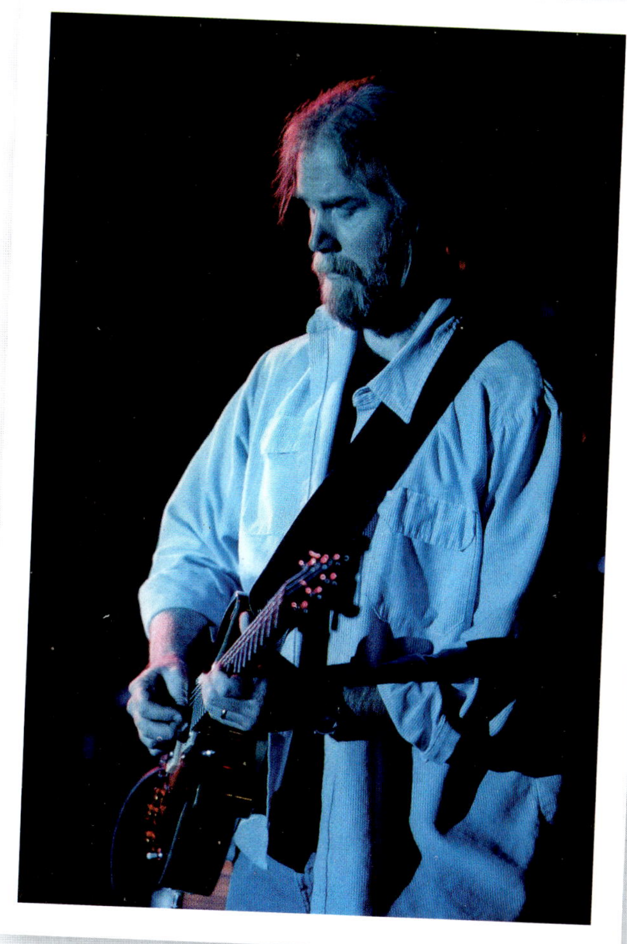

Jimmy Herring performing with Jazz is Dead before becoming the lead guitarist for Widespread Panic. Exposure setting not recorded.

Chapter 4 is all about the gear you need to do this work in a variety of shooting situations, including the best lenses for the job. Scott Diussa, concert photographer and my co-instructor for the Kelby Training Concert class, offers great insight here.

Chapter 5 gives an important overview of the basics of exposure settings, especially how they relate to concert photography. Shutter speed, aperture, and ISO are covered along with exposure modes and metering modes. Concert photographer Drew Gurian lends his advice in this chapter.

After exposure, we cover composition in Chapter 6. Focus, timing, emotion, and the different instruments of a band are all addressed here. Hali McGrath, concert photographer and photo editor, offers her voice and pro tips here.

Chapter 7 launches the venue-specific chapters with the place in which most of us start: bars. Bob Minkin, San Francisco-based photographer and designer offers his take on this shooting environment.

Chapter 8 ups the ante a little with information on photographing in your local club. It includes pro tips by Susana Millman, a concert and dance photographer, with whom I've shared many a photo pit.

The bigger and brighter concert halls are covered in Chapter 9. Lighting Director Groove explains his approach to lighting a stage, which can help you figure out how to time the lights to your advantage..

Chapter 10 hits the big time. This focuses on the bigger shows—the rock spectacle—and there's no one better to give advice on shooting here than Charles Jischke, a concert photographer who's spent the last few years on the road with Billy Idol.

Find information on photographing all-day or multi-day festivals in Chapter 11. Chelsea Lauren, a southern California wire service photographer who photographs festivals on a regular basis, lends her thoughts on this topic. On a personal note, I think it's great that she agreed to do this while we were in a photo pit at a festival.

Chapter 12 contains tips for those coveted occasions when you get to shoot backstage or side stage, and there's no one I know who spends as much time backstage and on stage photographing as Jay Blakesburg. He offers terrific insight to how to photograph in these situations.

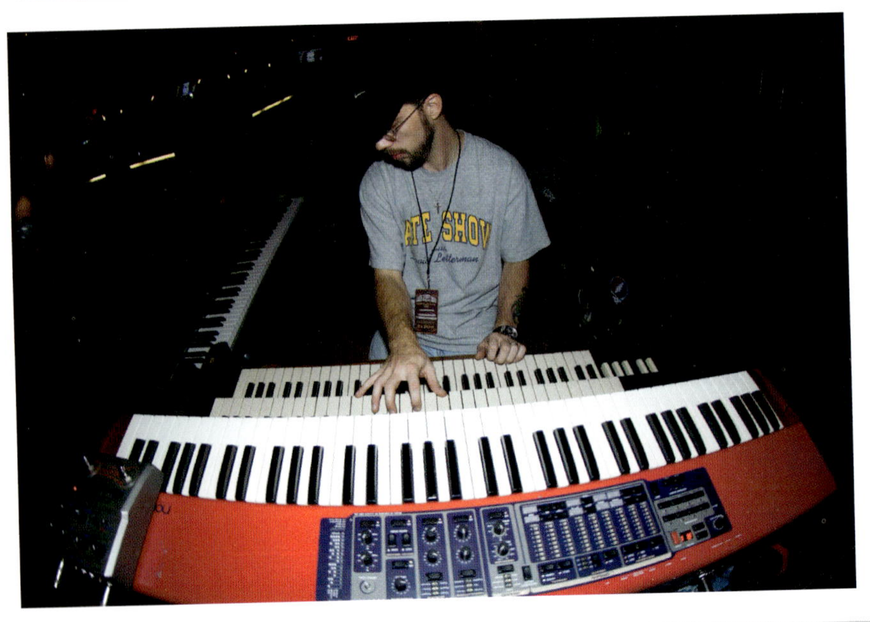

John Ginty warms up before a show. Using a fisheye lens and getting in close gives the image a little different perspective.

Taken at 1/80 second, f/2.8, and ISO 100

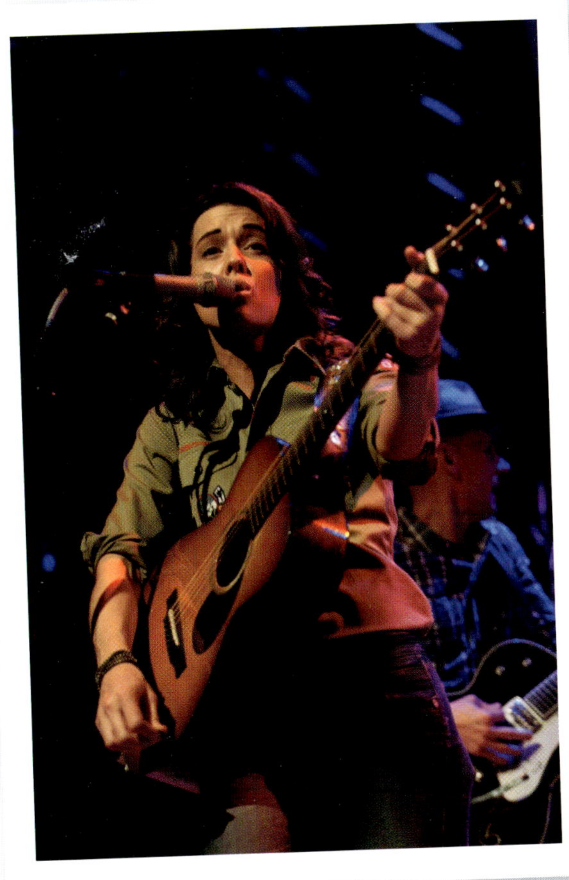

Brandi Carlile performs in San Diego.
Taken at 1/160 second, f/2.8, and ISO 1600

Similarities in the different types of music and what you can probably expect and look for when dealing with various types of musicians is packed into Chapter 13. Friend and concert photographer Brad Moore shares his thoughts here.

In Chapter 14, find information on post production, capped off with helpful tips from musician Mark Karan. I feel privileged to call Mark a friend, but before he was a friend, he was a subject. Want to know what a musician looks for in photographs of their performances? Well, this is the place to find out.

There are also three appendices; they cover Accessories, Copyright, and Resources.

Before we really get started though, I want to say something about the images used in this book. Some of these photos are my favorites, and they hang as prints my house; others are used because they illustrate a point well. But the one thing that all these images have in common is that I am legally allowed to use them. Many were taken at shows, where I was given permission by the band to use them for my own purposes. And I shot them with an All Access laminate, Working Pass, or Photo Pass in hand … and without signing a release. Others were taken when I worked for a wire service, and those image are still for sale on the PR Photo website.

What you don't (and won't) see in this book are images I've taken that came with a restrictive photo release. Many of these releases allowed for the images to be used for a specific publication or venue. For example, recently photographed performances by Katy Perry and Taylor Swift … to name just two. And while I love the photos, none are used here because they were shot specifically for the venue and not for this project.

But back to what is here. This book provides tips and information on how to shoot concert images and get the best results every time. This is not a coffee table book or a book of concert images to be paged through and admired. I hope you will use, read, mark, dog-ear, and highlight this book … and use the information to improve your career as a professional concert photographer.

Ready? Let's go.

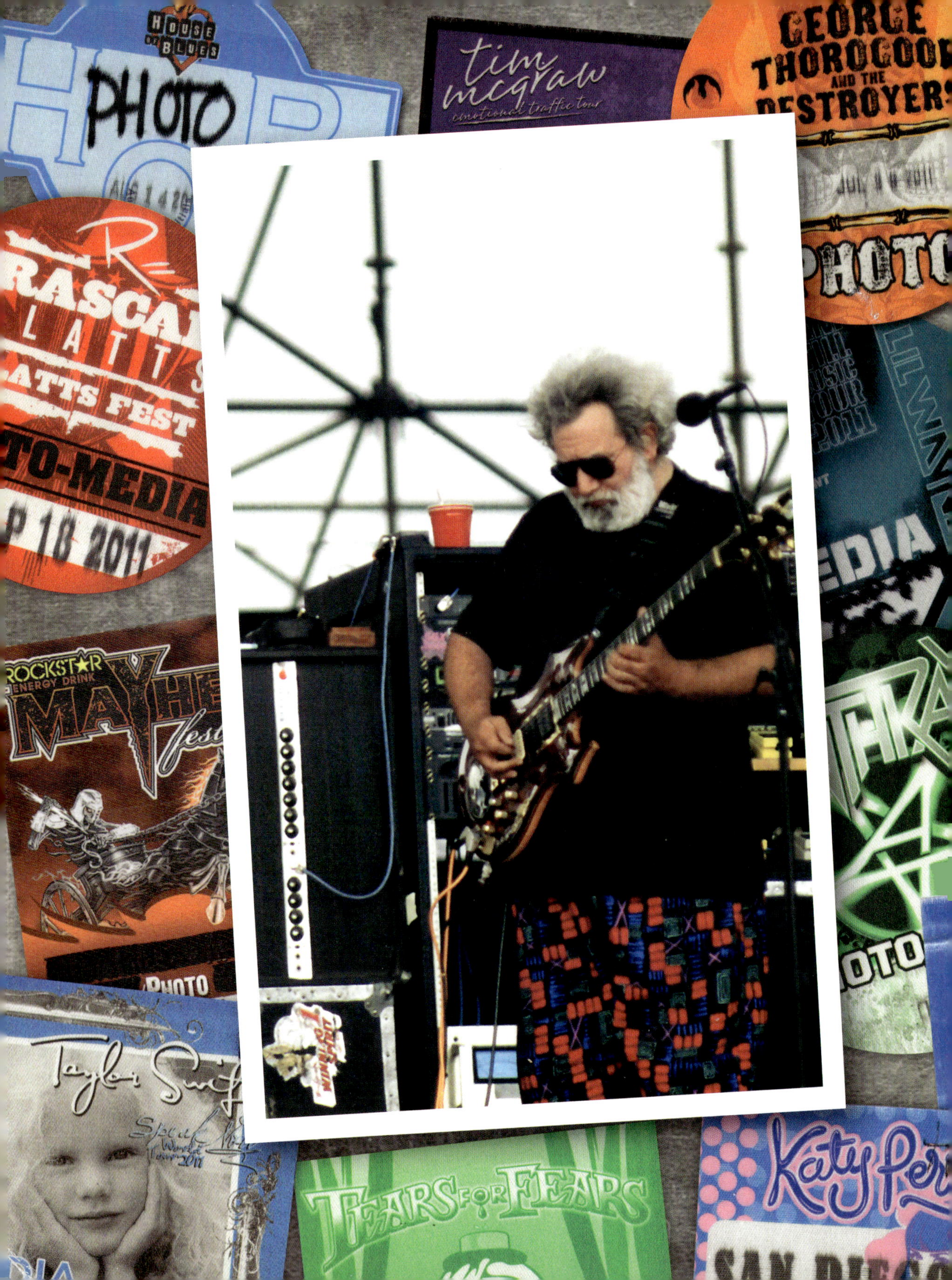

HOUSE OF BLUES
PHOTO
tim mcgraw
emotional traffic tour
GEORGE
AND THE
ATTS FEST
ROCKSTAR
ENERGY DRINK
PHOTO
TEARS FOR FEARS

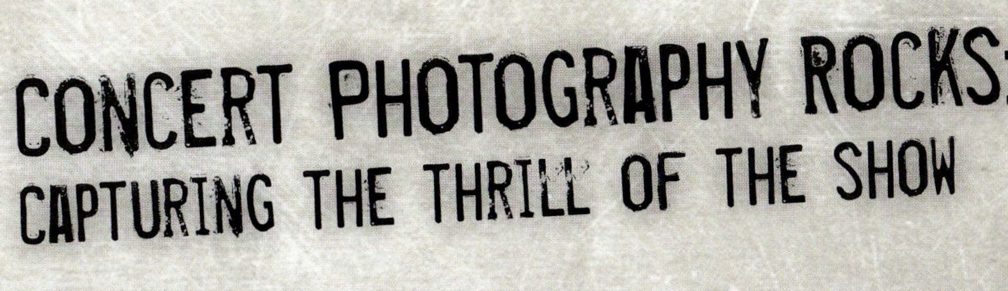

1 CONCERT PHOTOGRAPHY ROCKS: CAPTURING THE THRILL OF THE SHOW

Being in a photo pit at a cool venue when the house lights go down and the musicians take the stage is one of the most exciting moments in a photographer's career. The show is going to start right now. There are no second chances.

Am I ready? Are you?

Ready, that is, for the most challenging and exhilarating time of your life... in 10- to 15-minute increments?

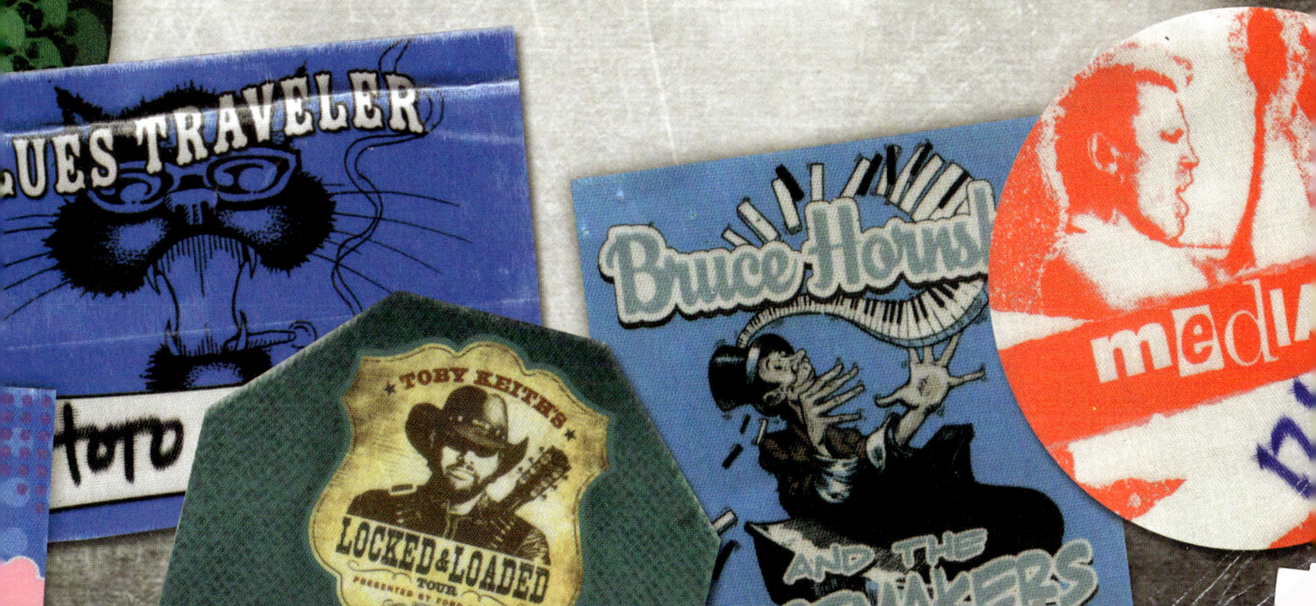

Even after years of shooting concerts, I still feel nervous at that moment, when there is no turning back, when the crowd starts to cheer, and the first notes ring out from the stage. It doesn't matter if it's a band down at the local bar or big-name act in a 20,000-seat amphitheater, the feeling is the same for me. It's another concert shoot, another opportunity to capture the thrill of the show.

PICTURE A MUSICAL JOURNEY.

Let me back up a little here and start at the beginning. My interest in performance photography started with the music, especially the live show. I grew up in a home where there was a lot of radio and little television. That wasn't because my parents didn't believe in television or wanted to deprive their children. On the contrary, they gave us kids a great childhood. But I grew up in South Africa in the 1970s, and there just wasn't any television … at all.

When television finally came to Capetown, it was 1976. I was already eight years old and had been listening to my radio for years. I had a green radio with a big dial on the front that you had to turn to tune in the stations. I had made little marks on the dial to show where the best reception was for my favorite stations. Man, I loved that radio. And I grew up listening to it a lot—listening to *music* on the radio. And I grew up in a family that liked music, especially rock and roll.

Then, on August 28, 1983, at the age of fifteen, I went to my first really big concert. I had been listening to Simon and Garfunkel for many years, and now I was going to see them perform those hit songs live! It was amazing. And as I sit here in late 2011 writing this, I can still close my eyes and see that stage out there in the middle of the field at Jack Murphy Stadium. The energy was incredible. From then on, I was hooked on concerts. Simple as that. And to this day I would rather listen to a live recording than a studio album, and I'd rather go to a concert than just about anything else.

It was during my time in college that the experience of seeing live music and the art of photography started to merge together for me. I was looking for classes that would fill my art requirements, and photography looked like it might be fun. I signed up for the Intro to Photography class.

I wish I could say that I had a great teacher who inspired me or took me under his wing and showed me the ropes, but that just wasn't the case. I sat in the back of the class and did the bare minimum to get by. But there was something about how photography allowed me to combine the very technical and logical controls of shutter speed and aperture with the creative side of composition to produce compelling images.

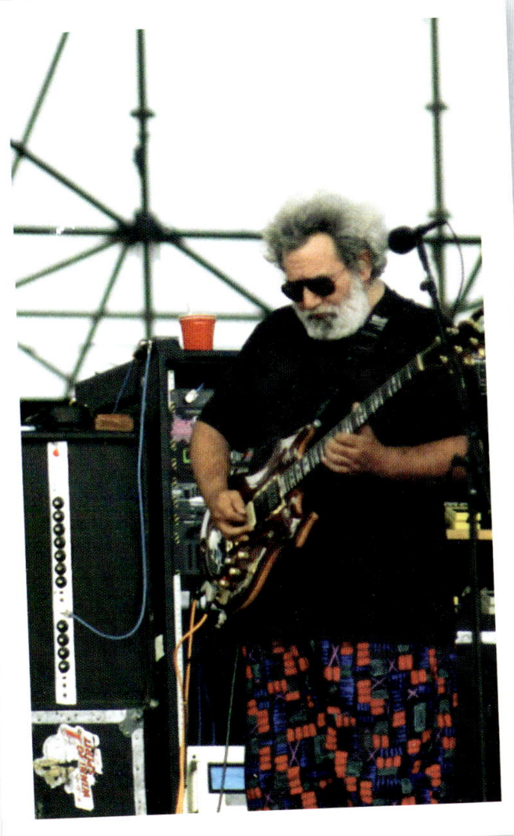

To me photography seemed to be art for people with logical thinking, and that suited me just fine. But it wasn't until I took my camera to a concert that real passion entered the picture. That was back in the mid 80s, and there was this little band called the Grateful Dead … with a very liberal camera policy.

Anyone could take a camera into the band's concerts and shoot all the photos (s)he wanted … as long as you didn't disturb the fans (also affectionately known as *Deadheads*). So I took my camera to a Grateful Dead concert and caught a very bad case of concert photography fever.

Around that same time, a friend started playing in a local band every weekend at a bar. I went along because it was fun. I took my camera once in a while and photographed the band under the stage lights. And there was very little pressure on me to produce

This is one of the only photos that I still have from my days of photographing the Grateful Dead from the audience. Back then, it was tough to keep track of the negatives and prints. This was before the digital age, when copies of images can be created with the push of a button and stored easily on the Internet.

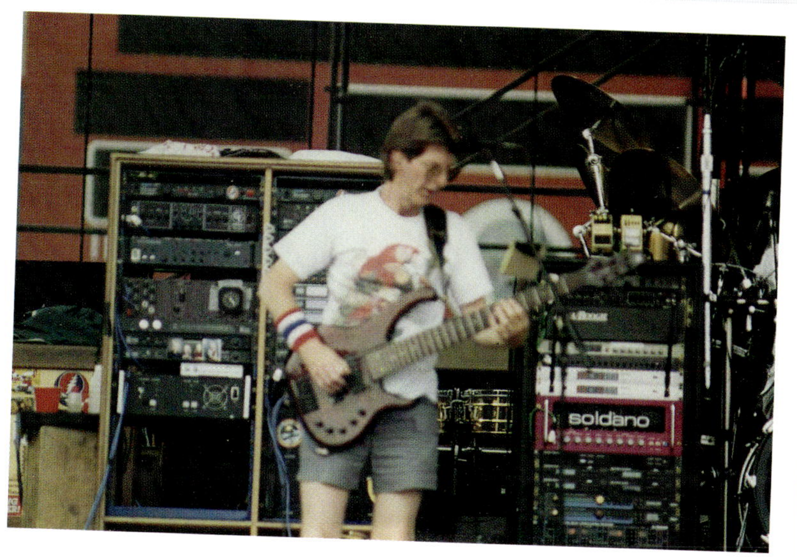

I was sure that I got Phil Lesh in focus when I took this, but with no way to check the image before developing it, I didn't know for sure. Imagine my surprise when I got this back from the developer to see that my focus was off.

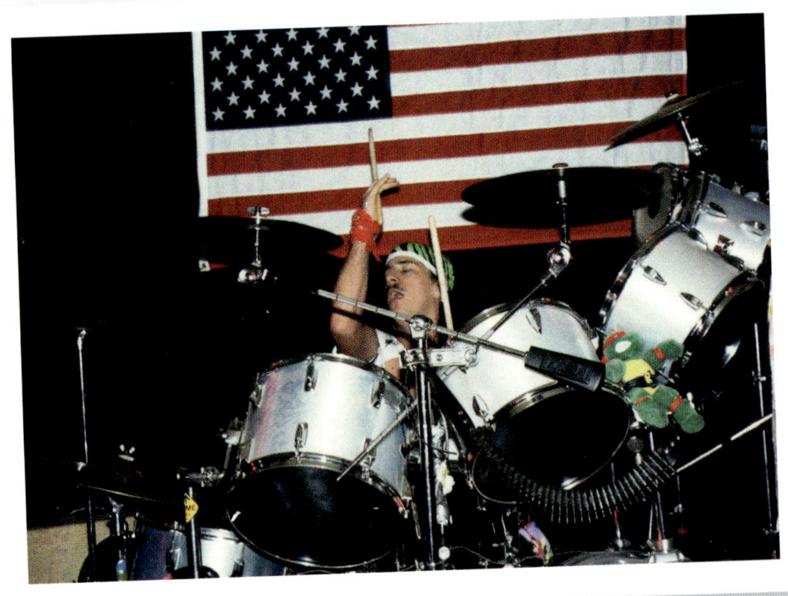

Here's my buddy Ron behind the drums in college.

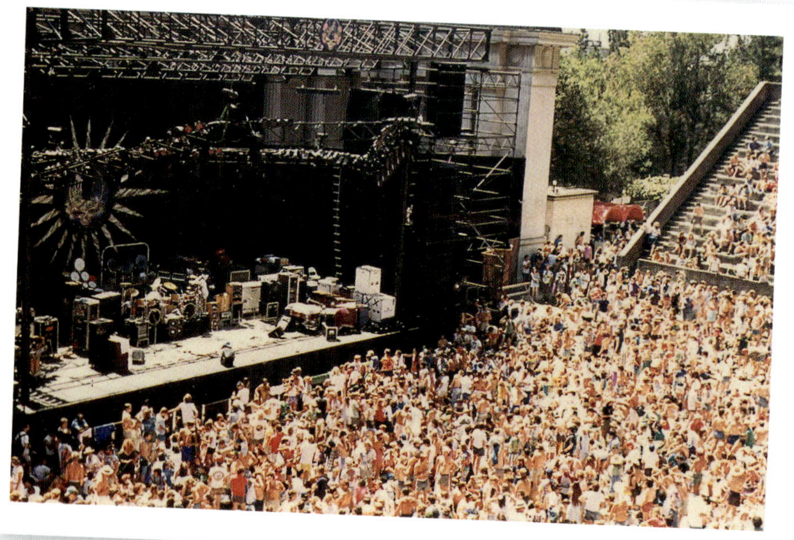

This was my usual spot for taking photos. It got frustrating to shoot from the crowd, even though cameras were allowed.

any kind of results. My buddies were just happy to see themselves performing in any photos. I know that seems strange now, but this was before there were cameras in everyone's cell phone. Actually, it was before everyone … or *anyone* … even had a cell phone. So casual photos weren't rampant as they are today.

Eventually, I started to get frustrated with taking my camera to shows and shooting from the audience. I wanted to get closer, a lot closer, to the performance! During these years, I should tell you, I was sneaking my camera into shows that didn't allow photography. I was a rebel, a rule breaker, and it was pretty easy to shoot my bootleg photos. Of course, this was before venues had metal detectors at the doors.

Well, this frustration finally motivated me to request permission to take photos of some bands. I heard a lot of no's, but finally a yes and then another yes. And soon, the number of yes replies outnumbered the no's! It was thrilling.

Then two things happened that would change my life. But, of course, I didn't know it at the time. These chance encounters just prove the value of always acting professionally and being nice to the people around you. You never know what might happen down the line and who will eventually really matter to your future. I'll run through the two events in the order that they happened.

IT'S WHO YOU KNOW.

The first of the two events happened because I had started listening to a certain band during my last few years of college. The band was called the Cardiff Reefers. They played reggae around San Diego and toured around the country a couple of times.

I saw them play so many times when I was home in San Diego on breaks from school that I became friends with the guys in the band. I even went on the road with them a few times. I usually had a camera with me and would take a couple of photos at their shows. Sadly, they disbanded in 1995 and went onto other careers, got married, and so forth. I lost touch with them. But then Facebook came along, and we got back in touch.

Well, it turns out that the lead guitar player now works for a company that does large format printing, and one of his clients is a large concert venue that was looking for a new house photographer. He suggested me!

You never know who can help you later in your career, so make sure you treat everyone with respect, and always act professionally.

I now count that venue among my clients and I've shot a variety of acts there, including Taylor Swift, Katy Perry, and Ricky Martin—all for the house. I never would've known about the job if not for my connection to the Cardiff Reefers and lead guitarist Matt Hale.

Now I know this might seem like nothing but luck, but there is more to it than that. It shows you how important it is to make connections with the musicians you're shooting when you can. Obviously this is much easier when they're just starting out than when they're already famous. So treat the local bands well. You never know where they'll end up. And even if they don't become the next big rock band, they just might end up in a position to help you anyway.

The second chance meeting that ended up being a real career-changer for me started at a three-day concert put on by a local promoter. When I found out about the show, I contacted the promoter and asked for full access to photograph the event. For that privilege, I offered him a selection of photos from the event to use for promotional purposes for future events.

The promoter took me up on the offer and the three days went by really fast. When the event was over, I gave him a selection of the images, and he liked them. We stayed in contact. Years later, that same promoter went to work for a big venue and needed a photographer. He called me. Because of that connection, I've photographed acts that range from the Smashing Pumpkins to Robin Williams.

Keep in mind that the reason this guy called me when he needed a professional photographer was because I acted like a professional when we worked together. It wasn't a big festival he put on back then, but it was important to him and to the musicians. And, for those reasons alone, it was important to me.

Yet neither of these relationships developed overnight. They took years of interaction. So remember that a good first impression is invaluable; equally important is protecting a good reputation with solid performance as a professional.

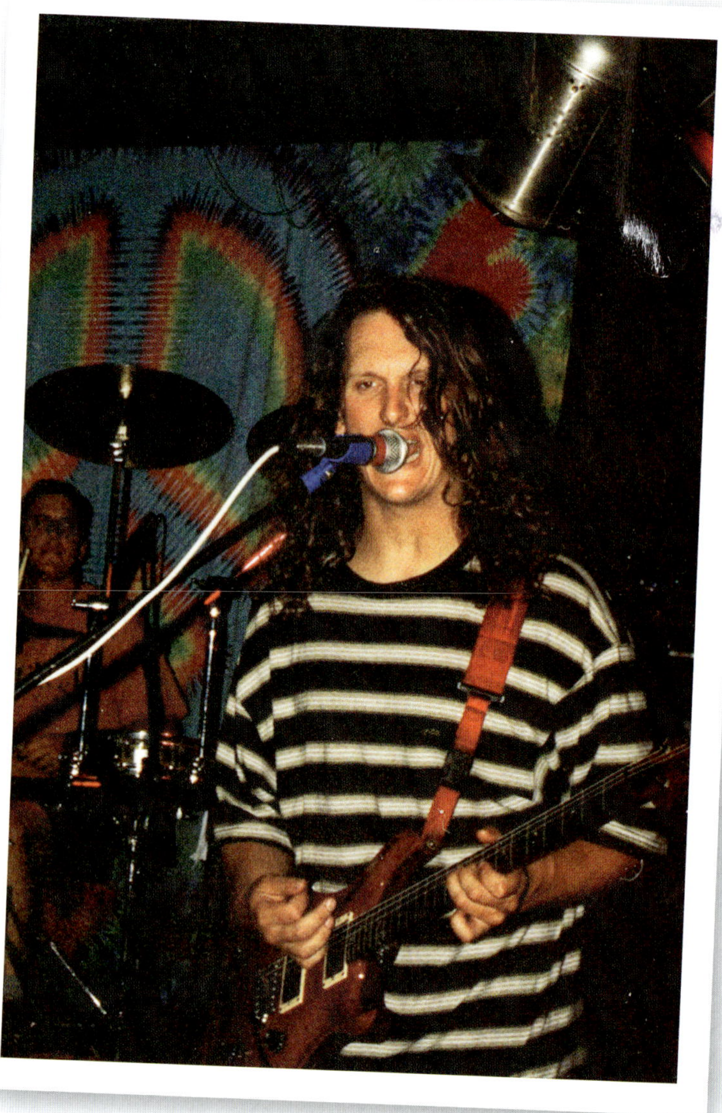

I photographed Matt Hale on guitar back when I was just starting out.

BE READY FOR THE PRESSURE.

As you begin to work for others, the pressure on you to get great shots increases significantly. There's definitely more pressure on my performance now than when I was starting out, because the images I take are no longer just for me and my own enjoyment. They're usually for a website or a wire service or a venue. In some cases, my images go directly to the band members

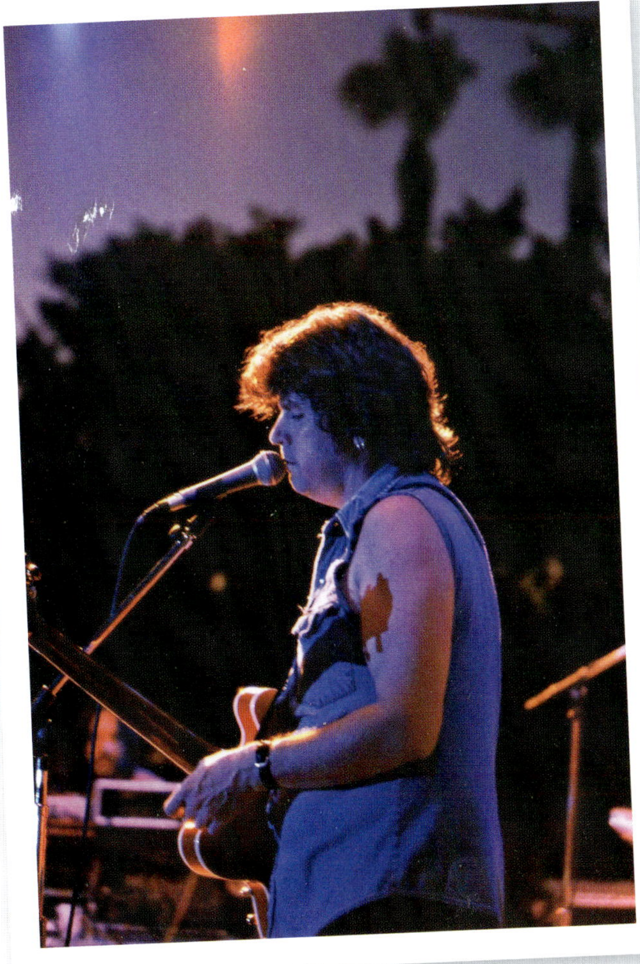

This is the very first time I photographed Mark Karan, and it was during a three-day show put on by a local promoter. I sent a copy of this photo (and others of the show) to Mark along with my contact information shortly after the concert. He liked them, and I now count Mark Karan among my close friends.

themselves. That can be a little stressful. The photos need to be great in many ways.

So nowadays, when the music starts and the band is ready to go, I know I need to capture images that are technically perfect and portray the energy of the show—no matter what's happening with the lighting or if there's a real photo pit or how much (or little) time there is to shoot.

Being a successful professional concert photographer means getting the shot every time … without fail … no matter what the conditions. That's tough. And it's why I wrote this book. I want to share with you some experience and advice that I didn't have when I was starting out. This is important to me, because I don't think this information should be secret or hidden.

When I was getting started in this line of work, there weren't any concert photography books or training. And many of the photographers I met back then were not very keen on sharing their settings or insights. But being able to pass along the insights I've gained from my experience helps to strengthen the business of concert photography. Informed photographers take better pictures and leave a better impression. And, on a selfish note, I hope that my tips will create a better working environment in the photo pit, where more photographers are polite to each other and work together better in this amazing place … even when it gets stressful.

Honestly, when you look at concert photography logically, it isn't very appealing. The craft requires you to beg for permission to take your photos and, at times, there's a release form that seriously limits how you can use the photos you take. You have no control over the lighting; no control over the subjects; and very little control over where you'll be positioned when you shoot. And there are no second chances to make it right if you blow it.

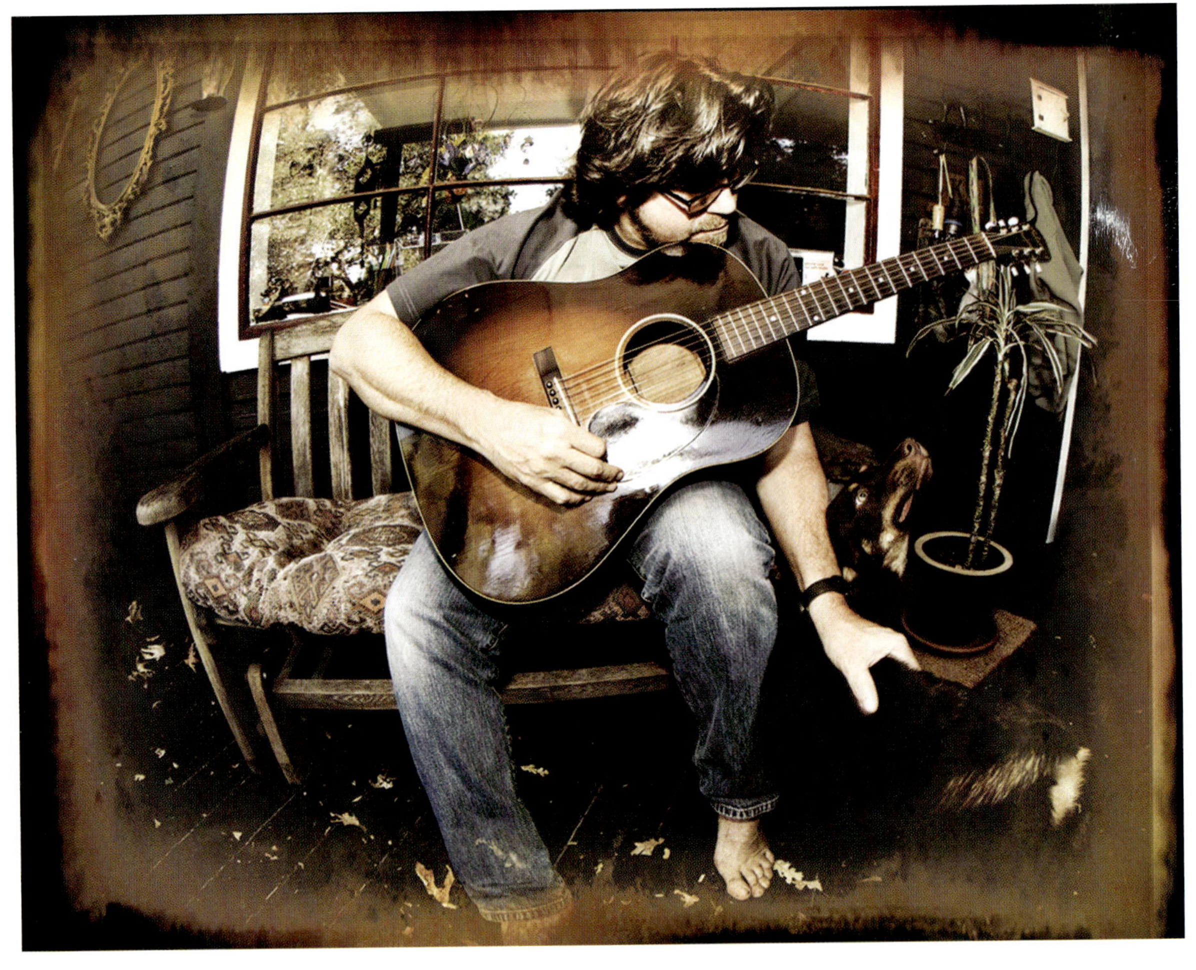

This photo of Mark Karan was taken years after my first shot of him, and it was used as the back cover of his *Walk Through the Fire* album. This shot would have never happened if not for those photos I took—and shared—back at that three-day festival.

So perhaps the one thing all concert photographers have in common is an ability to ignore all the negatives and stay focused on getting great shots of a music performance.

But it's not always easy. There've been many times, after really looking forward to photographing a certain act, that I've left the photo pit frustrated, slightly angry, and disappointed after the three-song shooting time. Sometimes it's because the lighting was all green or red; other times it's because the lead singer hid from the audience the whole time. In fact, at a recent show, the lead singer decided he was shy and asked that the lights be turned down to near darkness for the first song!

I'm just saying that you need to be prepared to work hard and feel frustrated to do this work. Photo pits are sometimes overcrowded to the bursting point, and maybe the photographer next to you will keep moving in front of you with his camera held over his head, trying to get really up close and personal with the band. Whatever the specific situation, concert photography is a tough and unpredictable way to work. And it takes a certain level of patience, fortitude, and skill to do it well.

IT'S A BALANCING ACT.

The world of concert photography is a tricky balancing act. There's a need to find balance in the soft skills of photography, like listening to the music and detaching from it enough to capture the visual aspects of important moments. But you also need to strike the right balance on technical aspects, like camera settings that freeze action and provide proper exposure.

The exposure balancing act takes practice (lots of practice) to master. Learning to adjust your camera settings in low light is key to getting the best photographs, even as the light continues to change. You can't lose control.

So here's a quick tip that can help you get centered and ready before a show starts. In the photo pit, before the band takes the stage, raise your camera to your eye and press the shutter release button halfway down to active the autofocus. Then take some shots. Check the exposure. Make preemptive adjustments and assure yourself that the camera is working properly. And later, when you go to import your images into the computer, these practice shots make it easy to tell which card was used first.

ON THE COVER OF *ROLLING STONE*....

One final thought before we get into this: I've never had a photograph published on the cover of *Rolling Stone* magazine. But I approach every concert as if I'm shooting for this cover, because it puts me in the right mindset to do great work.

It's all about the attitude and approach to photography. If you treat every shoot as the most important shoot ... and every band as the most important band, then the images you produce will be the best images you can create at the time. And that's the attitude I want when I wait in a photo pit for a show to begin.

Okay .... the house lights are going down, the crowd is cheering wildly, the band is walking onto the stage, and I can feel that excitement build as I raise my camera to my eye.

I really love my job.

BILLY MORRISON

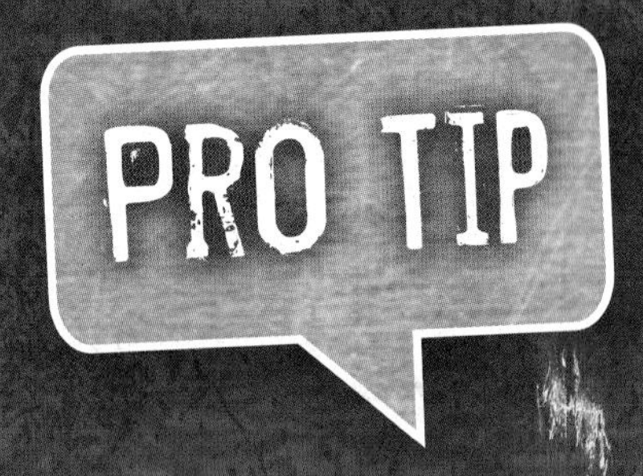

The guitarist for Billy Idol and the LA-based all-star band Camp Freddy, Billy Morrison is no stranger to being on the other side of the camera. And if he isn't on stage, chances are he's out on a motorcycle ride or acting on television or the big screen. Recently, Billy was honored with a Billy Morrison Signature model Gibson Les Paul.

www.billymorrison.net

Do you pay attention to photographers during a concert?

The GREAT live photographers do their job without being noticed. Occasionally I will notice photographers in the pit, but I'm usually lost in the moment, concentrating on what I'm playing/singing. But the shots I like from shows come from photographers who capture an intimate moment—a moment when an artist is lost in the performance. To do that, the photographer cannot be intruding in that moment.

Do you pay much attention to the photos you see of yourself on the Internet?

Only if it's a bad one!! Most artists are their own worst critics. And most good photographers know what shots portray an artist in the best light. So by default, I tend to like the photographers who post good shots. But these days there are cell phone pictures all over the web. I tend not to worry or care about them, because it's part of the job. If you run around, play hard, feel the music, and tap into the emotions of the gig, then you will have moments when you look less than perfect. But that's what rock and roll is about. It's meant to be passionate, emotional, loud, dirty. If every shot of you looks the same, then you are not doing your job as a musician.

Would you rather see a few great shots or tons of good shots?

I would absolutely prefer to see one or two great shots than a whole ream of badly lit, uninteresting pics. I call that the Facebook gallery. It's full of a bunch of out-of-focus, badly framed, badly lit shots of gigs. And the amount of bad ones detract from the one or two good shots that are in the set.

Do you have one piece of advice you would give someone starting out as a rock and roll photographer?

Only post your absolute best work. Artists get emails all the time saying, "Hey I saw you at so and so. Here's some pics." And it's more of the same. If you've been playing for a while, you've seen thousands of pictures of your shows and the ONLY thing that captures your attention is something different—something that you haven't seen before or something that's undeniably a great shot.

If I see one more shot of me taken with a flash, from the side of the stage … aargh!! I would also say do not shoot upwards. If the stage is high, move back. I've never seen an upward shot that I like.

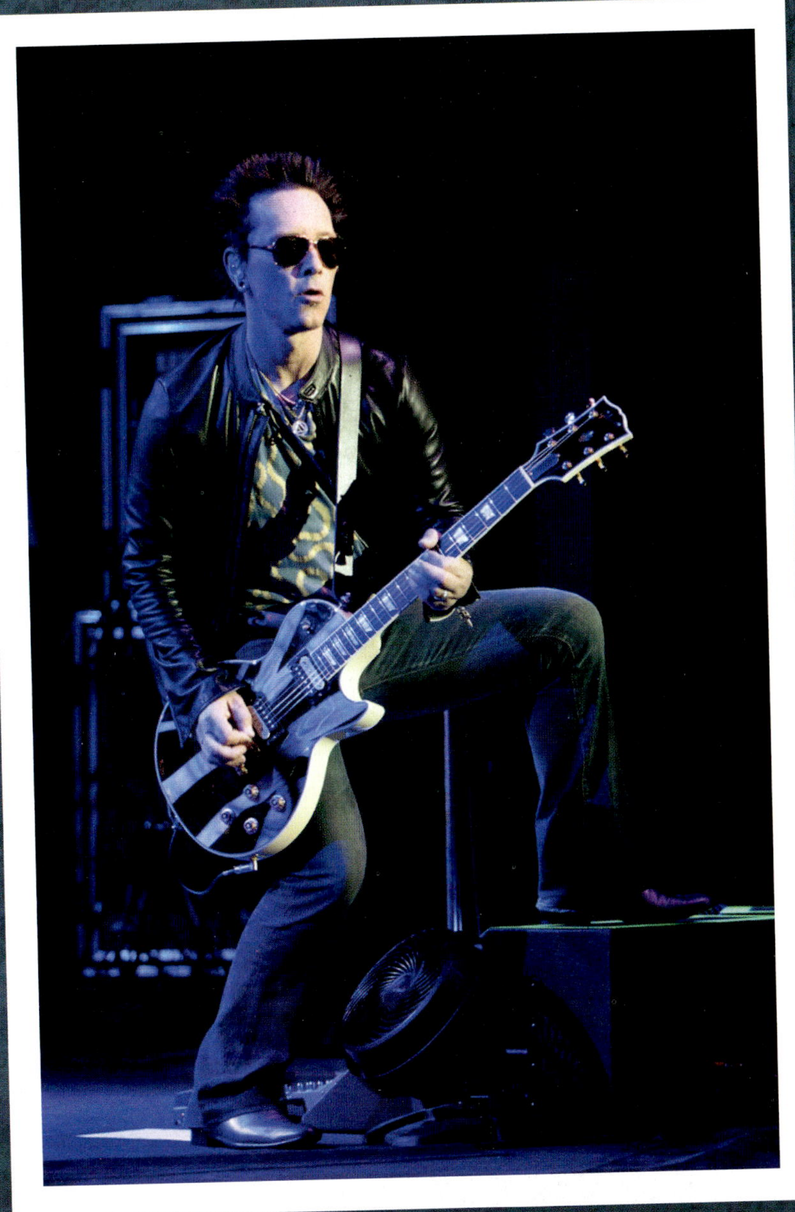

Billy Morrison

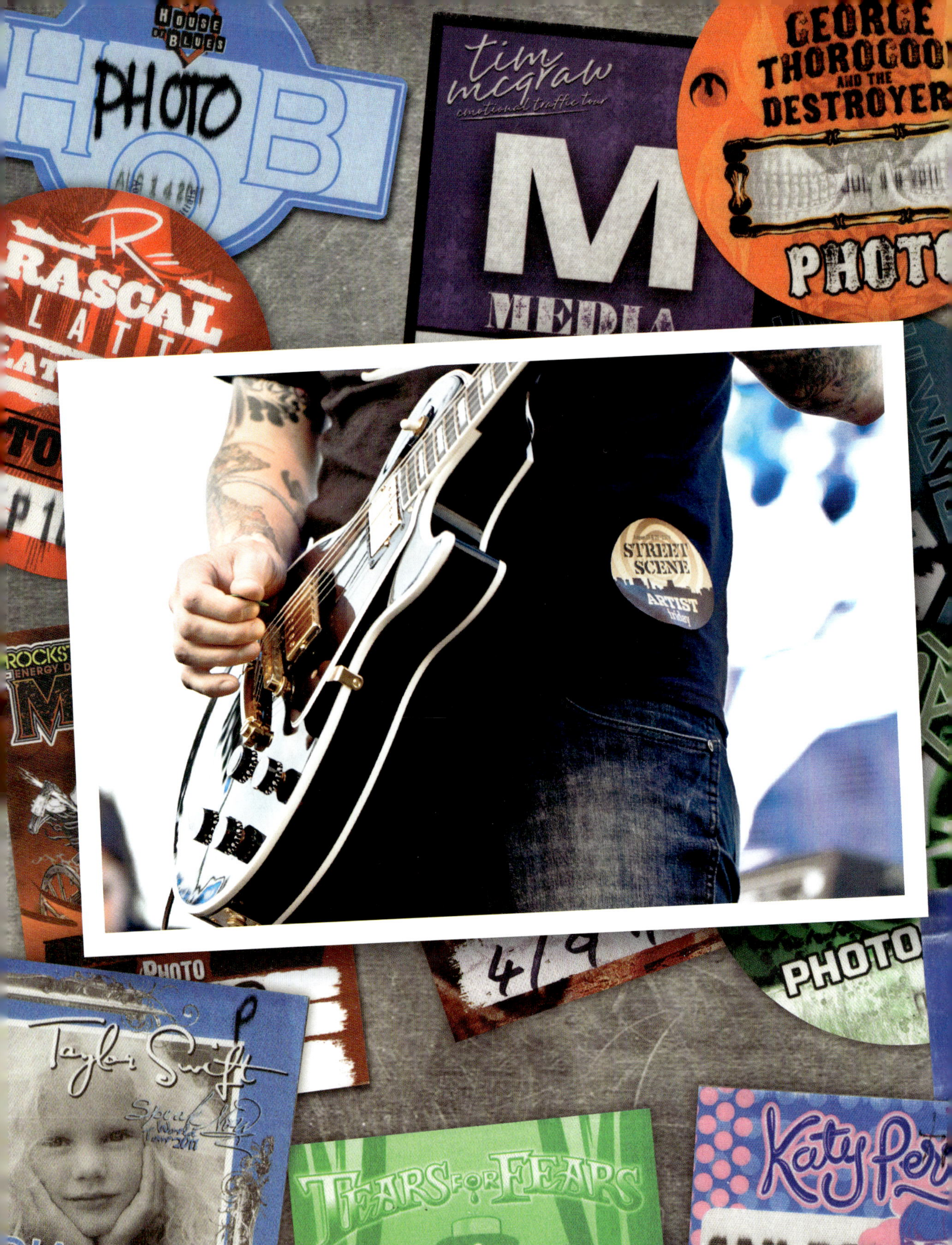
HOUSE OF BLUES
PHOTO
HOB
tim mcgraw
emotional traffic tour
M
MEDIA
GEORGE
AND THE
RASCAL
STREET SCENE
ARTIST
PHOTO
PHOTO
PHOTO
Taylor Swift
TEARS FOR FEARS

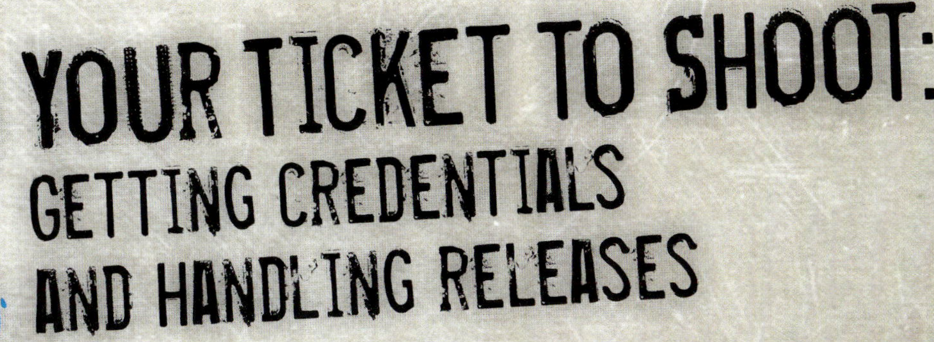

2 YOUR TICKET TO SHOOT: GETTING CREDENTIALS AND HANDLING RELEASES

This chapter is not about photography, but it does cover some of the more commonly asked questions about concert photography. The main one being *How do you get to photograph concerts?*

I mean, there you are, reading your favorite local newspaper or magazine. You see that one of your favorite bands is going to be playing in town, and you want to photograph them! Who do you ask? What do you ask for, exactly, and when should you ask for it? These are all great questions, and this chapter answers them.

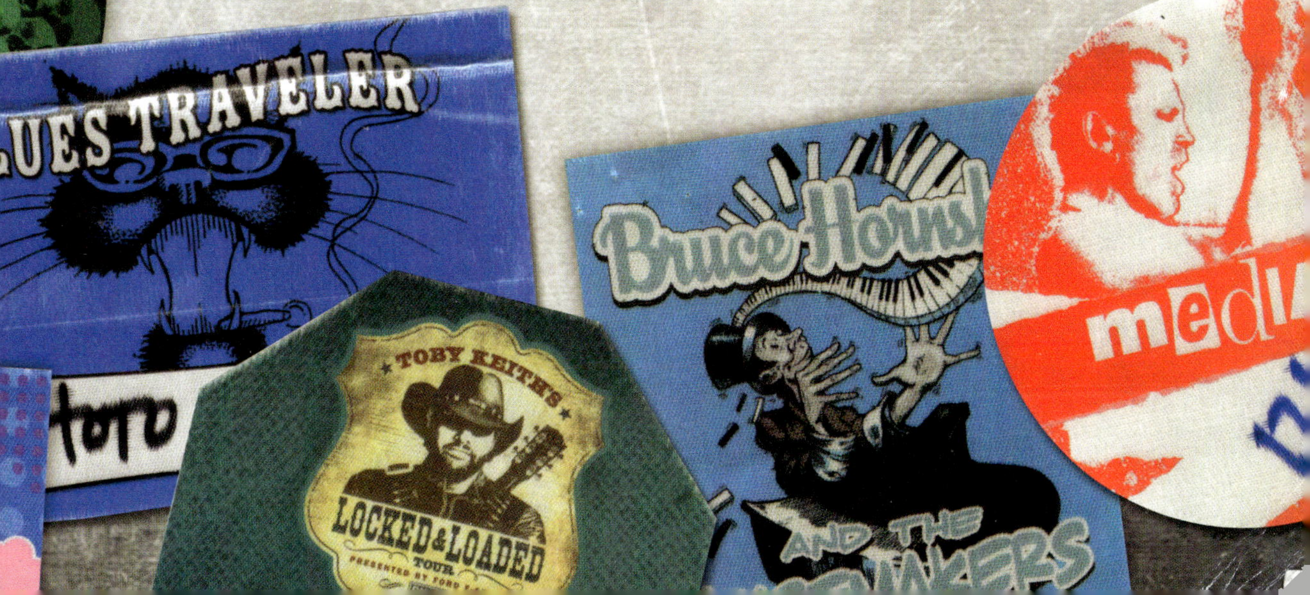

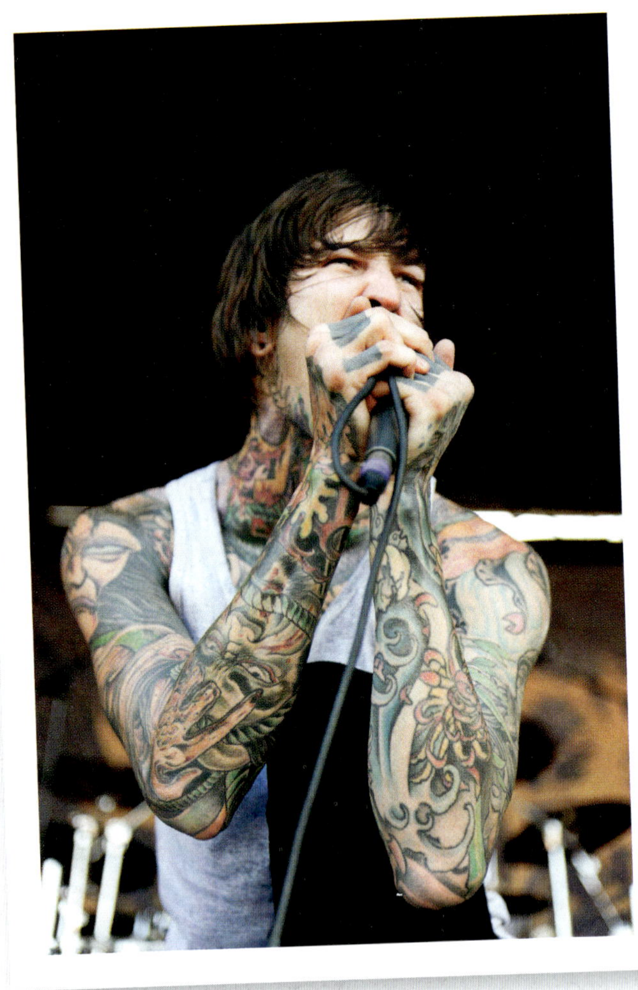

The only way to get up close to a performer with a camera at most shows is to have the right credentials. When I photographed Suicide Silence at the Rockstar Energy Drink Mayhem Festival, I had credentials that allowed me to shoot the side and main stages from the photo pit. This allowed me to get in close.
Taken at 1/400 second, f/2.8, and ISO 200

Without a doubt, the number one question I get is *Can I be your assistant*? This usually comes after someone sees that I've photographed his/ her favorite band. (The answer is always No, by the way.)

The second most common question I hear is *How do I get my camera into a concert so I can photograph the show?* or, more accurately, *How do I get a photo pass?* And while the process for every show is slightly different, there's one thing that all shows have in common: To obtain a photo pass, you have to ask for one.

In this chapter, we'll go through a series of questions and answers that can help you get a pass. The first step is to find out who to ask.

WHO TO ASK

When it comes to asking for a photo pass, there are a number of different people who might be able to help you. The most common roles and positions of these people are described below. Keep in mind that the person in charge of handing out photo credentials usually depends on the size and type of the show and the popularity of the band.

THE BAND'S PUBLICIST

Many bigger bands have their own publicist, whose job it is to make sure that the band is getting positive publicity. Publicists write press releases and control the band's interviews and photo opportunities. They are the best people to contact for photo credentials, because they control press access to the band. And a good publicist wants the band to show up in photos.

It's helpful to understand that sometimes a band's publicist is part of a firm that handles many different bands; other times it is a single person who deals with one or two bands exclusively. And, obviously, before you can ask for a photo pass, you need to find out who the publicist is for the band you want to shoot.

Fortunately, the Internet makes it quite easy to find this information, especially since publicists are not trying to hide. There's usually a link to the publicist from the band's website or Facebook page. If there's not a link, then try to find access to the publicist (the individual or the agency) using a search engine.

I usually start this process by searching the Band's Name plus "publicist." This often reveals press releases that contain the agency's and/ or publicist's name, firm, and contact information. Over time, I've been able to compile a list of band publicists and publicity companies, which makes it much easier to find a contact when I need it.

There are pros and cons to dealing with a company that handles a lot of artists. The biggest pro is that as you shoot more and earn a better reputation, the company is more likely to give you a photo pass versus issuing it to someone they don't know. For this to actually work in your favor though, you need to make sure that your behavior is always professional and above board (more on that later).

The biggest drawback to dealing with a big company is that it can be difficult to make personal connections. And that is the name of the game in this job. When dealing with an individual or a small publicity company, it's much easier to build a strong working relationship. But since individuals and small operations typically deal with only a few clients, you might work with them just once or twice a year.

MANAGEMENT/ PUBLICITY COMPANIES

Red Light Management

www.redlightmanagement.com

Artists include Phish, Tim McGraw, and Bruce Hornsby.

Each artist listing will give publicity information.

Mitch Schneider Organization

msopr.com

Artist include David Bowie, Slash, and Smashing Pumpkins.

This company deals with individual bands and also handles publicity for some of the bigger festivals and events, including the Big 4 concerts and Stagecoach: California's Country Music Festival.

Big Hassle

www.bighassle.com

Artists include Joss Stone, moe., and Primus.

This company also handles the press at large events, like Bonnaroo and Outside Lands.

Madison House Publicity

www.madisonhousepublicity.com

Artists include Robert Johnson, Keller Williams, and The String Cheese Incident.

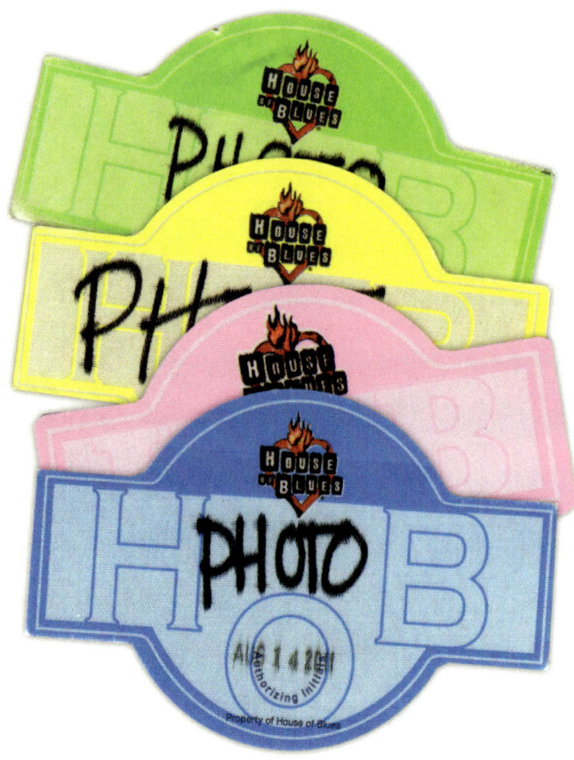

Different-colored passes keep people honest. I've been asked how a venue knows if a certain pass is for the right day. Many bands and venues use different colors for passes that change each day, so passes issued for a certain night are likely to be different from those issued for another one. For example, these passes from the House of Blues are just a small sampling of the different passes I've been issued over the years. The venue knows what color is the right one for any given night. As a backup, the passes are usually stamped with the date of the show.

THE PROMOTER

The person or company that's putting on the show—that is, the folks who are putting up the money to make the show happen—can be an excellent resource for things like press passes, because promoters need images to ... well, *promote* their shows. So this can be a great way to gain access to the photo pit.

Of course, there are promoters at all levels, but you probably only hear about the bigger companies. Look at the local level and try to work with up-and-coming promoters. Check out posters that are advertising local shows and see if they mention a production company. To find out who to deal with at a particular company—and how (s)he wants to be contacted—do a search on the Internet and check out the promoter's website. Based on my experience, email tends to be the go-to method.

When it comes to local promoters, I've found that email and phone are often the easiest ways to make contact. Make sure that you have all the information about the show on hand and be clear about what you want.

THE VENUE

One of the best concert photography jobs is House Photographer for a concert venue. If you hold this position, you get to shoot the concerts ... perhaps all of them. And you don't worry about requesting a photo pass; the venue usually deals with this for you.

But even if you're not a house photographer, it's possible to get permission to shoot a concert from the venue directly, especially if it's a bar or small club. In fact, this can be one of the easiest ways to ask for a photo pass, because you know exactly where the venue is and how to contact the office. Yet it's the least likely source to help you actually get the pass for a big show.

In other words, it's pretty easy to ask your local bar if you can take a few photographs during the performance of a local band. A yes is likely. But if you ask a local arena if you can take photographs during the next U2 show, your answer will probably be no.

THE RECORD LABEL

Record labels need publicity so their bands will sell lots of albums, and everybody can earn a living. So be aware that some bands don't have their own publicist but are represented instead with a publicist who works for the record label to which the band is signed. Check out the record label's website and see if there's a publicity contact for the act you want to cover. There's usually an email address for a contact at the label or a contact form.

One of the problems of dealing with a record label though is that there're usually many different artists signed, and one person could be dealing with many acts. Good luck with this one.

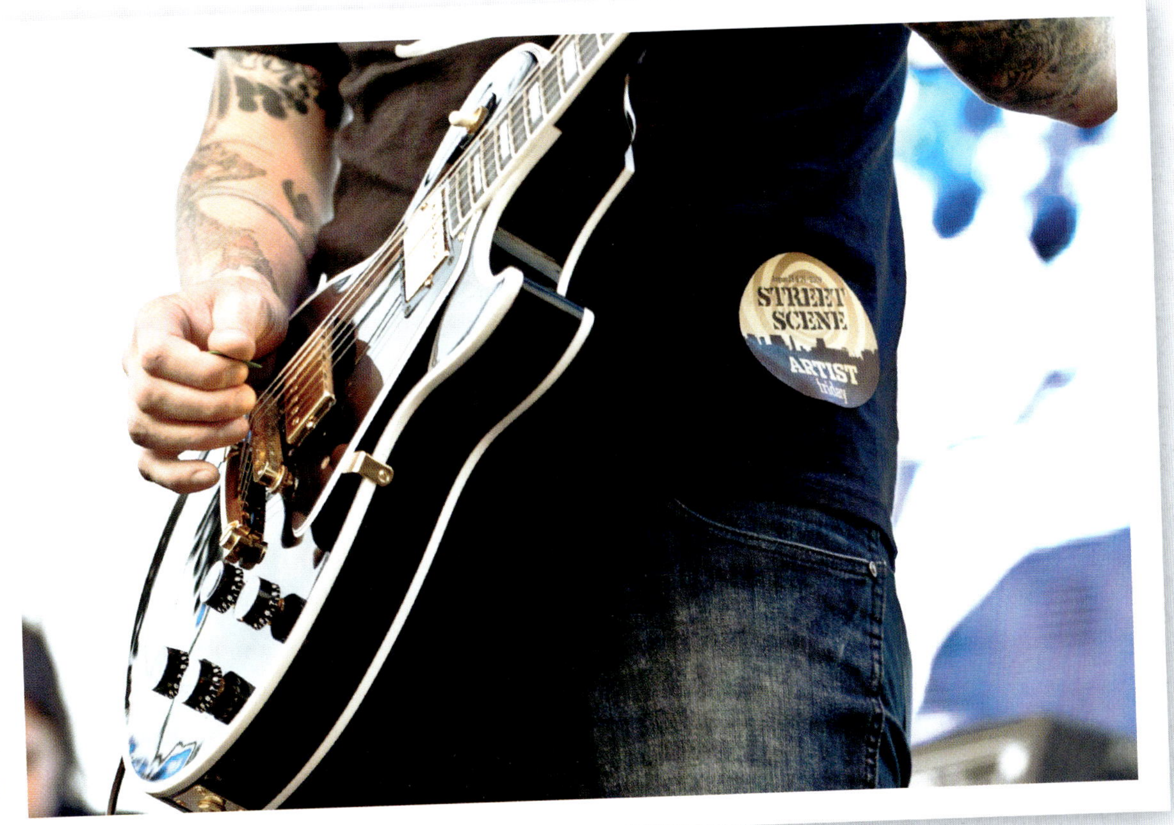

Many times band members need to have passes as well. Some bands have their own, but when it comes to festivals or venues that have tight control over access, the band has to follow the same rules as the rest. They need to wear their passes so security doesn't wonder who they are.

THE BAND ITSELF

Being friends with the band is a great way to get permission to photograph them. This is one of the best ways to get credentials to shoot a band, but it works best when you're really good friends with them and can actually call someone on the phone or email a band member directly.

But a big problem with getting photo passes from the band is that it's sometimes very difficult to get ahold of them when they're on tour, and they can easily forget or get the day wrong. A myriad of other things can go wrong, too. So this isn't the most solid option … no matter what your relationship is like with the band.

Once you discover who to ask for photo credentials, it's time to actually ask for the pass. So let's explore the different types of passes that you may see when photographing a show.

REWARDS OF GOOD BEHAVIOR

If you expect to receive more than one photo pass in your lifetime, there are some good working habits to practice. The way you interact with people and treat the opportunity is important, and people notice. So when it comes to working directly for a band or band member, consider this advice.

- **Treat the job seriously.**
  Musicians take their music seriously, and you should, too. Just because you're (probably) not shooting them for *Rolling Stone* doesn't mean you shouldn't approach it as though you are.
- **Share only the best shots.**
  There is no reason to share photographs with the band (or public) that don't show the band at their best and support their image. But definitely let them see photos that make them look good.
- **Give and take.**
  When you photograph a concert, it's one of the few situations in which I think it's a good idea to give away some work for free. I mean, you get to see and photograph the show for free, and the band might need a new photo or two for its website or Facebook Fan page. Share. Everyone wins. And the band will likely remember you favorably for the next show.
- **Start small.**
  Look for local bands to photograph when you're just getting started with concert photography, because it's much easier to build a relationship with bands that are going to play lots of local shows than those that come and play only once a year or less.

WHAT YOU WANT

There are basically four different types of passes at most shows. And while they are all pretty cool, only one will really get you what you want. The four passes are:

- All Access Pass
- Working Pass
- VIP/Aftershow Pass
- Photo/Media Pass

What you want to ask for and receive is the Photo/Media Pass, but let's take a look at what each of them do ... and don't do.

ALL ACCESS PASS

I won't lie, these are the coolest passes you can get. The All Access Pass gets you everywhere—on stage, backstage, dressing rooms, and even the clean backstage bathroom. But the one place that the All Access Pass might not get you is in the photo pit ... with a camera.

It's true. I've worked shows for which I had the All Access laminate and still needed to get a separate pass to actually photograph the show. There are venues that do not allow photography from the stage no matter what and other venues where union rules control the stage. So even the All Access Pass won't allow you to use a camera on the stage.

All that being said, the All Access Pass does come into play—and is quite helpful—when working for a band and shooting backstage. (That's covered in Chapter 12.)

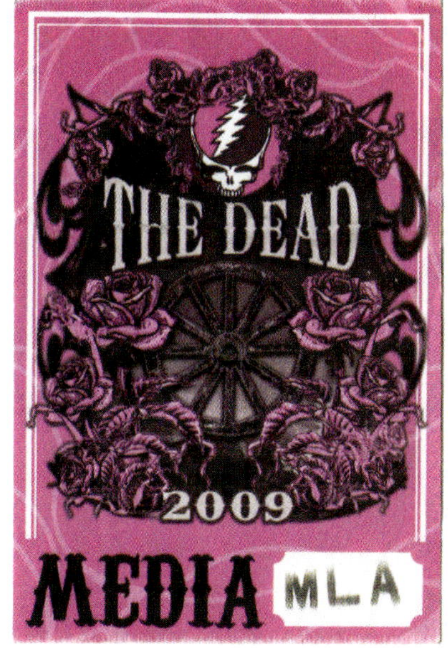

When The Dead went on tour in 2009, the band used separate passes to indicate Working access and Media access. The two kinds of passes were different sizes so security could easily tell them apart. The passes were a different color each day.

WORKING PASST

Bands give the local crew a Working Pass so they have the access they need to do their jobs. A Working Pass can actually have more leeway than even an All Access Pass, because folks with a Working Pass need to be exactly where they are, doing exactly what they are doing at any given time. So these pass holders are rarely questioned about their location and activity at a show.

To get one of these passes as a photographer is unusual. I've been given a Working Pass on only a few occasions, and it's been in conjunction with a Photo Pass each time. For example, when I was photographing The Dead on the last night of the band's tour in 2009 at the Gorge Amphitheatre in Washington State, I needed to access the photo pit for parts of the drum performance and the encore, but I needed to be in other parts of the venue at different times during the show. So I was issued a Working Pass as well as a Photo Pass for this concert.

VIP/AFTERSHOW PASS

These are the passes given to friends of the band, guests of the venue, and guests of the promoter. They're even sometimes used as prizes for radio giveaways and other special promotions. A VIP/Aftershow Pass might allow you to access a special area or upgrade your seats, but it will not allow you to shoot the concert or give you access to the photo pit. These passes are fun to have and they may allow you to meet the band; but to a photographer, these passes are close to worthless.

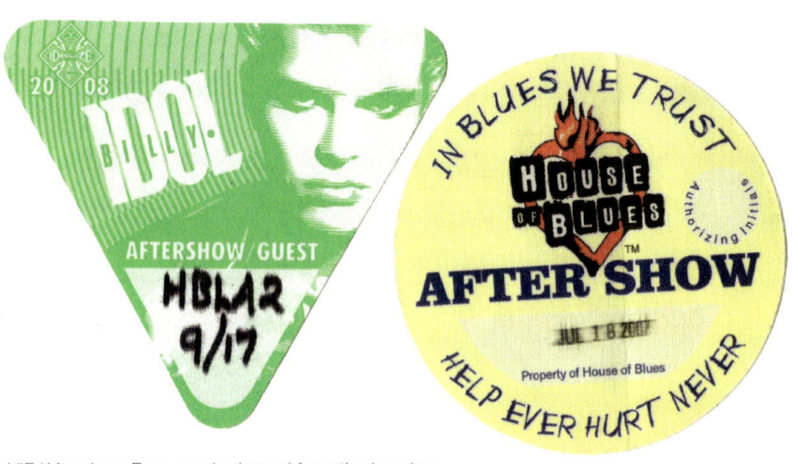

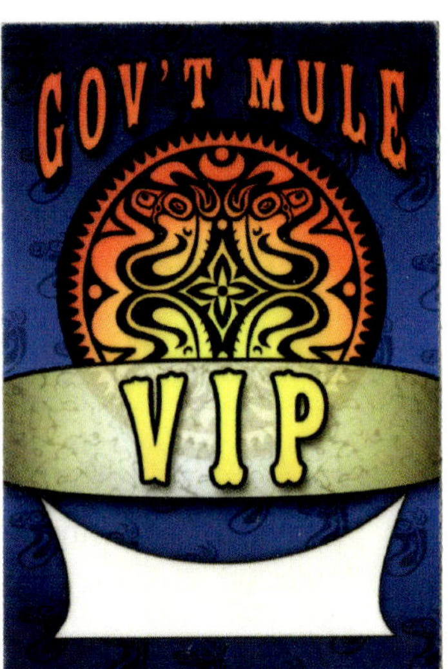

A VIP/Aftershow Pass can be issued from the band or the venue, and it usually allows the holder to access a special area or stay a little longer after the show.

PHOTO/MEDIA PASS

If you're a concert photographer, then this is the pass you want. The Photo Pass—sometimes called a Media Pass—is the credential that allows you to take your camera into a venue and legally photograph a show.

Think of the Photo Pass as a legal contract between you and the venue/band/promoter. In exchange for permission to photograph the performance, you agree to follow the rules they've established. The rules usually include a specific period of time to shoot and a static location from which to work.

Many times the Photo Pass is accompanied by a photo release form that needs to be signed (or not) that states what can and cannot be done with the images you shoot. (Photo releases are covered a little later in this chapter.)

So, to ensure that you receive the right access for the work you want to do, it's important that you specify, when you put in a request to photograph a concert, that you want to photograph the show and are looking to secure a Photo Pass. Here's why. The band's publicist/contact person is probably very busy and (s)he's unlikely to spend much time trying to figure out what it is you actually need. If you just say you want a Media Pass, then you might end up with a reviewer's ticket but no photo credential, and this will not allow you to bring your camera in to the show. Oops. Shoulda been more clear!

I know this seems obvious, but I've seen it happen over and over again. A photographer shows up at the Will Call window, or the media representative comes out with the passes, and a photographer is not on the list for a Photo Pass. Instead (s)he's issued a reviewer's ticket, because (s)he didn't ask for the right thing. Too bad. At that point, it's too late.

So now that you've found the right person to ask for your Photo Pass and you know what kind of access you need to request, it's time to figure out the best time to ask for credentials.

WHEN TO ASK

The timing on this can be a little tricky. If you ask too early, you could get forgotten. If you ask too late, the photo list could be full or closed. But I've found that asking about three weeks before the show tends to work well.

This doesn't mean that you'll find out if you are *approved* for the pass three weeks ahead of time, but this timing gives the people you're asking adequate time to decide whether or not to grant your request ... without being rushed or bothered with an event too far away.

Ask for a Photo Pass about three weeks before the show.

An exception to this suggested timing is for big festivals. These events usually have a standard application process for photographers, and it needs to be followed. So when you see a festival coming your way that you want to shoot, check the festival website and find out who's handling media and what the process is for obtaining photo credentials.

Be forewarned: A frustrating part of concert photography permissions is that the final okay typically comes just a day or two before the show. Sometimes it's less than 24 hours before showtime when you find out that you can photograph a concert. And while this can be frustrating, especially for long-term planning, it means that sending a reminder email about your pass request about 48 hours before the event can be successful.

And never be afraid to make a request or follow up the old-fashioned way—via telephone. Yes, you may actually have to speak to a live person, but this can often be the most efficient means of communication. Again, professionalism and standard telephone etiquette apply.

Alright, so at this point you should have the who, what, and when information on acquiring a Photo Pass. Now comes the biggie: Why should *you* get a Photo Pass? What's in it for the band?

WHY YOU?

The biggest hurdle in getting a Photo Pass, especially if you don't work for anyone or aren't on assignment, is explaining why you should get one. It's really easy to ask for credentials if you work for a newspaper or if *Billboard* sends you out to cover a show, but it's tougher to get a pass if you're just a fan and/ or working as a freelancer.

To overcome this, the key is to start small and local. Hit local clubs, local bands, local musicians, local promoters, and local events. Shoot like crazy and build a solid reputation as a quality photographer.

I started my concert photography career by photographing friends' bands while I was still in college. Around that time, I approached a local promoter here in San Diego about shooting a small festival he was putting on. After showing him my portfolio of images, we worked out a deal where he gave me access to the event in exchange for permission to use a few of my photos to advertise the next year's festival.

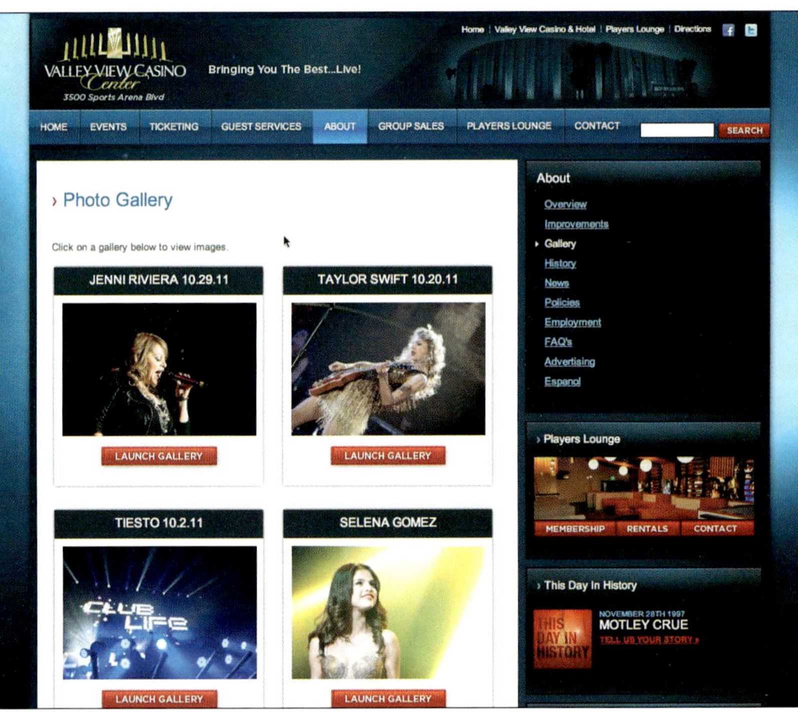

As a photographer working for this venue, many of my images end up as galleries on the Valley View Casino website. I send images after a show, and the marketing folks post them on the site.

This situation allowed me to expand my portfolio, and I ended up with a very good working relationship with the promoter. So when he went on to bigger and better things, he never forgot the work I did with him when we were both getting started.

Today, if you are just starting out and don't have a traditional outlet behind you, look to the new generation of media platforms that might be able to use your work. Here are some ideas:

- **Fan Websites**
  Every serious band out there has a fan club, and that fan club has a website, and that website needs and wants photographs … of the band. To get your photographs on this platform, it helps to be a fan yourself, but that's not totally necessary. Start by approaching the fan site administrators to ask if you can name the site as an outlet for images when you apply for photo credentials for the band's show. Just remember to send photos to the fan site if you get the credentials.
- **Music Websites**
  There are a large number of music-based websites out there, and they're all competing for the attention of music fans. These sites can be a great place to get a foot in the door, but they usually don't pay very well (if at all). The bigger sites have a recognized name and credibility in the music industry, and they can usually get photo credentials for a photographer who is assigned to a show. It's not easy to get a gig with this type of outlet though, because the bigger sites keep a list of photographers who are ready to work for them. But stick with it. Continue to build your portfolio and keep your name on the site's list of people who want to shoot. You never know what might happen … and when.
- **Music Blogs**
  By *music blog*, I mean a section of a bigger website that's dedicated to covering live events. Many of the traditional media outlets, like local television stations and newspapers, now have an online presence and they need content. These photography positions are usually unpaid, but they have a well-established name behind them, so their requests for photo passes tend to get approved.
- **Your Website**
  It might sound a little crazy, but if you are serious about shooting music, then why not start your own website magazine? The start-up costs are minimal, especially compared to what it used to take to launch a paper publication, and it might end up being a source of income for you … or, at the very least, a great way to show off your images.
- **Tablet Magazines**
  One of the newest forms of media is a newspaper or magazine that's created to be viewed on a tablet computing device, like an iPad. I expect to see this new niche market expand as the tablet devices market continues to grow.

YOUR PORTFOLIO

It's really important to show your best work in a portfolio. I firmly believe that a strong portfolio gets you more work and makes it more likely that you are taken seriously as a concert photographer. A portfolio is your lifeline in this business.

Especially if you're an unknown concert photographer, you need an online outlet to show your work. This makes it possible for people to check out your images when you request a Photo Pass. Your portfolio doesn't need to include a lot of big name artists (that doesn't hurt, of course), but it does need to include great images. Remember, the person looking through the portfolio is probably responsible for making sure the band looks good in public. (S)he's going to want to see, in your images, that you've done it for other bands.

When I was starting out, I shot a lot of photos of my friends in bands, and my portfolio was full of those images. Clearly, these were not big rock stars. They were just guys who played music together on weekends or who were trying to make a go of it by touring the bar music scene. I owe a lot to the guys in *Born Naked*, *The Travel Agents*, and the *Cardiff Reefers*, because if they hadn't let me photograph them, it's unlikely that I'd be doing what I do now.

Oh, and make sure that you update your portfolio often. When you get a great shot, replace one of the older not-so-great shots with it. The replace part is important. You don't want your portfolio to be too big ... or repetitive. If any of your shots look similar to another, pick the best and cut the rest.

To ensure that the publicist, promoter, venue staff, record label rep, or band member sees your work, be sure to add a link to your portfolio on your Photo Pass request.

Don't get discouraged if you don't have an outlet for your images. Definitely still ask for the pass if you want to photograph a show. The worst that can happen is that your request will be denied, and you end up exactly where you started. No harm done. But if you never ask for a pass, then you will never get a pass. You must give issuers an opportunity to say yes!

THE REQUEST

Here is the typical Photo Pass request that I send out. Note that this is a generic form that I modify depending on the show, my relationship with the band, and why I want to cover the show.

TO: publicist@band.com
Cc: Assignment_editor@outlet.com (if applicable)
Subject: Photo Pass request for BAND at VENUE on DATE

Message:

Hi there, NAME:
My name is Alan Hess, and I'm a freelance photographer based in San Diego. I'm hoping you can provide me with a photo pass to shoot BAND at VENUE on DATE.

The photos will be used for (If on assignment, then mention it here with a link to site or publication) or (if just a fan, mention it here).

If interested, visit LINK TO PORTFOLIO to take a look at my portfolio of past work.

Thank you for your time.

Alan Hess
Photographer
WEBSITE
PHONE NUMBER

If I've shot the band previously, I link to that specific gallery of my portfolio. And/or if I've photographed a different band that's represented by the same company, I add a specific link for that. The key is to make sure that you're very clear and concise, so that the publicist can determine what it is you want. And be sure that you present yourself as a respectful, polite, and professional photographer.

THE PHOTO RELEASE

Earlier, I mentioned that a concert Photo Pass is much like a contract between the band and the photographer. And sometimes, there is another, more legally binding contract for the photographer to sign. This is the photo release. It stipulates in legal terms what can and cannot be done with the images you shoot.

Photo releases range from the good to the bad … and to the really, really bad. There are photos I've taken that I would love to include in this book, but cannot due to the terms of the related photo release. For instance, I've shot shows as a house photographer that I never would have been approved for in any other capacity. The clause below is the thing that makes those photos unusable here. (But, to be fair, I was paid for my photographs, and this release really isn't too bad.)

> *The Photographs shall be submitted only to the Publication and shall not be submitted elsewhere... All rights in and to the Photographs shall belong to the Photographer. No party other than the Publication shall have the right to publish, exploit or use the Photographs.*

Later in the release, there is a clause that allows the images to be used as part of my portfolio for the sole purpose of getting future work. So that part's nice. Would I prefer to be allowed to do anything I want with the images? Of course. But that's not always going to be the case. And there are certain opportunities that outweigh the delights of full control.

The way photo releases work in concert photography is a little different from other kinds of photography businesses. Here's why: If there is no photo release, then there are usually no restrictions on the image use. A photo release in concert photography specifies the conditions of use. Many times those conditions are pretty simple; they define where the image(s) can be used.

For example, many concert photo releases do not allow images to be used in a publication or book featuring the musician(s) without the individual or the band's permission. Other times, the release stipulates that the images cannot be used commercially to make and sell collateral, like mugs, calendars, t-shirts, and so forth. Other restrictions may not allow for the images to be used in advertising. But photo releases usually allow the images to be used in portfolios, news publications and magazines, and for other kinds of editorial purposes.

Be very aware though that there are some photo releases that should not be signed at all. Among these are releases that ask the photographer to assign image copyright to the artist or the artist's representative without compensation. This is bad for the photographer, because it means that (s)he relinquishes all rights to the images ... giving them away for free, so the band can do whatever they want with them. Uh, no!

Another type of photo release that I won't sign is one that gives the artist or the artist's representative editorial rights over what can and can't be published. I find this type of restriction akin to allowing the people who make the news to write the news. Can anyone say *too much bias*? Since I never show anything but my best work, I've never found this type of restriction to be worth the effort.

While it's not always possible, it's always a good idea to ask for a copy of the photo release in advance—ask if it can be sent to you before the show—so you can read it and decide whether or not to sign it before making the drive to the venue.

FOLLOW UP WITH THANKS

After the show, be sure to thank the person who approved you for the Photo Pass. And send him/her a photo or two (or a link to the outlet that assigned you to the shoot).

Here's what I do for every show I shoot. (I even do this when working for venues, which will get copies of all the images later on anyway.) As I'm processing images from the show, I grab one that catches my eye and do a quick edit in Adobe Photoshop. I resize the file to about 600x400 pixels and email it to the person who supplied the Photo Pass with a heartfelt thank you.

The image I send might not be the very best one from the whole show, but it will probably be in the top ten. That isn't the most important part of the gesture, but showing a great shot from the show doesn't hurt. My goal is to make sure that the appreciation for allowing me to photograph is tied with an image that shows my work. And it needs to be sent in a timely manner.

If everything goes as planned, I try to send this follow up within the first 24 hours after the concert. If nothing else, this shows a level of professionalism and politeness that will be remembered. For me, those follow up emails have generated new business opportunities and other photo shoots. Well worth the effort.

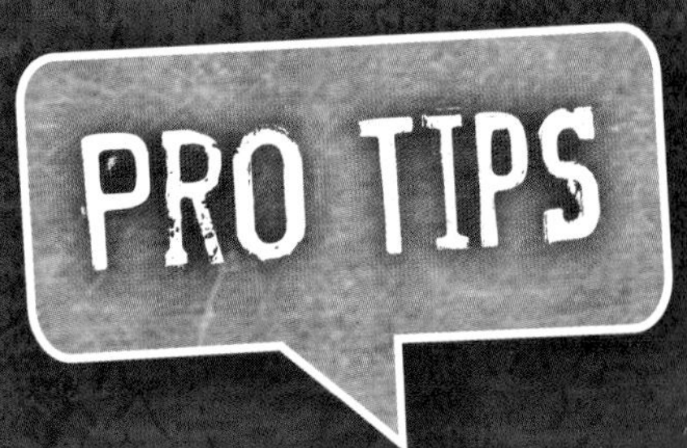

Dennis McNally

Publicist for the Grateful Dead, Bob Weir and RatDog, and more

What is/ was your title with the Grateful Dead, Bob Weir, and RatDog?

Publicist

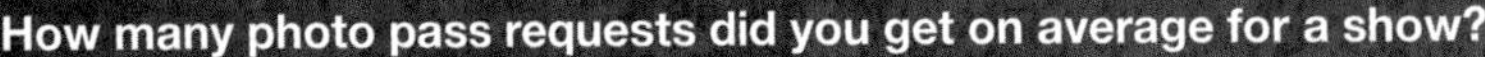

How many photo pass requests did you get on average for a show?

Well, that varies greatly. For the Grateful Dead, it was anywhere from 5 to 15; for smaller bands, more like 2 or 3.

How did you decide which ones to approve?

My inclination was to say yes to as many as possible. If I knew, on site, that the area in front of the stage was tiny, that would affect how many I'd be able to accommodate.

How much weight was given to the outlet the photographer was shooting for?

Of course, the *New York Times* or the main daily of any town is always going to get in. But a smart publicist takes a long view; the guy shooting for a college paper could be somebody you'll see in a few years shooting professionally. Generosity is always rewarded.

What about fan photographers?

I am fortunate to be able to say that my bands permitted fan photography and were usually general admission, which meant I could smile, wave, and not have to worry about it.

What were the photography rules for the Grateful Dead? RatDog?

While I retained flexibility and could overrule myself if I felt like it, the basic rules were the traditional and obvious ones:

- three songs (which could be half an hour)
- no flash (that was ironclad)
- don't break the plane of the stage (as in leaning your elbows on a low stage, which can look as though you're climbing onto the stage)
- no cameras on the stage (it's not your desk)

What happened if a photographer didn't follow the rules?

Depends on mood. If I thought I was being gratuitously ignored, a loud eviction. Otherwise, friendly advice.

What is one tip you can give a photographer who is just starting out in the concert photography business?

With digital cameras everywhere, even in phones, everyone in the world thinks that they can take pictures, which makes it harder to try to do it as a business. So I can only say, *good luck*. The one tip would be to be nice and to listen to the publicist, who is in that moment your co-worker … probably good advice for anybody in any work situation.

Heidi Ellen Robinson-Fitzgerald

Publicist for Anthrax, Slayer, Rick Rubin, and more

How many photo pass requests do you get on average for a show?

There really isn't an average; it depends on the artist and the city. In some cities, we can get twenty requests; in others, just one or two.

How do you decide which ones to approve?

Our policy is to credential photographers who are on assignment from a legitimate media outlet for a review of the show. In the past ten years or so, the definition for the word *legitimate* has expanded.

How much weight is given to the outlet the photographer is shooting for?

Quite a bit. You can credential only so many photographers. Barricades hold only so many people. You have to take into consideration the fact that security is also in the barricade and need to move around if there's a problem, especially with a show like Slayer, where lots of kids crowd surf into the barricade. Photographers also need to be able to move around to shoot from different angles, and you don't want to degrade the experience for the kids in the front row. So the outlet the photographer is shooting for is a big part of getting a credential.

What about fan photographers?

While we have credentialed some over the years, it's not something we normally do. If you credential one fan, you've got to credential all of them, and we can't do that.

What are the photography rules for your bands?

The standard is "first three songs, no flash." There are circumstances when we'll push for select photographers to shoot more than the first three songs—maybe give better access, such as onstage, from the soundboard, and so on. If a media outlet is doing a major feature on the artist, we'll want to provide special access so the photos will be the best they can be.

What happens if a photographer doesn't follow the rules?

When we issue photo passes, all photographers receive a very detailed email ahead of time, informing them of all the rules: what, when, where, and for how long they can shoot. If someone decides not to follow the rules, I suppose they could be tossed out of the barricade, or even out of the venue.

What is one tip you can give a photographer who is just starting out in the concert photography business?

I'm not a photographer, so I couldn't offer any technical or artistic advice, but I would say that "Practice makes perfect." So shoot, shoot, shoot, shoot, shoot. You can put two photographers in a pit and have them shoot the exact same show at the exact same time, and one photographer will press "click" at all the right times, while the other will shoot in between the great moments. It's an art form; and I think, as with any art form, there is raw instinct involved in getting those truly magical photos. But practice definitely helps.

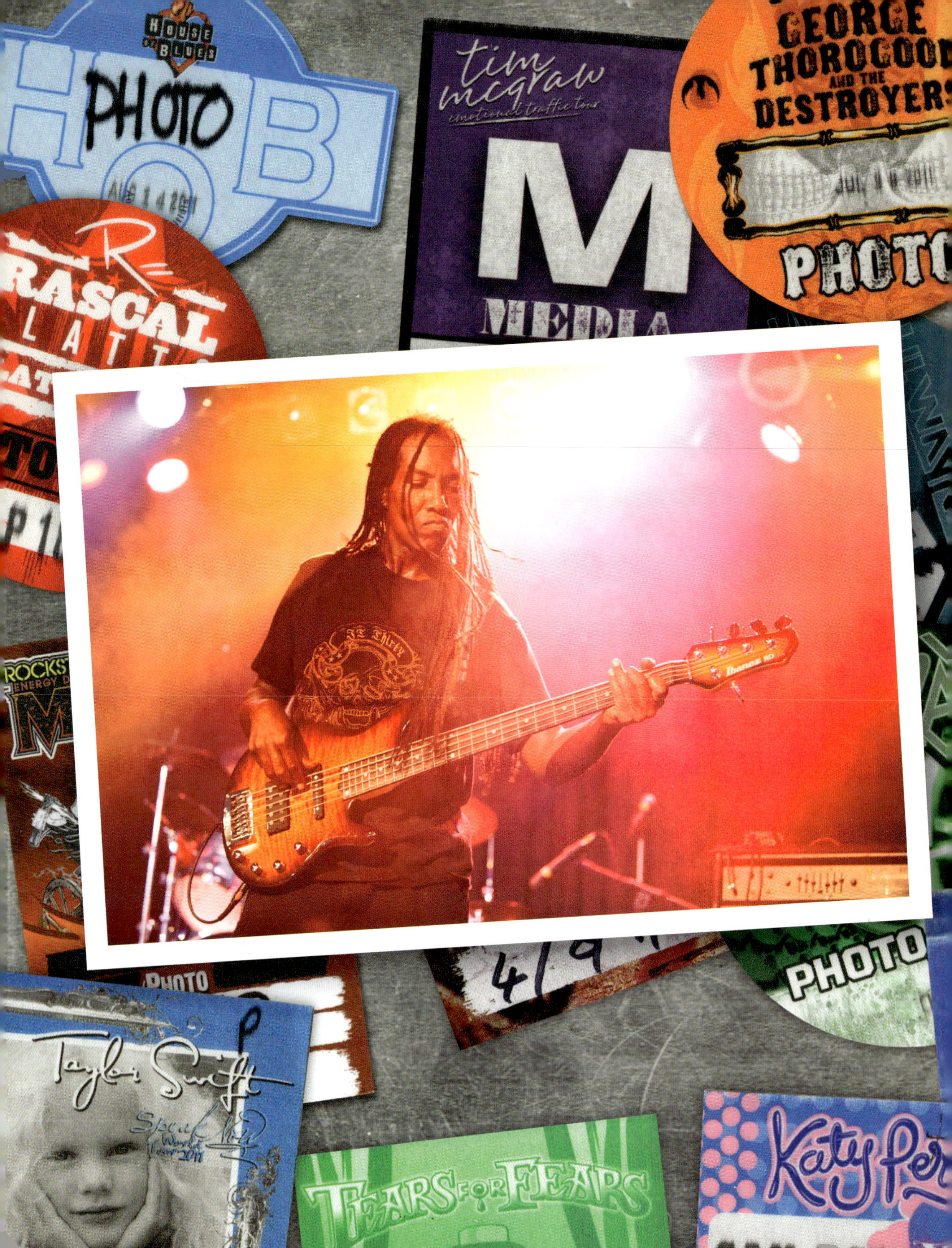

HOUSE OF BLUES
PHOTO
HOB
tim mcgraw
emotional traffic tour
M
MEDIA
GEORGE
AND THE
PHOTO
RASCAL
Ibanez
PHOTO
PHOTO
Taylor Swift
Speak Now World Tour 2011
TEARS FOR FEARS

3 PIT RULES: BEHAVING LIKE A PRO

In this chapter, we still don't get into photography techniques and camera settings. Instead, we cover perhaps an equally important kind of information: etiquette. That is, we explore all the things a concert photographer should do (and not do) once (s)he has a Photo Pass in hand. How do you behave well, so you have a shot at getting invited back?

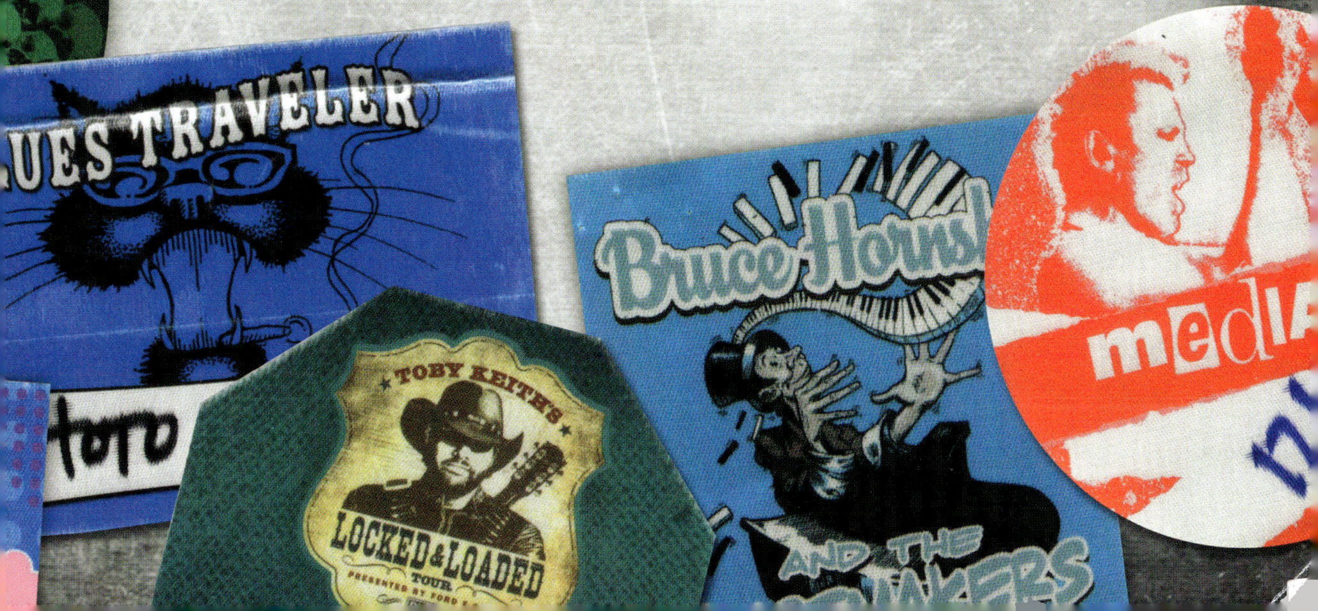

So many little things can make a shoot go really well ... or turn it into a nightmare. And it's stuff that's not always obvious or foreseeable. I've had shoots that I dreaded. They started out foreboding, like they were going to be a big hassle, but then they turned out to be great. And, similarly, I've had shoots that went from great to terrible in less time than it takes to change a lens.

To make your experience a positive one, my suggestion is to start with the people involved with your shooting gig. That's why we cover them here first. And then we move on to the photo pit, the workspace of the concert photographer. Soundboards and shooting from the crowd are also covered for shows that don't involve a pit or pit access.

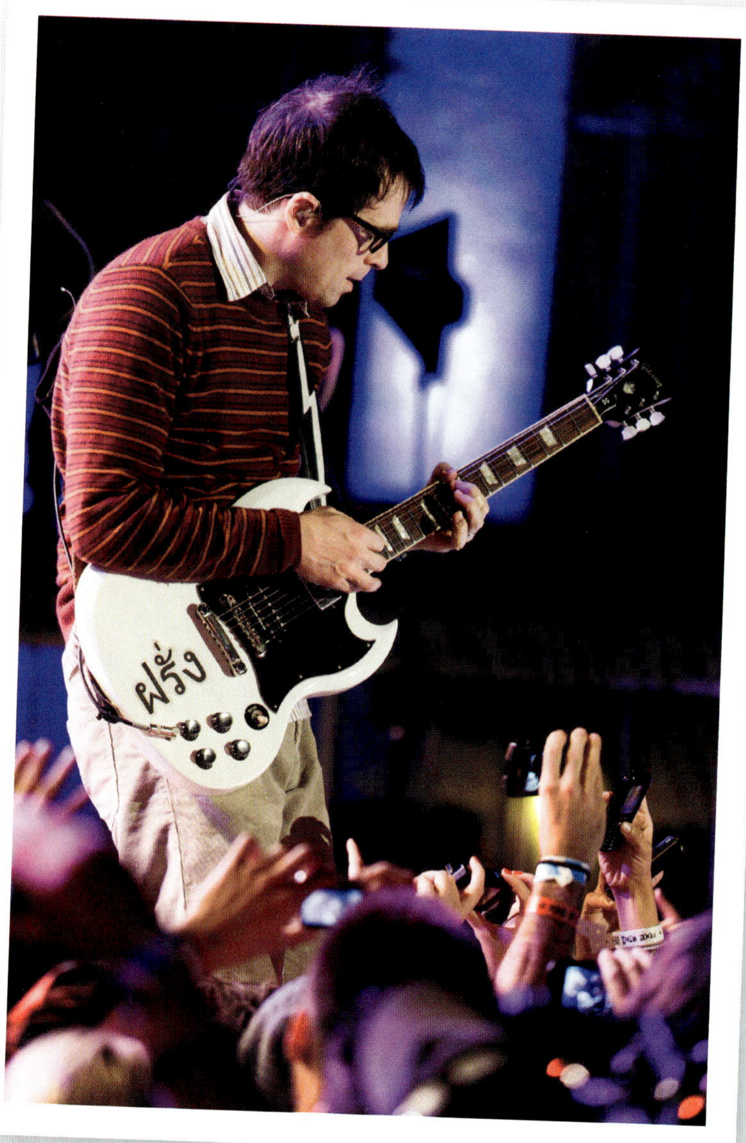

You don't have to be in the photo pit to get a great concert shot. Sometimes a different angle can give you a different, and better, view. Capture the interaction between the performer and the crowd, for example. In this shot, try to count the number of fans with cameras getting a shot of Rivers Cuomo of Weezer.

Taken at 1/500 second, f/2.8, and ISO 1600

THE PLAYERS

A lot of people are involved with your ability to photograph a concert. Of course, not all those listed here are going to be at every show, but you can count on running into each of them at some point if you do this type of photography for very long. And obviously some of these players will be at every show, because … well, it's not much of a concert without the band and some fans.

MUSICIANS

Musical artists are usually the subject of concert photos; they're the reason you're there, right? But most of the time, you won't have any direct interaction with the band. Your interaction will happen exclusively through the lens. But that doesn't matter. They're still the most important people in the room, because nothing happens without them.

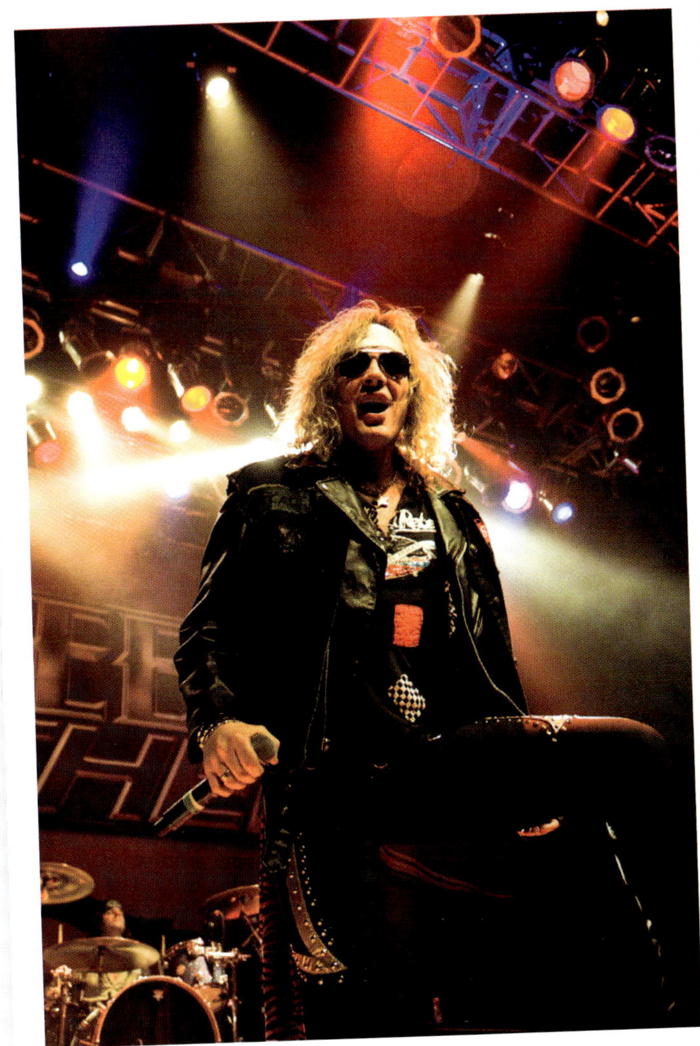

Being up front allows some great angles. As a photographer, it's your job to show the band in the best light, and that's really easy when the band performs for the crowd and photographers. Here is Steel Panther performing at the House of Blues in San Diego.
Taken at 1/160 second, f/2.8, and ISO 1600

Sometimes musicians will work with photographers and play to the cameras. Other artists seem to go out of their way to make sure that photographers get the worst possible images. You never know how it'll be, but it helps to remember that musicians are just people. They have moods and bad days like the rest of us. So when a band seems to be having an off day or to be purposely antagonistic to the photographers, I suggest shooting from as far away as possible. Doing this allows you to focus on the whole scene and maybe avoid the performers attention.

For example, when shooting Marilyn Manson, I stayed off to the side as he threw water out over the photo pit and crowd. And I was glad I did. Other photographers at the show ended up with water on their camera gear.

FANS

The concert crowd can make your life easy or difficult. Either way, you have to remember that the band is there for the fans, the paying patrons—not you. So when you photograph a show in a venue that has a photo pit, stay mindful that you're in front of the fans. Make sure you don't block their view too much.

I received some good advice early in my career. A publicist told me not to stand directly in front of the lead singer of the band for too long, because it's not fair to the fans that end up with a blocked view. I've tried to follow this advice as much as possible over the years.

Two of the most obvious ways to avoid blocking a fan's view of the performers:

- **Stand off to the side**, especially before the band takes the stage and when you're not shooting.
- **Crouch down** when possible.

For venues that have no photo pit, fans can make your life easier by letting you up front to snap a few photos. Ask politely and hand out business cards, so people can check your website after the show to see the photos. Heck, you never know … some might actually buy a print or two, making this necessary interaction a source of revenue.

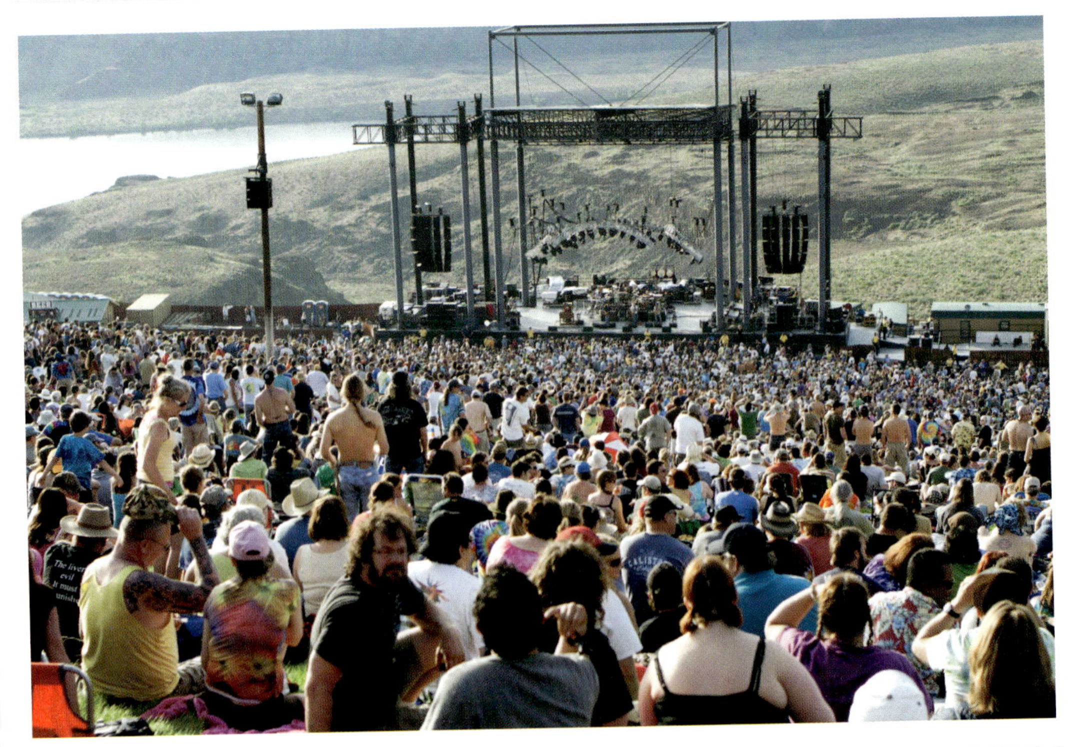

Ask any musician and (s)he'll tell you that the show is all about the fans. Here, fans wait for The Dead to take the stage at the Gorge Amphitheater.
Taken at 1/320 second, f/5.0, and ISO 200

EDITORS

When you're shooting on assignment, it's very important to remember the goal of the shoot—even in the excitement of actually photographing the show. When you're not shooting on someone else's assignment, give *yourself* an assignment and keep your goal(s) in mind during the shoot.

For example, if shooting for a band to get images for its website, then make sure to capture each of the members in a solo shot. If shooting for the venue, then capture the individual performers and get shots of the stage and the show. And, of course, if you're photographing a show for a guitar magazine, concentrate on getting great images of the guitar(s) and guitarist(s).

In fact, every time you raise the camera to your eye, think about the purpose of the image. Listen to that voice in your head—the one telling you to do good things!—before pressing the shutter release button. The editor you're working for is usually not at the show when you shoot, but sometimes it helps if you pretend (s)he is.

PUBLICISTS

At times, the band or record label publicist will actually be on the road with the band. This is a really good thing for you as a concert photographer, because it allows you to meet him/her in person, and it gives you a chance to present yourself as a professional. Another plus to having the publicist at the show is that (s)he'll probably make sure that the rules are being followed. This means that security staff will allow credentialed photographers in the pit and for the full allotted shooting time.

MEDIA ESCORTS

These important folks sometimes don't get the recognition they deserve. Media escorts are usually hired by a venue or promoter or even sometimes a band to deal with members of the media on the day of a show. They escort photographers (and videographers) into the building and into the photo pit or soundboard to shoot.

An example: When I arrive to shoot at one of the local venues in San Diego that's run by Live Nation, a representative meets me, hands me the photo pass, and escorts me to and from the venue's photo area. Many times the onsite media escort is not the person who approved the pass, but (s)he's in charge at the show. Good relationships with media escorts can be invaluable. When credentials are not in order, for instance, these people can often vouch for you or contact tour personnel.

PHOTOGRAPHERS

The chances of you being the only photographer at a show are slim, but it does happen. You just never know. I've been in photo pits with one other photographer, and I've been in pits with seventy-five others. And while you'd think that photographers would treat each other well, that's not always the case. We'll cover photo pit etiquette a little later in this chapter. For now, just know that you will most likely be working alongside other photographers who are all just trying to get their shots—like you.

VENUE STAFF

Ushers, waitresses, and other event staff are working for a living, and they don't need you in their way. I've included these venue staff people on this list, because your paths will eventually cross, and it usually happens when you're in their space or they're in yours. Someone ends up feeling put out.

At some venues, the wait staff use the photo pit to serve drinks to fans in the front. And while they usually try to stay out of photographers' way, it's best to keep an eye out for them. I mean, a tray full of drinks falling into your camera bag will result in a very bad shoot.

Some of the more experienced staff will understand that you're there for just a short time and they'll either wait for you to leave or try to work around you. In any case, be polite and courteous. Everything will go smoother that way.

Ushers are a different story. Many of them believe that they are also functioning as security—even if they're not. So they might try to stop you from entering a certain area or walking down an aisle. I try very hard to introduce myself to these folks early in the evening and explain that I'm working the event, like they are. This usually serves me well. If you've talked with an usher, (s)he's much less likely to stop you while you're working.

SECURITY

If there's one group of people that can absolutely set the tone for a shoot, it's the security staff. They have a tough job and really don't want you to become a problem. If they think you *are* causing problems, they will remove you from the photo pit, and there will be nothing you can do about it.

Security usually has the final say about who goes where during a show—and rightfully so. They are responsible for the safety of the band, the fans, the crew, and the photographers.

I go out of my way to introduce myself to the security personnel at a venue, especially those working at the stage. And that's a good habit, because the more you shoot concerts, the more likely you are to see the same faces in security jackets. And it goes both ways. So make sure yours is a face they want to see. If the security staff knows you and likes you, then you'll have an easier time getting your shots of the show. You might even get extra access if you're known as a photographer who acts in a responsible and professional way.

One way to get on security's good side is to offer them earplugs. They usually have them already, but they appreciate the gesture. And be sure to always do what they say and follow the rules.

THE PHOTO PIT

The photo pit is where I go to work. And I think one of the coolest things about being a concert photographer is being able to photograph from the photo pit. This is the area in front of the stage between the fans and the band. And there's just no denying it: the photo pit is the coolest seat in the house.

It's all yours for three songs, right?! Ha. A lot of photographers think that's the case … until they find themselves crammed into a tiny area with thirty other photographers as well as a large contingent of big-muscled security personal, a media rep or two, and sometimes even the friends and family of the band who've been given media credentials.

That's right, the photo pit can be the greatest place from which to shoot a show and the most frustrating. Your experience here depends on a bunch of different factors, including the size of the pit, the possible shooting angles, the stage layout, the security staff, other photographers, the band, the fans, and even the height of the stage. The one thing you can count on is that the pit is never the same twice—even at the same venue. It's configured based on the show.

GOING NOWHERE

At some shows, I'm the only photographer. But other times, the pit is so crowded that it's impossible to move at all. When I was photographing the Stagecoach Country Music Festival in 2011, for example, the main stage photo pit was exactly one person wide. There was a break in the middle, so if you went in on the left, you stayed on the left; if you went in on the right, you stayed on the right. Because the pit was so narrow, the photographers had to stand in single file and, once in position, it was nearly impossible to move. This meant that every shot had the same angle, and if a musician stayed on the other side of the stage, there was no way to capture him. Bummer.

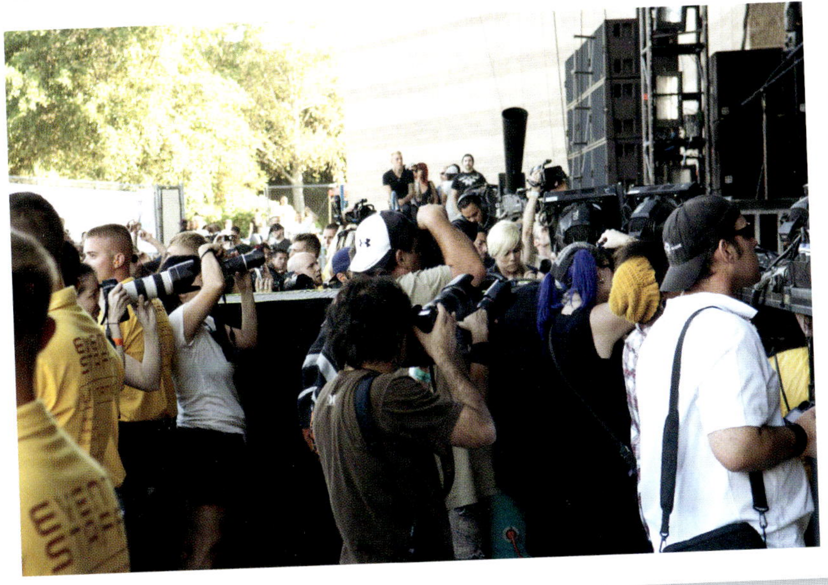

The photo pit at the Mayhem Festival Main Stage was packed with photographers. Most of them were clustered around the center of the stage.

DO'S AND DON'TS

Wouldn't the world be a great place if everyone got along all the time? Ahh … Well, you can start by making the photo pit a better place—for yourself and the other people in it—by following a few simple rules. These are not rules I just made up randomly. They come from years of experience in thousands of photo pits with other photographers, security people, video guys, and assorted other people. Most are common sense and basic tenets of respect. Of course, not everyone in the pit will observe this code of conduct, so to speak, but following it really does pay in the long run.

- **Be polite to the fans.**
  This is the most important thing to remember when shooting a show, and it should be in the back of your mind at all times. For me, this means trying not to stand directly in front of a fan for too long and being considerate about where I walk and stand. Remember that the fans are the ones paying for the tickets that keep shows happening.

- **Respect security.**
  Working security at a concert can be a tough job. At some shows the crowds are extremely energetic and really make security people work for their money. For instance, crowd-surfing fans sometimes come flying feet first into the photo pit (wearing boots!). Ouch. You'll be grateful when security stops this. And some fans will do about anything to get on the stage to meet their favorite musician(s) in person. I've seen fans get on the stage … only to be quickly escorted off the stage and out of the venue. But for some reason, there are people who still think that it's a good idea to climb up on stage during a show.

  The best way to deal with the security at a show is to make sure they don't have to deal with you. This means staying out of the way and not being a problem—even when they're wrong.

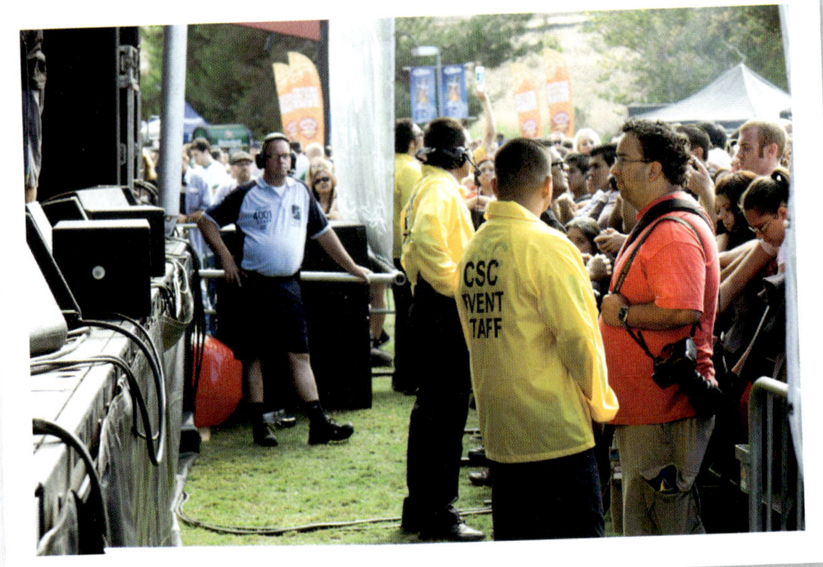

There will be security personnel in the photo pit, and it pays to be nice to them. Don't forget that they are the ones in control. At this side stage, there was plenty of space for photographers … even with the security people in yellow and blue.

- **Be kind to other photographers.**
  This one can be tough, because other photographers are your competition, right? I know the photo pit can seem like a very competitive place, but it doesn't need to be that way. It helps to develop your own style for concert photography work and understand that the photo pit is a place you need to share. One way to help foster a better working environment is to always walk behind other photographers when they're shooting. A small tap on the shoulder can let them know you're there.

- **Don't camp in one spot.**
  If there are lots of photographers in the pit, it's likely that most of them are trying to get the same kind of shots. So when you get a great shot from a certain location, move around and let someone else shoot from there. If everyone does this, each shooter there can get images from the good spot(s).

- **Respect the rules.**
  Be sure that you uphold all of a venue's rules—all the time. If they restrict you to shooting from the left side only, then shoot from the left side. If they say you can shoot during the first three songs only and not shoot the audience, then do your work in three songs and don't photograph the audience. Even if the venue staff asks you to leave the photo pit before the allotted time is up, then leave the photo pit.

  Sometimes it can be upsetting or frustrating to follow rules that you don't understand, but I've never come across a situation when it's worth it to break rules in the photo pit. Being allowed to shoot again at a venue where you broke rules is unlikely.

- **Leave when you should.**
  Photographers try to shoot just a little more after the allotted time ... all the time. Don't be that guy. Nothing drives security, publicists, and media escorts more nuts than a photographer who tries to push the limits. Don't do it, especially if you want a concert photography career with any longevity.

In summary, these are the people skills that will help you out in the photo pit. And trust me, being nice, polite, and professional will serve you well for future opportunities.

SOUNDBOARD SHOOTS

Sometimes you won't be shooting from a photo pit—either because there is no photo pit or because photography at a show is limited to another shooting location at the request of the band, venue, or production company. Many of the big shows now require photographers to shoot from the soundboard or the back of the room.

Being at the soundboard means you're working next to the people responsible for the sound at the show. It's very important that you to watch your step and don't inadvertently unplug something or get between the sound engineer and the stage. The best course of action is to make sure that you are in the right spot before the lights go down and not to move. If you're allowed to move, be very very careful about where you step.

And while it's unlikely that you'll ever be excited about the prospect of shooting from the soundboard, it's possible to get great shots from this position. It just requires a little preparation.

LENS LENGTH

The first hurdle to overcome is the distance to the performer, which is usually quite far from the soundboard. The main problem many photographers face with this distance issue is that their lenses are just not long enough. That 70–200mm f/2.8 lens suddenly doesn't offer the reach needed to get great shots. And this, unfortunately, is when concert photography can become a very expensive endeavor. Long lenses cost a lot of money.

Shooting from a soundboard usually requires a 300mm lens or longer. And since the light is low—it's still concert lighting, after all—that 300mm lens needs to have a maximum aperture of f/4 or wider.

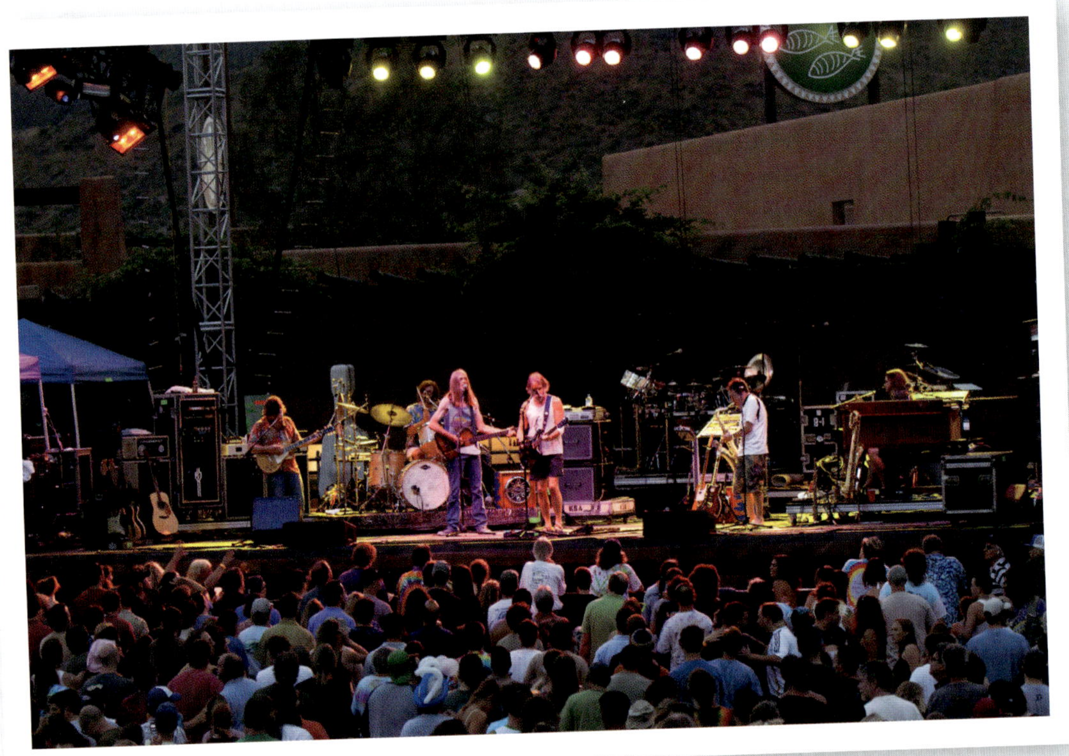

Shooting from the soundboard can result in good overall views of the band, but the distance can make it tough to get a great shot of any individual musician without a long lens. This photograph was captured with an 80–200mm f/2.8 lens, which just wasn't long enough to get in close from the soundboard.

Taken at 1/80 second, f/2.8 ISO, and ISO 400

In my experience, the perfect lens to use for shooting from the soundboard is a 400mm f/2.8. But that's going to be a pipe dream for a lot of people, because it costs about $9000. Yes, you read that right: $9000 for a lens that you get to use for three songs once in a while. Fortunately, there are options.

For starters, you can rent a lens from a local camera store or one of the online rental businesses. Here are two of the biggest online lens rental places:

- **Lens Pro To Go** (www.lensprotogo.com)
  This company rents cameras and lenses and sends them anywhere in the United States. The lenses and cameras can be rented for 4 days, 10 days, 14 days … all the way to 30 days. The best things about Lens Pro To Go is that the company does not charge a security deposit and it has a lot of gear. Take the Nikon 400mm f/2.8 lens for example. You can rent it for 4 days for $340.00 or 14 days for $690.00. That's a whole lot less than the $9000 buy-it price.

- **Borrow Lenses** (www.borrowlenses.com)
  This company has a ton of gear for photographers, and its minimum rental period is only 3 days. So the rental cost is less than Lens Pro To Go, but you get the gear for less time. Here, the Nikon 400mm f/2.8 lens rents for $299.00 for 3 days, which is $40 less than Lens Pro To Go. But keep in mind that you have to pay a little more for a longer rental period.

Another option is to use a less expensive 300mm lens that opens to a maximum aperture of only f/4. These lenses are much more affordable than the 400mm lenses, but they are still quite pricey. And an important drawback to note is that these lenses require photographers to push up the ISO, because they don't open up as wide as an f/2.8 does.

MONOPOD

When you shoot from the soundboard, especially with a longer lens in hand, it's a very good idea to use a monopod to support the lens. This will help you reduce camera shake, which is key to getting clear shots. Remember, the longer the lens, the more obvious it becomes in an image if there was any movement of the camera during capture. The slightest movement in this setup will result in a blurry image. And since it's nearly impossible to hand hold a big lens for a long period of time—those lenses get really heavy very quickly—the monopod can feel like a lifesaver to a concert photographer.

Since you're not moving around in this situation and the monopod will not be in the way, this is the one time I recommend bringing it. Using a monopod in the photo pit is close to impossible and it's much more of a hindrance than a help, because it's bulky and heavy. And most times you won't be allowed to use one in the photo pit anyway due to the space limitations.

COMPOSITION

Truly, the main problem with shooting from the soundboard is achieving good composition in your photos. Because of the distance and the fixed shooting position, there is usually very little that can be done to make photos look much different from one another. And this problem is exaggerated if the performer doesn't move much.

Unfortunately, there's not much you can do in these situations, except watch for any changes of expression on the performers' faces or changes in the background.

Yeah, I'll admit that when it comes down to it, shooting from the soundboard is not much fun. But it's not an impossible situation with the right gear. There's more on gear in Chapter 4.

SHOOTING FROM THE CROWD

It'll happen … eventually. You'll show up to shoot a show, expecting a photo pit, and you'll find out that there isn't one. And while most bars and some clubs don't ever have photo pits, this is also (surprisingly) the case on some big tours—gigs at which you expect to have plenty of space to shoot. Instead, you might discover that the stage has been changed or flat-out isn't there, because of the nature of the performance.

When I was asked to photograph John Legend for the RIMAC Arena, I was told a few hours before the show that there would be no photo pit, that we would be shooting from the side aisles and the soundboard. This was because John makes his entrance down the middle of the floor seats, and he walks up steps to the stage. So no photo pit. No dedicated space for photographers to shoot the show.

It's just important to realize that all kinds of venues can remove the photo pit or make it very small. It depends on the band, the crowd, and any other reason that might exist. Concert photographs are wise to anticipate a changing circumstance and prepare to be flexible.

Here are some things you can do to prepare for an unknown shooting situation. While none are perfect, these actions will enable you to get the shots you need for a successful session.

GO EARLY AND WAIT.

This is a much more appealing solution if you actually like the band you're photographing, because you will be hanging out with the other fans for a while, sometimes a long while. This also only really works at General Admission shows; otherwise you'll need to buy a ticket for a seat up close. But the trick is to get to the venue early enough to be close to the front and then stand there and wait until the band starts.

When I was starting out, I used to do this a lot at venues that allowed cameras. I would position myself just off center and as close to the stage as possible. Once the show started, I'd photograph until I believed I had all the shots I wanted. Then I'd pack my camera in a bag and either leave or watch the rest of the show. The downside to this method is that your photos are all taken from the same position, and this can get a little boring.

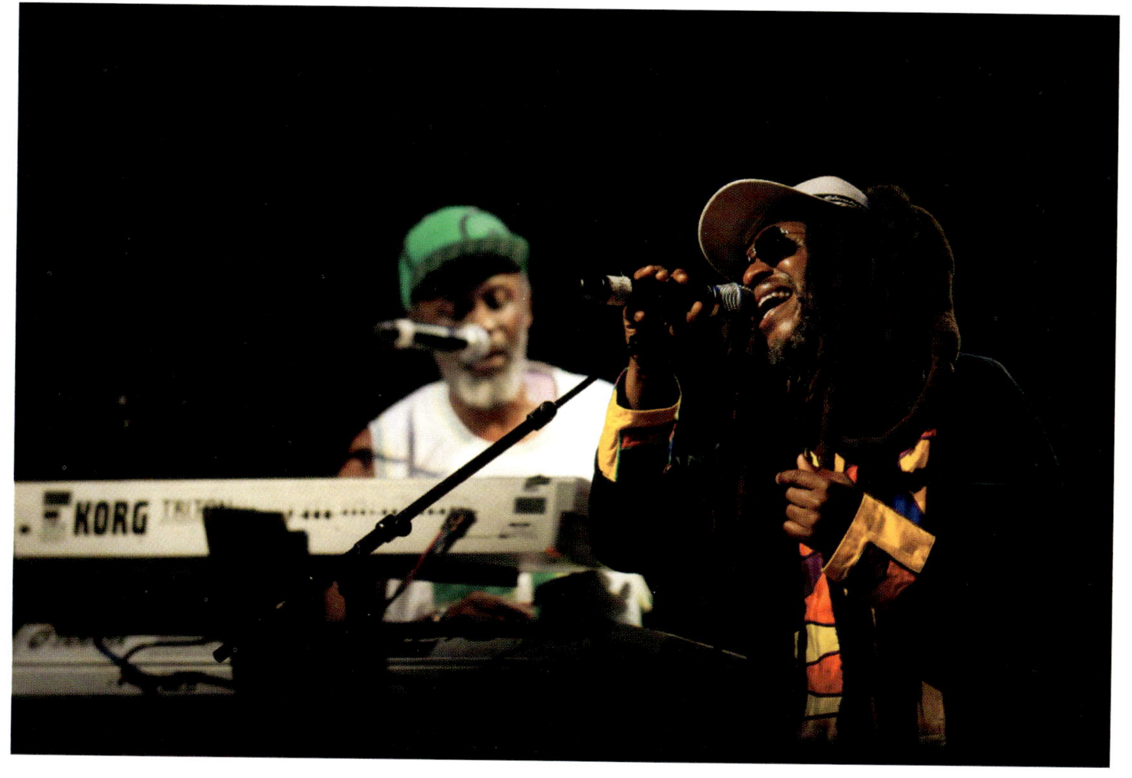

I have been photographing the reggae band Steel Pulse for years, but to get a shot with both David Hinds and Selwyn Brown, I had to shoot from the crowd with a longer lens.
Taken at 1/200 second, f/2.8, and ISO 3200

SHOOT AND MOVE.

Many fans will allow you to get in front of them for a few moments to take a photo, especially if they know they'll get to see the photos afterward. For this to work, you need to be very polite and carry a ton of business cards. You also need to be able to take rejection very well. The idea here is to tell a fan that you'll be in his or her way for just a second and that the photos will be online. Be sure to hand the person a card with your website so (s)he can access the images after the show.

For this to work, you need to shoot and move. Do not block the fan's view for more than a minute or two. When finished, say thanks as you move to a different position. This method allows you to get a wide variety of shots, but it can fail, which means you might end up shooting from the back of the venue.

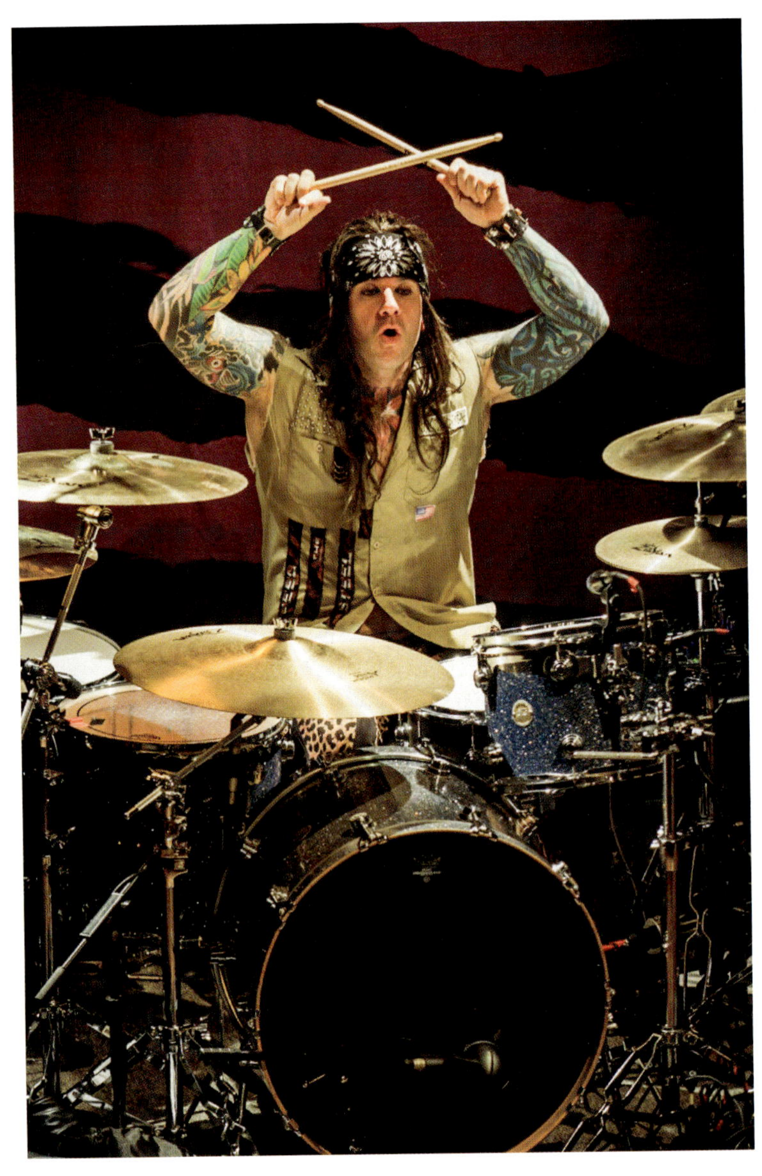

The balcony is sometimes the best place to shoot from, especially for getting those elusive drummer shots. This photograph of drummer Stix Zadinia was taken from the balcony at a club with a 70–200mm f/2.8 lens at 200mm.

Taken at 1/200 second, f/2.8, and ISO 2000

USE A LONG LENS.

The main advantage of shooting a concert in a bar or small club is that you can usually get pretty close to the stage. In this situation, a 70–200mm f/2.8 lens is perfect for getting in close … even from the back of the room.

In a bar, look to shoot from the soundboard. I know it seems odd to voluntarily choose to shoot from the soundboard; but in small venues, this area is usually raised a little so the sound tech can better see the stage. This works in your favor, because it allows you to reduce the number of fan heads in your photos.

If the venue has a balcony, try to get upstairs and shoot from there. The distance is likely greater than from spots on the floor, but you'll get better angles. It's also usually less crowded on the balcony and easier to get to the front. The same tactics that you use on a crowd on the floor can work for a crowd in the balcony. Just remember to be polite and gracious for any inconvenience you may cause a fan.

CONSIDER THE SIDE VIEW

Some bars and small clubs have another option for concert photographers. There may be a way to shoot from the sides of the stage, especially if there's a section for a monitor mixing board. The angles for your shots in this position are not as good as those from the front of the stage, but with some patience, timing, and luck, your photos can be great.

A little sign language with the monitor tech may allow you to get up tight and take a few shots. Just make sure that you don't get in the way of the musicians or crew.

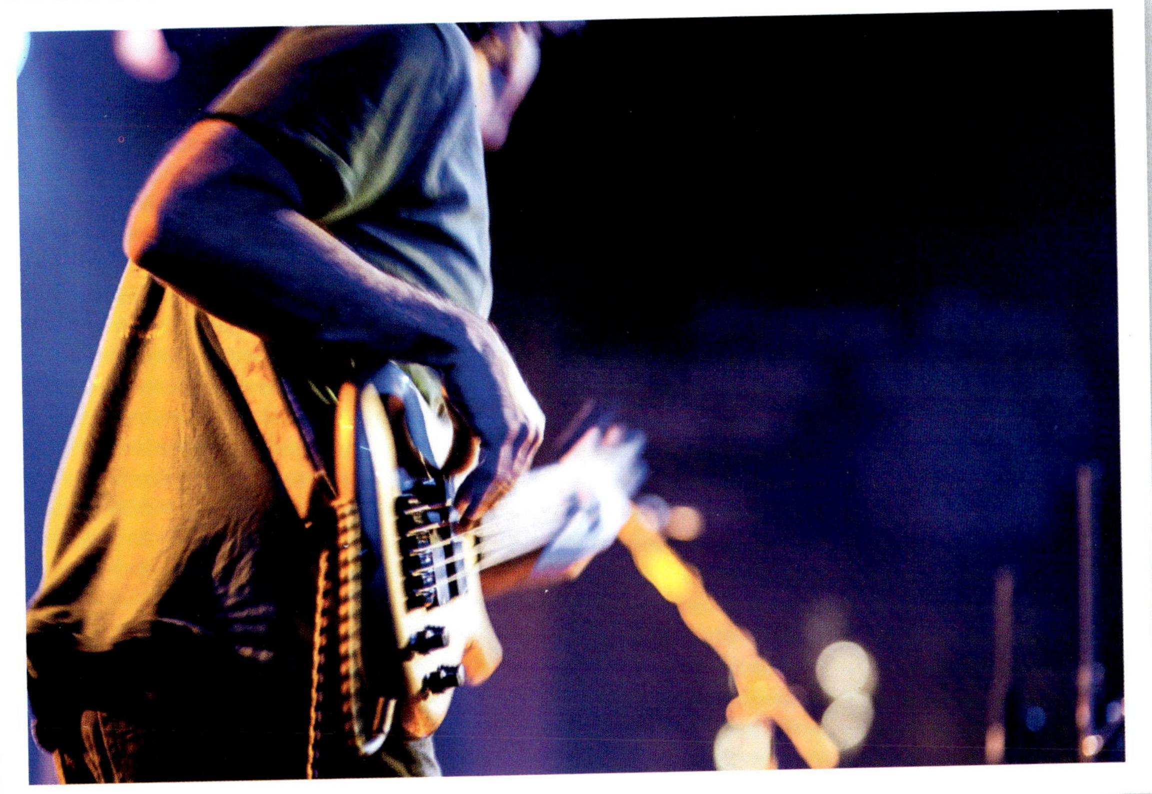

Shooting from the side of the stage gives you opportunities to experiment, and it gives you angles that are just not available from the front.
Taken at 1/30 second, f/1.4, and ISO 1600

Allen Ross Thomas

Concert Photographer

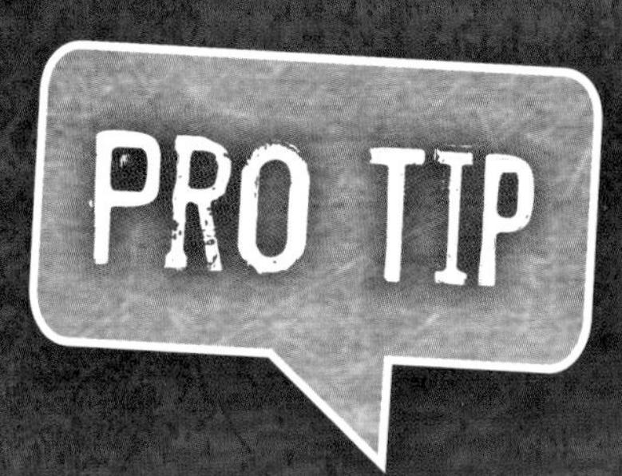

How long have you been shooting concerts?

Seven years.

What's the most important thing about working with other photographers in the photo pit?

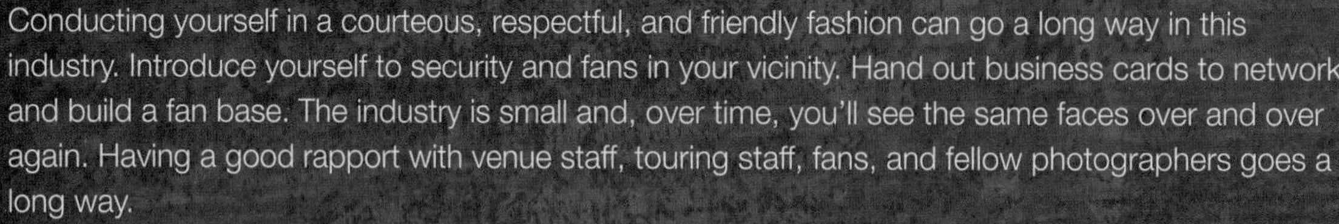
Conducting yourself in a courteous, respectful, and friendly fashion can go a long way in this industry. Introduce yourself to security and fans in your vicinity. Hand out business cards to network and build a fan base. The industry is small and, over time, you'll see the same faces over and over again. Having a good rapport with venue staff, touring staff, fans, and fellow photographers goes a long way.

And when the shooting begins, shoot with conviction and pass other photographers from behind with a light tap. Do not review photos during the active shooting period. You are there to photograph, not to edit. Do not chase a moment that has already happened; instead, anticipate the next big moment and be positioned for it.

What do you do when there is no pit?

There are two general scenarios when shooting without a photo pit. There's either an open standing-room floor or reserved seating. In both cases, I prefer not to share a position at the front of the stage that's packed in with fans, and I don't want to be intrusive to front row ticket holders.

When working from an open floor, I begin shooting house left or house right at the stage edge, where fan density tends to be at its lightest. From this position I primarily focus on artist profiles and headshots with a long zoom and catch crowd interaction with a wide zoom. After the first couple of songs, the crowd tends to settle from the rush to stage front, and this allows me to do a slow pass across the stage. I cross a row or two back from stage front.

When shooting among reserve seating, I take a similar approach. I start at house left or house right. And my pass along the front of the stage is more like a crawl across the floor. I stay low and unobtrusive as I try to capture a series of frames from a kneeling position.

How do you prepare for soundboard shoots?

When preparing for a soundboard-bound shoot, I approach the assignment just as I would approach any concert assignment. I research the performance, research the positioning, and review shooting notes from past assignments at the venue. From this, I determine if my gear is suitable or if I need to rent a lens with longer reach for the evening. Investing in a collapsible step stool is a good idea, because photographers are often at the same level as thousands of fans. A small stool can

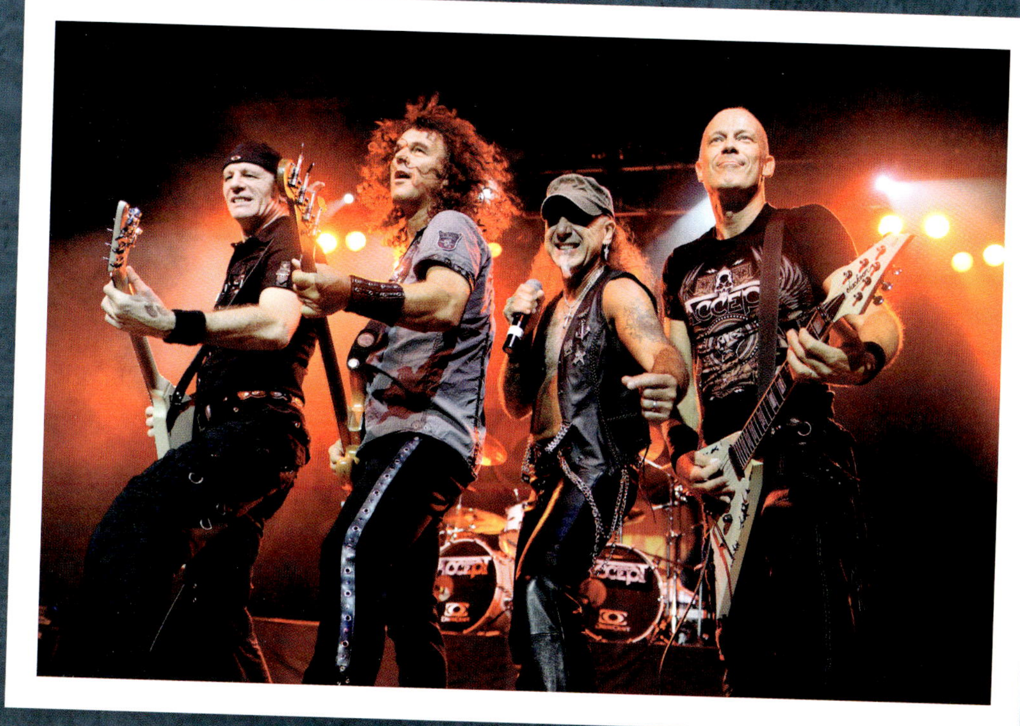

© Allen Ross Thomas

provide a little extra height for increased audience clearance. I also look for positioning variety that may be available around the soundboard. Try shooting from the sides, behind, in front of, and as far left and right from the plane of the soundboard you can.

What is the one tip you would give to photographers who want to get into the concert photography business?

Find a few local clubs that are camera-friendly and go there. Treat these excursions as assignments. Always shoot in manual and learn the technicals of shutter, aperture, and ISO. Review EXIF data to understand why certain settings worked well … or didn't. Internalize these with your memory of the lighting scenario. Also seek key or peak moments in an artist's performance and frame them cleanly with minimal obstructions.

And remember to introduce yourself to venue staff, fans, and bands; then follow up with these people with an aggressive edit of your best shots. Develop a portfolio of 15–20 examples of your best work and submit it to local street press and webzines. Ask to be a contributor and to keep you in mind for future assignments. Lather, rinse, and repeat.

This process stays the same as your career progresses—even as the venues get better, the restrictions tighter, the media outlets larger, and the artists more widely known.

Maile Hatfield

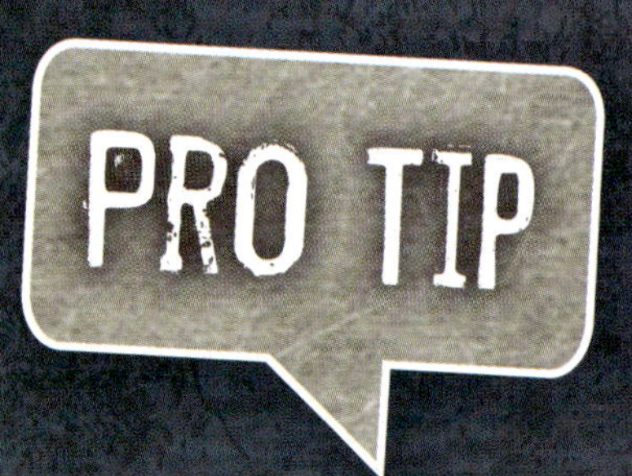

Band Manager, Tour Manager
Twitter: @seemaile

How important are good images to your bands?

Critical. Today's world is show-and-tell ... emphasis on *show*. People want to see what their experience will be. Think: What does the room look like when there's a live show? What does the energy of the performers feel like? For my primary client, soul and emotion are two things we try to convey, as they are the driving force in the live shows. You can hear that on the audio and see it on video. But if you have to send one still image to convey that, it better be compelling.

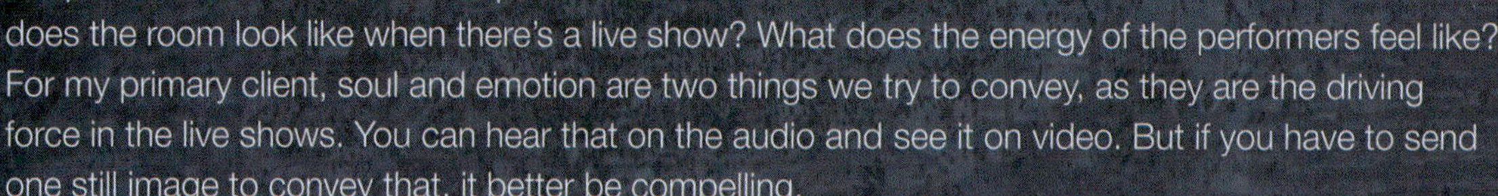

What do you expect from photographers when they are photographing your bands?

To be professionals, to communicate in advance, and to follow the venue rules. I also expect them to want to show the artists in the best light possible. No secret shots from the dressing room. No "artful" angles that make the musicians look unattractive. I call those the "Today Show" shots—shots from the ankles looking up. No one looks good in those shots. And the fisheye isn't always the best choice either. As a rule, look at the photographs on the artists' websites. If yours aren't equally as flattering, they won't be used. Lastly, EDIT. The fastest way to be ruled out is to send a gallery of all four hundred shots you took, especially when half are out of focus or blurry. Send me three amazing shots and ten good ones.

What are the rules for photographing your bands?

No flash. No in-your-face shots that distract the musicians from doing their jobs. Respect the fans. As a courtesy, if it's the first time we've worked together, I prefer to see a photographer's work before it's released publicly. In larger venues, the three-song rule allows the need for photography while protecting the performance from distraction. Word of advice: [After the first three songs is a] GREAT time to go shoot the audience, the hallways, the scene outside, the marquee, and other aspects of the show.

When a photographer asks to shoot one of the bands, what should they say?

"I'd like to come shoot the band ... for (magazine/website)." Large bands or venues won't let amateurs into the photo pit nor will they issue credentials without a publication. The band is giving you access; what are you giving the band? Hopefully not more mediocre pictures of them online.

Or (for smaller bands) say, "I'm a photographer trying to gain more experience in live concert photography. May I come shoot your show?" In either case, explain how the images will be used, if they'll be sold, if you grant management final approval. It also helps to share where your work has appeared and a link to your site or online portfolio.

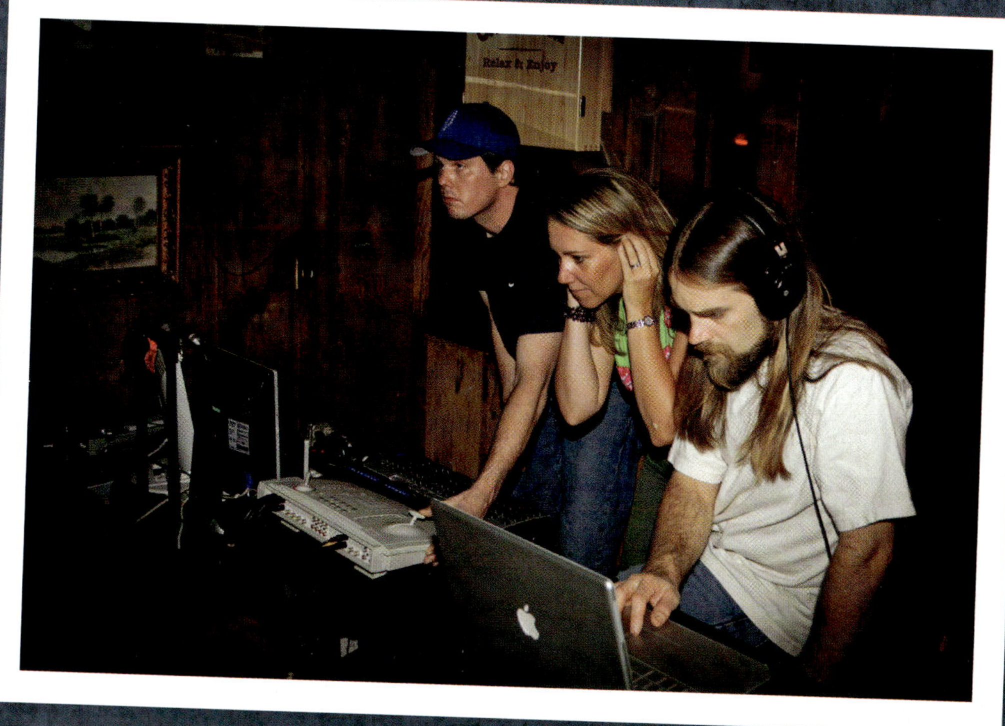

What is the one piece of advice you have for a photographer who's starting out in the concert business?

Offer to shoot the band for free or at least for trade. The band gets to use some images for its website and you build a portfolio. If the images are to be used for products, then make sure you discuss that up front and that everyone understands the licensing involved and the payment structure.

Do good work, follow management/venue rules, and follow up with a gallery link of a few incredible images. Remember to edit the collection. If you do good work, you'll be invited back for more intimate moments, like aftershow, backstage, warming up. You'll likely become friends with the artists, as creative professionals do. Once that happens, the band will likely pay you to come shoot their next album cover/press photo, or whatnot. Just remember: What goes on the road stays on the road. You should never EVER photograph something you intuitively know you shouldn't.

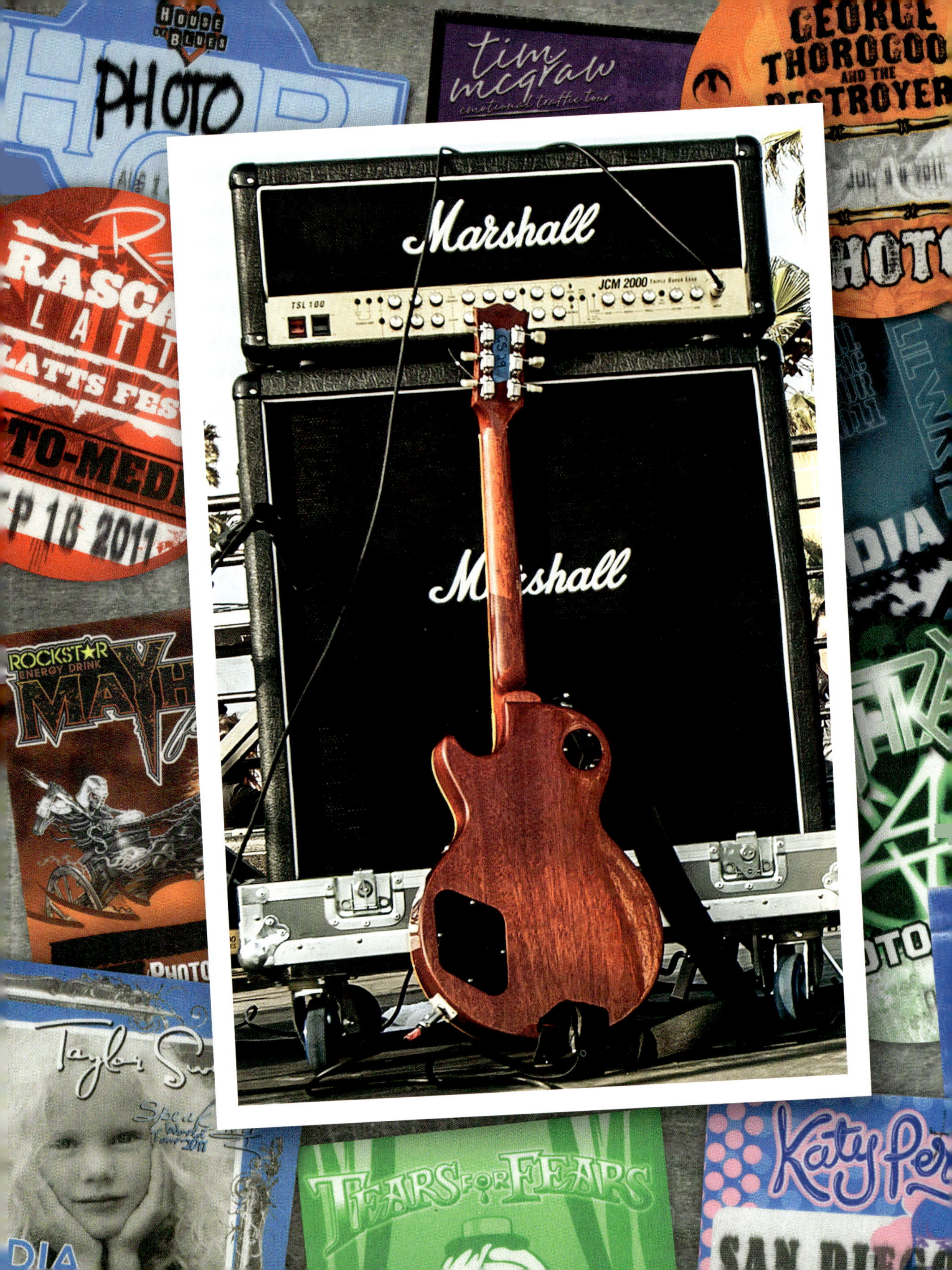

HOUSE OF BLUES
PHOTO
tim mcgraw
emotional traffic tour
GEORGE
AND THE
Marshall
JCM 2000
TSL 100
ROCKSTAR
ENERGY DRINK
TEARS FOR FEARS

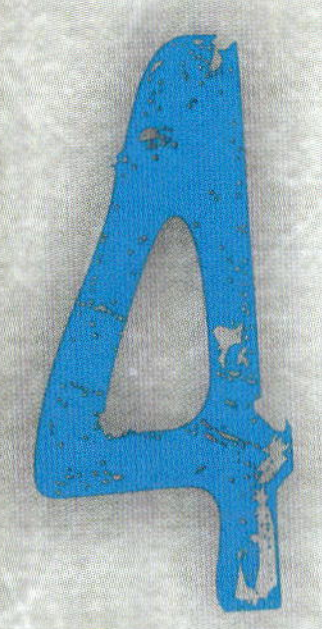

OH THE GEAR: WORKING WITH THE BEST CAMERA AND LENSES FOR THE JOB

To create photographs, you need a camera and a lens. And some will say that good photos can be taken with *any* camera and lens. But I'm here to tell you that when it comes to photographing concerts in low light, that's not always true.

The kind of camera you choose to use for concert photography is important, especially its ISO range and the amount of digital noise it produces at the higher ISO settings. And the lenses needed for concert shooting have wide maximum apertures. Unfortunately, these are not cheap.

Let's think about camera selection first.

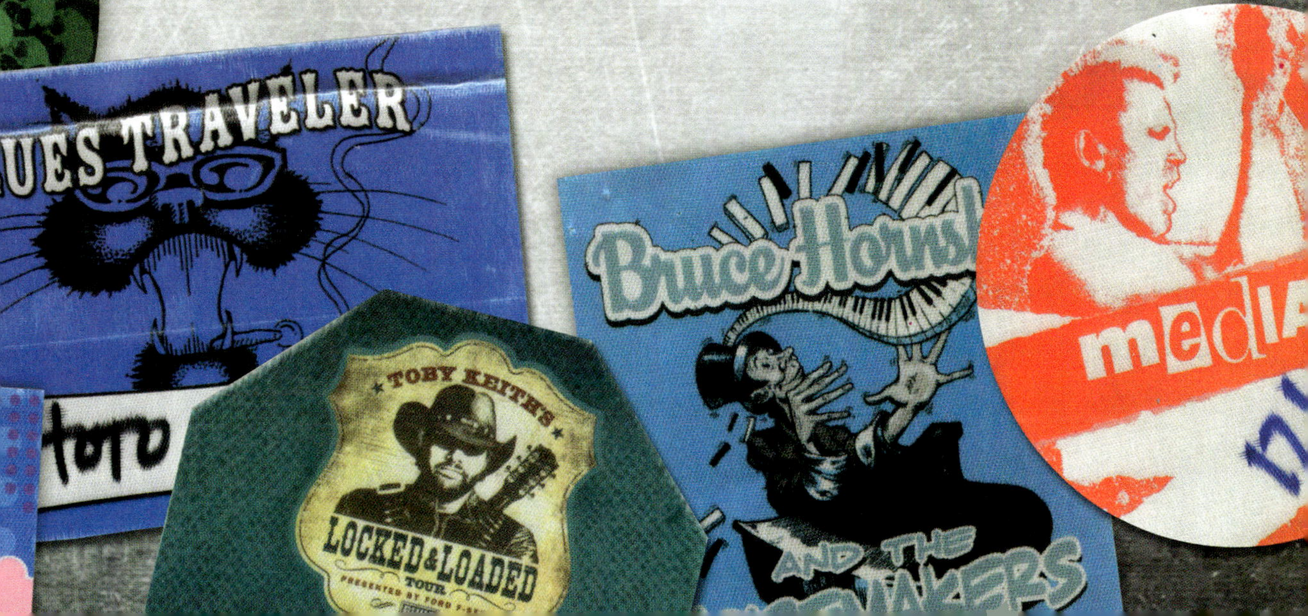

CAMERAS

Picking the right camera is a tough job these days. Years ago, before digital photography, a camera really just needed to move the shutter and allow light coming through the lens to reach the film. Then it needed to advance the film to the next frame. Everything was mechanical, and every camera did the job the same way.

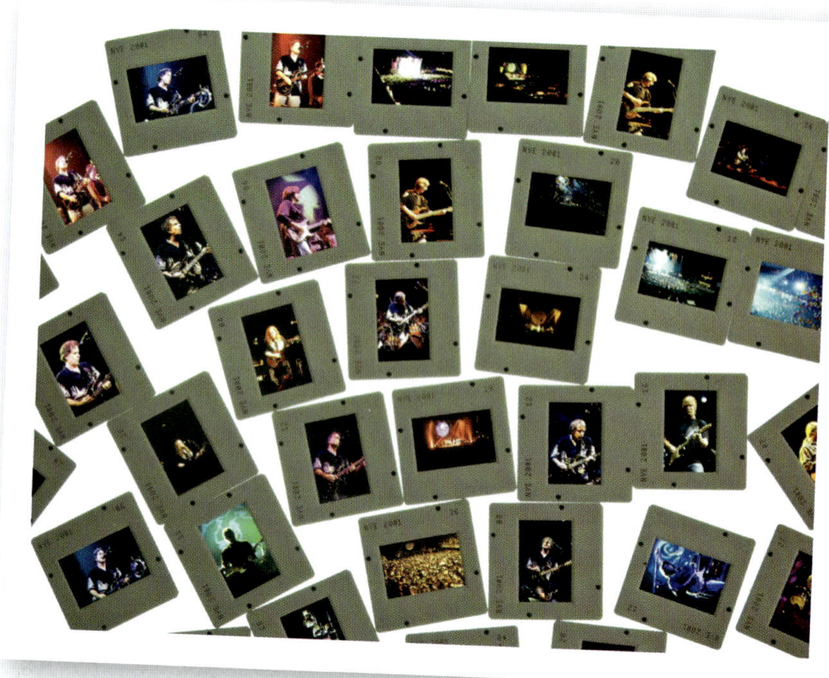

Before digital, I shot concerts using slide film. The sorting process then wasn't much different from today's process. But instead of a computer, photographers used a light box and a loupe.

If you needed to shoot in low light, you bought film with a high ISO, and you shot 12, 24, or 36 frames. When done with a roll, you put in a new one. If you wanted to photograph in black and white, you used black and white film. To make the colors in your images look more saturated, you used a film that made color look more saturated. It really was a different era of photography. Oh, and you didn't get to see the photos until after they were developed and printed, which could take hours or days! Herein lies the primary advantage to digital photography: you get to see the image right away. You know instantly if you got the shot; no more waiting for the photo lab.

When digital sensors started to replace film, the choices in camera bodies became more important, because they dictate the kind of photography you can create. In other words, the camera itself began controlling more aspects of the final image. With no film, any options related to a photograph must be built into the camera from the onset.

But look beyond the camera's body when buying a new camera, especially your first camera. Be sure to consider the whole system. Be sure you're comfortable with the body, its features, *and* the brand's related accessories. Because once you start spending money on lenses, you'll pretty much be locked into a camera brand … unless you're in a position to spend a lot of money to re-purchase lenses for a different system.

PATIENCE

Buying a new camera can be stressful. Cameras are not cheap, and the truth is that concert photography doesn't pay too well. So every dollar *has* to count. I really try to weigh the pros and cons of every piece of photography gear I buy, especially when it comes to a camera. Cause here's the deal: Once you buy a certain make of camera and a couple of lenses for it, you'll probably stick with that brand for a long time. This can be frustrating, as camera companies are always competing for your business. They keep coming out with new cameras and cool features. But I've noticed that if one brand comes out with something really great, chances are your brand will offer something competitive very soon. You just need a little patience.

MEMORY CARDS

It might not seem very important to know what kind of memory card a camera takes if it's your first camera, but this issue of compatibility might play a large part in your purchase decision if you've been using a camera that takes a specific card type. You'll have money invested in those cards.

For example, I have a lot of CompactFlash cards that cost a considerable amount of money, and I'd rather not have to buy all new memory cards. Especially if a new camera is going to be a second body or a new main body, then I like to make sure that the two cameras take the same memory cards. I don't want to carry two different types of cards with me on a shoot.

USER CATEGORY

There are different categories of cameras. Some are aimed for the casual consumer; some are designed for the advanced hobbyist; and others are professional-level cameras. Deciding which one is right for you is probably more complicated than you think.

One of the main differences is price. Pro-level cameras cost pro-level prices. But the functional differences between a pro and consumer camera model are the build quality and materials. Camera manufacturers know that professional photographers use (and abuse) their cameras more than the average shooter.

Here are some key differences between consumer, prosumer, and professional-level cameras:

- **Shutter Actuation**
  Digital Single Lens Reflex (dSLR) cameras have a mechanical shutter that moves out of the way when the shutter release button is pressed. And the shutter speed setting determines how long it stays out of the way. Well, that shutter mechanism is a mechanical one, and mechanical systems break down.

A big difference among the different levels of cameras is the expected number of shutter actuations—that is, the number of times the shutter is moved when the shutter release button is pressed. Pro-level cameras are rated for more shutter actuations than consumer cameras. But how important this is to you depends on how many photos you take before upgrading to a new camera. If you tend to keep a camera for a year or two ... and only shoot casually (not hundreds of photos a day), then a low shutter actuation rating is probably fine for you.

If you're curious to know the shutter count of you camera, you can go to www.myshuttercount.com and upload a photo. Right now, the Nikon D3 that I use as a main body has a shutter count of 44,069, and the Nikon D700 that I've been using for a lot longer has a shutter count of 144,223 ... and it's still going strong.

- **Weather Sealing**
  Pro cameras tend to be better sealed against dirt, dust, and the elements. And they need to be, because part of the pro-level price is a reasonable assurance that the camera's going to work everywhere and all the time.

  Many consumer cameras are built well and can hold up in the elements, but they usually don't have the same level of protection as a pro model. For example, I was photographing a show when it started to rain. I covered my gear as well as I could, but my cameras still got wet. I didn't worry, because the cameras were sealed and a quick wipe with a dry towel was all it took. They were fine. A consumer- or prosumer-level camera may have had more trouble, but there's no way to know for sure.

- **Focus Points**
  Many professional cameras have more focus points than their consumer counterparts. For example, the pro-level Nikon D3 has 51 different focus points, while prosumer Nikon D7000 has 39 points and the consumer level Nikon D3100 has only 11. A high number of focus points means you can fine tune where the focus is in an image. More importantly, a high number of focus points helps the camera when tracking a moving subject.

- **Buffer Size**
  Back in the days of film, an image's exposure was created and saved at the same time—at the moment the film was exposed to the light. But with digital photography, the sensor captures the image when it's exposed to the light, but the image then needs to be written to a storage device (the digital film/memory card). And this takes time.

  Camera manufacturers design cameras with a built-in memory buffer that stores images as they are written to the memory card. A bigger buffer means more images can be stored before the camera has to stop and write the image files to the memory card. On professional cameras, this buffer is much bigger than it is on consumer models, and this allows a photographer to capture more images before the camera forces a pause while the buffer empties.

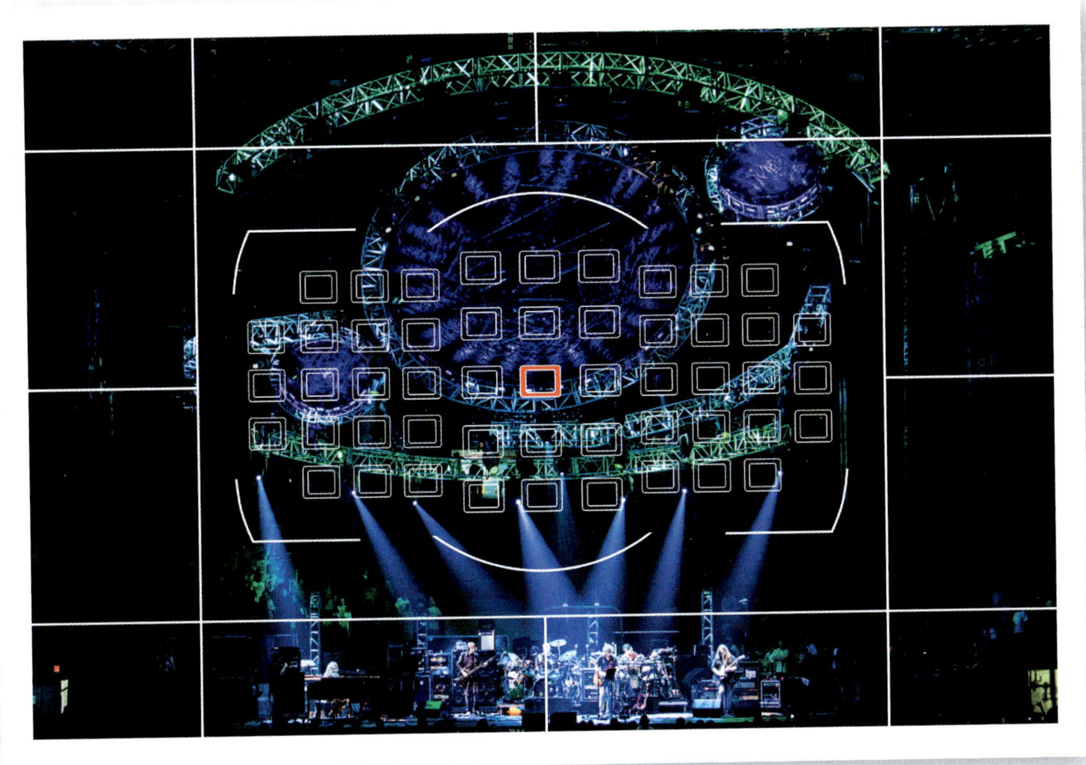

The Nikon D700 has 51 focus points, allowing you to pick exactly where the camera should focus … as long as it's in the center area of the frame. The active point is marked in red.

It's also important to know that the speed of your memory card can affect your shooting time as well. That is, the speed of the card can decrease the time it takes to transfer images from the buffer to the card. Unfortunately though, some consumer cameras don't take advantage of the newest technology and can't use the highest-speed cards at their highest speed. So be sure to make note of this when choosing gear.

- **Scene Modes**
  Many of the consumer and some prosumer cameras have scene modes that automatically adjust the camera for specific situations, such as Sports or Macro or Landscape. These are great for beginner photographers who want a preset other than the basics (Manual, Shutter Speed Priority, Aperture Priority, and Program Auto). Professional cameras don't have these modes, because manufacturers assume that pro photographers don't need these alternate versions of auto mode.

- **Built-In Flash**
  Most professional cameras do not have a built-in flash, because it's unlikely that most professionals would use a built-in flash if it *was* there. The light from those units is just so unflattering. But that

doesn't mean it's useless to have a built-in flash. To the contrary … a built-in flash can be used to trigger an external flash. But for that to happen with a pro-level camera (without a built-in flash), you need to use a separate commander unit or separate flash mounted on the camera.

The worst experience I ever had with a pop-up flash is when it unexpectedly popped up during a concert shoot and fired in a photo pit! I was mortified. But I solved that problem by using a small piece of gaffer tape to keep the flash down … even if the flash button is pushed by mistake.

Now, I know (I am human!) that when a photographer heads out to purchase a new camera, the pull toward a professional-level model is strong. Who doesn't want the biggest and the best? But hold on for just a second and think it out for a minute. There are some real advantages to buying a consumer-level camera: frequent upgrades and a lower price. It's smart to remember that camera manufacturers tend to upgrade consumer-level cameras

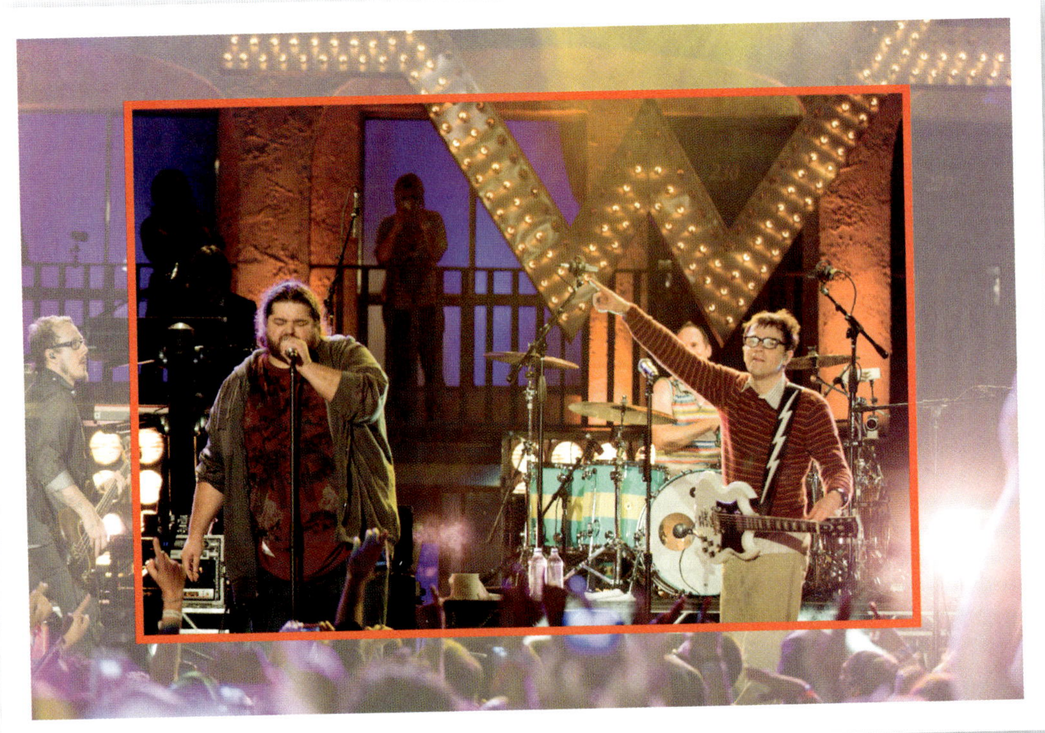

This image was shot with a full frame sensor. If it had been shot on a cropped sensor, the image would only contain the parts inside the red box.

Taken at 1/400 second, f/2.8, and ISO 1600

more often than their pro versions ... and because a consumer-level model costs a lot less than a pro camera, it's possible to upgrade more often and stay at the forefront of technology.

SENSOR SIZE

Digital sensors come in a variety of sizes, but they can be broken down into two basic categories: full frame and cropped frame. A full frame sensor is the same size as a full frame of 35mm film; cropped frame sensors are smaller. There's a lot of difference between the two types of sensors, but concert photographers are primarily concerned with the sensor's effect on focal length and its low-light functionality.

When you use a camera with a cropped frame sensor, it records less of the scene in front of the camera than a full frame sensor does with the same lens. So when you compare images taken at 200mm—one with a full frame sensor and one with a cropped frame sensor—you'll see that the cropped sensor seems to get you in closer, a real advantage when shooting a big show.

MEGAPIXELS

There was a time when digital cameras were judged on their number of megapixels. More megapixels meant a better camera, according to the camera manufacturers engaged in the megapixel war. But is this true?

First, let's define *megapixel*; it's one million pixels, and it's the term used to describe the number of elements on a camera's sensor. So a 10-megapixel camera has more image sensors than a 6-megapixel camera, and a 10-megapixel camera creates image files that are much bigger than a 6-megapixel camera. But the problem with jamming as many megapixels onto a chip as possible is that, to fit, the individual sensors must be small and placed close together. This tends to produce more digital noise when the signal from the chip is amplified.

In 2003, Nikon released a professional-level camera that the company tried to market to photojournalists and sports photographers—instead of pushing for more megapixels. This camera also worked great in concert environments because it was only 4.1 megapixels and produced very low digital noise at the higher ISO settings. This camera, the D2H, allowed photographers to shoot 25 RAW images or 40 full size JPEG images before the buffer was full—something unheard of at the time. This product was a refreshing sign that camera manufactures were going to start looking at improving other features of cameras and get away from focusing solely on megapixels.

Yet there is a case to be made for more megapixels. Since each megapixel captures additional information about a scene, more of them (within reason) ensures that every frame you shoot has a data density that allows you to, say, crop the image if you want and still get a print with a

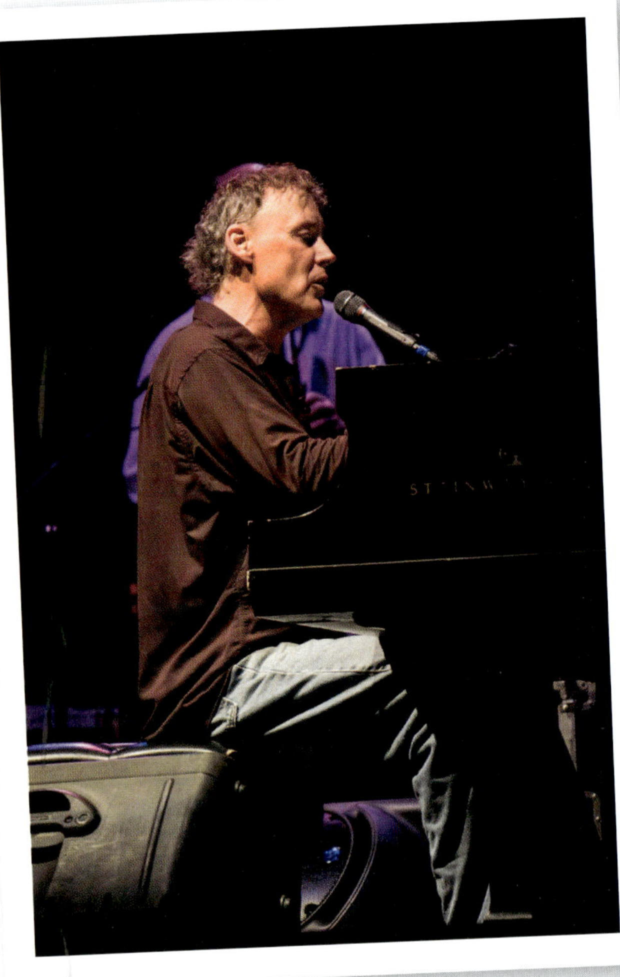

I photographed Bruce Hornsby in concert with a Nikon D2H, a 4.1-megapixel camera that produced a great-looking image that can't be distinguished from the 12.1-megapixel D700 image of Steel Panther.

Taken at 1/100 second, f/3.2, and ISO 500

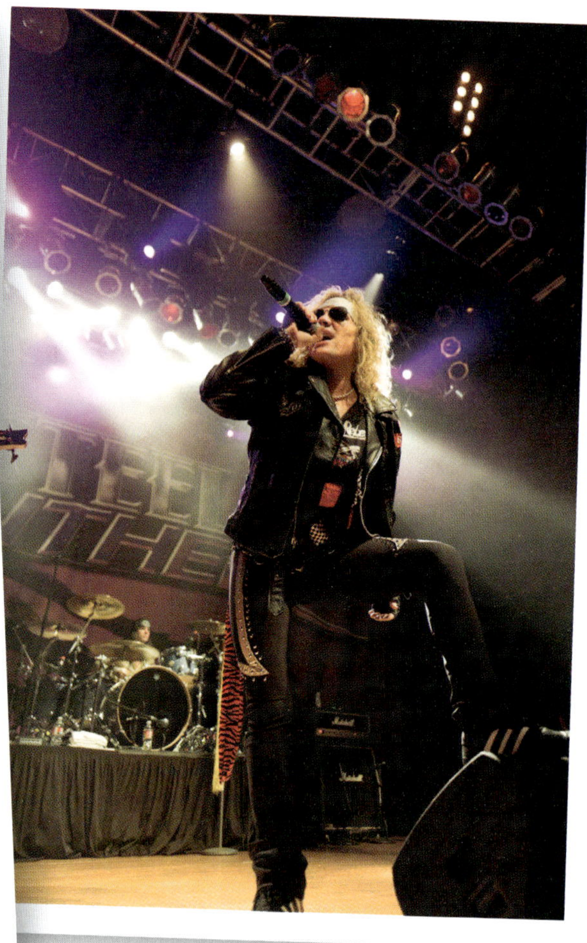

I photographed Steel Panther with the Nikon D700. This camera has a 12.1-megapixel sensor, which captures more information than the D2H 4.1-megapixel camera used for the Bruce Hornsby image. But those extra pixels don't matter when printed at this size or even at 11x17, so depending on the intended use, the number of megapixels might not matter much.

Taken at 1/125 second, f/2.8, and ISO 1600

good quality image. For example, if a camera has 36 megapixels, then you can crop an image it produces in half and still end up with a huge 15 megapixel file that's full of image information.

Technology is also improving sensor chips with every new generation of cameras, so the noise created by shooting at high ISO settings is diminishing. This is excellent news for the low-light shooters, like concert photographers.

ISO

The most important thing to look for in a camera that you're going to use to photograph concerts is its ISO capabilities. Look for the camera's ISO range and how much noise is visible at the high ISO setting.

This, by the way, is not a concern when shooting with film cameras because the ISO is determined by the film used, not a camera setting. If you want a higher ISO in that situation, you just put in a higher ISO film. But when it comes to shooting digital cameras, the film (sensor) cannot be changed—just its sensitivity settings.

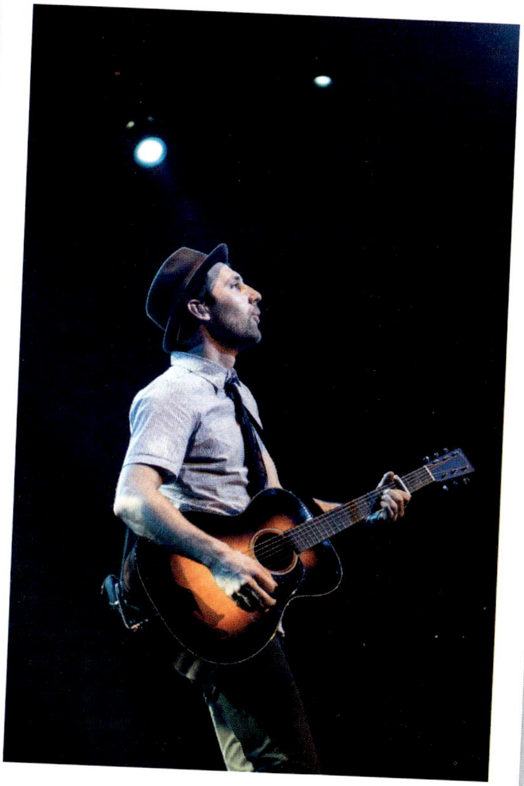

Because most concert photography is shot in low light, having a camera that can use high—even very high—ISO values without a lot of digital noise is important. This photo of Mat Kearney was shot using ISO 3200, an ISO higher than any film I ever used.

Taken at 1/160 second, f/2.8, and ISO 3200

ERGONOMICS

I use Nikon cameras and have for many years. When I pick up a Nikon, it feels right in my hands, and I know where all the buttons, dials, knobs, and levers are positioned. These considerations are part of the camera's ergonomics ... and what I've gotten used to using.

Many of my friends—some who've contributed to this book as part of the Pro Tip sections—feel the exact same way ... about their Canons. So this is not about what camera system is better overall. It's about determining which one feels better in your hands.

So before buying a camera, go to a camera store and pick up one. Hold it in your hand; hold it up to your eye; change lenses; snap a few frames. If you're not really sure if you've found the right one, I suggest that you rent a camera and lens for a few days and work with it. Before you buy, make sure it feels right.

SUPPORT

Nothing beats a good local camera shop except maybe having a good friend with the same gear as you. The big camera chains are really great, and many have service departments. But a local camera store will have gear that you can hold and test. Also, many of the major camera companies have programs for their pro shooters, so if concert photography (or any other type) becomes a main source of income for you, check that out.

For more resources that you may find helpful when purchasing a camera, see Appendix C: Resources.

LENSES

Cameras are important, but lenses are even more important. A good lens will last a lifetime, but chances are you'll trade up in cameras every two or three years. I have lenses that I've owned for a very long time. I bought them when I was shooting film and I still use them all the time. The 85mm lens that I purchased more than ten years ago, for instance, is still one of my go-to lenses for bar shoots. The lens is as sharp as ever; it focuses like a charm; and, because I take the time to clean the lens regularly, I expect it to last for many more years.

FAST GLASS

When it comes to choosing lenses for photographing concerts, you need to think about low-light situations. Of course, there are concerts that take place during the day as well as shows that start in the day and end at night. But you need to be sure you have the equipment to handle low-light scenes. That's the most common scenario for concert photography.

So when you hear concert photographers talk about *fast glass*, it helps to know that this term describes lenses with a very wide maximum aperture. These lenses allow you to get the maximum amount of light through the lens, which makes them a necessity when shooting in low light.

PRIME VS. ZOOM

There are two types of lenses: those that have a single focal length and those that cover a range of focal lengths. Both types of lenses are useful and have their place in your concert photography camera bag.

- **Prime Lenses**
  Prime lenses, or fixed focal length lenses, have a single focal length. This type of lens has two advantages over zoom lenses:
  - Prime lenses can have a wider maximum aperture than zoom lenses.
  - Prime lenses can be cheaper than the zoom equivalents.
  - Prime lenses can be sharper than zoom equivalents, especially older zooms.

Prime lenses have fewer moving components than zooms, and they're often lighter and smaller.

Take a look at my main prime and zoom lenses.

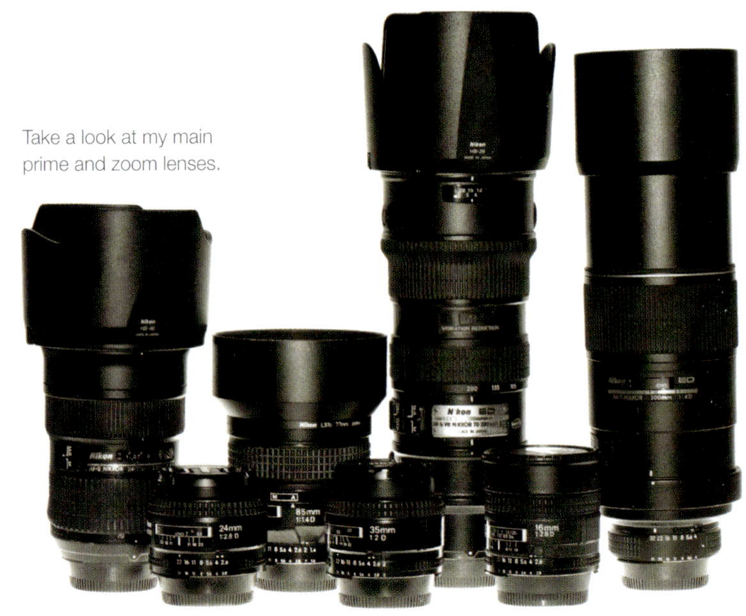

What this means is that you can get a prime lens that opens up really wide for less money than a zoom that opens as wide, if one's even available. Let's take the 50mm focal length for example: The Nikon Nikkor AF-S 50mm f/1.8 lens sells for less than $250. That's not a lot of money for a very fast piece of glass. But if you go to get a zoom lens with the widest maximum aperture and a focal length of 50mm, you'd need to spend well over a $1000, and the widest maximum aperture would be f/2.8.

This doesn't mean that all prime lenses are cheaper than zoom lenses though. The longer prime lenses are really expensive. For example, the Nikon 400mm f/2.8 lens retails for close to $10,000, while the 80–400mm f/4.5–5.6 retails for about $1600—a huge difference in price.

There is also a belief that prime lenses are sharper than zoom lenses, and this might be true, especially at the edges of an image. But I've never really noticed this … probably because the edges of the images I take during a concert are usually dark.

- **Zoom Lenses**
  Zoom lenses cover a wide range of focal lengths, making them very versatile. This is perfect for concert photographers in a photo pit, because you usually can't move around too much. In this shooting situation, you'll be grateful for a lens that can help you capture different versions of a scene without too much moving around.

APERTURE

There are two types of zoom lenses: variable aperture and constant aperture. It's critical that you know the difference between them and understand how your choice can affect your photography.

Some zoom lenses have the same maximum aperture no matter what focal length is being used (constant); on others, the maximum aperture changes depending on the focal length setting (variable). Let's take a closer look at these options.

- **Variable Aperture Zoom Lenses**
  These lenses have a different maximum aperture depending on the focal length used. The maximum aperture gets smaller as the focal length gets longer. For example, a Nikon 55–200mm f/4 - 5.6 G ED AF-S DX Zoom lens has a maximum aperture of f/4 at 5mm and a maximum aperture of f/5.6 at 200mm. This means that the exposure settings at the shorter focal length are different from those at the longer focal length, and there is nothing you can do about it.

  So say you're shooting in manual mode and have the lens set to 55mm, and the camera settings are 1/100 second shutter speed, f/4, and ISO 800. If you zoom in from 55 to 200mm, the camera settings will change to 1/100 second, f/5.6, and ISO 800. Note that this is a full stop difference, so your image will be underexposed by a full stop. To correct the exposure, you need to drop the shutter speed by a full stop or raise the ISO by a full stop.

It takes a lot of work to make sure that the exposures stay consistent when using these lenses, so why do photographers buy them? The answer is two-fold. First, a variable aperture zoom lens is cheaper and smaller than the constant aperture counterparts. Second, most photographers don't need to access the maximum aperture of a lens like low-light photographers do.

As a concert photographer who *does* need to use the maximum aperture, there are three things you can do to make the variable aperture lenses work for you.

- Use the lens at its widest focal length only, and use your feet to get closer or farther away from your subject(s).
- Use the manual exposure mode and set the aperture value as the maximum aperture for the longest focal length only. So, if using the 55–200mm lens mentioned earlier, use f/5.6 as the aperture no matter what focal length you need.
- Make sure you know how to increase the ISO by a full stop as you zoom in so that the exposure stays the same. The images might have more digital noise but that's better than being badly exposed.

Most kit lenses are variable aperture, so it's helpful to know how to make these lenses work for you. They can be used in the pit to capture great images as long as you know the limitations. However, there's no question in my mind that for concert photography, a constant aperture lens is best. Here's why.

- **Constant Aperture Zoom Lenses**

  These lenses keep the same maximum aperture no matter what focal length setting is being used. And most of them have pretty wide maximum apertures. These lenses are often used by professional wedding, sport, and event photographers. And although they're great, they do have three drawbacks that you need to understand.

  - These lenses are expensive. The 70–200mm f/2.8 lens, for example, which is a staple in concert photography, costs more than $2000. And the 24–70mm f2/8 lens costs about $1700. That means you'll spend more than $3700 for two constant aperture lenses to cover the 24–200mm focal lengths. You can pick up a 18–200mm f/3.5–5.6 variable aperture lens for under $800—a $2900 difference.
  - Constant aperture lenses are bigger and heavier than variable aperture lenses. The aperture of a given lens is determined by a mathematical equation that considers the size of the opening in relationship with the focal length. To get the widest possible maximum aperture, the lens needs to be physically wide, which means it's bigger and, in most cases, heavier than lenses with smaller maximum aperture settings. The 70–200mm f/2.8 lens, for example, is much larger than the 55–200 f/3.5–5.6 lens.
  - The range of focal lengths is more limited in constant aperture lenses than they

are in variable aperture lenses. Since the size of the opening needs to be constant throughout the whole range of focal lengths, the physical limitations of this lens makes it tough to cover a huge range of focal lengths. Just look back at the example used to explain the cost factor. It takes two lenses with constant apertures to match one variable aperture lens.

Yet, even with these drawbacks, if you can afford it and are serious about your concert photography, then you'll need to invest in some constant aperture zoom lenses. Here are some advantages to these lenses for concert photographers:

- The constant aperture throughout the focal range of the lens means that you don't have to change the exposure settings when you change the focal length.
- These lenses work well in low light because they have a larger maximum aperture than variable aperture lenses in general.

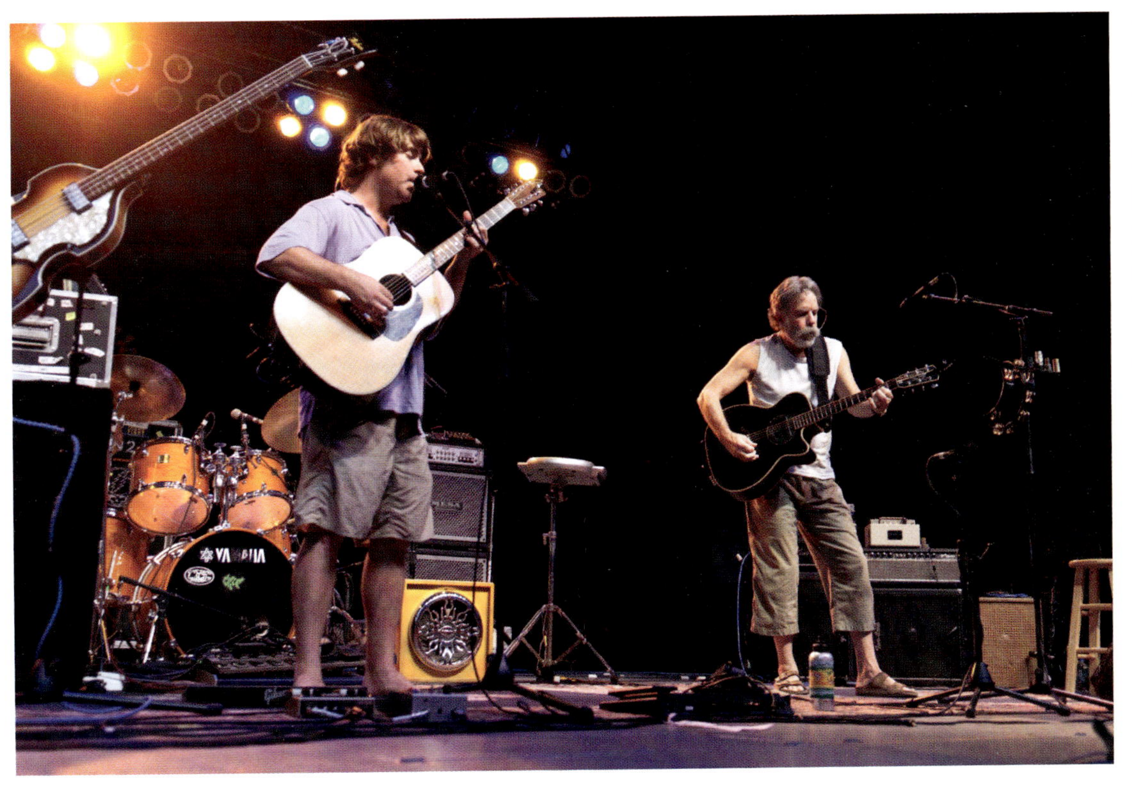

The 24mm focal length allows for wider angle shots, even when really close to the stage. This images shows Keller Williams and Bob Weir.
Taken at 1/100 second, f/3.5, and ISO 320

- An image in the viewfinder can be brighter and the autofocus can work faster when using these lenses because more light is allowed to reach the sensor.

The two lenses that I use for most of my concert photography are a 24–70mm f/2.8 and a 70–200m f/2.78—each on its own camera. This allows me to set the exposure once and have it the same on both cameras for all focal lengths.

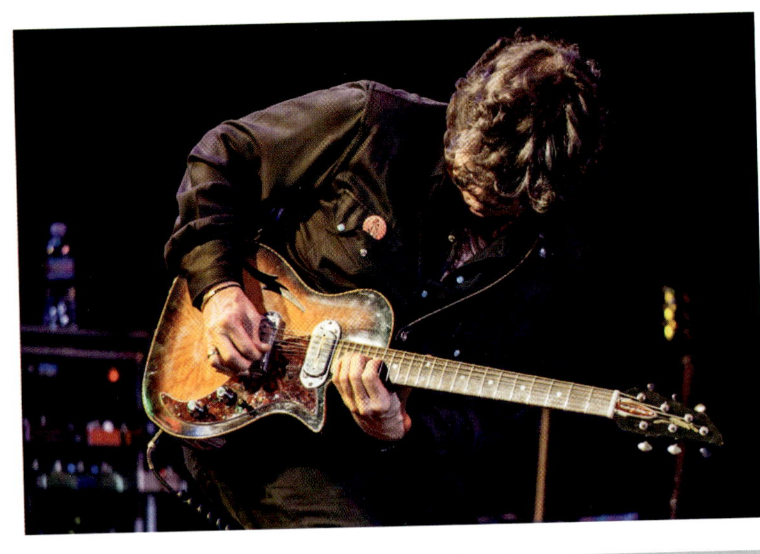

A 200mm lens allows you to get in close and fill the frame with the subject.
Taken at 1/250 second, f/2.8, and ISO 1600

VIBRATION REDUCTION/IMAGE STABILIZATION

Vibration reduction (VR)/Image stabilization (IS) technology tries to counteract the slight (or not-so-slight) movements that show up in images as blur when a photographer is using slower shutter speeds. Image stabilization was introduced by Nikon back in 1994, and it has constantly improved ever since by allowing photographers to get sharp images at low shutter speeds.

Today, there are two types of image stabilization: one is built into the camera, and the other is built into the lens. No matter where it resides though, VR and IS systems compensate for image blur that's caused by *camera shake*—a term used to describe the movements that happen when handholding a camera. This movement tends to be more pronounced at longer focal lengths, where even the slightest movement is visible in an image.

Well, one way to deal with camera shake is to use a shutter speed that is high enough to freeze the action and these small movements. The speed needed to accomplish this is usually 1/the focal length. So, if you're shooting a 200mm lens, for example, the lowest shutter speed you can use to negate camera shake is 1/200 second. A second way to deal with camera shake is to set the camera on a tripod.

Unfortunately, neither of these solutions work well for concert photography. Tripods are not allowed in most venues, and there are times when the light is too low to use shutter speeds of 1/200 second.

So enters VR technology, which measures any movement that may cause blur and then works to correct it. It calculates the amount of movement up and down and left to right and then uses a microcomputer to adjust the built-in motors to keep the image sharp.

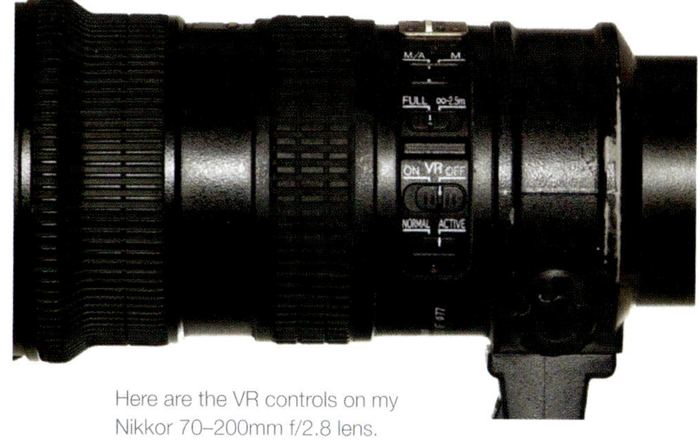

Here are the VR controls on my Nikkor 70–200mm f/2.8 lens.

This is awesome technology that may or may not help you when it comes to concert photography. The biggest problem with this tool is that there is a very small pause (when the VR is turned on) between pressing the shutter release and the camera taking the photo. It's a really small delay, but I notice it and it bothers me so much that I turn off the VR function.

There are times I'll turn it back on, but only for shooting a static subject (stuff that doesn't move) or for wide angle shots, when I want to capture the whole stage at a lower shutter speed. But when it comes to capturing a musician in the moment, I rely on my ability to hold a camera steady.

FLASH

Standard concert photography rules state that a photographer with credentials may shoot the first three (sometimes two) songs—no flash. So why bother to dedicate space in this book to flash? Well, there are times when you'll want a flash with you, and you'll need to know how to use it to get natural-looking shots.

When it comes to lighting, here's the rundown:

- The smaller the light, the harder the light will be. This means it will create harsh (unflattering) shadows.
- The bigger the light source, the softer (and more flattering) the light will be on a subject.

The size of light is based on its proximity to the subject. For example, the sun is a very big light source, but it is very far away. This makes it a small light source. Look at the hard shadows created by the noon-day sun as an example of hard light.

When buying a flash for use in portraits or backstage shots, make sure you get one that has a flash head that can rotate and tilt. This is important because you want to be able to aim the flash away from your subject and bounce the light off the ceiling or a wall to make it bigger and thereby softer.

If you start to take lots of backstage portraits, there are a few other things you might want to consider. You'll want to know how to trigger your flash remotely and even what flash accessories can help you.

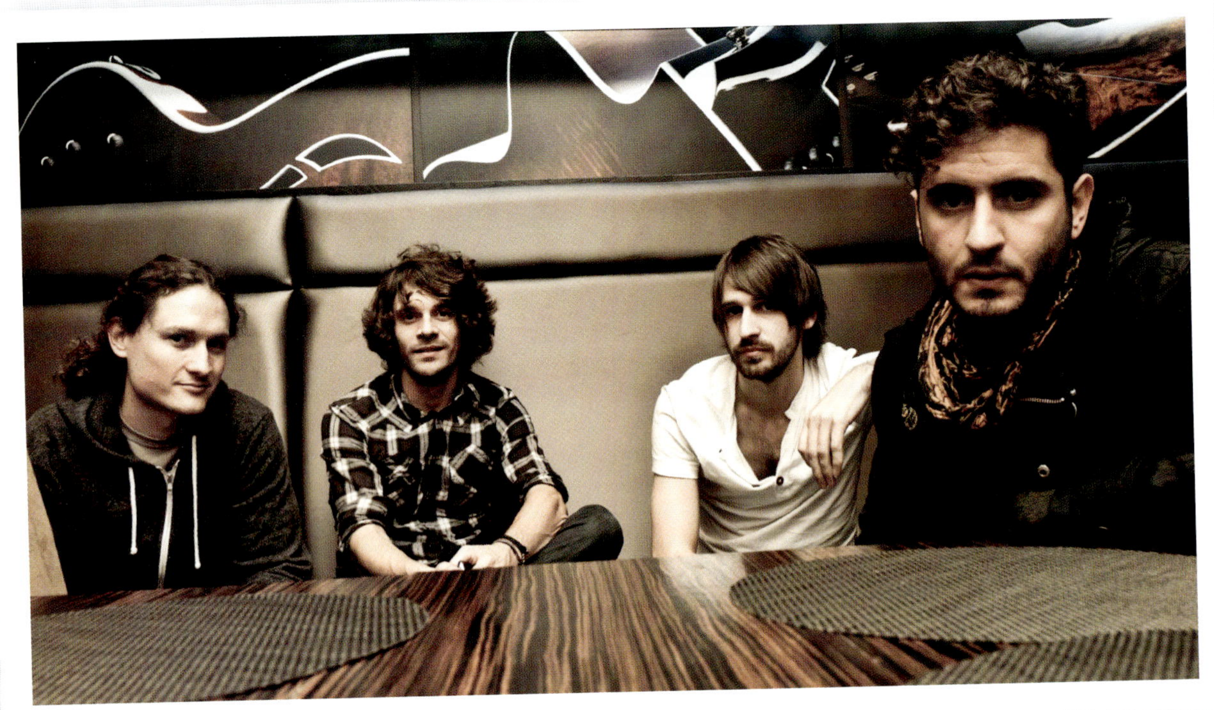

Given a few minutes to photograph the band One Eskimo before a show, I used a Nikon Sb900 flash with a Rouge FlashBender on it to create a bigger, softer light.

Taken at 1/13 second, f/6.3, and ISO 500

REMOTE FLASH

Getting your flash off the camera and triggering it remotely will help you get better portraits. This allows you to aim the flash and the light where you want it instead of straight from the camera. Let's take a look at how to achieve this with remote triggers and built-in controllers.

- **Remote Triggers**

  This type of control allows the flash to be triggered from the camera no matter where the camera or the flash is located. I use a set of Pocket Wizards. One is attached to the camera's hot shoe and the other is attached to the flash. When the shutter release button is pressed, a signal is sent to the flash and it fires.

  In this method, the flash is triggered by radio waves (not line of sight), so it can be positioned anywhere. It doesn't have to see the camera to work. On the downside, the flash power cannot be adjusted remotely in this setup. If you need to increase or decrease the output, you need to do it on the flash itself.

- **Built-in Controllers**

  Camera systems today allow users to trigger a flash unit remotely by using the built-in flash or an external flash mounted on the camera to trigger a remote flash. This type of system has some real advantages, because the external flash and the camera communicate with each other. So the camera can tell the flash how much power to use ... remotely. And, in most cases, you can set up the flash where you want it and fire away.

  This is important because, when you're shooting backstage, you're lucky to get even a few minutes with the band. For the shot of OneEskimo, I had a total of three minutes to get the shot before the band went on stage, so I had to make sure everything was set up quickly and working well.

  The downside to the built-in system is that users are limited on placement of the flash; it is line of sight that enables the external flash to see the camera and function with it.

FLASH ACCESSORIES

The light from small flashes is small and hard, making it quite unflattering. Fortunately, there are a few small flash accessories that can help convert that into a bigger and softer light.

- **Dome Diffuser**

  A dome diffuser is a plastic piece that fits over the front of the flash and helps to scatter the light. The nice part about these diffusers is that they usually come with the flash. If they don't, you can get one like the StoFen Omni bounce, which is pretty inexpensive. You can also keep the dome diffuser on the flash so it doesn't take up space in your camera bag.

- **Softbox**

  There are great little softboxes, created by companies such as LumiQuest, that are made for external flash units. They attach over the head of the flash and are held in place with hook-and-loop fasteners. These softboxes fold up flat, so they fit easily in a camera bag. This is really helpful, especially if you're also carrying a laptop. The LumiQuest Softbox LTp is actually designed to fit in a laptop pocket. The LTp stands for *laptop*.

- **Rouge FlashBenders**

  This is one of my favorite flash accessories. Rouge FlashBenders are shapeable, bendable light modifiers that strap onto the flash with the built-in strap. FlashBenders come in different sizes, but I've found that they all can be bent, folded, and stuffed into a bag easily.

  For the One Eskimo image, I used the big FlashBender, and it turned the small light into a much bigger light, creating a softer and more pleasing light.

Scott Diussa

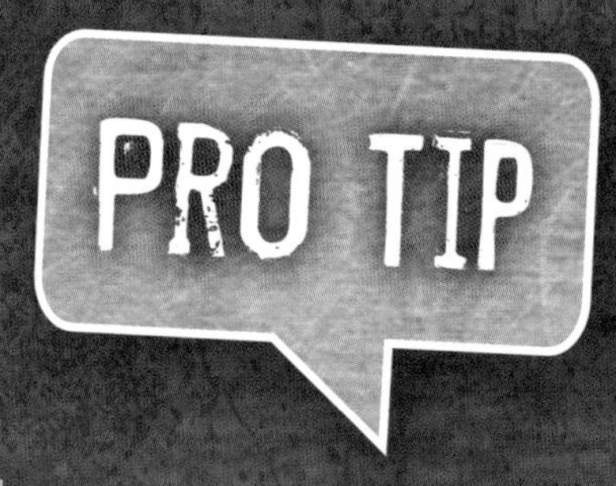

Field Operations Manager, Nikon Professional Services
www.scottdiussa.com

How long have you been shooting shows?

The first show that I remember shooting was in 1991, and it was Cheap Trick and REO Speedwagon at a fair in Palm Beach, Florida. I was working at a camera store at the time and borrowed a Nikon 6006 with a 75–300mm lens, and I think that was when 800 ISO film had just become popular. That was my first lesson in what it takes to get sharp images in that kind of light.

After that, in 1994 and 1995, I got hooked up with a club in Orlando, Florida. I shot a lot of shows of bands that I liked from the 1980s. I shot Warrant, Dokken, Night Ranger, Cheap Trick (again), Yngwie Malmsteen, Slaughter, and even Eddie Money! That's when I really learned how important it is to shoot with the right gear. At the time, I was using a Nikon N90s with a 28–70mm lens and a 70–200mm 2.8 lens. For years after, I didn't do too many concerts … and then it started all over again in 2007 with a string of shows for the Nikon Live website. That led to an opportunity for me to teach a concert photography class with Alan Hess at Photoshop World and to create a concert photography class for Kelby Training online. So in total I have about twenty years of on and off experience.

What was your favorite shoot?

My favorite shoot would almost have to be the one I just shot! Each one I learn more and more. Some are easier than others. Some are only a song or three. Some are an entire show. Some are full arenas with great lights, and others are small shows with challenging lighting and no photo pit. But as long as I come out of a show with some good stuff, it's a favorite.

That said, some of my favorite bands to shoot are the those that put on the best shows. Bands such as Accept, Y&T, Papa Roach, Nickelback, and Poison have great stage presence and really play to the camera. And I think one of my favorite shoots of all time was for Accept at the Grammercy Theater in New York City in May of 2010. It was the first show of the band's tour to support the first new CD release in like fifteen years with a brand new lead singer. So it was a very pivotal moment for the band, and they gave it their all!

This was just an amazing show, especially given that the band hadn't toured in quite some time. They are top-notch professionals who gave 100%-plus to both the crowd and the cameras up front, and they let photographers shoot the whole show. They aren't the prima donnas that worry about how they look after the first few songs. And the images from the second half of the show are by far the best of the night. I have so many "keepers" from that concert, and the band ended up using a bunch of my images from that show as well. It was an all-around great experience, and they are a really nice group of guys.

How important is the gear?

You need to have equal parts of good gear and good instinct. If you have a great eye for shooting concerts but your gear can't handle the situation, then you're limited. You can, on the other hand, go out and spend a small fortune on the best gear out there and still take crappy pictures if you have no instinct for how to shoot a show. Sure, sometimes technology in cameras can save you if you have no clue about what you're doing, but live performance shooting … along with indoor sports … have to be the hardest types of photography to master.

When it comes to camera gear, the camera body isn't nearly as important as the camera lens choice that you make. Fast, or wide aperture, lenses are essential. These are lenses with a maximum aperture of f/2.8 or even lower. You need as much light as possible to come into the lens in order to get the shutter speed you need to stop the action. And that's reliant on the camera's ISO setting range as well.

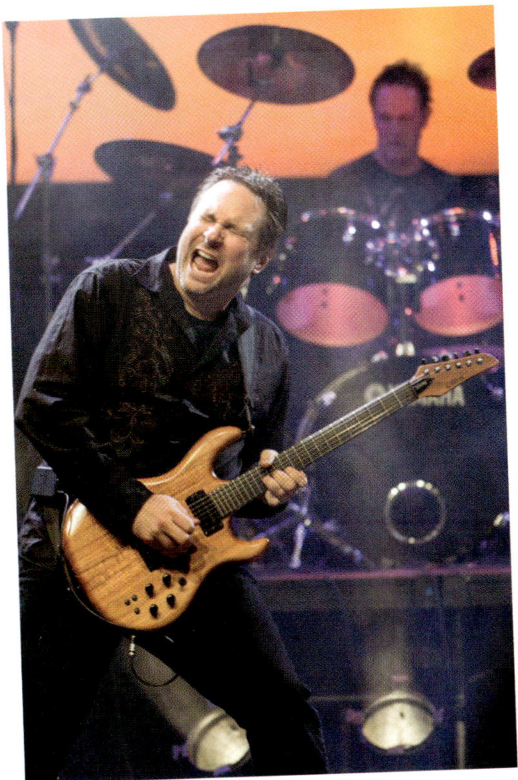

Scott is playing guitar during the live shoot of the Photoshop World Concert Photography Pre-Con. Taken at 1/250 second, f/2.8, and ISO 1600.

Most cameras these days really do a great job at high ISO settings—1600, 3200, or even 6400 and higher. ISO 1600 at f/2.8 and about 1/250 second is about the starting point for any show. If you can't achieve that with your camera gear, then you need to get gear that can.

So, I think having the proper camera gear for concert photography is a serious investment, but equally important is the investment of time it takes to get into the shows and gain experience with shooting them.

What makes your own style of concert photography different from other concert photographers you know?

I shoot concerts differently from other photographers I know because I'm a musician. I've played the guitar for 27 years and grew up with posters of various guitarists on the wall in my room.

I guess that since I always wanted to be like them, I took notice of how they looked best in the pictures I saw. So I shoot musicians to create what I'd like to see of me if I were some famous Rock Star! (Yeah right!)

Actually, having knowledge of who plays what instrument in a band and the uniqueness of how (s)he plays the instrument is very important. Many musicians have signature moves. Take guitarist Pete Townshend from The Who, for example, with the signature "windmill" move he makes with his right arm. Capturing that moment is key.

Also, how you frame images in the camera gives you a style. I tend to shoot very tight, and that means that I crop inside the camera to exactly what I want to see. Sometimes this can be detrimental, because I may frame a guitar neck too close and cut off the end … or something like that.

Some photographers shoot loose (or wide) and then crop to how they like it. But I actually do the opposite. I'm not entirely sure why; it's just me. I also like experimenting with crazy angles, especially with bands that are rather boring on stage. It makes them seem a bit more interesting.

There are many small pieces to the bigger puzzle of how you create your own style of shooting concerts. You just have to get out there and find out what you like.

Favorite piece of gear?

My favorite piece of gear... earplugs! I like to be able to hear when I get home! It's crazy to shoot concerts without them. As far as other gear goes, I'd have to say my Nikon 70–200 2.8 VRII lens. It's a rock-solid, comfortable, sharp lens that always produces great images.

Favorite camera bag?

My favorite camera bag is one I haven't designed yet! I'm a bit of a camera bag-a-holic, and every bag has some feature I wish was on another bag. I personally use Lowepro bags 90% of the time. I like my Lowepro Pro Roller X200 if I'm going to be keeping my gear in my car and working out of my car trunk.

I've also been experimenting with the Lowepro Lens Exchange bag, which can hold a single lens. With this bag, if you're shooting a show with one body and two lenses, then you can easily swap lenses on your camera. It has a unique design that allows you to put a lens in one side as you take a lens out of the other. So you can change a lens without having to stick one under your arm or between your legs or something like that. Too many lenses get dropped that way. It's a great design.

I also have a plain old wide-open Domke bag from many years ago that has been soaked with beer on the floors of shows so many times that it can pretty much take any abuse, while also protecting my gear. It simply holds one camera and lens while I'm shooting with the other camera and lens.

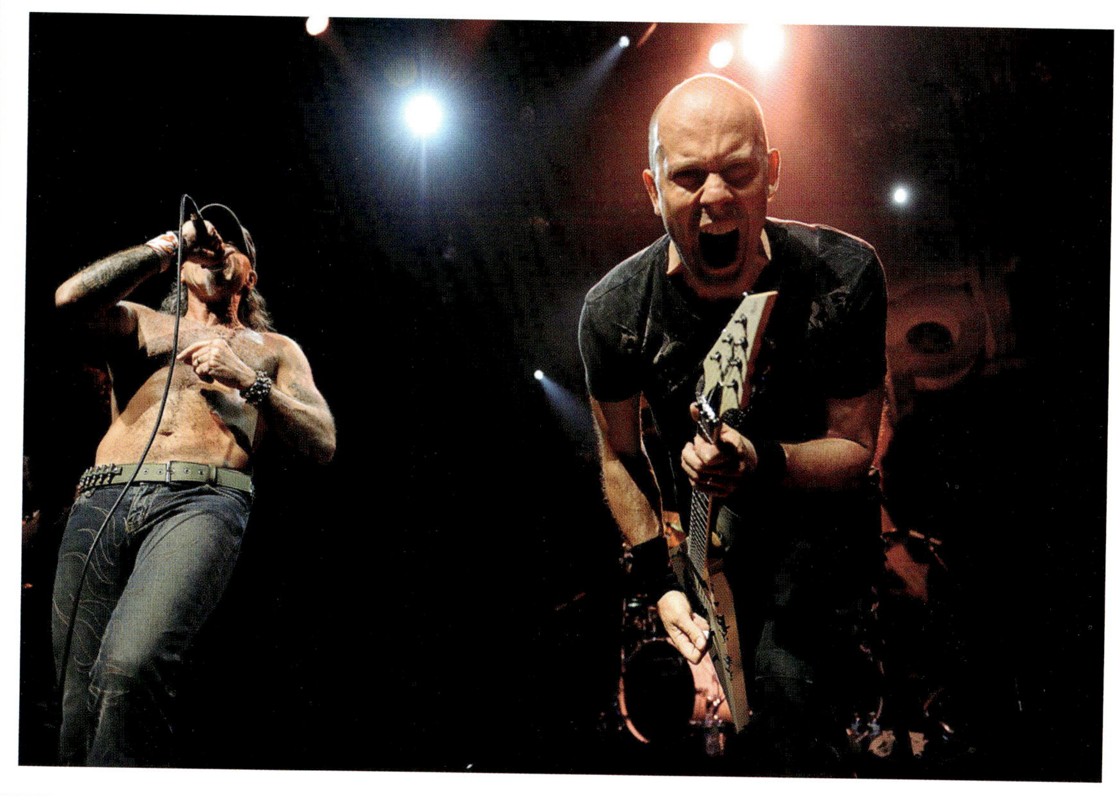

The band Accept puts tons of energy into their shows, making it a fun group to photograph.
© Scott Diussa

Tip for a beginning concert photographer?

My suggestion for anyone who wants to get into concert photography is to practice on a small, local level to gain knowledge and experience before attempting to shoot a large show. Any type of stage performance will be good experience. If you don't have a local band that wants some good live images to use for its website or Facebook page or something like that, then find a theatre company that's putting on a play. Shoot the dress rehearsal for them when there's no one else in the theater.

If you get some good stuff, you'll start to build a reputation … and experience with shooting in stage lighting conditions. School plays, dance recitals, and anything with stage lighting can provide good practice. Then you can move up from there. If there is a good club or theater that gets some big name bands, get to know the concert promoter of the club, and offer to give him/her images to use in exchange for the experience. If you produce good stuff, you may end up creating a great win-win relationship that can last for years.

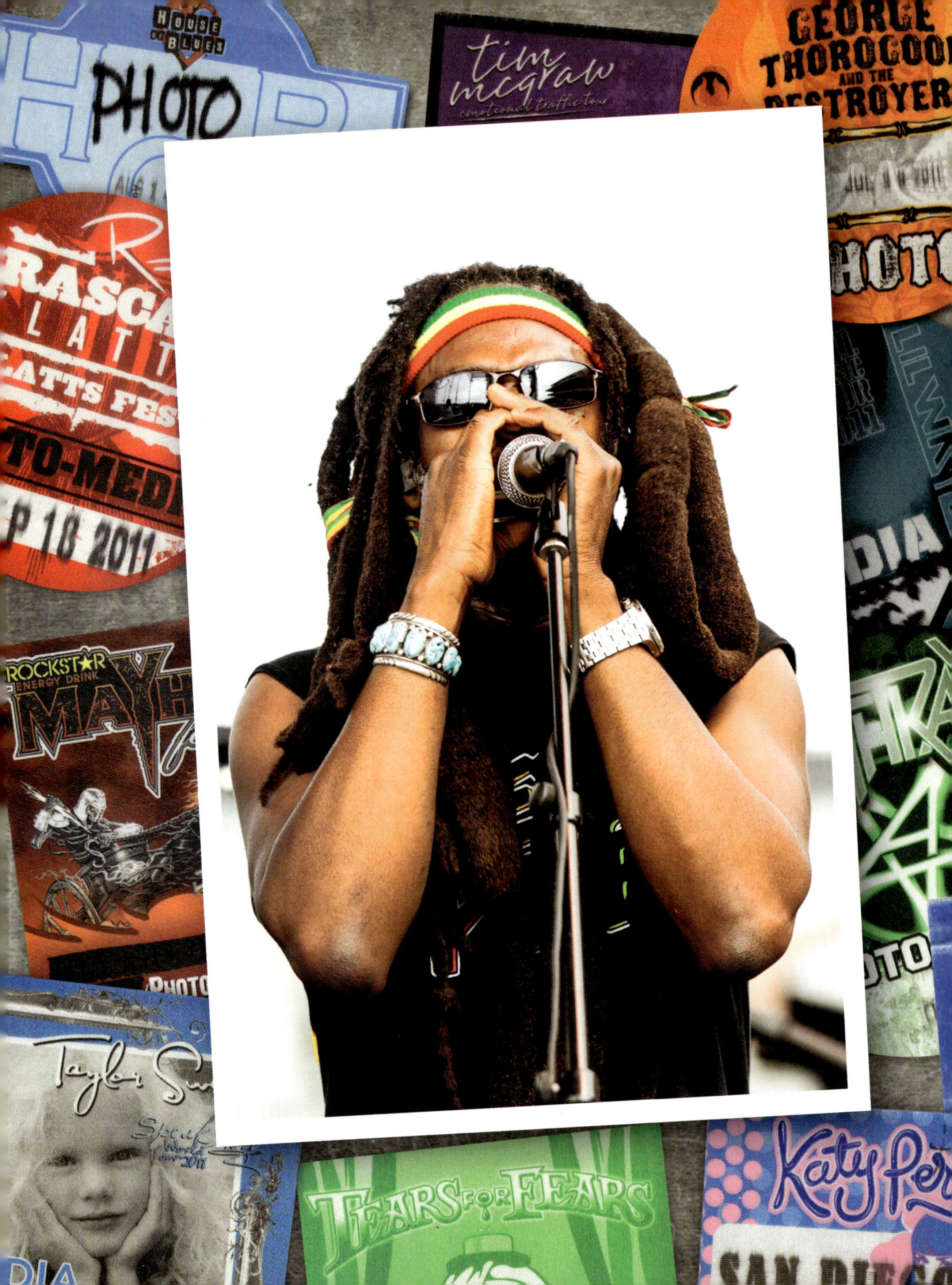
HOUSE OF BLUES
PHOTO
tim mcgraw
emotional traffic tour
GEORGE
AND THE
ROCKSTAR
ENERGY DRINK
TEARS FOR FEARS
P 18 2011

5 LIGHTS OUT: EXPOSURE BASICS FOR CONCERT SHOOTERS

So far, we've talked about photo passes and shooting restrictions, limited access, awkward angles, and bad lighting. But before any of that actually comes into play or starts to impact your ability to shoot concert images that people want to see, you need to master some important techniques of photography.

This means dealing with the settings and issues of exposure, which include shutter speed, aperture, and ISO as well as the different shooting modes on your camera. It also means tackling decisions related to metering modes, focus modes, and white balance. Stop! No throwing books! We'll get through this ...

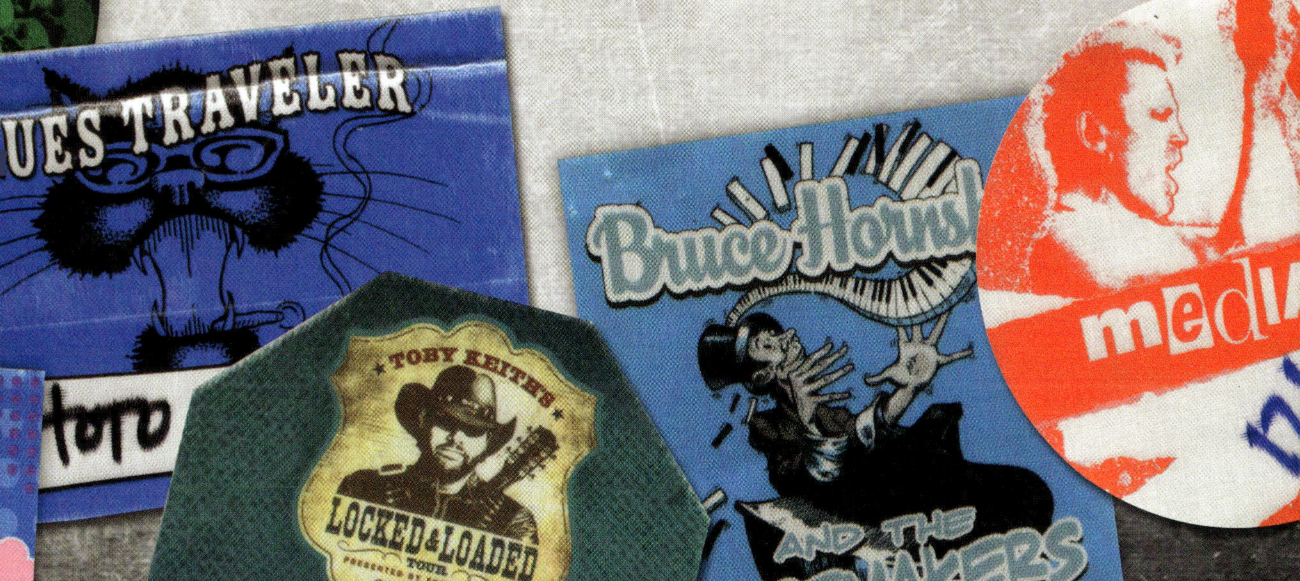

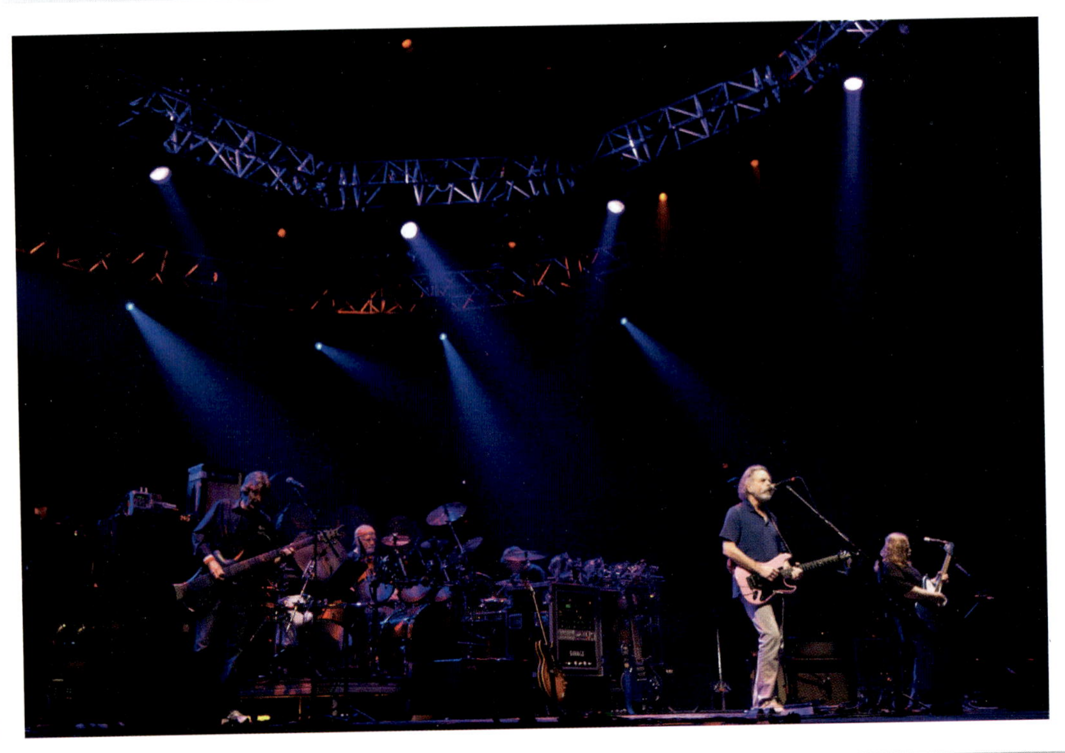

This photograph shows The Dead under the band's impressive lighting rig. There are thirteen visible light sources using four different colors and coming from a variety of directions in this image.
Taken at 1/80 second, f/2.8, and ISO 800

I understand. I know all this technical stuff might feel like high school trigonometry and it's definitely less exciting than actually shooting a show, but without this basic knowledge and the skills to use it, successful concert photography is close to impossible.

Don't sigh. I know that anyone can grab one of the new dSLR cameras, set it on full auto, and walk into a big show and get some great shots. But to do that time and time again in a wide variety of lighting and shooting conditions is another story. So let's commit to doing it right from the start. We'll start from the top.

MEASURING LIGHT

Photography is the process of capturing light. If you get too much light, your image will be *overexposed*. This means that the image will be too bright and light areas will appear washed out. Too little light results in an *underexposed* image, and the effect is too dark. With concert photography, especially the shows that take place indoors or at night, the most common exposure problem is underexposure.

The key to achieving a proper exposure is knowing how much light is present, so the correct camera settings can be used to capture the right amount of light to illuminate your scene. Measuring the light is done using a light meter, and your camera has one built right in. More on using the light meter and the different metering modes a little later.

For now, just note that when it comes to concert photography, one of the main challenges is measuring the light, because it's constantly moving and changing in intensity during a concert. The stage lights rarely stay the same for more than a second or two. So it's really important that you start to develop a feel for concert lighting. Don't worry; with experience, you'll be able to look at the lighting and, for all practical purposes, measure it in your head.

METERING MODES

Your camera has a built-in light meter that assesses the light in a scene. But instead of relying on a single way to read the light, your light meter has at least three different modes. These modes may have different names depending on the camera you use, but they function the same way I'll describe in this section.

The three modes on your light meter read the light in different areas of a scene and then uses that information in various ways, depending on the exposure mode you set. This gives you control over what's factored into the meter's reading. More importantly, it allows you to determine what's left out of the equation. Find more on exposure modes later in this chapter.

In concert photography, the scenes that you photograph are usually quite extreme in terms of the range of light present. Certain areas are usually very well lit and others are not lit at all. Take a band on a stage, for example. The lead singer might have a bright white spotlight on her, while the rest of the band is in the shadows.

To get a proper exposure of the lead singer, you need to ignore the vast areas around her; but to get a properly exposed photo of the whole band, you need to deal with the whole scene. Finding the right metering mode is important, and it takes practice. After shooting for a while though, you'll be able to meter the light just by looking at it. You'll get pretty close anyway.

The three light metering modes are

- spot metering
- center-weighted metering
- multi-pattern metering

SPOT METERING

Spot metering refers to the reading of a very small area of a scene. In older cameras this area is at the very center of the frame, but newer cameras tie the spot metering area to the focus point. This means that the camera's metering system looks only at the area right around the focus point, and this is very useful for concert photography.

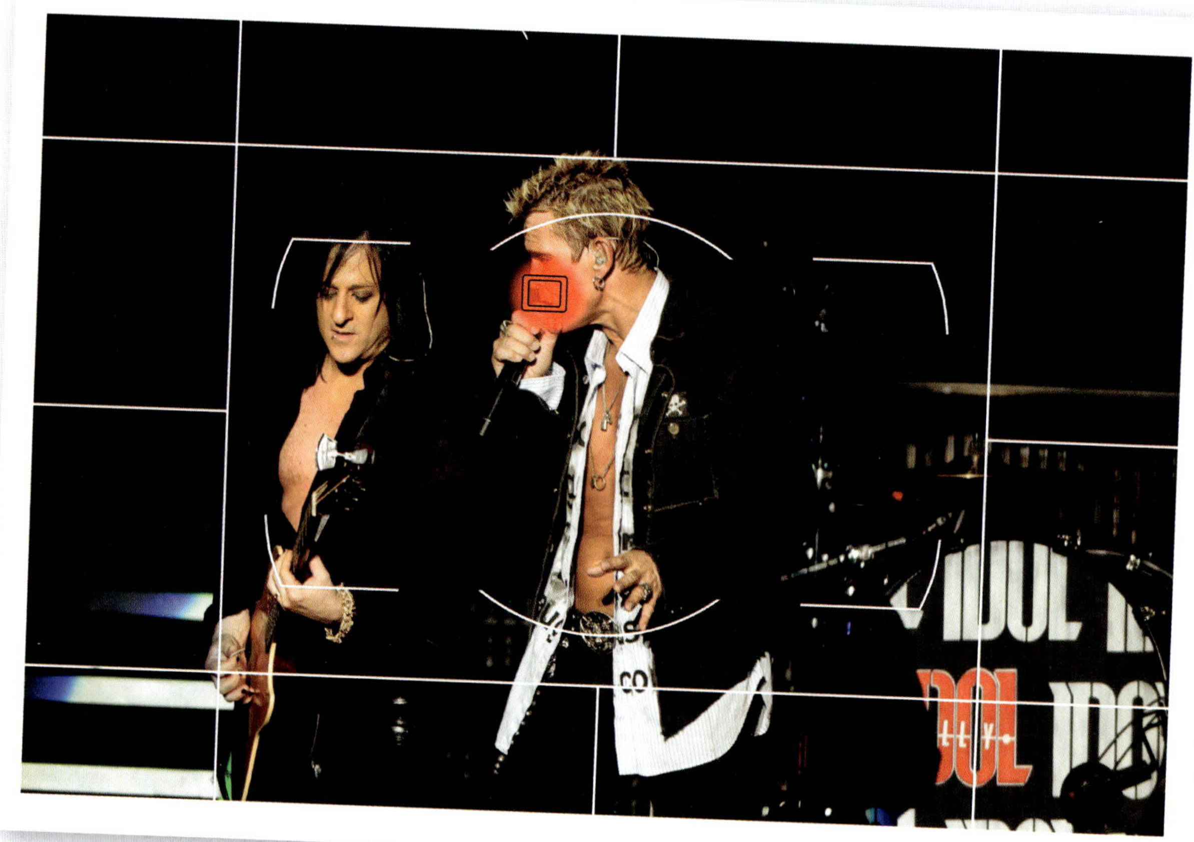

This photo of Steve Stevens and Billy Idol has a large area of black in the background, so I needed to make sure that the built-in metering looked only at what I wanted it to evaluate—the face and microphone in this case, which are covered by the focus point. The red area is an approximation of the area used for the metering.

Taken at 1/250 second, f/2.8, and ISO 1600

Just understand that this mode is the hardest to use, because even a slight change in the focus point results in a whole new set of exposure values from the meter. Yet this is the mode I use for 99% of all my concert photography.

CENTER-WEIGHTED METERING

This metering system places a higher value on the information it receives from the center area of the frame versus the edges. The center metering mode takes a bigger area of the scene into account than the spot metering mode, and it ignores the very edges of the scene. It can give you an accurate reading if you keep the performer in the middle of the frame. In reality, I don't use this mode, because spot metering is more accurate for photographing concerts.

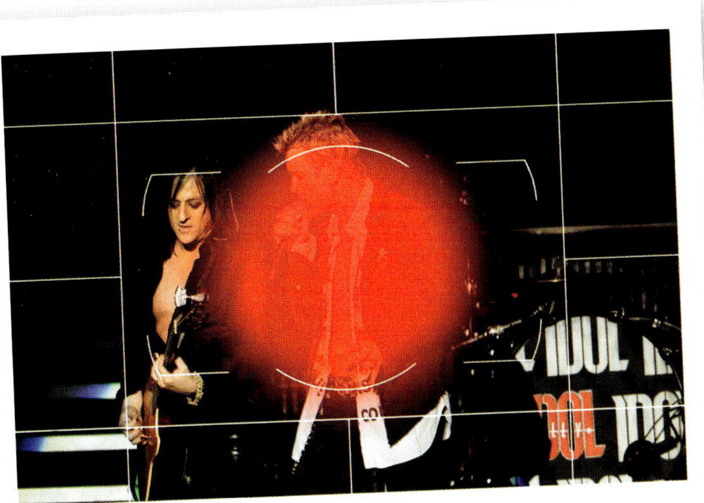

If I had used center-weighted metering for this shot, the area covered in red would have been considered by the built-in meter. This mode would have factored in the bright white shirt and dark jacket, yet these are things I needed to avoid.

Taken at 1/250 second, f/2.8, and ISO 1600

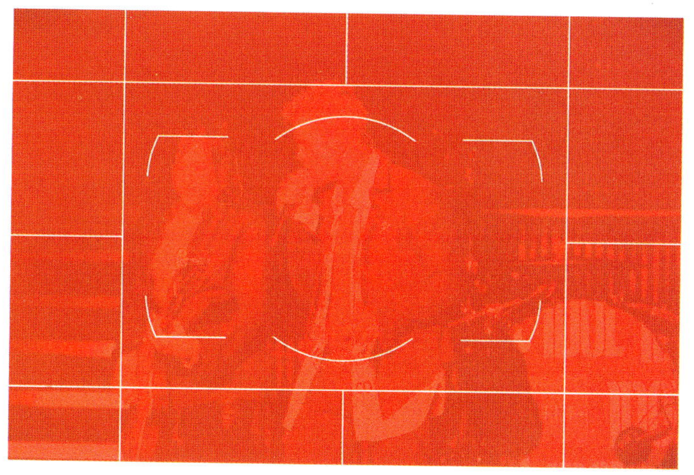

This mode considers the whole scene, as shown by the red overlay. Would the camera have figured out that it was two musicians playing against a black backdrop? I doubt it.

Taken at 1/250 second, f/2.8, and ISO 1600

MULTI-PATTERN METERING

This third metering mode is called *Matrix* metering in the Nikon system and *Evaluative* metering in the Canon system. It takes in the whole scene in front of the camera and breaks it into different pieces, or segments. Then it tries to actually *see* the scene and match it to a built-in database. In other words, the camera tries to figure out what you're trying to capture to give you the best exposure for every scene.

This works great for many shooting situations, but concerts are not one of them. It's very rare that the whole scene of a performance shot will have information that's important to the exposure. Rather, it's more common to have huge areas of darkness and some very bright spots. This kind of scene does not meter well with the multi-pattern metering mode.

Now that we know about the three built-in metering modes, and what they're looking at, let's look at what we mean by *proper exposure*. As photographers, we try to capture a scene the way we envision it, and balancing the lighting in a scene is a key aspect of this.

PROPER EXPOSURE

When you take a photograph, you want it to have the proper exposure. Generally, this means that there's detail in the brightest—and the

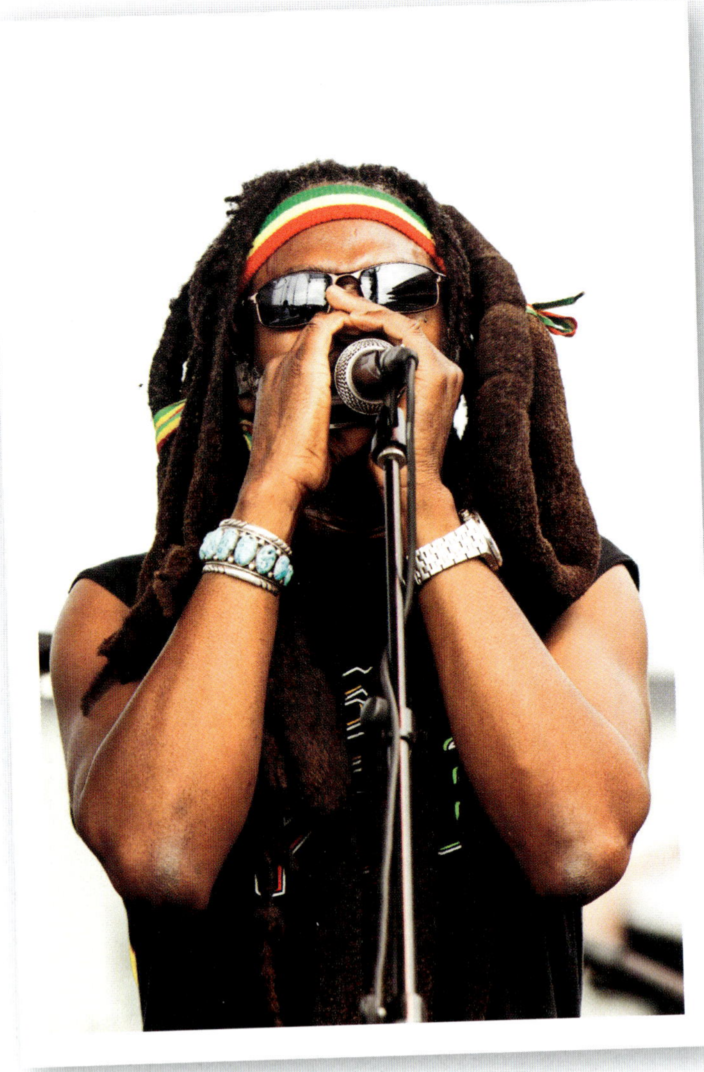

A proper exposure in a concert image might have areas of solid black or, in this case, solid white. The bright sky in the background is not important to the image. If I would have exposed for the sky, the subject, David Hinds of Steel Pulse, would have been severely underexposed.

Taken at 1/200 second, f/4.2, and ISO 200

darkest—parts of the image. That is, you want to avoid the bright areas showing up as pure white and the dark areas being pure black. In an image that's properly exposed, a viewer can see detail in both extremes of the lighting spectrum in a scene.

Now this gets a little tricky when it comes to concert photography, because what's considered a proper exposure in other types of photography doesn't always apply to this kind of work.

In concert photography, there will be a lot of images that show areas as pure white and pure black ... and they can still be considered *properly* exposed. For example, if you're shooting a show and the lights are behind the performers and they come forward and are captured in your image, the stage lights will most likely be pure white in your image. And that will be correct. Similarly, if the background is black, then you'll probably want it to show as black, pure black, in your image ... without details. And that will be correct as well.

The thing is, when it comes to photographing concerts, don't forget that the lighting director isn't lighting the stage so you can see everything. Instead, (s)he creates interesting visuals for a live audience by selectively lighting the stage.

HISTOGRAM

A histogram is a visual representation of the tones in your image. The information provided by a histogram is often misused by photographers to determine if an image is good or bad. But there are no good or bad histograms. The information shown by a histogram is just that: information. If an image is predominantly black, then the histogram needs to show that. If an image is taken outdoors in the bright sun and it has a lot of very light areas, then the histogram needs to show that as well.

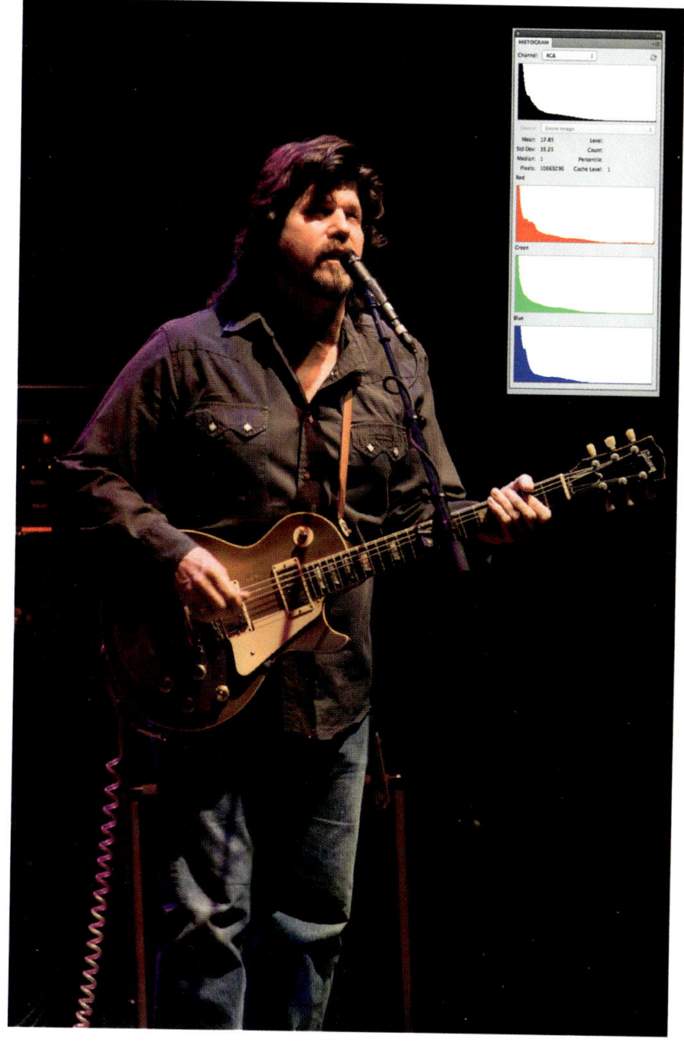

This photo of Mark Karan playing lead guitar was taken against a black background, and the histogram shows that. Since there is no pure white in the scene ... or even any light tones ... I would expect to see a lot more info on the left of the graph than on the right. This is okay.

So, to get an image that's well-exposed, use a combination of ISO, aperture, and shutter speed settings (described in the next section). These settings work together to capture the light that's present in a scene. And to select a combination that works, your best bet is to pick your settings by using one of the exposure modes based on information from your metering modes.

EXPOSURE SETTINGS

Photography is not very complicated; there are only three controls that affect your exposure: shutter speed, aperture, and ISO. And it's the huge variety in possible combinations of these three settings that provides creative control over an image.

SHUTTER SPEED

The shutter speed setting determines how long the camera's shutter is open, allowing light to reach the sensor. When a shutter speed is slow, the shutter is open for a long period of time, so more light is able to reach the sensor. A fast shutter speed means the shutter is open for less time, which allows less light to reach the shutter. Easy enough, right?

Well, each time the shutter speed halves or doubles, it allows in twice as much or half as much light. For example, if you go from shutter speed 1/100 second to 1/200 second, the shutter is open for exactly half the time, so half as much light gets to the sensor. This change is called a *stop,* and a full stop of light is exactly one half or double the amount of light of the next or previous stop.

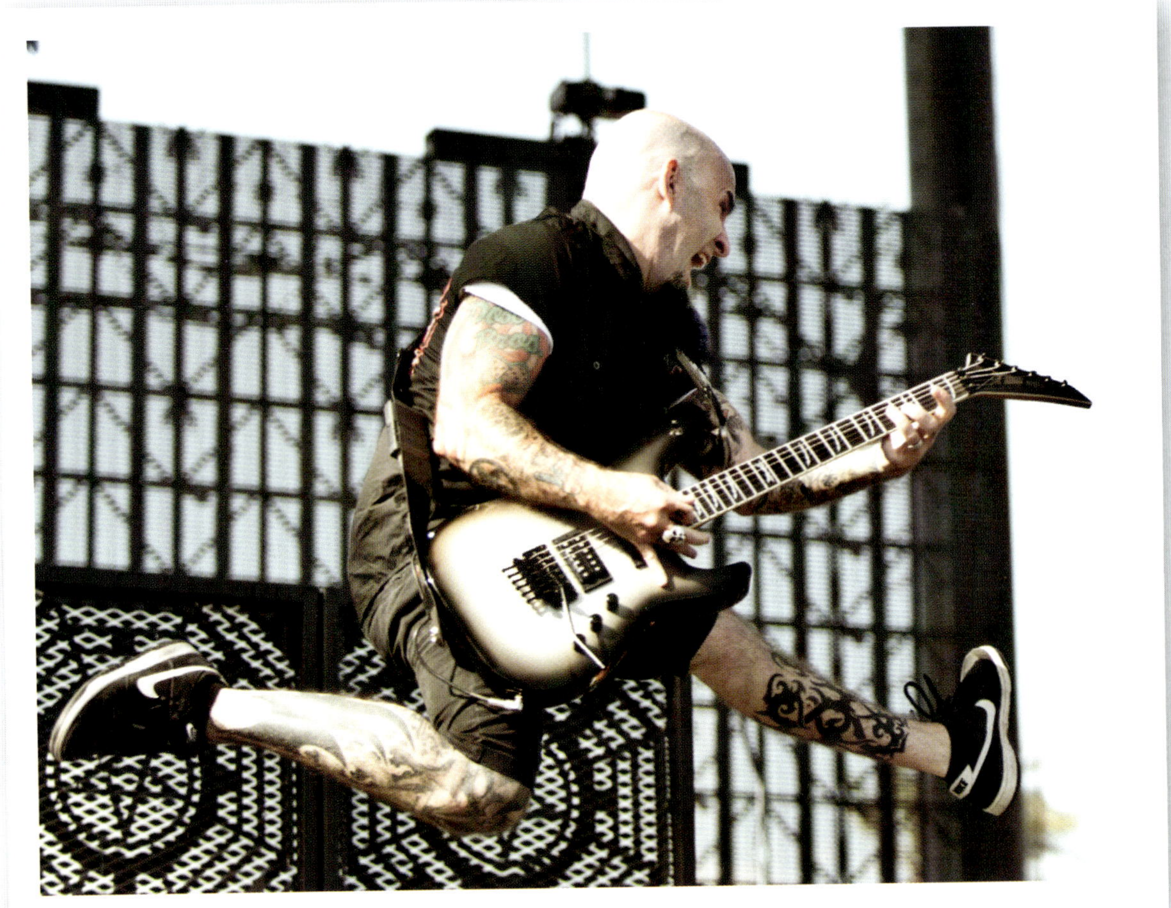

Sometimes you want to freeze the action in your concert photographs. This is Scott Ian, rhythm guitarist for the band Anthrax, shown leaping through the air. *Taken at 1/1000 second, f/2.8, and ISO 200*

The following fractions are shutter speeds in full stops. As you go from left to right, the amount of light allowed to reach the sensor is halved. Conversely, as you move from each stop on the right to the left, you double the amount of light that hits the sensor. Note that shutter speed is measured in seconds or, for concert photography, more usually in parts of a second.

1 1/2 1/4 1/8 1/16 1/30 1/60 1/125 1/250 1/500 1/1000

Think of shutter speed as a way to control how time is represented in your images. Fast shutter speeds allow the shutter to be open for only very short periods, which freezes action and gives you sharp, in-focus photos. Slow shutter speeds keep the shutter open for a longer period of time, which means that movement by a subject (or camera) is captured. This can create a feeling of motion, but it means that subjects might not be in sharp focus.

Most of the time, I try to use a shutter speed that freezes the action. That's a setting around 1/160 of a second, depending on the act. But sometimes I use a slower shutter speed to purposely blur parts of the image, like a hand strumming a guitar, to experiment with certain effects.

APERTURE

The term *aperture* relates to the opening in the lens that allows light to pass through and reach the sensor. A bigger opening allows in more light. A smaller opening permits in less light.

Each time the aperture increases by a full stop, it lets in exactly half as much light as before. This means that f/4 allows in half as much light as f/2.8, and f/8 lets in twice as much light as f/11. Each is a full stop difference.

Now, there's another aspect of aperture, and it's how aperture controls the depth of field in an image. *Depth of field* is the area in an image that's in acceptable focus. It starts at the focal plane and extends a third of the way in front of it and two-thirds of the space behind it. The wider the aperture, the smaller (or *shallower*) the depth of field.

In practical terms, this means that when you use a wide-open aperture to get as much light as possible through your lens—and this is a very common scenario in concert photography—the depth of field in your resulting image is very shallow.

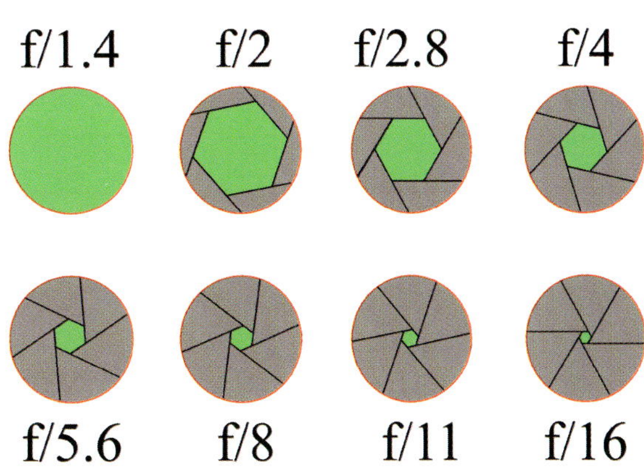

As you can see, the size of the aperture can change drastically; f/1.4 is much larger than f/11.

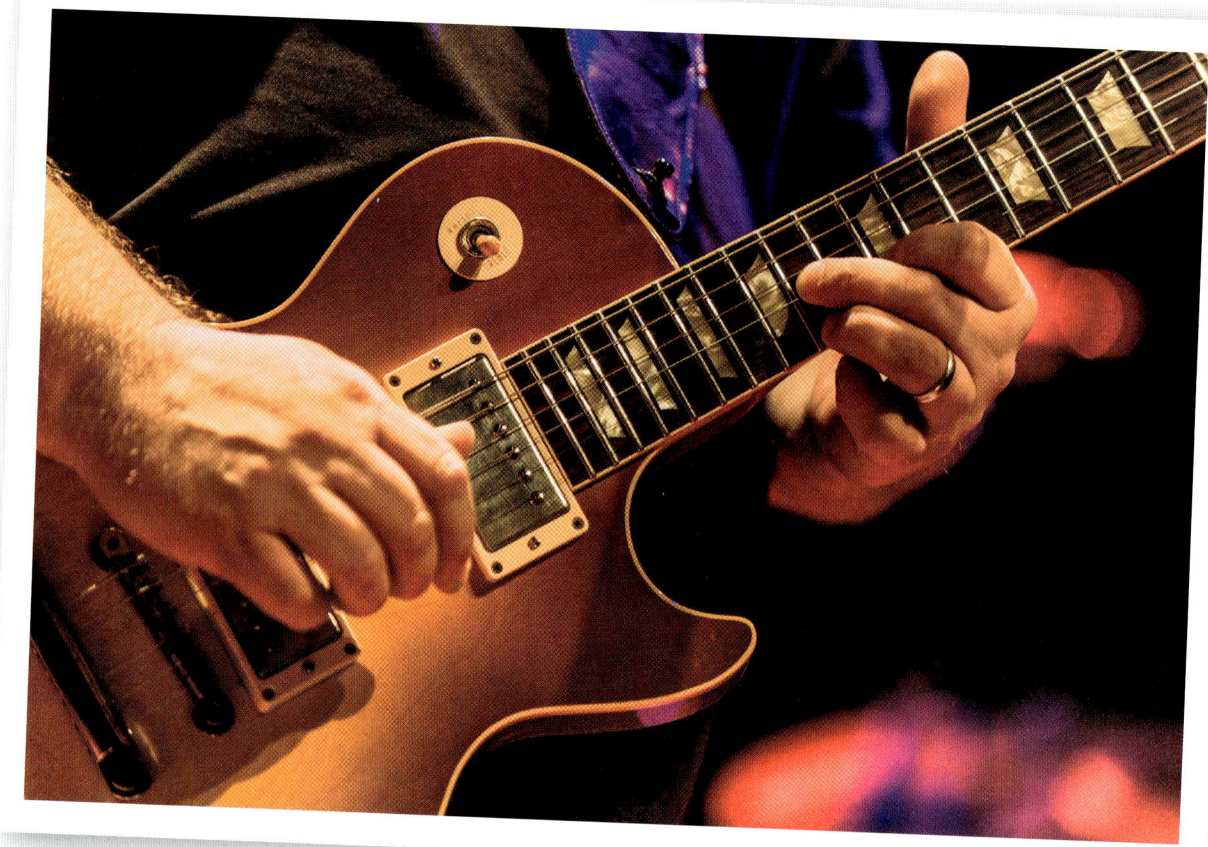

The depth of field in concert photography can be very shallow due to the use of wide apertures. This makes it critical to focus properly. This photo is a great example of a shallow depth of field. The guitar is in focus, but the playing hand is not.

Taken at 1/160 second, f/2.8, and ISO 1600

ISO

Use your camera's ISO setting to standardize the sensitivity of its sensor. Think of it this way: If there was no way to determine how sensitive your sensor is to light, then it would be impossible to calculate exposure values. In this regard, the ISO setting on digital cameras comes from the days of film.

The basics are simple. A high ISO rating on a roll of film means that the film is more sensitive to light than a roll with a low ISO rating. In digital cameras, you can't actually change the sensor as you can with film. Instead, the electronic signal from the sensor is amplified as you increase the ISO, and this makes it seem like the sensor is more sensitive to light. The level

> **ISO 400 is exactly twice as sensitive to light as ISO 200, and ISO 3200 is twice as sensitive to light as ISO 1600. Each of these changes represents a full stop.**

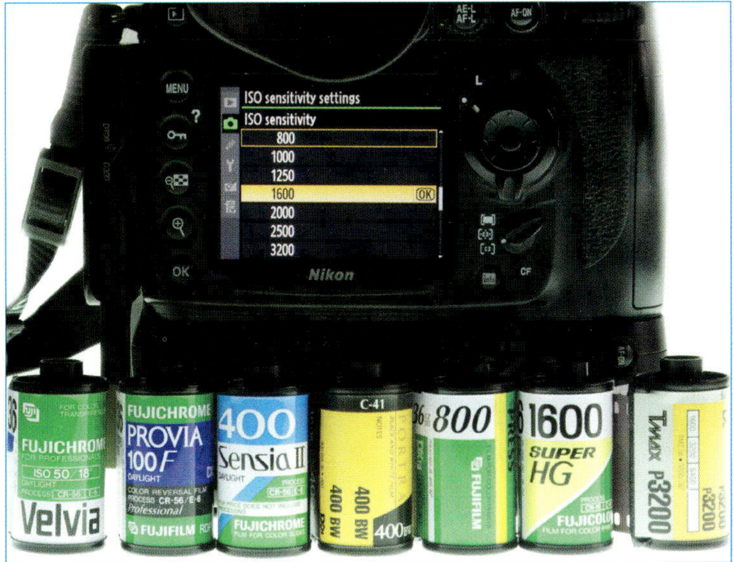

When shooting with film, we had to change the roll in order to adjust ISO. But now, just change the ISO setting on your camera body.

of amplification is designed to make the sensor in a digital camera behave the same way as high ISO film does. So when you dial in an ISO setting of 800 on your digital camera, it acts the same way as a roll of ISO 800 film.

Like shutter speed and aperture, ISO settings are measured in stops. A full stop adjustment means that the sensor's sensitivity to light is exactly double or halved. Since the ISO is measured in plain numbers, this is easy to see. Typical ISO settings are 100, 200, 400, 800, 1600, 3200, and 6400. Notice that each number is double the previous number, if you go from left to right. (Moving left, each setting is half the previous number.)

There are a couple of real advantages to digital photography over film photography. The first is that you can change the ISO with every image. (With film, an entire roll needs to be shot at the same ISO.) And newer digital cameras can use ISO values that are higher than any film. Since concert photography takes place in low-light venues most of the time, being able to use high ISO settings is extremely important. The higher the usable ISO, the less light you need.

DIGITAL NOISE

Most things in photography require a trade-off. For example, when you pick a wide aperture, you get a shallow depth of field. If you need a deep depth of field, then you need to use a smaller aperture. You can't have a deep depth of field *and* a wide aperture.

In the case of ISO, there is a cost to using high settings, and it's digital noise, which appears as graininess in a photograph. Digital noise is created in a variety of ways, but the most common culprit for concert photographers is use of a high ISO setting due to the low light. A high ISO amplifies the signal from the sensor, and increased amplification magnifies digital noise.

Sometimes this is okay. Digital noise has been compared to the grain you see in a photograph that was shot with high ISO films. But really, it's way more distracting. Digital noise shows up as unwanted spots of color in your image. So you can only push the ISO so high. At some point, the amount of noise in your image becomes so distracting that the image becomes unusable.

The good news for photographers who use high ISO settings on a regular basis is that camera manufacturers are creating cameras that product significantly less noise than

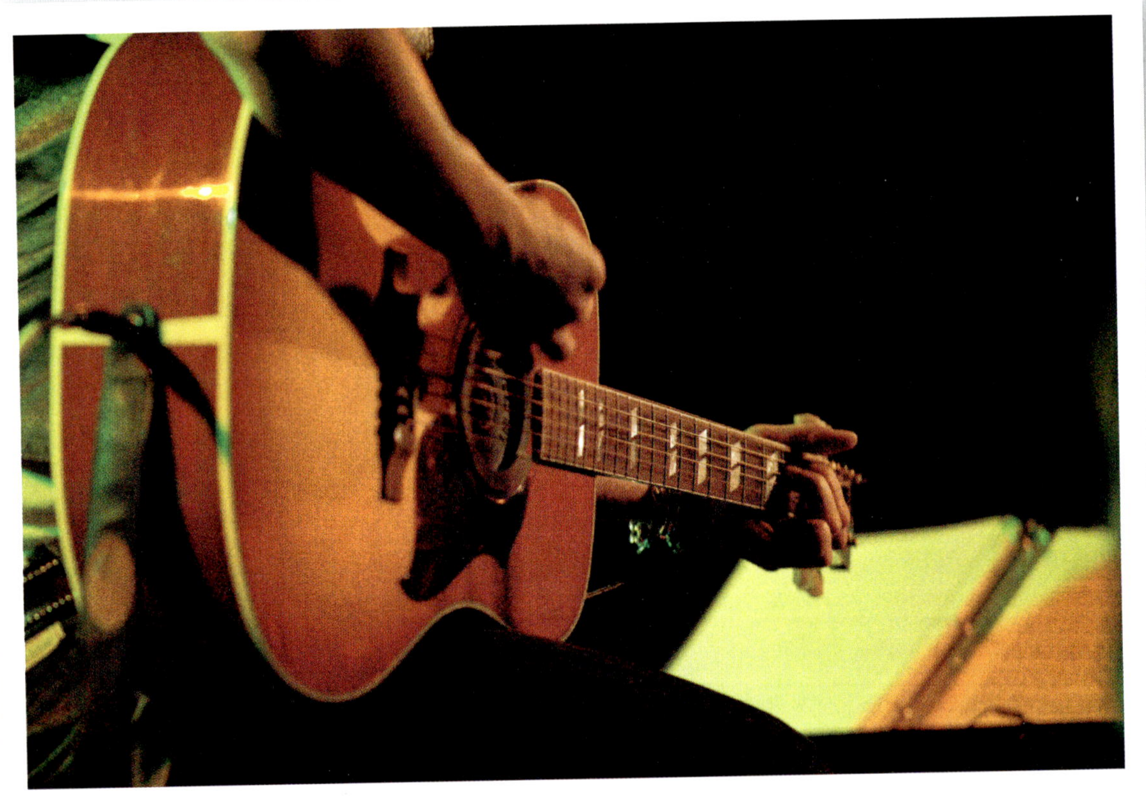

Images taken at high ISO settings will have digital noise. Noise shows up as unwanted spots of color in this image as a result of the ISO 6400 setting. The good news is that cameras are performing better all the time; ISO values that were unusable years ago are producing nice images now.

Taken at 1/125, f/2.8, and ISO 6400

previous generations. An image shot at ISO 800 on a Nikon D3, for example, has a lot less noise than an image shot on a Nikon D2x at ISO 800. The cameras are only one generation apart, but the technology is dramatically different. So it's fairly safe to say that the newer the camera, the less noise you'll have in your images at similar ISO settings … due to advances in technology.

It's possible to reduce the effect of digital noise using software in post production, but the noise-reducing methods can also reduce the sharpness of the image. So if you're applying a lot of noise reduction to an image, remember to also add some sharpening in order to keep the details in your images well-defined.

EXPOSURE MODES

Your camera has at least four exposure modes. Many cameras also have a set of scene modes that usually include *sports* or *macro* or *portrait*. But don't worry if you don't have these, because I won't be covering them and you don't need them. Instead, the four exposure modes that you need to understand are:

- Manual
- Shutter Speed Priority
- Aperture Priority
- Program Auto

Exposure modes can be broken down into two different categories: those that use the metering information from the camera and those that don't. Well, there's really only one mode that ignores the metering information, and that's the manual mode. The other three modes use the information from the built-in light meter to pick your camera settings. Let's take a closer look.

MANUAL MODE

Manual is the mode I use most often, because it relinquishes complete control of the camera to the shooter. When using manual mode, *you* set the shutter speed, the aperture, and the ISO—not the camera—even if those settings are going to result in an image that, by technical standards, is incorrectly exposed.

In other words, the camera won't change anything. And this is really important for concert photography, because the lights can change all the time. If the camera is in control of any of the exposure settings, it will use the built-in light meter to set exposure control(s). And with constantly changing light, that can be a mess.

SHUTTER SPEED PRIORITY

When using shutter speed priority, the photographer sets the shutter speed, and the camera uses the built-in light meter to assess the light in the scene and set the aperture. In this mode, the exposure settings can change from moment to moment depending on the light present and the metering mode selected.

APERTURE PRIORITY

Here, you set the aperture and the camera uses data from the built-in light meter to set an appropriate shutter speed. The shutter speed can drop automatically in this mode, so images may end up blurry. And because the built-in meter is reading the light—nothing else—the settings can change quickly.

PROGRAM AUTO

This option's similar to setting the camera on full auto and letting the built-in light meter and metering mode select a shutter speed and ISO setting and, in some cases, even the ISO automatically. There are times when this mode can be useful, but if you want consistent results, then this is not the mode to use.

Truly, the only real difference between program auto and a full auto mode is that you can adjust the shutter speed or aperture for each image in program auto. This makes it a little more useful than full auto … but not much.

Keep in mind that, in theory, none of the modes are better or worse than any of the others; but when it comes to concert photography, the best mode to use is the manual mode. If you want to use one of the other modes, I suggest trying aperture priority set at the widest aperture possible and with the spot metering mode. You can also try the shutter speed priority mode, but be prepared for underexposed images. The camera, when in shutter priority mode, will use the shutter speed you pick no matter what.

To find out how to set the exposure mode on your camera, check your camera manual.

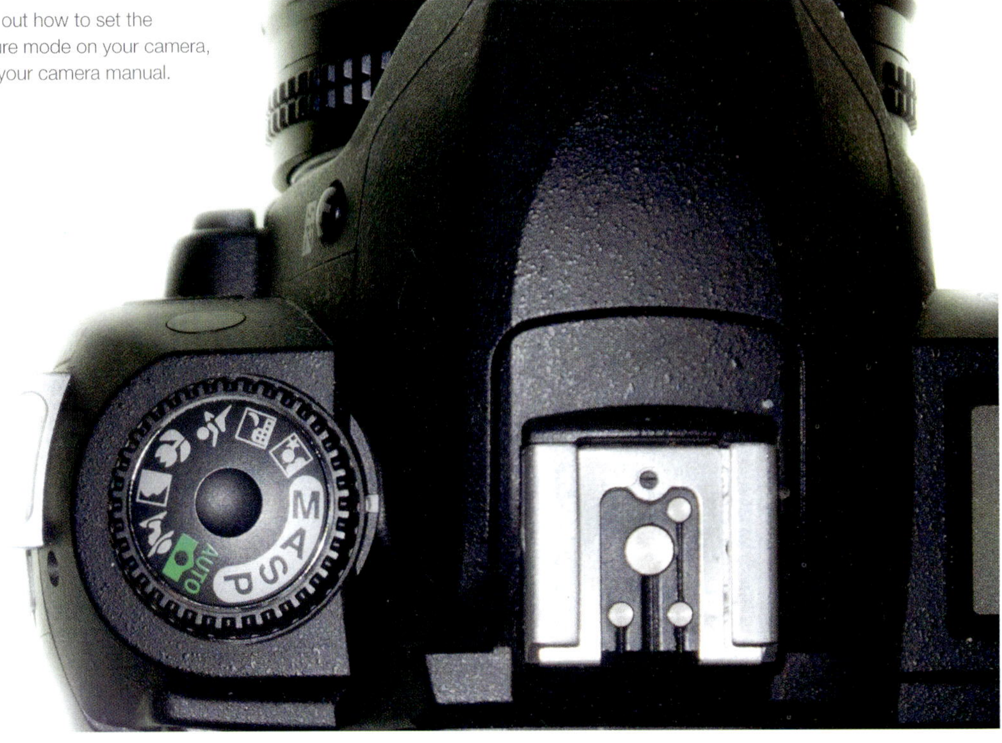

FOCUS MODES

My first camera with autofocus changed my life. Well, maybe that's overstating it a little, but it sure made my photography work easier. And it's kinda hard to believe that there are now several different focus modes on most cameras—usually a set of autofocus modes and manual focus.

The autofocus mode I use for concert photography is continuous autofocus, which is designed for capturing moving subjects. On the Nikon system it's called AF-C or Autofocus Continuous; on the Canon system it's called AI Servo focusing. All the same, this mode constantly adjusts the focus as long as the shutter button is pressed down halfway.

The continuous auto tracking autofocus tool will always try to focus on the subject that's closest to the camera.

There are also settings that allow you to tell your camera where to focus and whether or not to activate focus tracking, a feature that tries to keep your target subject in focus as it moves. This is amazing technology and can work great if you keep one very important factor in mind: The continuous auto tracking autofocus tool will always try to focus on the subject that's closest to the camera. So if you're tracking a musician and (s)he steps up to the microphone, the camera might focus on the microphone. This is just something to keep in mind. For more on the different focus modes available to you, check out your camera manual.

WHITE BALANCE

Different types of lights have different colors. This might seem obvious when talking about the colorful and often elaborate lighting sets you see at a concert, but it applies to all light sources—even the sun. And it's important to know that there's a big difference between how our eyes and brains deal with the various colors and how a camera records them.

The easiest way to explain how this works is for you to try a little experiment at home. Take a piece of white paper and go outside. Stand in the sunlight. The paper still looks white, right? Well, now take that same piece of paper and go stand in the shade. After a minute or two, your piece of paper still looks white, I bet.

So now … here's the big test: Take that paper inside and walk around your home or office. Look at the paper under a variety of lights, and you'll notice that it looks white everywhere, especially after a few moments in each condition. This is an example of our brains and eyes working together to accurately represent color to us under a variety of different lighting conditions.

Cameras don't work the same way; the camera sensor just records the light it sees. Sometimes it has a blue cast; sometimes orange or red; and sometimes it's true white. Well, the camera setting that deals with the color of light is called the *white balance*. It tries to shift colors so they look correct in your images under the different types of light.

This is the one setting that I adjust least often. I don't use it much, because when I shoot a concert, I *want* the images to have the color cast of the stage lighting. That doesn't mean that some images don't need to be tweaked in post processing to get them to look right, but I generally don't worry too much about the white balance. I set my cameras to auto white balance most of the time.

Also, I shoot using the RAW file format. One of the reasons for this is that, if needed, I can easily adjust the white balance in post production. More on that in Chapter 14.

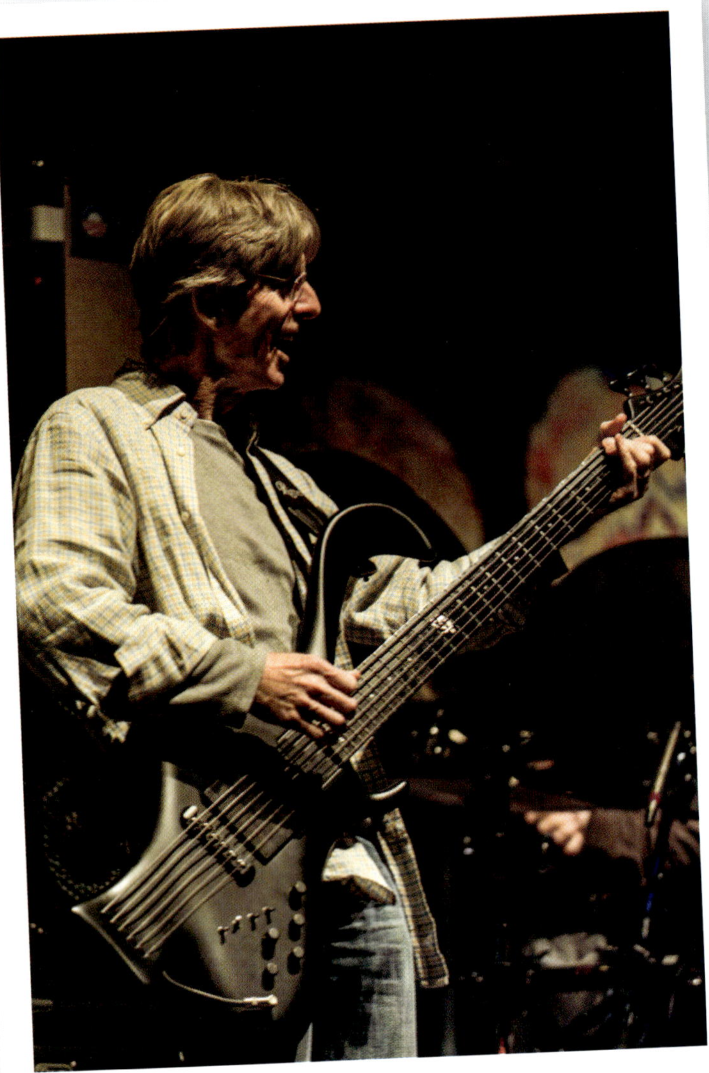

The auto white balance setting on my camera rendered the colors in this photograph of Phil Lesh as they were on the stage.
Taken at 1/200 second, f/2.8, and ISO 1250

ALL TOGETHER

To get a good exposure when shooting concerts, follow this series of steps.

1. Set your camera on manual exposure mode. This ensures that, no matter what happens with the lights, your settings won't change unless you change them.

2. Set the camera to spot metering mode. Even though this won't enable your settings to change, the built-in light meter readings can help you get a proper exposure.
3. When shooting inside, set the ISO to 1600, open the aperture up to f/2.8, and set the shutter speed to 1/160 second. When shooting outdoors, I suggest setting the ISO to 200 and using the other settings described for inside shoots.

Will this combination work for all your images? No, but we have to start somewhere, and these settings are solid.

I use these settings when I leave my house for a show, because I want my cameras to have the same initial settings every time I shoot. This allows me to adjust my camera during a shoot without needing to look at the info screen or any of the menu screens. One dial controls the aperture; the other controls the shutter speed. And, if needed, I can adjust the ISO. But when it comes to concert photography, you're probably adjusting the shutter speed and the ISO. The aperture will stay wide open.

ISO

Setting the ISO to 1600 amplifies the sensor information, as covered earlier in this chapter, and this is helpful in low-light situations, like a concert. The current generation of digital cameras can photograph at ISO 1600 with very little noise, especially compared to cameras from just a few years ago. In fact, you can increase the ISO to 3200, if necessary, but 1600 is a good place to start.

If the show is very bright, consider moving the ISO down to 800. For daytime shows, set the starting ISO to 200. Just be prepared to adjust the it up rather quickly to handle stage shadows and a setting sun as the day progresses.

APERTURE

I like to open up the lens as wide as it can go. If it's a zoom lens, that's f/2.8. If I'm using a prime lens that can open up wider, I set it for f/2.8 and go wider only if I really need to … like when I'm shooting in a small bar. I rarely adjust the aperture though, even when shooting in full light, because I prefer a shallow depth of field. I think it makes for a better backgrounds.

SHUTTER SPEED

The shutter speed setting is a guess, but I like 1/160 as a starting point because it's easy to go up or down quickly from there. Here's how I approach getting the right exposure at a show. With the camera set up at 1/160 second, f/2.8, and ISO 1600, I look around at the lighting and try to figure out if I'm going to need a slower shutter speed (to deal with low lighting) or if I might be using a higher shutter speed (for bright lights).

I know this doesn't sound very scientific, but as you gain more experience with photographing shows, you'll become more accurate in your assessments. Of course there will always be hiccups—a show might look like it's going to be very bright and end up being dark, for instance. But generally, look to see if there are follow spots or lots of stage lighting to get an idea of which way you'll likely be adjusting the shutter speed.

TESTING ... TESTING ...

Then take a quick shot of the stage before the band starts to see if your settings are in the ballpark. This works best for daytime shows, but you can do this to get a feel for the lighting at any show.

With the camera set to use spot metering, make sure the focus point is on a musician's face and press the shutter button halfway down to activate the autofocus and the built-in light meter. The viewfinder will have an exposure display that shows you how much the current settings are over- or underexposed compared to the reading that the camera gets from the spot metering area. Snap the photo and check it on the LCD screen. If it's too dark, then lower the shutter speed. If it's too bright, then raise the shutter speed.

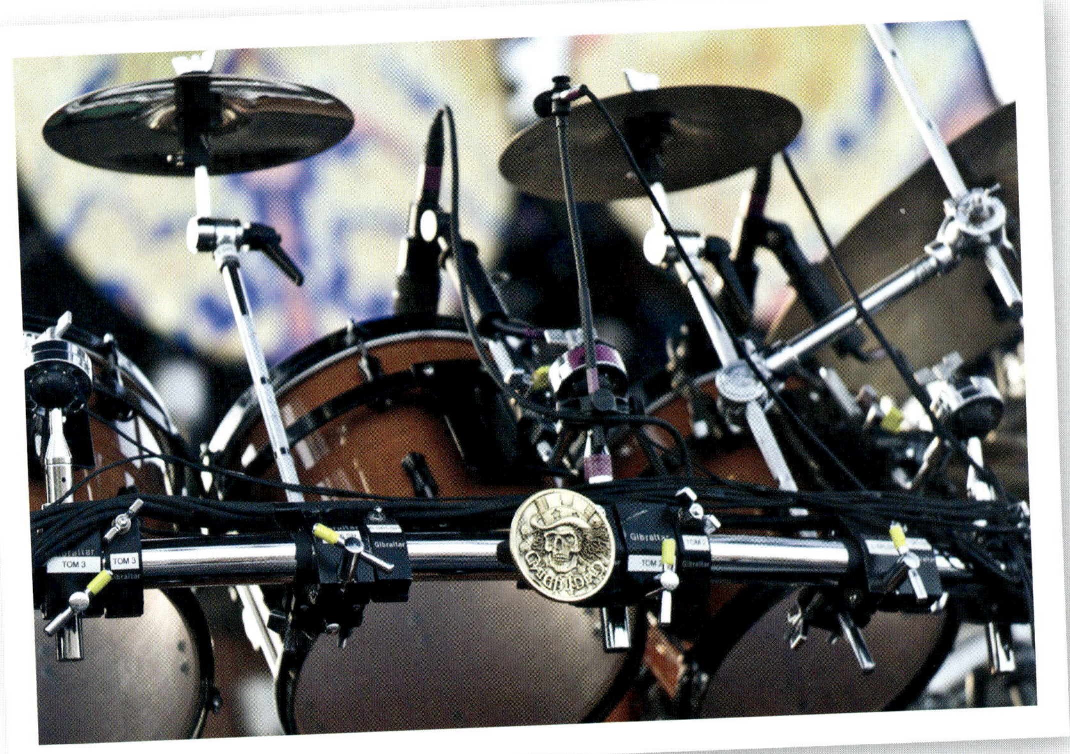

This shot of The Dead's drum kit was taken before the band hit the stage.

Taken at 1/125, f/2.8, and ISO 400

If the performers are moving fast and you want to freeze them in place, then you need to make sure that your shutter speed is fast enough and that you remember to raise the ISO if needed. Given the limited time to shoot at most shows, it's important that you're able to adjust the settings without checking the back of the camera. This means that you need to be able to judge the lights and adjust the exposure almost instinctively. So practice, practice, and then practice some more.

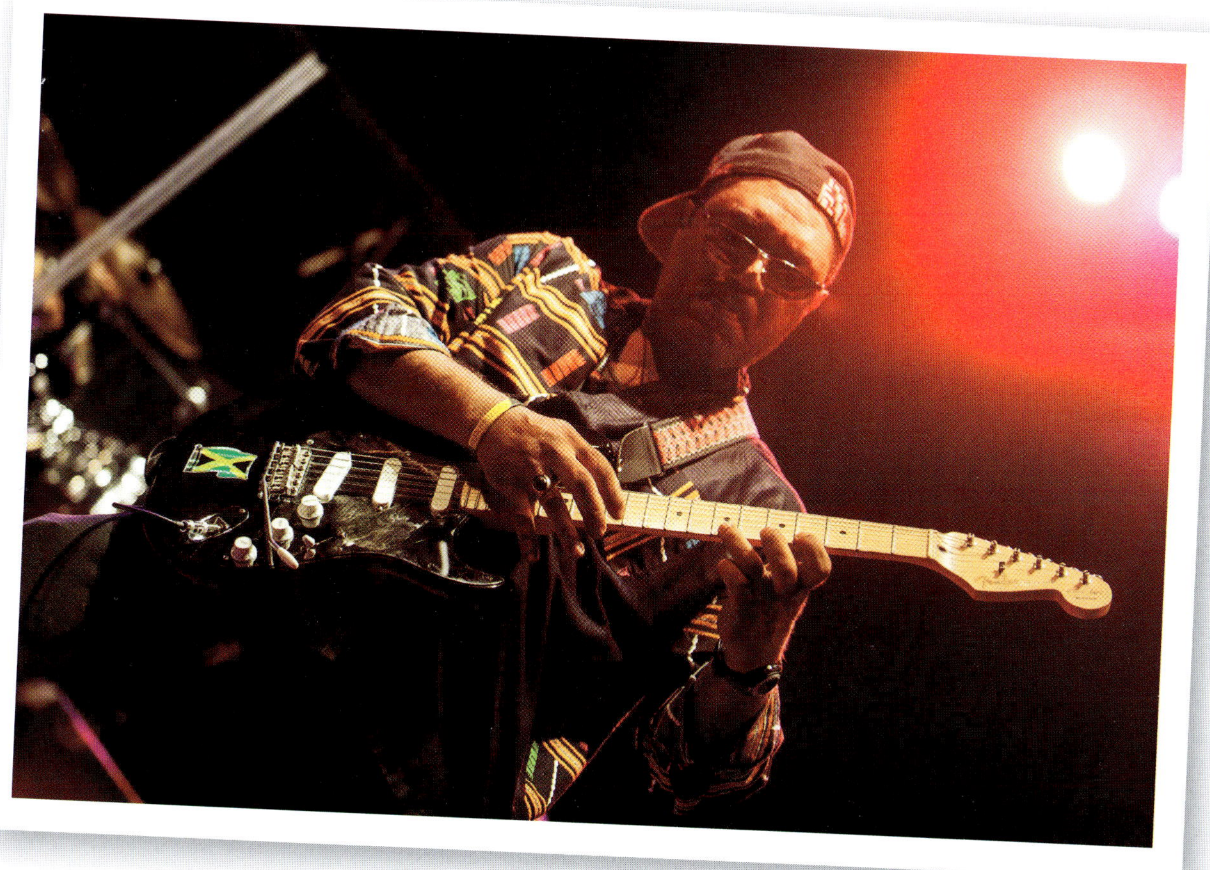

Practice and a familiarity with the band Steel Pulse made it possible to capture guitarist Donovan McKitty up close during one of his solos.
Taken at 1/125 second, f/2.8 and ISO 1250

Drew Gurian

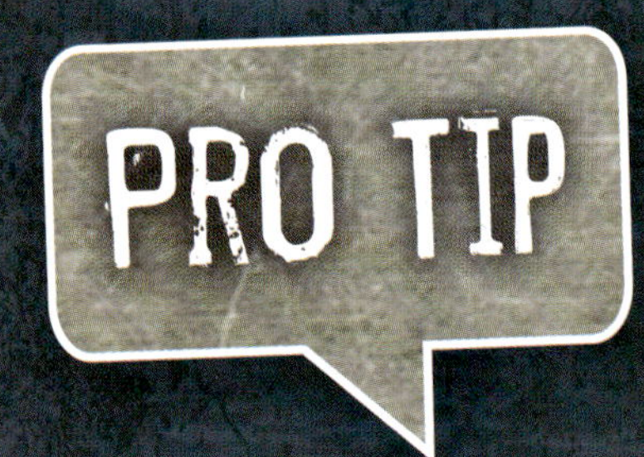

Drew Gurian is a New York City-based freelance music and editorial photographer. He spends a great deal of time traveling the globe, and he is always looking for new and exciting challenges.

www.drewgurian.com
www.twitter.com/drewgurian

What was the first concert you shot?

The first concert I ever shot was for a band called Guster, which was playing with G. Love & Special Sauce and Widespread Panic at New York's Jones Beach Amphitheater. I was a family friend of one of the guys in Guster, and they were gracious enough to hook me up with photo passes whenever I called. That's how I got started in the photo world.

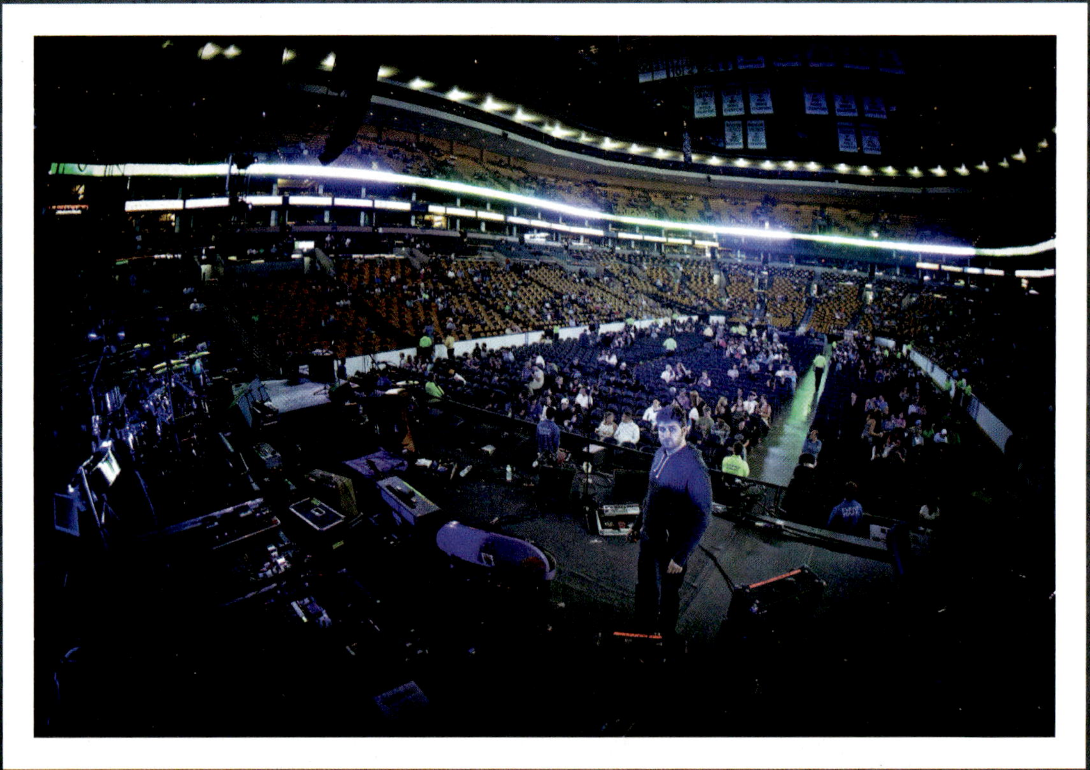

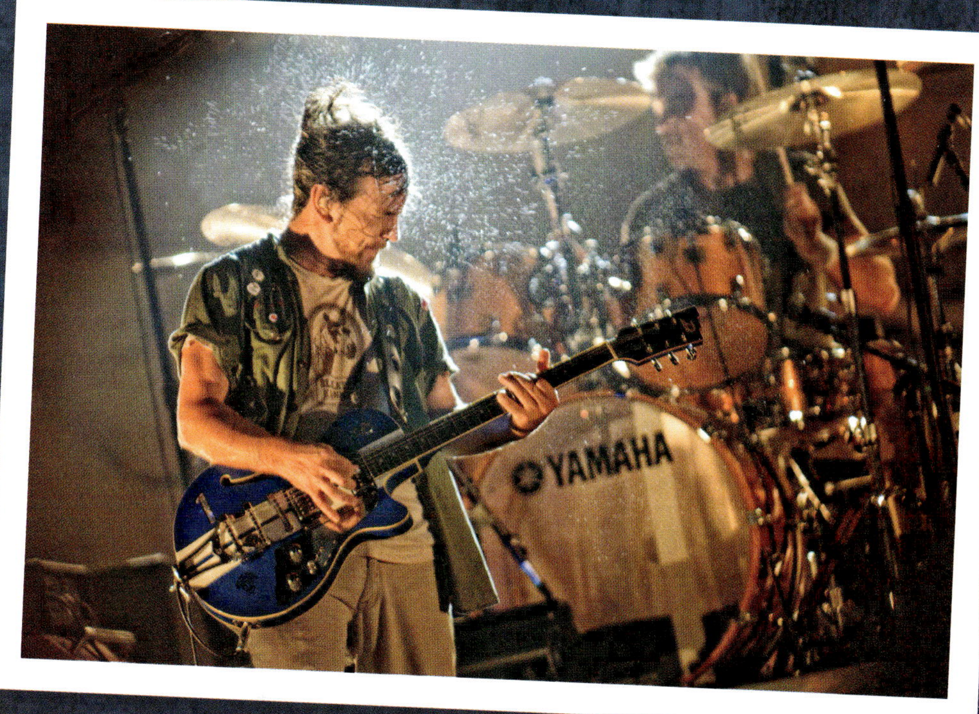

© Drew Gurian

What do you look for when shooting live music?

Having the opportunity to shoot musicians on or off stage is an amazing gift. Music has always had an incredibly important place in my life, so it's incredibly rewarding to be allowed into the life of those who create it. Musicians let everything out on stage, and it's our job as shooters to be as well-versed in our craft as they are in theirs ... and to capture peak moments. My best photos are those that show raw emotion. If I can capture that in a single, still frame, then I've done my job.

What gear do you use?

For live shooting, I tend to shoot with two Nikon D3s bodies and a few staple lenses: 14–24 f/2.8, 24–70 f/2.8, and 70–200 f/2.8VRII. I've been getting back into black and white film, so I'm shooting off-stage candids with a Leica M6 and occasionally a 1950s Rolleiflex.

Any advice to photographers starting out in the concert field?

The best advice I can give to anyone starting out is to shoot like crazy. That's really the only way to get great at this. And as hard as you may think you're working at it, there's always people working harder. When you're ready to start marketing yourself, make friends. Lots of my connections now are from bands and publicists I met ten-plus years ago, and I'm still working with them to this day.

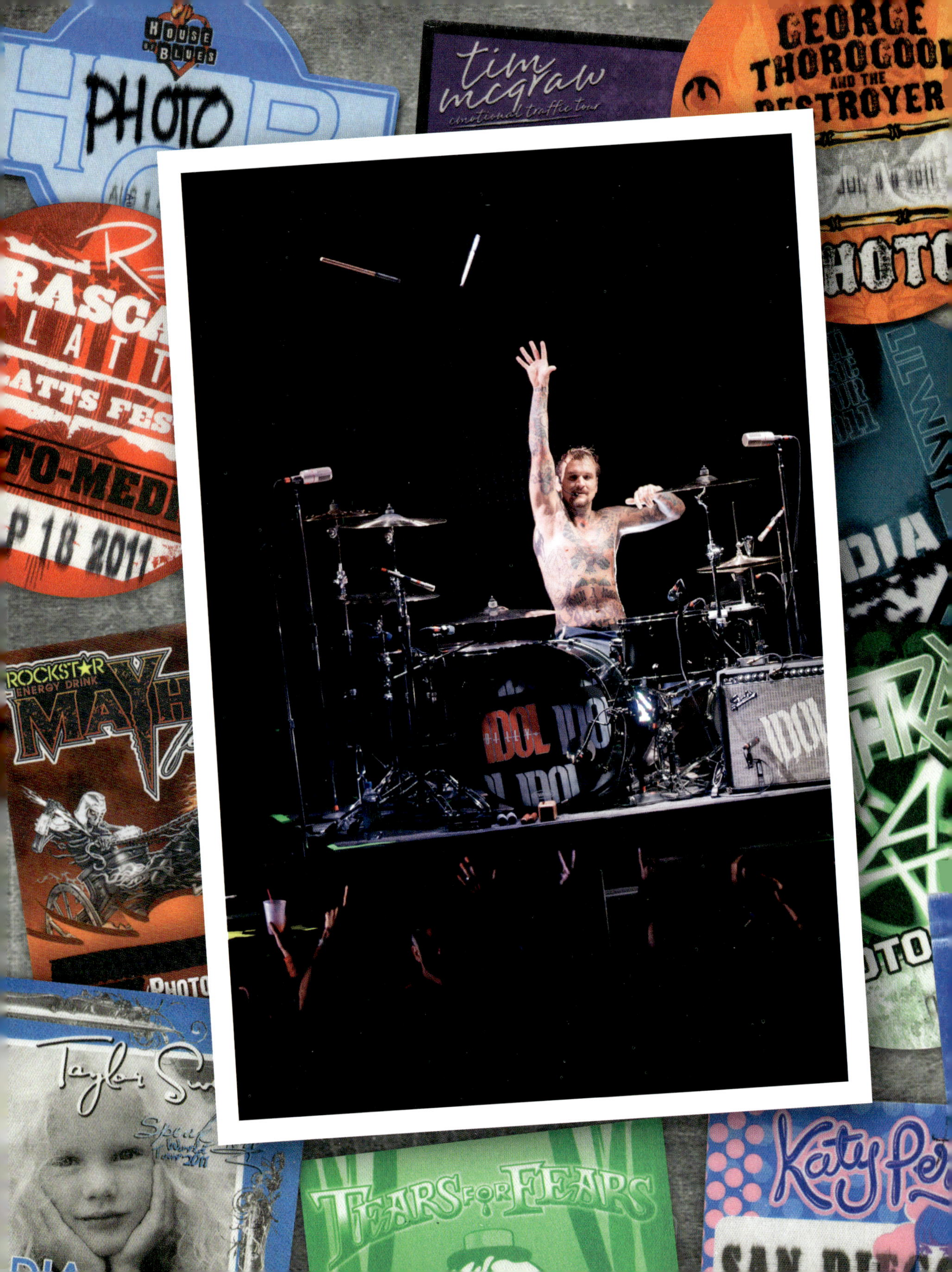

HOUSE OF BLUES
PHOTO
tim mcgraw
emotional traffic tour
GEORGE
THOROGOOD
AND THE
ROCKSTAR
ENERGY DRINK
IDOL
TEARS FOR FEARS

6 In the Spotlight: Composing Hot Shots for Live Music

Picture this. You're in a photo pit, and there are 75 other photographers all looking to capture the same band, at the same time, and from the same position as you. (Groan.)

To make it as a successful concert photographer, you've got to find a way to make your photos stand out from the rest . . . even in tough, competitive shooting situations.

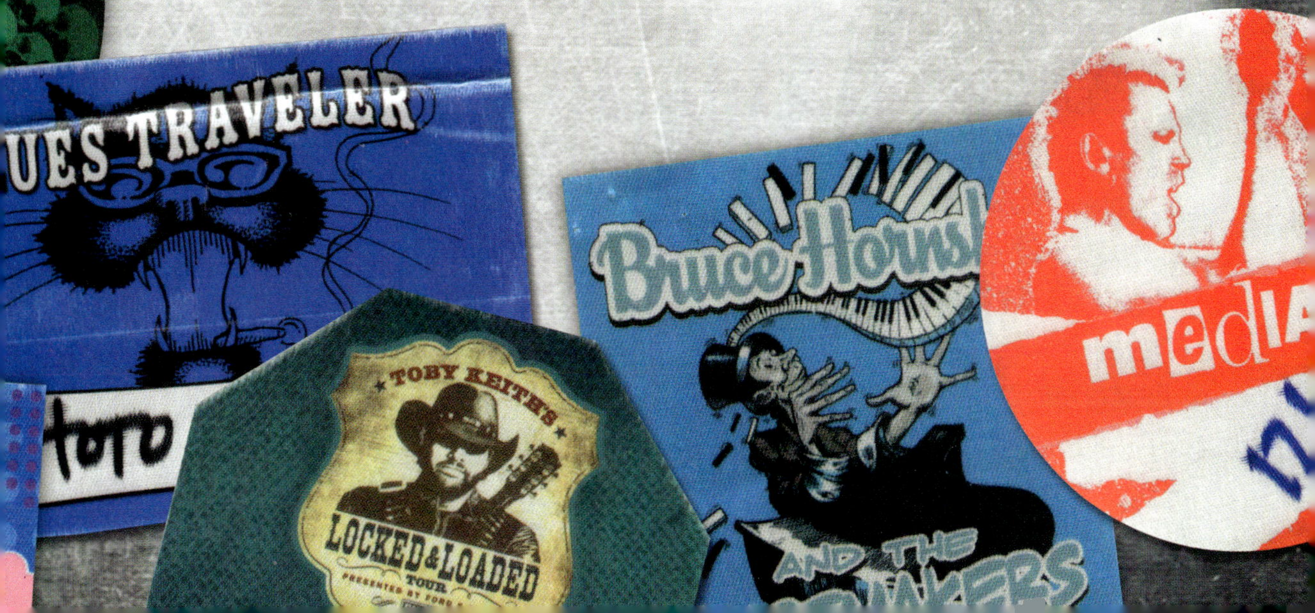

And the key is *composition*, which is comprised of what you choose to include (and exclude) from your image and where you place your subjects in the frame. Since it's extremely unlikely that performing musicians will stop and pose for you—and it can be nearly impossible to change your position in a crowded pit—the timing of your photographs and the emotion that you capture take on a whole new level of importance to your concert shots. But you also need to know how to capture the various instruments and situations of the live show. These are the pillars of good composition for performance-based images.

When considering these aspects of composition, always remember your client. Why are you there? What does your client need? Are you shooting for a guitar manufacturer or an amp company or drum manufacturer? Is the shoot for a magazine article or music website? Are the images for sale on a wire service or being used only by the band or a fan site? Whatever the case, keep the end in mind. As you press the shutter release button, be sure the composition suits the final goal of the photographs.

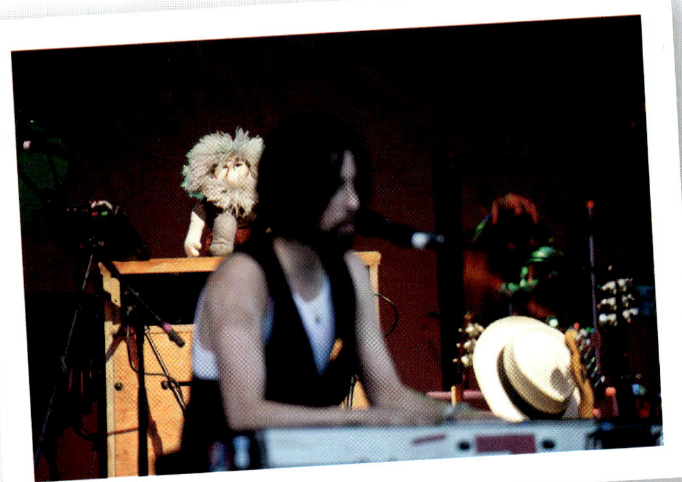

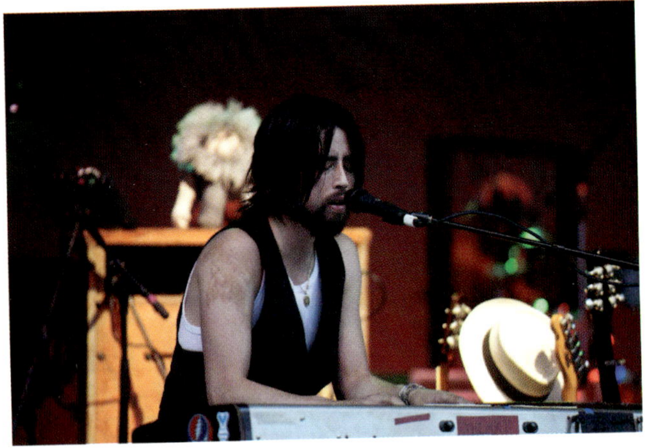

Pay close attention to the focus spot, especially when there is a shallow depth of field. Both of these images are of Jackie Green, but the focus is on the Jerry Garcia doll in the first photo and on Jackie in the second. The two elements are so close together in the scene that it's really easy for the camera to switch focus between them.

Taken at 1/125 second, f/2.8, and ISO 1600

FOCUS

One of the first aspects of composition to consider is focus. By this I mean both the central element of an image—what do you choose to highlight?—and the actual focus setting of the shot. When I first picked up a SLR camera back in the 80s, it didn't have autofocus. And I remember trying to keep the band members in focus while they moved all over the stage.

I do not miss those days at all. The dSLRs available now have great autofocus, and they get faster and more accurate all the time. They are

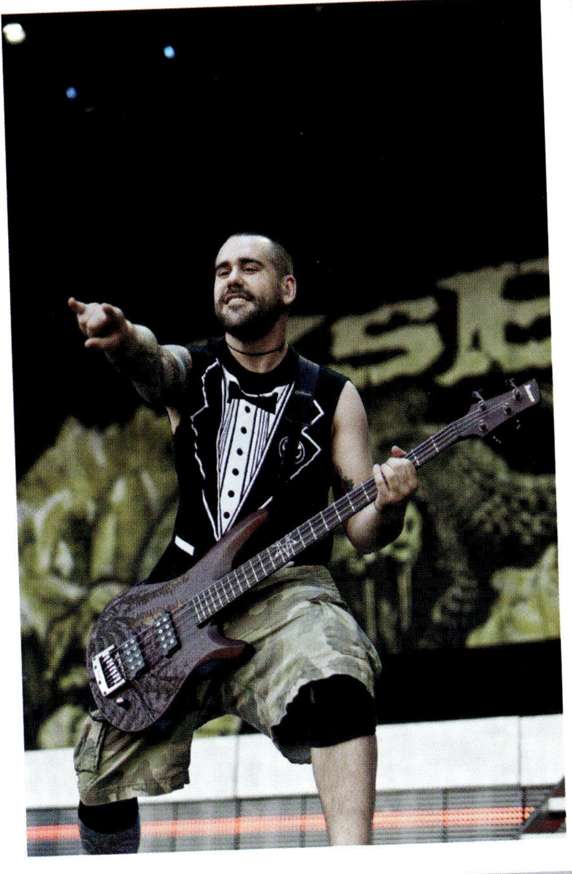

When shooting concerts and using a very shallow depth of field, you need to clearly define your subject. Take this image for example. The focus is on the face of the musician and not on the hand out front.

Taken at 1/800 second, f/2.8, and ISO 800

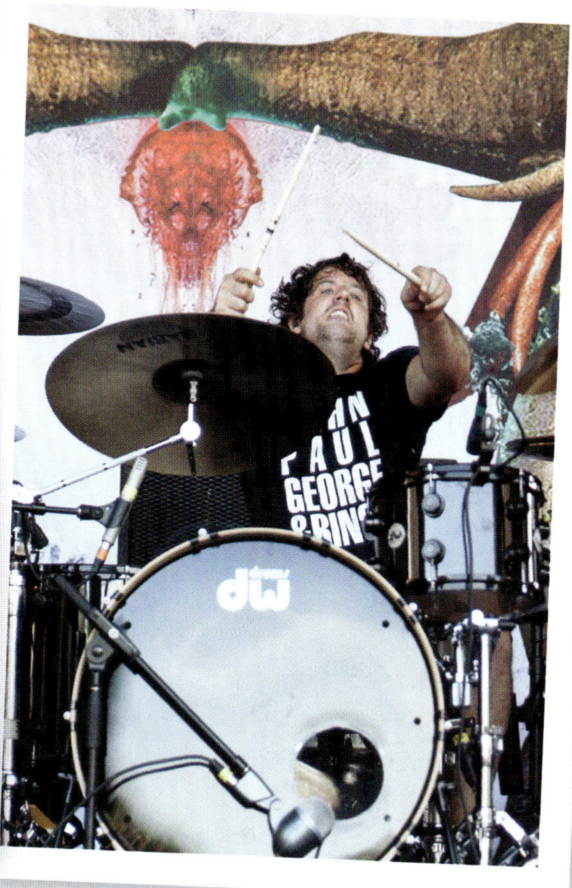

If the camera has control of the focus points, photographing the drummer can be a problem. But if you control the focus point, you can shoot past the gear and capture the drummer.

Taken at 1/500 second, f/2.8, and ISO 640

so good, in fact, that I can't recall the last time I needed to manually focus when shooting a concert.

Nevertheless, you need to know how the autofocus in your camera works. Because you are shooting at very wide apertures due to the low light, you end up with a very shallow depth of field. This means that your focus better be exactly on your subject. So I use the continuous autofocus with single point selection as my autofocus setting. This gives me the best results.

Make sure that your camera is set on continuous autofocus, so autofocus will adjust as the subject moves. (On the Nikon system, this is called Continuous Servo Auto Focus; on the Canon system, it's the AI Servo mode.) Then use single-point autofocus to manually move the focus point onto whatever you want to be in focus.

I know many concert photographers who use dynamic area autofocus, which tries to track the subject as it moves. The only downside to this is that the dynamic autofocus will lock onto whatever is closest to the camera. And many times, that ends up being the microphone stand and not the singer using it.

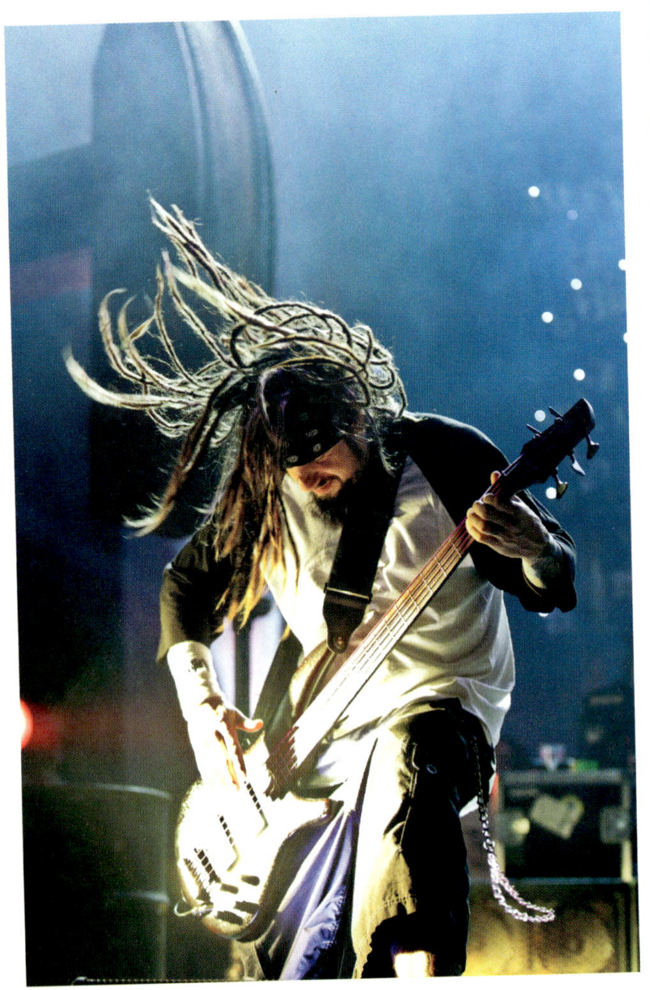

The autofocus is so good on my cameras that it allows me to carefully consider the composition and follow the action on stage without worrying about my focus settings. When shooting Korn at the Rockstar Mayhem Festival in 2010, I was able to capture the flying hair by keeping the focus point on the face of Reginald "Fieldy" Arvizu.

Taken at 1/400 second, f/2.8, and ISO 2000

It takes some practice to determine which setting works best for you. But I've found that by picking the focus point myself, I can hone in on, say, a drummer without the drums getting in the way of a clear focus.

TIMING

As they say, *timing is everything*. With everybody in a single location (the photo pit or soundboard) and shooting the same band under the same lights, the one thing that can really set you apart is great timing. This is knowing the exact right moment(s) to press the shutter release button to capture a memorable scene in front of the lens.

Timing is something that comes naturally to some. But don't worry if yours is a little off. It can also be learned. Here are some things that can help with the timing of your shots:

- **Study the band.**
  Digital photography and the Internet have made it really easy to see a lot of photos of just about any band. When preparing for a concert shoot, check the band's website or search Flickr and Google images to see what the band looks like. Check for a consistent look to the images and, if possible, watch some live video clips. All of this homework will help with your timing when shooting live.

- **Know signature moves.**
  Some bands and musicians do a certain action over and over again. If you know what that action is, you can be ready to capture it. For example, Scott Ian, rhythm guitar player for the band Anthrax, usually leaps into the air during the third song in the set. To get the height he wants, he does a very distinct walk right before the jump. Knowing this has helped me to capture the jump every time I photograph Anthrax.
- **Shoot in burst mode.**
  Digital cameras and big memory cards mean you can take a lot of photos and not worry about running out of film. When I see something cool, I shoot in burst mode, taking three to five shots in quick succession. Know how many shots you can shoot in a row with your camera, and work on starting a burst shoot as soon as a series of special moments begin. And continue shooting though the action.
- **Use double vision.**
  Photograph with both eyes open. In other words, watch the scene with one eye in the viewfinder and the other open to the unfiltered view. This isn't as easy as it sounds; it can be a little distracting. But with practice, the technique allows you to switch your focus easily.
- **Know your camera settings.**
  I know I've said it before, but if you have to take the camera away from your eye to change settings, you will miss important moments. So it's important that you know what every button, lever, and dial does … and know it by touch, so you can change settings quickly in a dark music venue.

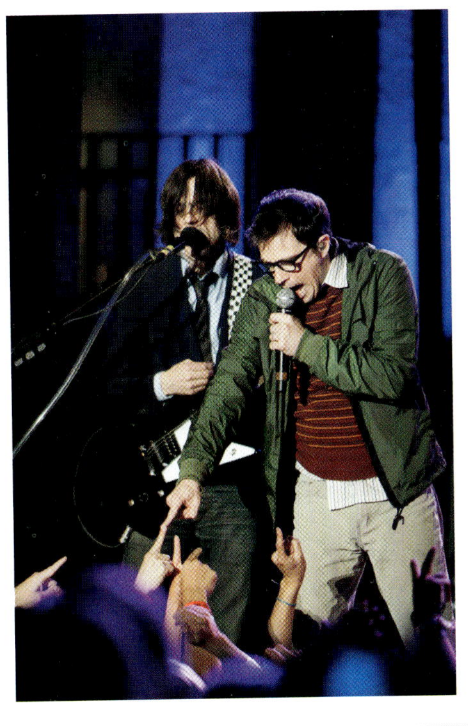

Here is a touching moment between a fan and Weezer front man, Rivers Cuomo. Getting this shot required me to watch the scene unfold in front of the lens and press the shutter release button at the right time.

Taken at 1/400 second, f/2.8, and ISO 1600

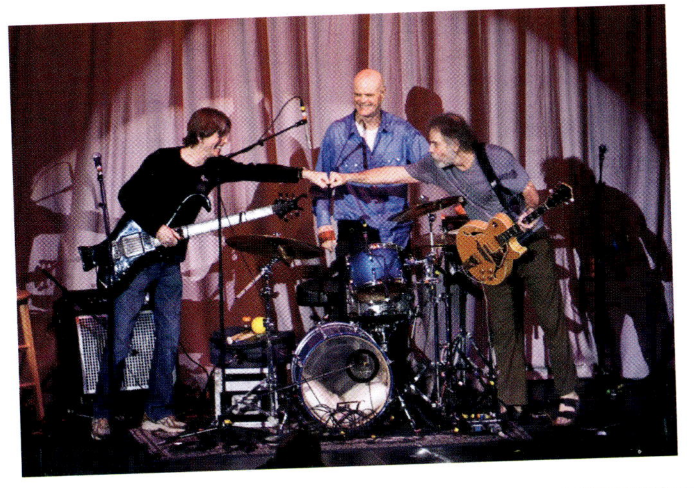

My favorite moment of the Phil Lesh, John Molo, and Bob Weir set came right at the end, when Bob and Phil had a little fist bump moment.

Taken at 1/200 second, f/2.8, at ISO 1600

The longer you photograph concerts, the more you'll be able to use your sixth sense. After seeing so many shows through the viewfinder, you start to see and feel the rhythm of the show. You get familiar with it and know what to expect. The performers will fall into patterns, too.

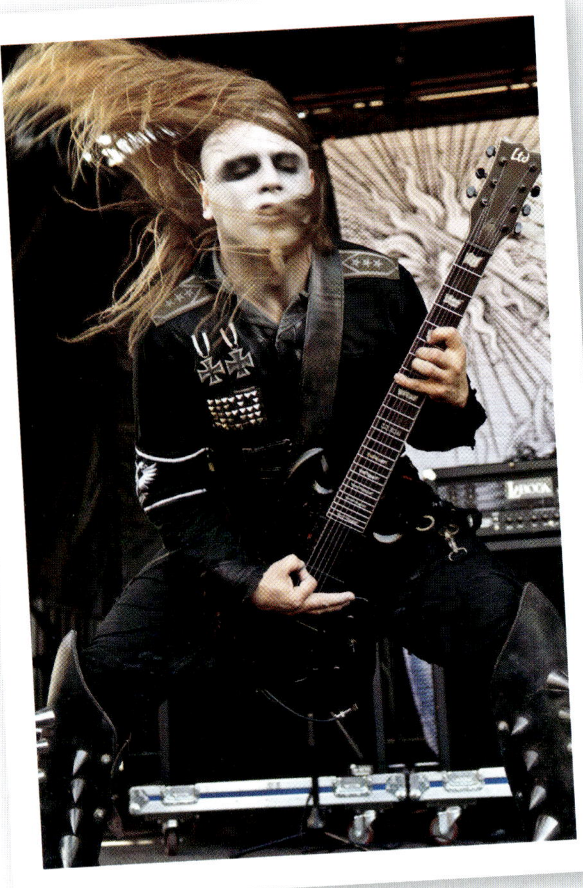

Three songs is enough time to get a feel for a performance. After a song or two, you'll notice how the guitarist pulls back when playing a lead and that the bass player turns to watch the drummer during a solo when he starts expecting the signal to get back into the groove. Use that information during the third song. And of course if you've shot the band before, use your experience to time your shots.

The last part of timing has to do with the lights. You need to be able to time them as they go from illuminating to hiding a musician. Very few light shows are random, and a good lighting director can really enhance the show. Here are a few things that stay pretty constant when lighting a band.

- **The "name" will get the light.**
  If you're seeing a big-name star that is a solo performer with a backing band, then you can bet that the light will be on her. For example, I recently photographed Taylor Swift; she had great light on her all the time. This is because people came to see Taylor Swift—not the bass player. There's nothing wrong with this, but you need to be aware of it; because if you want images of someone in the backup band, you need to either wait until (s)he has a solo or adjust your exposure settings to deal with the lower light.
- **The soloist will get the light.**
  If a member of the band is playing a solo, the light is usually on him. This allows the audience to figure out who is doing what on stage. Otherwise it can be tough to tell. It also makes it a lot easier to photograph the soloist. A musician is in full performance mode when playing a solo, andthat's where the audience is looking.

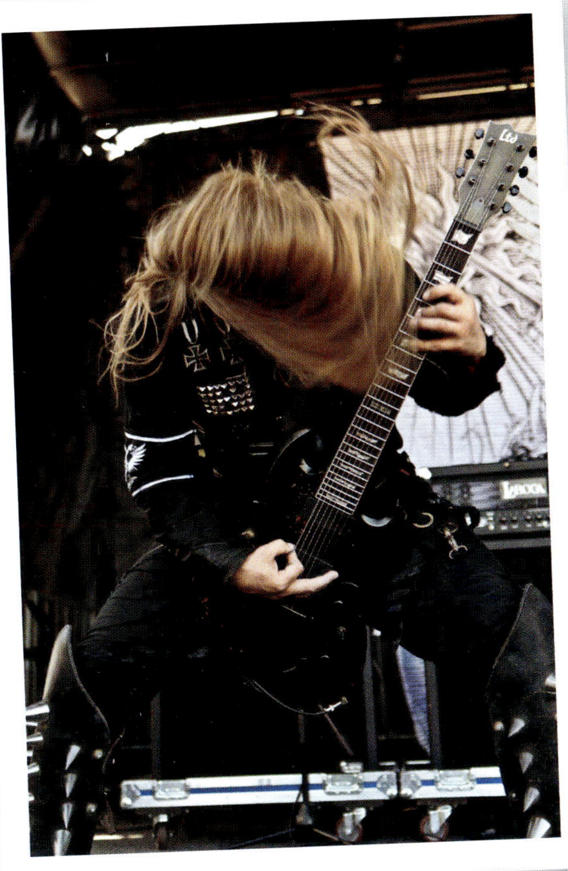

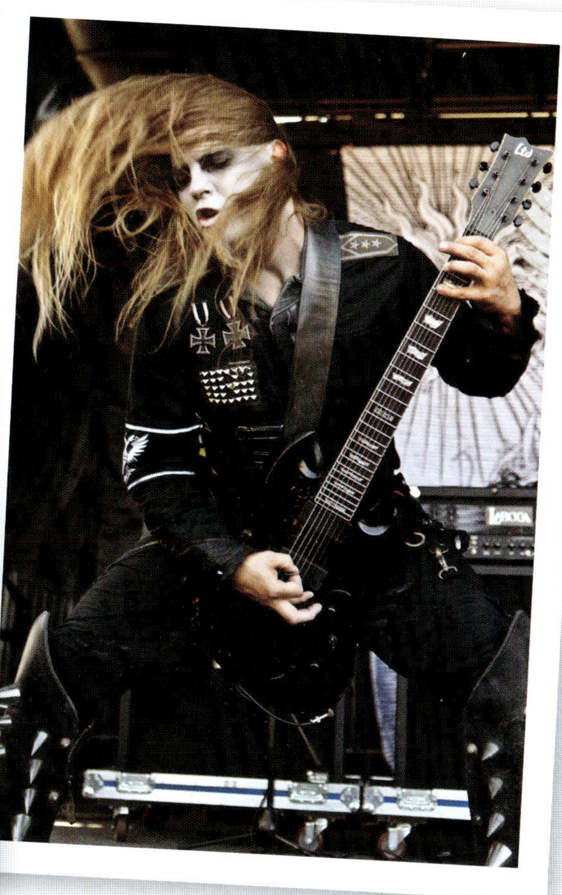

A sequence of images shot in quick succession can help get the one shot you want. When photographing Behemoth in concert, I started to shoot sequences of the guitar player in hopes of getting a clean shot of his face with the hair flying. It did work out in the end.
Taken at 1/250 second, f/2.8, and ISO 320

- **The main light can be boring.**
  The main spotlight is usually a bright white light that can be a little boring in photos. The first time you see it, it looks great, especially if you're used to shooting in reds and greens. But after awhile, it seems to have very little personality.

EMOTION

There's something magical about music. It can take you back to the first time you heard a particular song and bring certain emotions and memories to the surface … even after many years. Music has the power to lift your spirits when life seems to be at it darkest. And it can be reassuring to find out that other people feel the same way you do. Good music can make you feel really, really good.

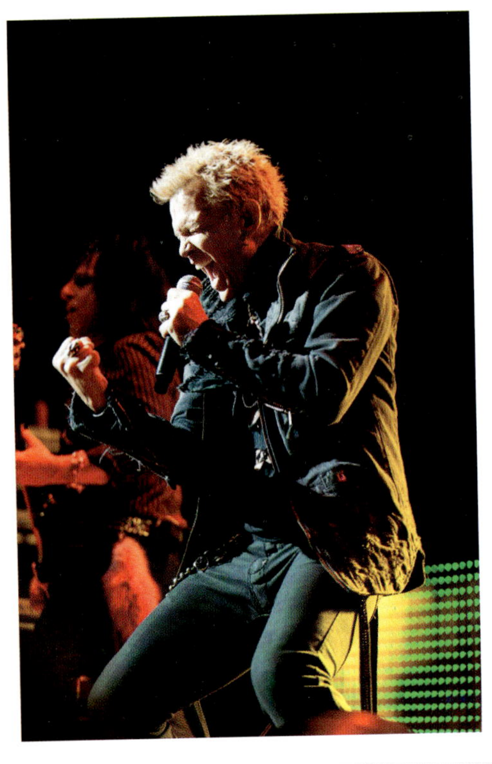

Billy Idol wears his emotions on his face, making it easy to capture great moments.

Taken at 1/125 second, f/2.8, and ISO 1250

There's a lot of raw emotion in music, and a great live show will have an emotional element that's present on the faces of performers. As concert photographers, we need to capture that emotion.

So watch the facial expressions of performers as you listen to their music. It's very easy to get caught up in the moment and miss a smirk or small smile, but if you keep watching, you'll see visible emotion. Be ready to capture it. Some performers are easier to read than others, but all great musicians are emotionally invested in their music … and show it.

Look for facial expressions that reveal an emotion or illicit an emotional response. A look of intense concentration or an ear-to-ear grin work well, as does a yell or scream. Also watch for the closed eyes of a musician who's lost in her own world.

Look, too, for emotions on the faces of fans, especially those that've been waiting all day to see their favorite band. They sing along to every song; they smile, laugh, and sometimes even cry. I really like to get some of the fans in my shots when I'm working in a small photo pit. Use a very wide-angle lens or even a fisheye to do this. If you can get a combination of a moment and an emotion in the same shot, it's a winning combination that just can't be beat. The resulting image will stand out from the rest and that's exactly what you want to happen.

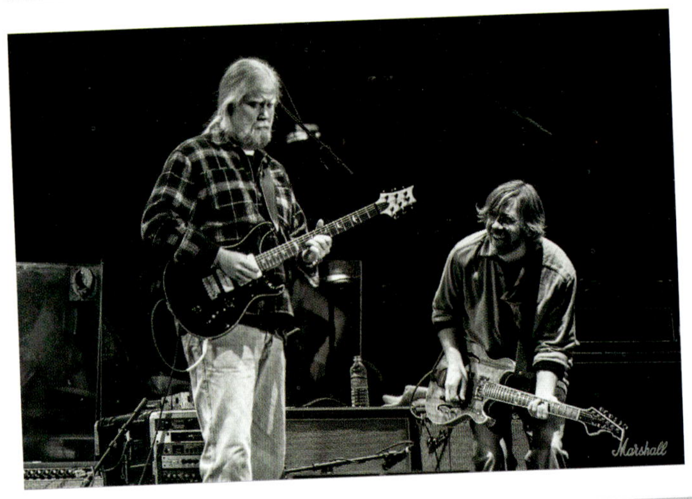

The look on Trey Anastasio's face as he watches Jimmy Herring play speaks volumes about the music being produced. He just looks happy.

Taken at 1/80 second, f/2.8, and ISO 500

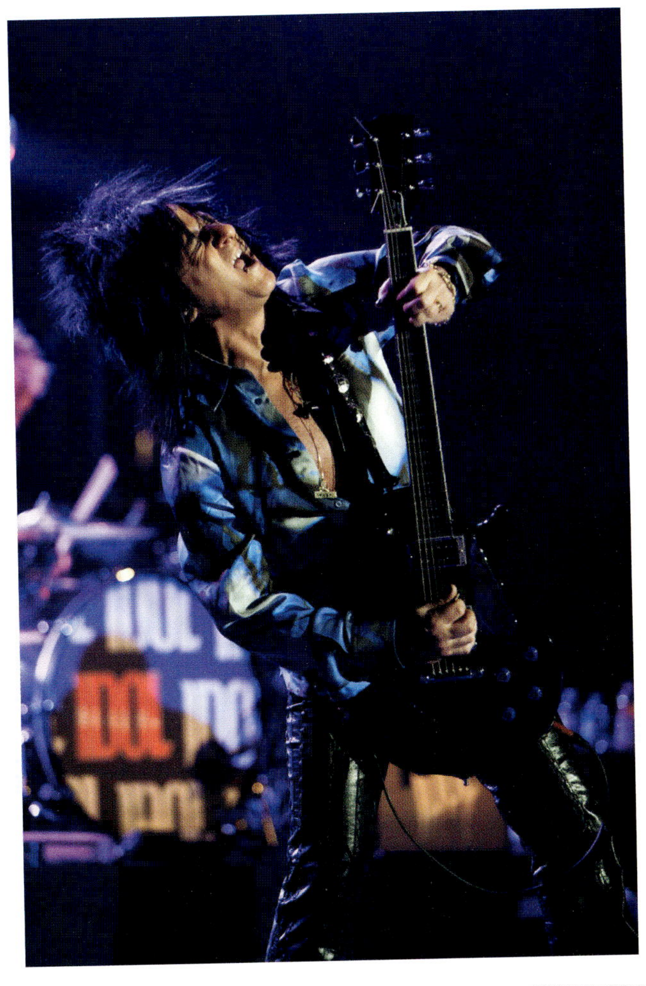

Watching Steve Stevens play is an amazing experience. He puts everything he's got into each note, every time. You can clearly see the passion on his face when he plays.

Taken at 1/320 second, f/2.8, and ISO 1600

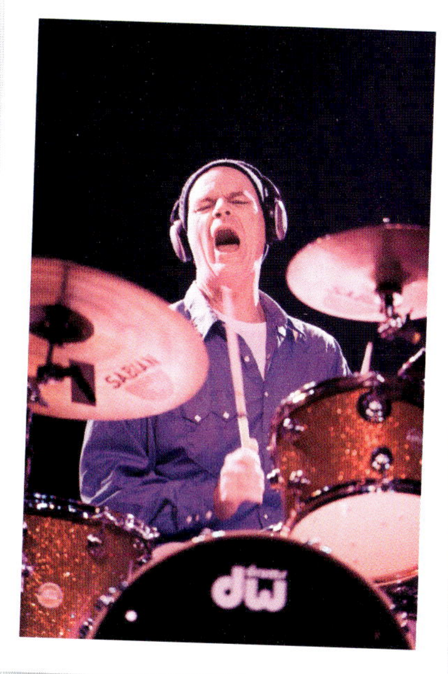

John Molo has always been a great drummer to watch, because his facial expressions are so animated and easy to read. The joy he's showing in this shot is really pure delight at the music being played.

Taken at 1/320 second, f/.28, and ISO 1600

The easiest way to capture emotion is to keep the focus point on the face of the performer. When practicing this, don't worry about anything else. Just look for and recognize emotions as they occur.

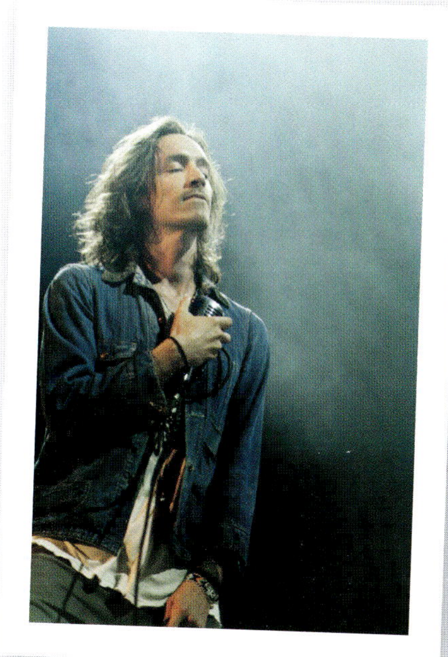

The emotions are clear on Brandon Boyd, lead singer of the band Incubus, even though there is no screaming or yelling.

Taken at 1/250 second, f/2.8, and ISO 1600

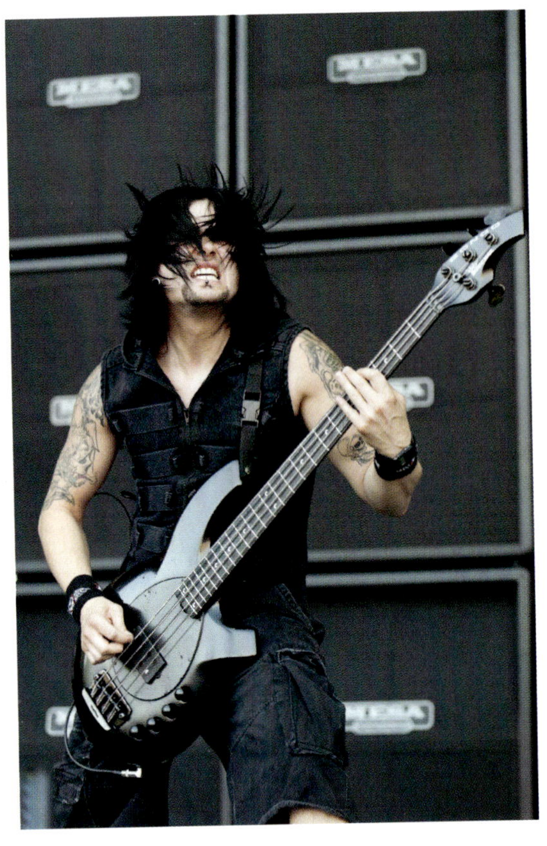

This is one of my favorite concert photos for two reasons. I love the hair and expression on Jason James' face (Bullet For My Valentine), and I love the clean Mesa Boogie background.
Taken at 1/500 second, f/2.8, and ISO 640

BACKGROUND

It's really easy to get caught up in the moment as a band is rocking. The light looks great, the fans are cheering, and the action in front of the lens has your full attention. Now is the time when a good shot can become a great shot ... or just another photograph that's really close to being great. It's time to consider the background.

FOCAL LENGTHS

Different focal lengths show more or less of a background. When you use a wide angle lens, you get a lot of the background in an image. When you use a long focal length, less of the background is visible. In other words, a wide focal length expands the background while a narrow focal length compresses it.

That's simple enough, but there's a little more to it. Your focal length and distance to the subject also affect the depth of field. A wide angle lens has a deeper depth of field than a telephoto lens; so if you use a wide angle lens, you fill more of the frame with the subject and capture less of the background. And your background will be more out of focus at the same exposure settings than on a telephoto lens. For example, if you take the same shot with a 16mm lens and a 70mm lens ... using the same shutter speed, aperture, and ISO for both ... the depth of field in the 16mm lens shot will be deeper than the 70mm lens shot. So pick your focal length carefully.

ANGLES

Slight changes in your angle can make a huge difference to how a final photo looks. This is especially important if you have a compelling background that you want to include in your shot. In this case, if you're shooting a band with musicians who tend to wander around the stage, watch as they pass in front of the background elements and away from equipment in the foreground.

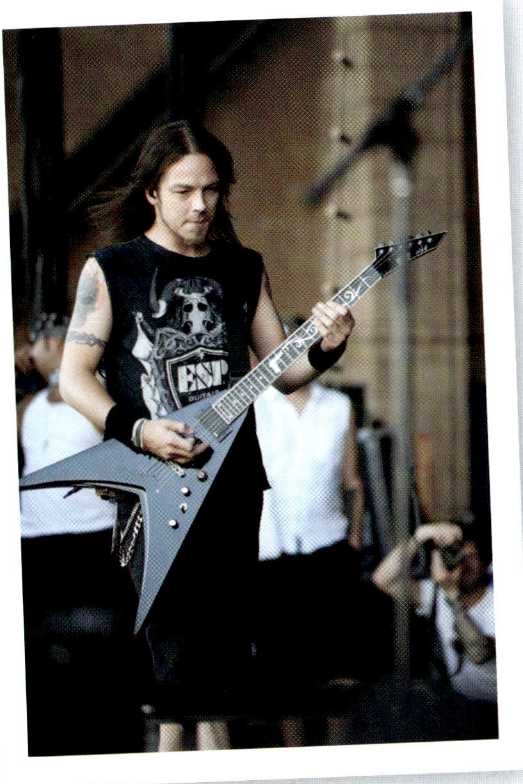

The background in the image of Mike Paget is really distracting. You can see the crew working ... and a photographer on the stage. Even using a shallow depth of field can't hide the bad background on this one.

Taken at 1/400 second, f/2.8, and ISO 640

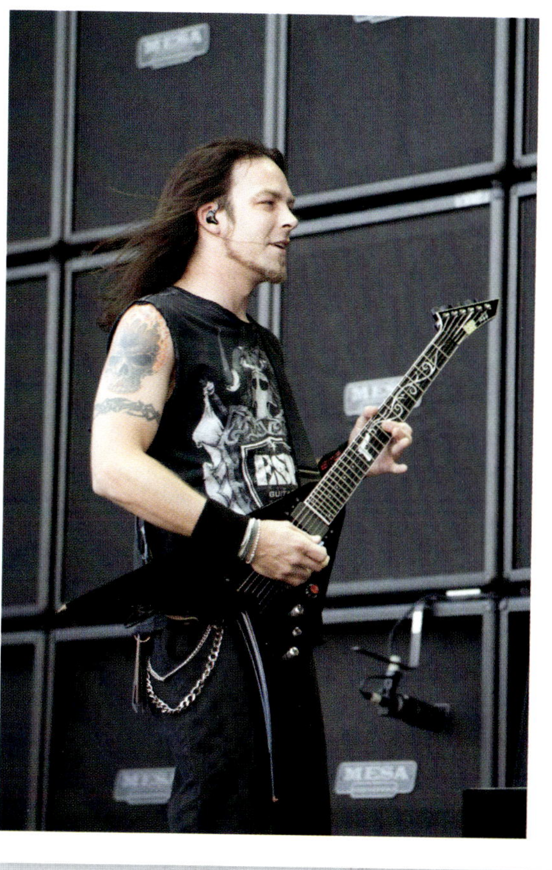

By waiting until Mike Paget moved a few feet to the right, I was able to capture this image with a much better background.

Taken at 1/400 second, f/2.8, and ISO 640

Areas to watch when shooting from the sides of the photo pit are

- **Side Stage**
  I'm not talking about shooting from the side of the stage here. I'm suggesting that you watch what happens on the side of the stage and try not to capture it. Nothing is as distracting to me when looking at a concert image than seeing the crew working on the side of the stage. It's a little like looking behind a magic trick and seeing how it works. As interesting as it may be, it detracts from the image. So try to move so your image shows the performer against the backdrop of the stage.

- **Across the Stage**
  Another option for the scenario described above is to move so you can shoot across the stage and capture a background comprised of fans. I think this kind of shot is great, and I try to get it, especially when a performer interacts with the crowd.

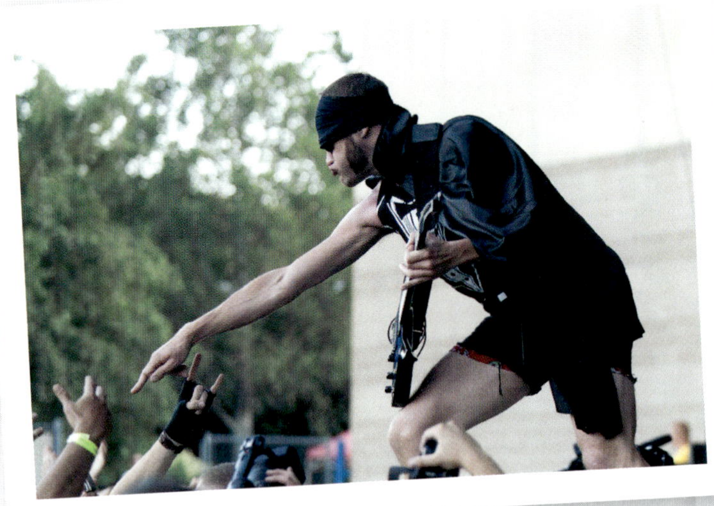

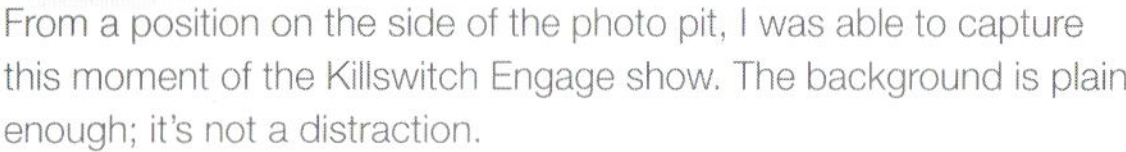

From a position on the side of the photo pit, I was able to capture this moment of the Killswitch Engage show. The background is plain enough; it's not a distraction.

Taken at 1/800 second, f/2.8, and ISO 800

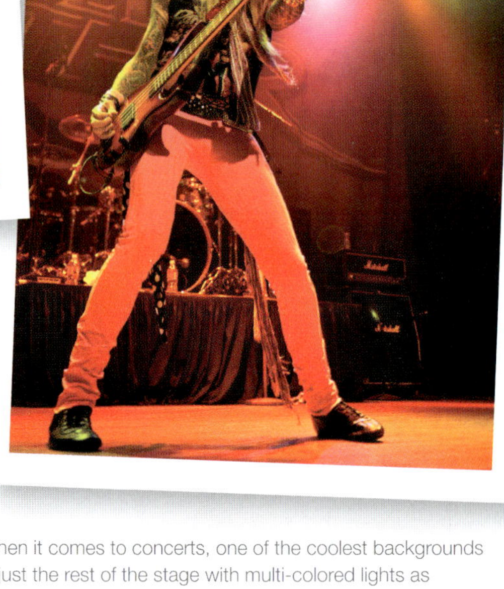

When it comes to concerts, one of the coolest backgrounds is just the rest of the stage with multi-colored lights as accents. Use a low angle to get the lights in the background. This is Steel Panther, by the way.

Taken at 1/200 second, f/2.8, and ISO 1600

GUITARS

There is something about a guitar that is just cool. I'll be the first to admit that I know very little about guitars, except that I like to see and hear them being played. I've been lucky enough to photograph some of the great guitar players in the world, and I'm always in awe of the sounds they get out of this instrument.

There are lots of different ways to capture guitars. In fact people debate for hours on where and when it's okay to cut off the headstock or cut into the guitar body at all. This goes for regular guitars and bass guitars, too. Of course the two instruments are played differently, but they have the same basic shape. So use the same set of rules (which we cover in just a second).

But keep in mind that the *rules* here are really just suggestions. They can be ignored to create great shots. Trust your vision. These are guidelines.

HEADSTOCK

The biggest concern with photographing guitars is where to cut off or bisect the headstock. Well, there are two acceptable places for cutting the headstock if it can't be avoided; but as a rule, try to avoid cutting the headstock or having anything in the foreground disrupt the view of it.

- **Don't cut the headstock.** If life was perfect, I would never cut off a guitar's headstock. Every guitar player photo would show the whole guitar, and no one would argue. But the reality is that sometimes composition suffers if you include the whole guitar in a particular shot.

  Remember who's paying you to take the photos. If you're shooting for a guitar company, then you definitely want to make sure that the whole guitar is in the shot. If your client wants to crop it later, then (s)he can do it in post production. This also applies to guitar players. If you're photographing the guitar player for a guitar-related product or for the guitar player himself, then you'll want to keep the guitar whole in your images.

- **Cut after the playing hand.** If it's impossible to avoid cutting off part of the guitar neck or headstock, make sure that the musician's hand is inside the frame. This allows the hand to become an anchor point, so leaving out some of the headstock doesn't look as weird or wrong.

- **Avoid object interference.** There are times when a microphone stand or other piece of stage gear bisects or otherwise interferes with the view of the guitar neck. Try to avoid this by changing your angle. But if that doesn't help, then try to get the whole headstock in the shot even with the bisecting line.

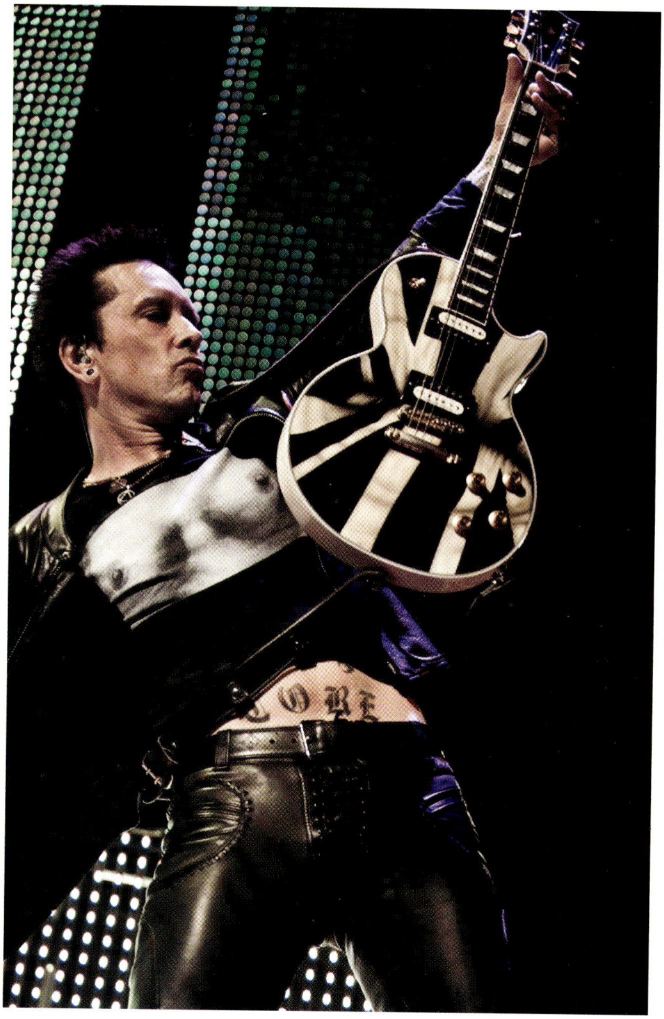

Billy Morrison is the rhythm guitarist in Billy Idol's band. I took this shot of him during the 2010 tour. When he lifted the guitar at the end of the second song, I zoomed out as quickly as I could and tried to get the whole pose in the image. I failed. I cut off the very end of the guitar, but the shot looked great anyway. More importantly, Billy liked it.

Taken at 1/160 second, f/2.8, and ISO 1250

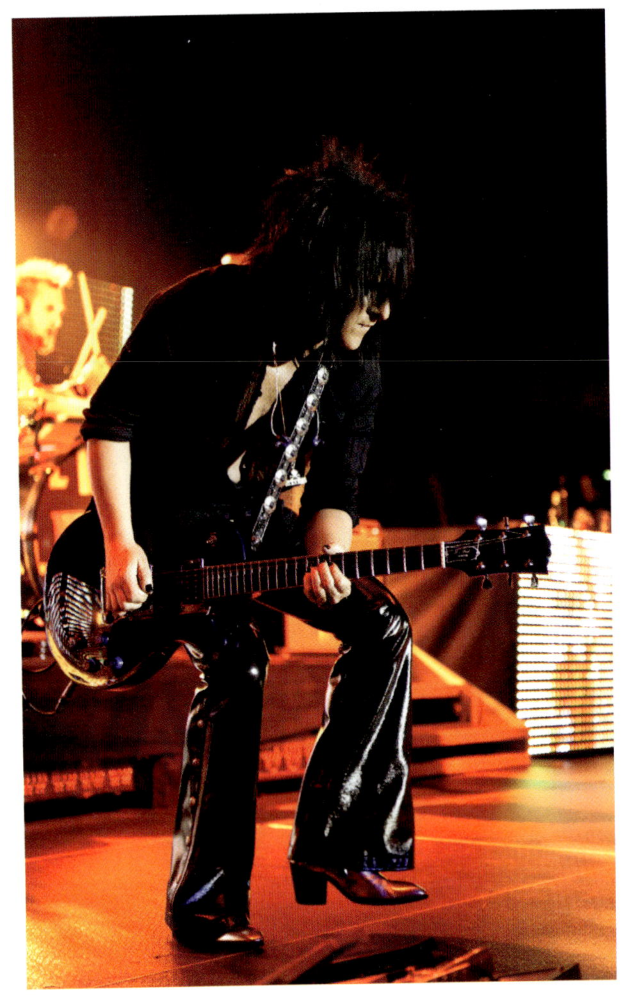

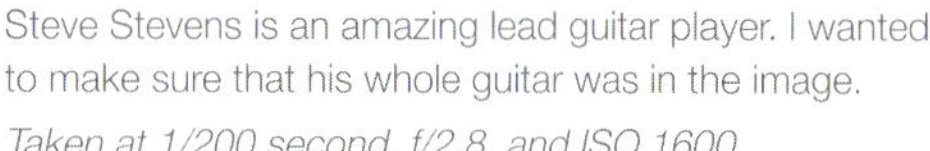

Steve Stevens is an amazing lead guitar player. I wanted to make sure that his whole guitar was in the image.
Taken at 1/200 second, f/2.8, and ISO 1600

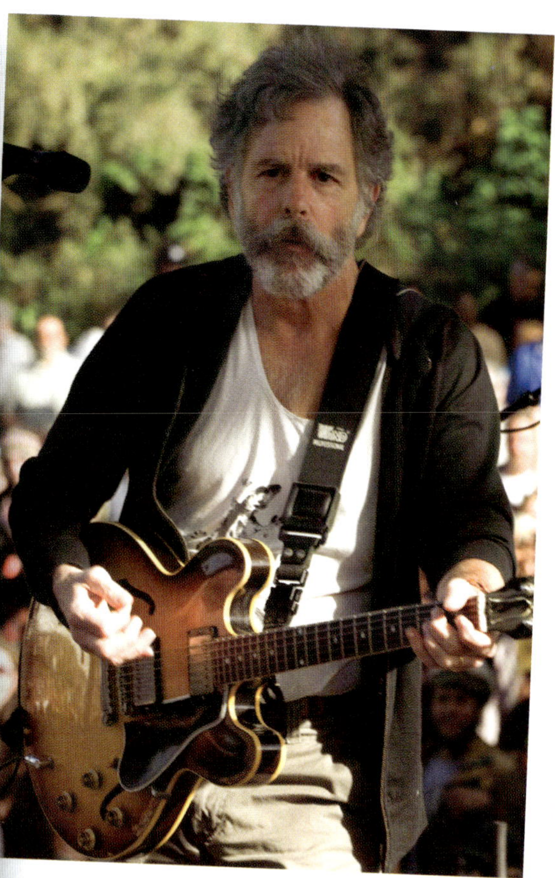

When Bob Weir turned to me right before the encore at the Green Apple Music Festival in Golden Gate Part, I took this shot. You can see some of the crowd in the background. I was cropped in tight but still managed to make sure that his left hand was in the image and that the guitar was cut after the hand.
Taken at 1/180 second, f/6.7, and ISO 250

One last thing here: It's especially important to keep the headstock complete when the focus of the image is the guitar itself and not the guitarist. Make sure that your image is clear about what it's featuring. If you shoot from the side of the guitarist's playing hand (from the right for right-handed players and from the left for left-handed players), watch how (s)he angles toward the playing hand. This makes it easier to capture the guitar.

DRUMS

Drums and drummers can be some of the most difficult aspects of a concert to capture, because they're usually positioned at the back of the stage and surrounded by stuff that gets in the way of a clean photograph. The lighting for the drummer tends to be an afterthought, too. It's not as bright or constant as it is for the lead singer or guitar player.

The problem of capturing drumsticks is particularly tough. If you capture the shot on the downbeat, then the sticks are usually hidden and your image just shows a guy sitting behind a drum kit. If you capture the drumsticks on an upbeat, you have to photograph against the natural rhythm of the music, which can be difficult.

I cover this again later in this section, but I suggest that you start shooting on the downbeat and keep shooting for a few seconds to capture the action after the stick hits the drum head. Hopefully this will help you capture a stick on the upbeat. It might end up in front of the drummer's face, but that's better than no stick at all in your frame. If this happens, change your angle if you can, so the stick is off to the side.

And sometimes, just *seeing* the drummer can be a huge challenge. When I was photographing Motorhead, for example, the drum riser was so high and the drummer was so far back on it that there was no way to see him from the photo pit. The only thing we could see from the photo pit was the front of the bass drum.

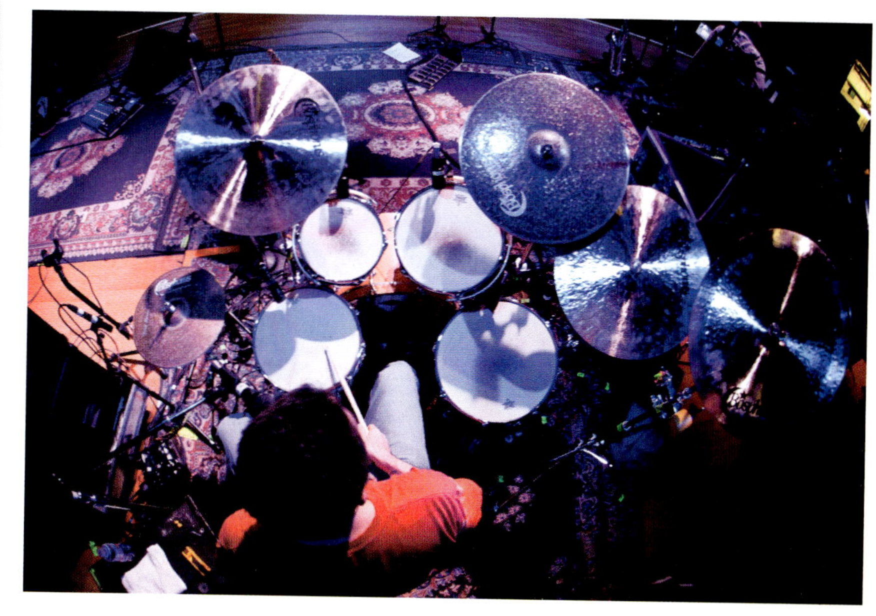

Some venues give photographers a view that faces down to the stage. And nothing is quite as cool as seeing the drums from a top-down view. This photo of Jay Lane from RatDog and Primus was taken with a 10.5mm DX fisheye lens.

Taken at 1/50 of a second, f/2.8, and ISO 320

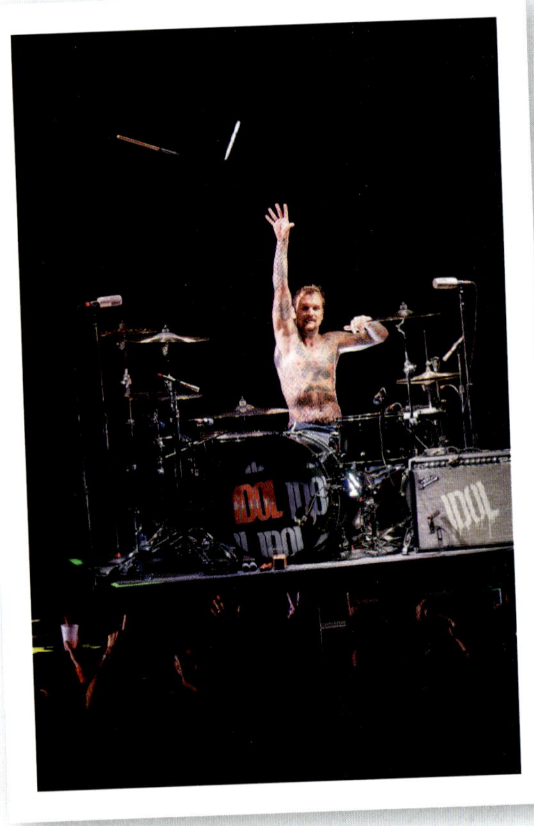

It took seeing and photographing Jeremy Colson numerous times before I was able to capture this shot of him during the drum solo. It might be my favorite drummer photo of all time, because it captures a special moment that's tough to get. The drum solo comes late in the show, and it took special permission to shoot this whole show. Capturing this specific moment took patience and being ready for the shot.

Taken at 1/500 second, f/4, and ISO 3200

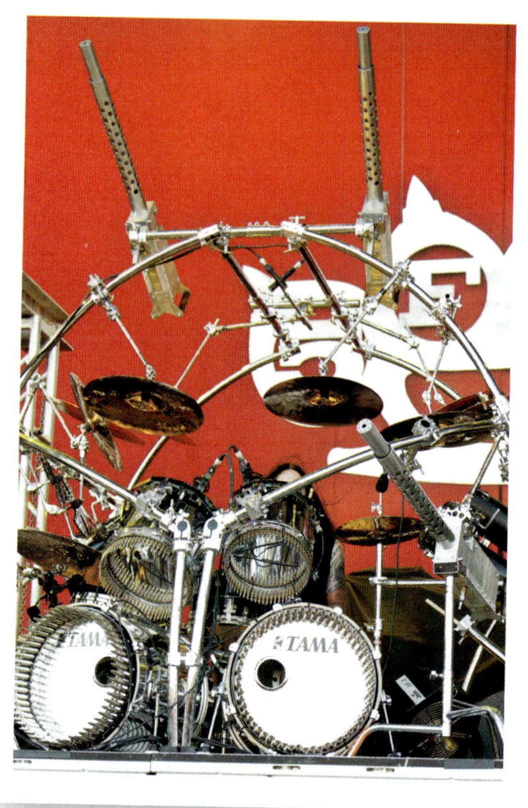

Sometimes it's nearly impossible to even see the drummer. This was the case when I photographed Fiver Finger Death Punch in 2010. The drum kit was built like an anti-aircraft gun kit with the drummer hidden behind hardware and guns.

Taken at 1/400 second, f/3.2, and ISO 800

In a situation like this, if you have more access and can change position—this is more likely if you're in a bar or a small club—then try to move back and get a side view of the drummer. But if this isn't an option and you're restricted to the photo pit, then try some of these suggestions:

- **Use a long lens.**
  Drummers are usually positioned at the back of the stage, so the first thing to do when trying to photograph them is to make sure you can reach them with your lens. This means using the 70–200mm f/2.8 lens at about the 200mm focal length. It's possible to crop the image in post production, but the closer you get in the original photo, the better.

- **Find a good angle.**
  Many times you need to shoot past other band members standing in front of the drummer and around parts of the drum kit. So the best angle for a drummer shot is usually front center of the drums. But that usually puts you right in front of the main member of the band. Look to shoot just left or right of center stage and, at times, up through the drum set. Focus on the drummer's face, because it's his expression—a drummer feeling the moment—that will make a great photo.

- **Shoot from the side.**
  The previous tip was to shoot from near-center to get the drummer pretty much straight on, but you can also shoot from the sides of the photo pit to get an extreme angle on the drummer. This works best if the drums are not buried deep in the back of the stage but are instead in line with the rest of the band.

- **Be patient.**
  I'll say it again: Capturing the drummer is tough work, and a lot depends on the stage layout and the lighting. But if you can see the drummer, you just need to wait for the right moment and be in a good position to capture the killer shot. Keep in mind that drummers are always moving, so you need to wait until they move to the right position for your picture. It takes some patience, but waiting can result in great shots.

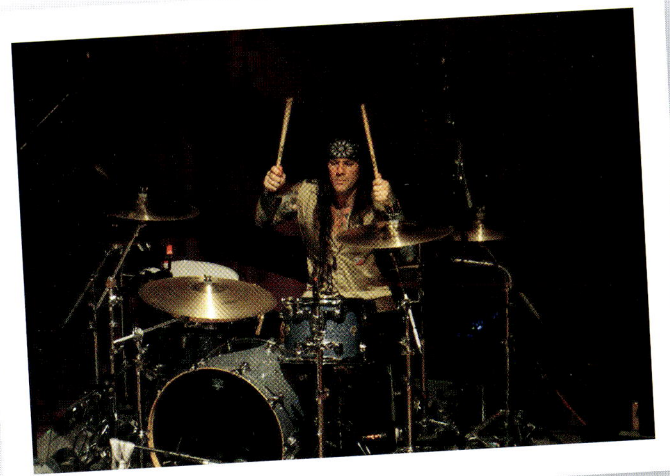

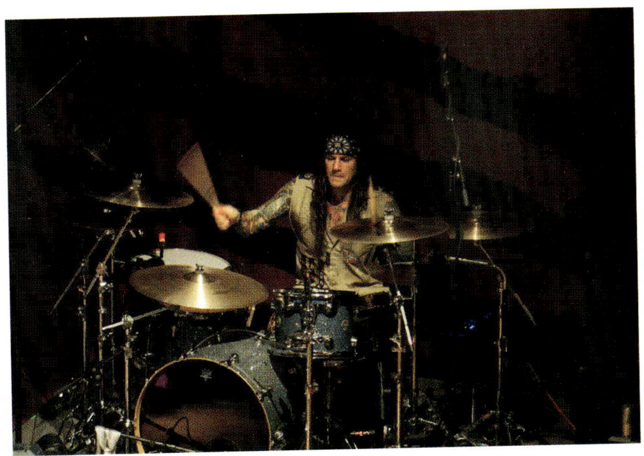

These two photos show the same drummer at the same show. A mere seconds passed between the shots. Do the drumsticks look better when frozen or when blurred? I like the slightly blurred look, because it shows movement; he is really playing the drums!

Taken at 1/160 second, f/2.8, and ISO 1600

To capture the drummer doing what (s)he does best, you have to be able to catch the drumsticks once in a while. At times the sticks will be caught, frozen in place; other times, the drumsticks will be moving so fast that they look like a fan instead of a stick. It's tough to get this right. But the idea is to use a shutter speed that's fast enough to freeze the drummer and slow enough to capture the drumstick so it looks slightly blurred.

Since a drummer might change his speed at any time, it can often feel like luck when you get this right. But there's one thing you can do to increase the odds of capturing a drumstick in the air, and it has everything to do with the timing of your shot. You need to watch for the sticks to come up from the drums and shoot them on the upbeat. If you shoot as the drummer is on the downbeat, you'll miss the shot. If you get too involved in the rhythm of the music, you'll probably press the shutter release button as you hear the beat, and that's too late.

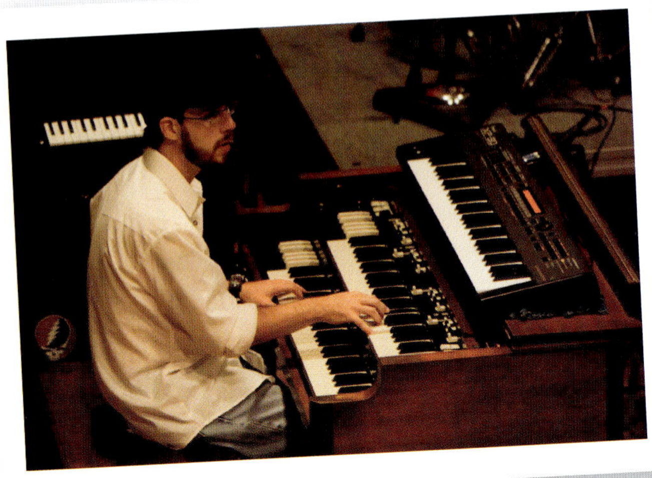

Photographing from the side balcony and down on the keyboards during a sound check allowed me to get this shot of John Ginty on tour with Citizen Cope.

Taken at 1/60 second, f/2.8, and ISO 800

KEYBOARDS

Drums and drummers are tough, but capturing great images of keyboards and pianos can be nearly impossible. Seeing the musician is no problem, but a keyboardist's hands are usually hidden. And when you try to get an angle that allows you to see the hands on the keys, it usually means that the face is hidden.

The best solution to this is to shoot from a balcony. The angle from this position is great and you can get the hands on the keys and, if the musician looks up, you can get the face in your shot as well. The real problem here is that there are not a lot of photo pits that have balconies. So unless you're shooting in a bar or club without a photo pit, it's unlikely that there will be a balcony angle.

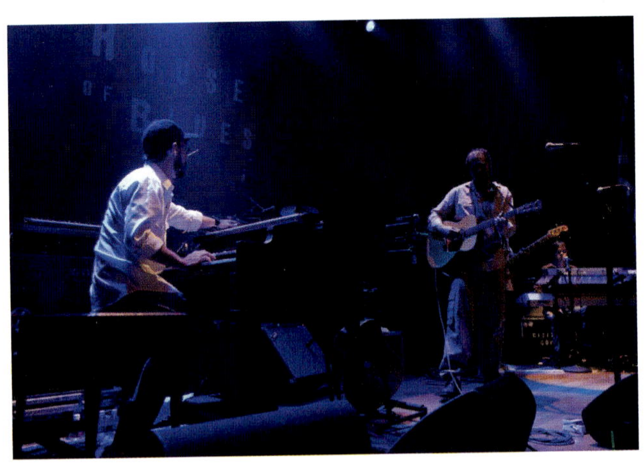

During the concert, access to the balcony was not possible. So I used a side view from the extreme edge of the photo pit to get both the keyboard and the action on the stage.

Taken at 1/60 second, f/3.2, and ISO 640

When you don't have a balcony, you need to really work on your floor angles to get a good shot of keyboards and the musician. I've found that the lens choice is really important in these situations. And you need to shoot either really tight on the hands or really wide to get the whole keyboard and musician in the shot.

Some bands will actually set up the keyboards on the stage at an angle to allow the audience to see the hands on the keys. When you have a situation like this, wait until the hands are actually on the keys to take your shot.

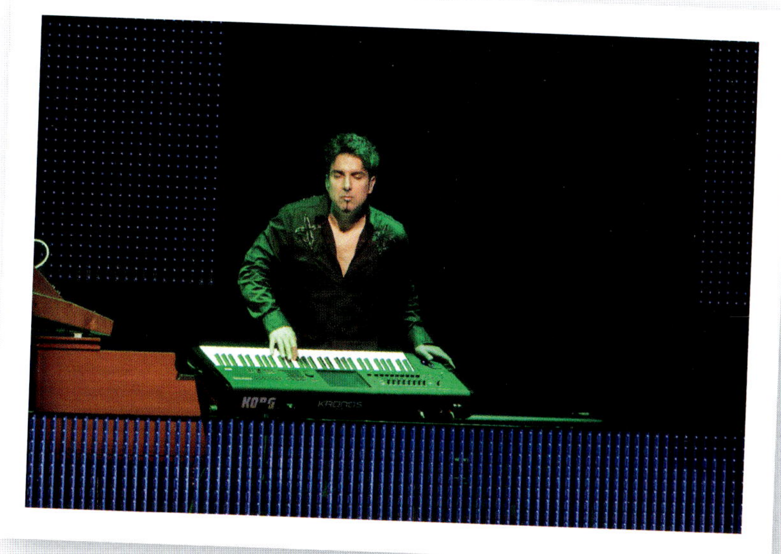

Derek Sheridian, playing keyboards for Billy Idol, has one of the keyboards set at an angle, so getting photos of him playing are a snap.

Taken at 1/200 second, f/4, and ISO 3200

VOCALS

The lead singer of a band is usually in the spotlight more than anyone else. This means that (s)he tends to have enough light for a great photo, and there are plenty of photo opportunities. There is a problem though, and it's a big one. To be heard at a concert, the lead singer needs to use a microphone, and the microphone often blocks the singer's face. And even if the microphone itself isn't blocking the face, it can cause ugly shadows.

There are some things that can be done to minimize the effect of the microphone on the face of a vocalist. These are more or less effective depending on where you are in the pit, how the microphones are set up, and where the light is coming from.

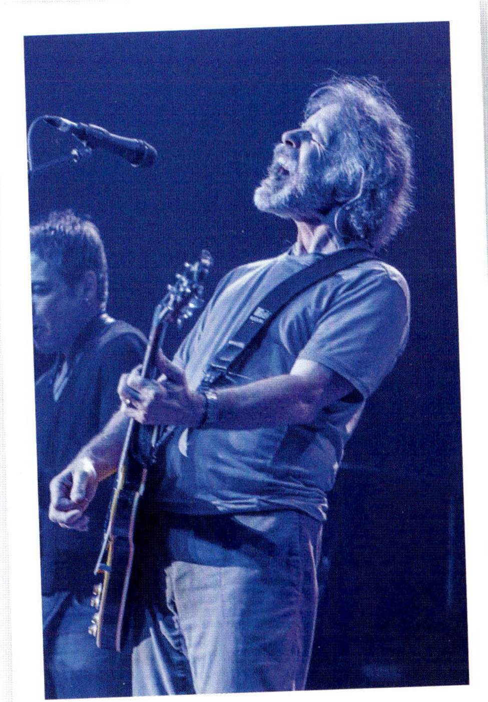

Shooting from the side, I waited until Bob pulled away from the microphone to shoot. But I kept the microphone in the shot to provide context.

Taken at 1/60 second, f/2.8, and ISO 1600

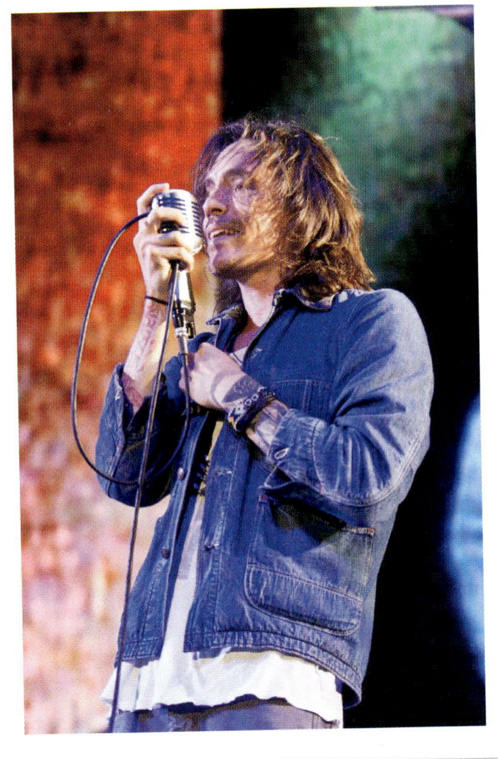

The lead singer of Incubus was photographed from an angle to get separation between the microphone and the face.
Taken at 1/200 second, f/2.8, and ISO 1600

- **Shoot from the side.**
  The easiest solution is to shoot off center—and sometimes *way* off center. One of the reasons I like to shoot from the sides of the photo pit is because it helps me to get a clean shot of the vocalist. This works if the singer is hand-holding the microphone or if the microphone is in a stand. And, of course, it's easiest when the microphone is in the stand, because the placement doesn't change and you can line up the shot before you shoot. But when the singer is holding the microphone, you need to wait until the angle is right. Most of the time though, the singer performs to the audience right in front, so being on the side works well.
- **Wait for high note.**
  Watch the way the singer is treating the microphone when singing different notes. Many times the professional performers, those who've done this for a while, know when to get closer to the microphone and, more importantly, when to back off from it. Watch him and time your shots for the moments when he backs off from the microphone. You can actually see how a vocalist does this before the show; just search for some live video clips on the Internet to see how he acts when on stage during a performance.

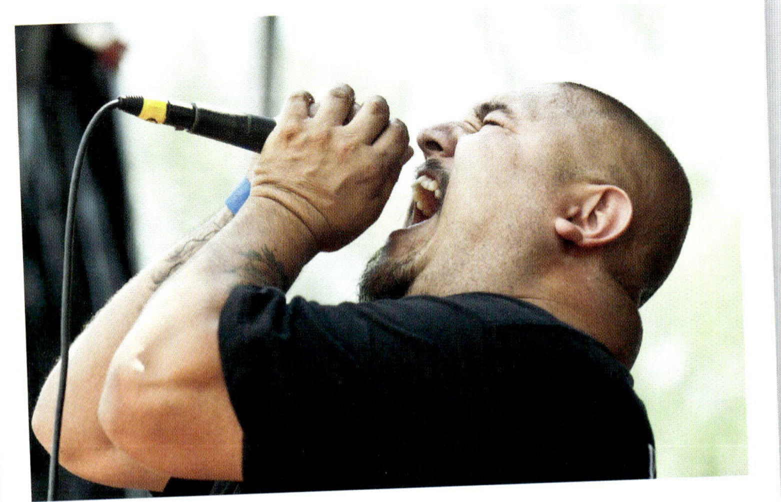

Shooting from the side of the photo pit allows for great shots of the vocals.
Taken at 1/500, f/2.8, and ISO 1000

- **Watch for the microphone drop.** Most vocalists won't drop the microphone to the floor, but they'll drop the microphone slightly at the end of a song or when there's going to be an instrumental part or solo. Watch for the slight drop and grab your shot.
- **Watch for the step-away.** When a vocalist is also a guitar player, (s)he'll usually step away from the microphone when concentrating on playing instead of singing. With some luck and timing, you can also get the microphone in the shot during an instrumental part.
- **Watch the shadows.** Even when the microphone is away from the face, it still might cast a distracting shadow on your subject. So watch as the shadows move and try to keep them off the chin.
- **Shoot from the weak side.** Another way to get a clean shot of a vocalist's face is to photograph it from the weak side, the side not holding the microphone. Some vocalists switch sides all the time, so be prepared to shoot when the microphone is on the other side … away from you.

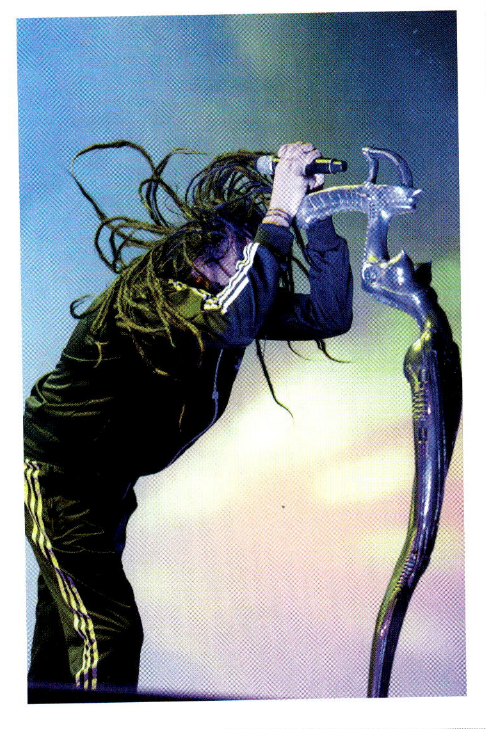

Even when you do everything right, vocalists can be tough to capture.

Taken at 1/500 second, f/2.8, and ISO 2000

GROUP SHOTS

There are two ways to shoot a full stage or group. The first is from the photo pit with a very wide angle lens. The second is from a position at the back of the venue. It's much easier to get a group shot from the back of the room or up in the balcony than from the photo pit.

There are two advantages to shooting a group shot from the back of the room. First, given the distance from the lens to the stage, even at very shallow depth of field, the whole stage and all the band members can be in focus. The second advantage is that when fans see this type of photo, it's usually the view they had at the show, so they relate … and they like the image for the familiarity it delivers.

The same concepts apply with all concert photos. You need to make sure there is something worth shooting when you hit the shutter release. And since the band is only a fraction of the overall frame, it helps if there's also some good stage lighting. Especially when shooting down toward the stage, it's nice if the stage is lit up or somehow interesting. The Grateful Dead put nice colorful rugs on the stage, and this added to the ambiance of the scene.

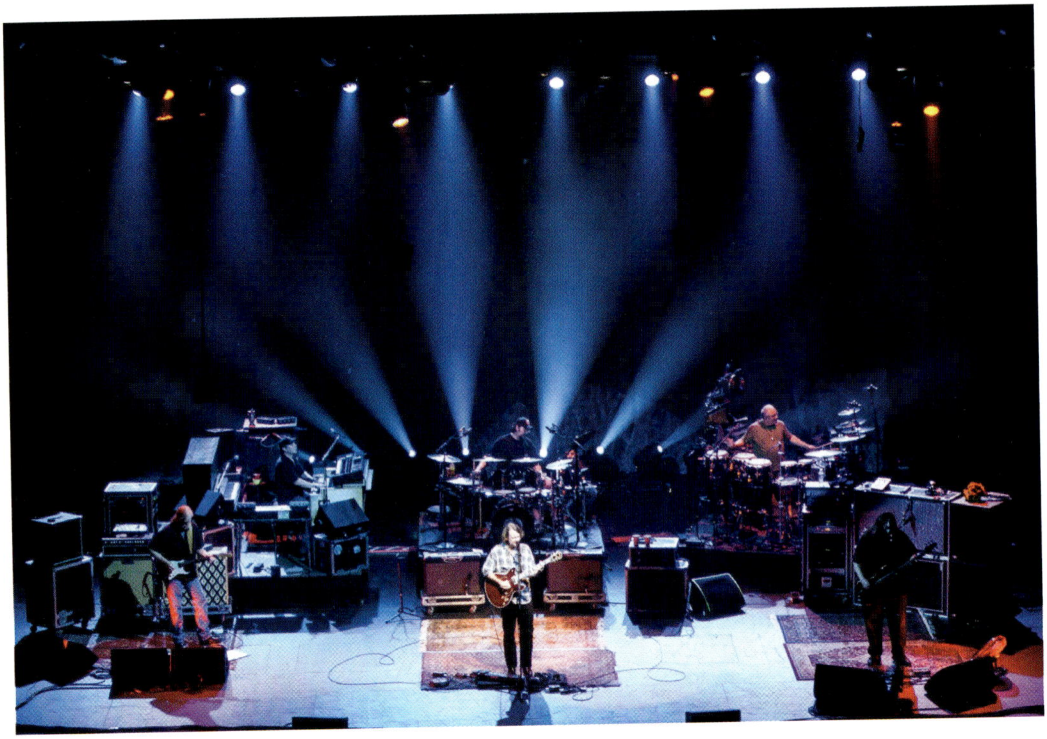

Widespread Panic at the San Diego Civic Center in 2008 allowed me to photograph the whole show and not just from the front. I got this full-stage shot during the first set from the back of the balcony with a 50mm lens on a cropped sensor.

Taken at 1/60 second, f/2.8, and ISO 200

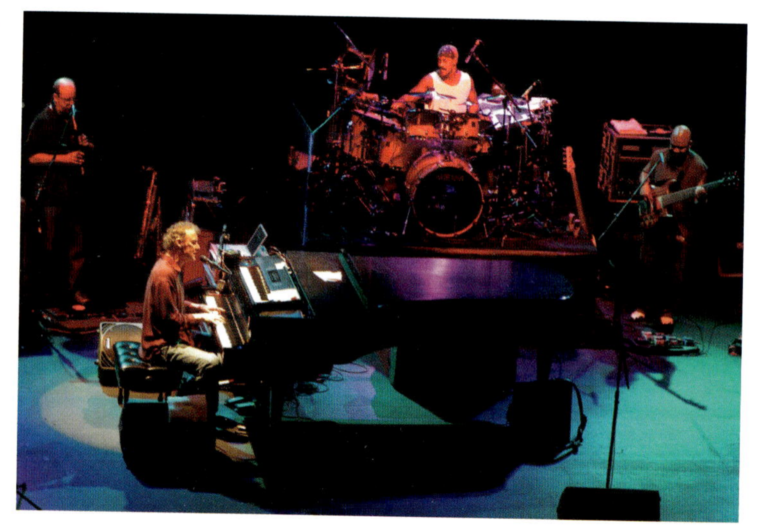

I photographed Bruce Hornsby and most of his band from the front of the balcony, which allowed me to get both the piano and the band in the same shot. I waited until the stage was lit to take the shot.

Taken at 1/30 second, f/2.8, and ISO 400

The problem is that you're often not allowed to shoot from the back of the room; you can only shoot from the photo pit. So it becomes very difficult to get a good shot of the whole stage due to the limitations of the light and the camera settings along with the placement of band members.

When using a shallow depth of field, band members need to be on the same plane to be in acceptable focus. And since most bands do not play standing in a straight line, this is a problem. One solution is to wait until they take a bow at the end of the show.

Not many photographers are allowed to shoot an entire show or can get back in the photo pit to shoot the final bow, but it does happen. Yet another solution for getting the whole band in a single shot is to use a seriously wide angel lens. The 14–24mm f/2.8 lens is good for this, but I like the 16mm f/2.8 fisheye lens on the full-frame sensors or the 10.5mm fisheye lens on the cropped sensors. This lens can get a whole stage and the whole band and, due to the short focal length, there is usually an acceptable focus on everything.

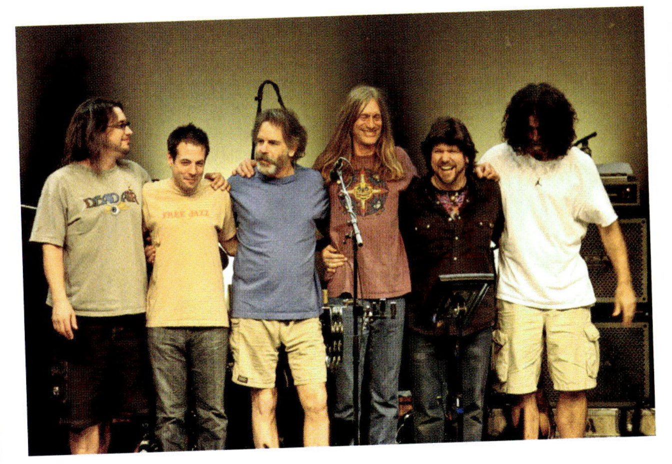

Bob Weir and RatDog take a final bow at the end of the show. This is a great time to get the whole band together.

Taken at 1/125 second, f/4, and ISO 800

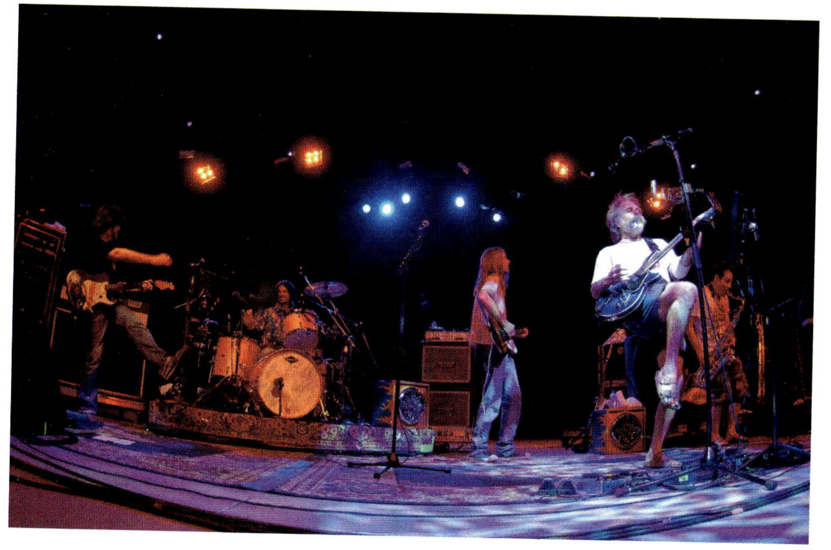

Bob Weir and RatDog were photographed with a 10.5mm fisheye lens from the photo pit, and the photo was cropped to remove the unwanted empty space from the edges.

Taken at 1/80 second, f/3.2, and ISO 400

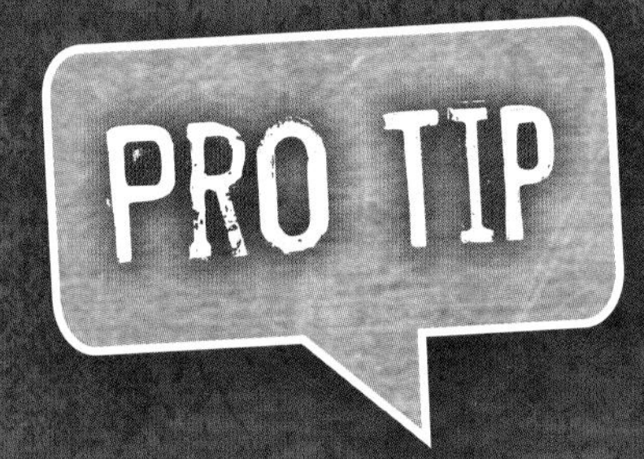

Hali McGrath

Hali McGrath is an 18-year veteran concert photographer (Australia and U.S.) and photo editor at SoundSpike Media (formerly LiveDaily.com). She is also a staff photographer at The Jazzschool in her home town of Berkeley, California. After the 2010 death of mentor Jim Marshall, Hali began working to launch an annual award for excellence in music photography—both to honor Marshall and to help raise appreciation for the art of music photography.

www.haliphoto.com

What do you look for when deciding what images to use on the website?

I have a set of criteria, a mental checklist really, that is so intuitive it's hard to deconstruct. Anything original definitely gets selected. I'm looking for eye-catching color and a face that's in focus, recognizable and showing emotion. I look for a sense of the energy in the performance; mid-air jumps are a favorite, because I know how very hard it is to capture them. Another thing I look for is variety in sight lines. If I'm selecting a single photo to represent the story of a show, I simply go with eye-candy. But when selecting a batch of slides, I'm interested in seeing at least one frame that includes the whole group and stage as well as fan-to-band or band-in-band interaction. Other than that, photos showing emotion are pretty much always keepers. Nothing beats shiny happy people.

What are the "have to have" shots?

It's really a case of knowing the band. If you know that the original bass player just rejoined the band after years of being elsewhere, you're going to want to get shots of him. Or maybe an artist has a signature move, like Roger Daltrey of The Who, who tosses his mic into the air and swings it high overhead. Personally, I am always a bit sad when a shooter doesn't give me any usable shots of the drummer.

Is it easier or more difficult to pick images when you know the band really well?

It's easier, because I can choose images that best represent the live show. Many musicians/singers have a signature move or mannerism; and if I know that, I can spot it immediately.

As a photographer as well as a photo editor, how much does your personal taste come into play?

As a photographer, if I'm shooting for myself, I'm very selective about who I photograph at this point. Nearly two decades in, I'm not trying to build my portfolio, and time is the most valuable thing to me. However, as a photo editor for SoundSpike, I leave my personal taste out of it. My job is to select and publish the most dynamic and compelling music photos possible—period.

What advice would you give someone starting out in the concert photography field?

If you are just starting out, I suggest connecting with those who are already working at it professionally. Say hello and shake hands when you show up at the venue. Find out what the protocol is for behavior in the photo pit, ask people who they shoot for, and exchange cards. Later, look at other people's work and follow up. Your fellow photographers are not the enemy. There is a palpable vibe of competition on location, this is true. And some shooters will not be friendly at first (or ever), but if you behave professionally, your character will speak volumes over time and that's all anyone really cares about. You never know when one of those photographers might need you to fill in on a gig because (s)he double booked, or maybe use you as an assistant to help cover a festival.

Understand that to be a music photographer, you have to make a lot of sacrifices—not least of which is financial. Camera repair alone can be enough to break the bank. It is also critical that you understand copyright law and photo asset management. Do you know the difference between a TIFF and a JPEG? Every single photo that you take needs to have your copyright info embedded in its metadata … ideally with the description field filled in, unless you have an elephant's memory.

Most of all, I say don't give away your self esteem to do this work. At first it won't seem like a big deal, but if you truly love shooting music, you most likely have the heart of an artist, and we are a sensitive lot. So guard it like your own imaginary security staff. And if it ever feels like you're being asked to grab your ankles, RUN!

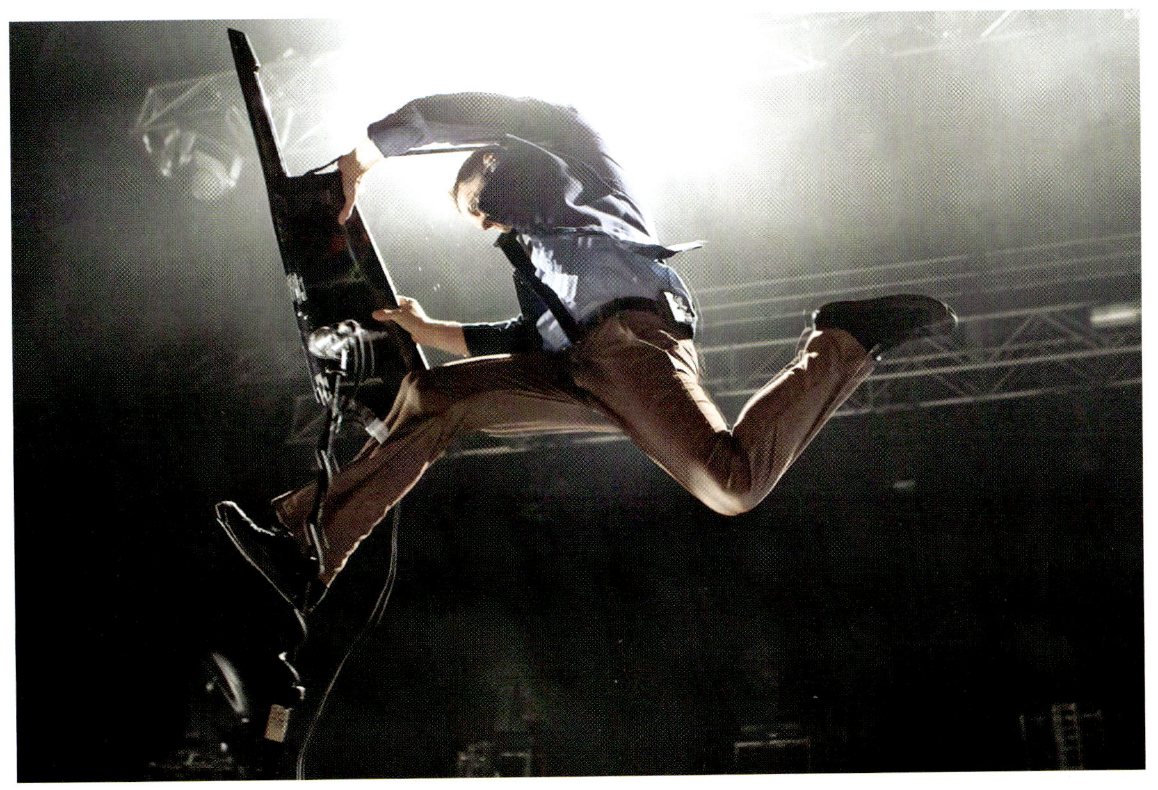

© Hali McGrath

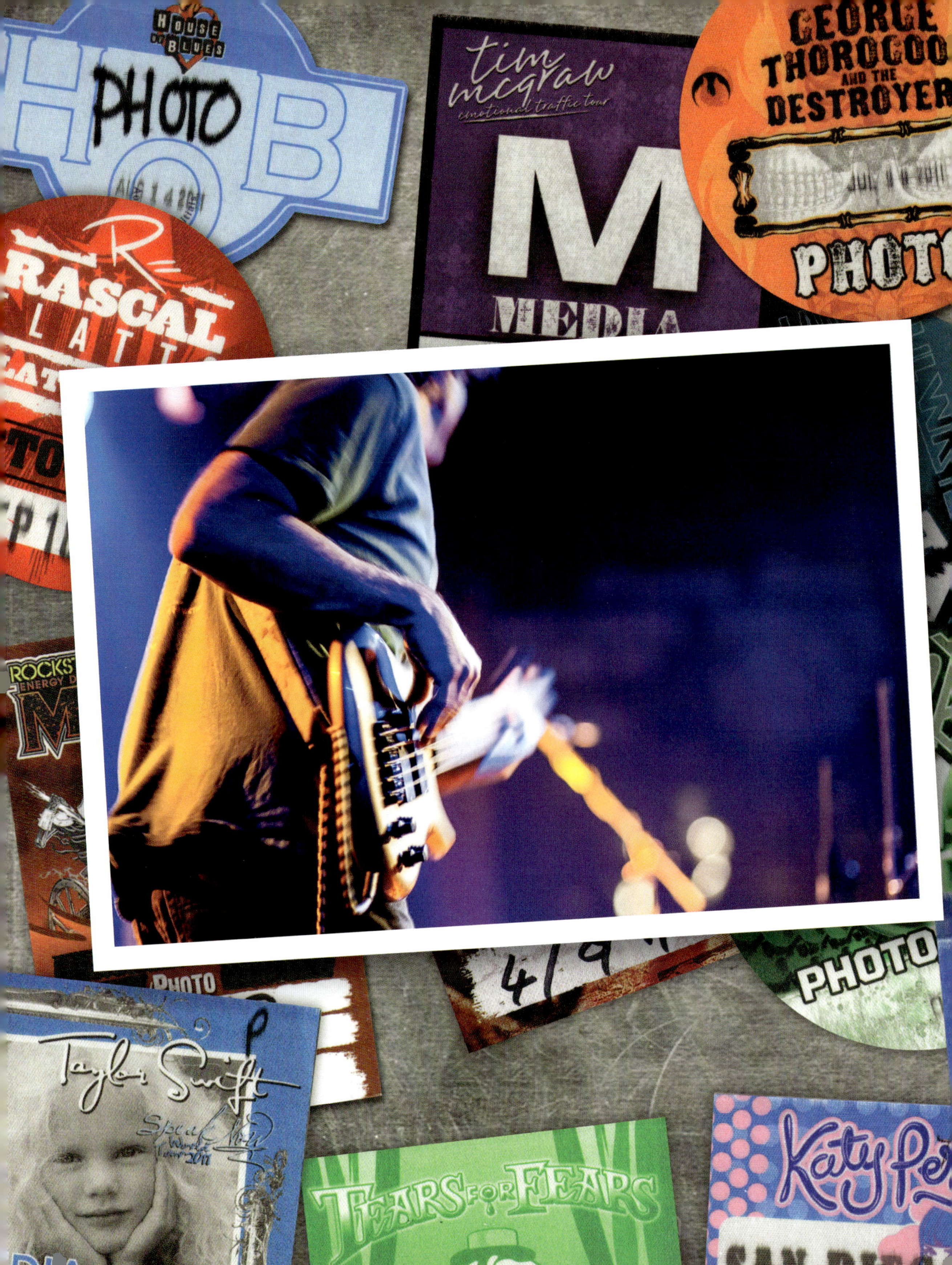

HOUSE OF BLUES
PHOTO
tim mcgraw
emotional traffic tour
M
MEDIA
GEORGE
AND THE
RASCAL
PHOTO
PHOTO
Taylor Swift
TEARS FOR FEARS

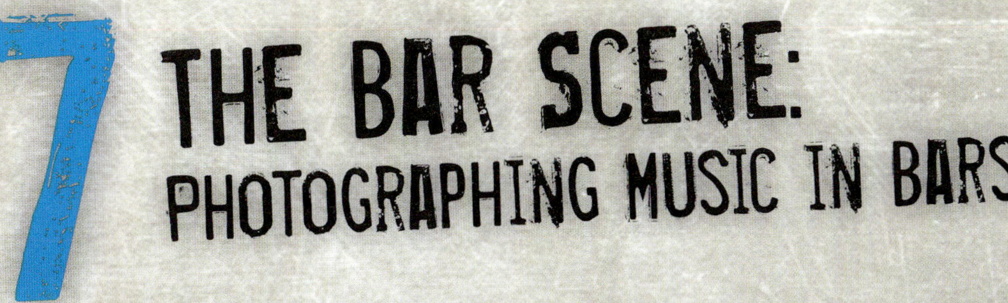

7 THE BAR SCENE: PHOTOGRAPHING MUSIC IN BARS

Imagine! The main lights go down and the stage lights come on as the Rolling Stones take the stage. There you are in the photo pit, ready to go. You've hit the big time!

Alright, well ... it's good to have goals. But the reality is that most concert photographers start in much less glamorous situations. And many never get to such a desirable place. So don't be too disappointed if your bread-and-butter gigs are local shows in neighborhood watering holes.

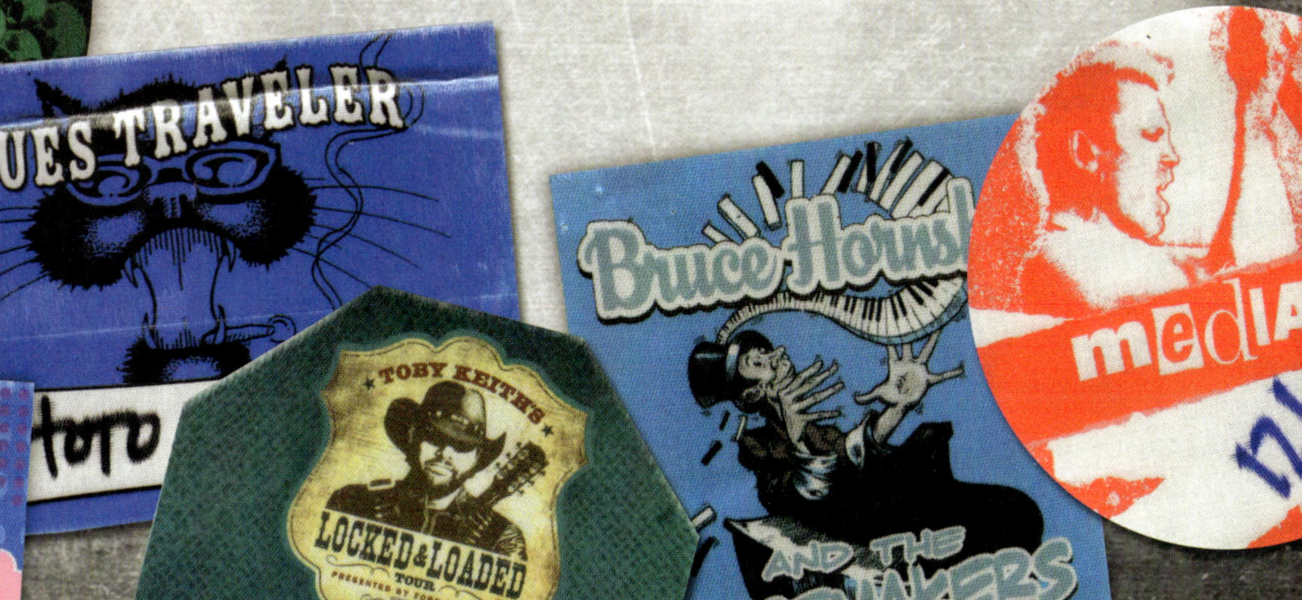

Most concert photographers, especially when just starting out, work in small bars with no photo pit, no real lighting, and pushy crowds. Working conditions can be pretty frustrating. True, photographing in a dimly lit bar while the crowd dances, drinks too much, and gets in the way of good clean shots can deter most photographers from this type of work altogether. But there are a lot of positives to this work, too!

The main upside is that it's a lot easier to gain access to shoot a local band in a bar than it is to photograph the Rolling Stones at the stadium. And the lighting conditions only get better from here. So once you master bar lighting, the rest of your venues will seem easy.

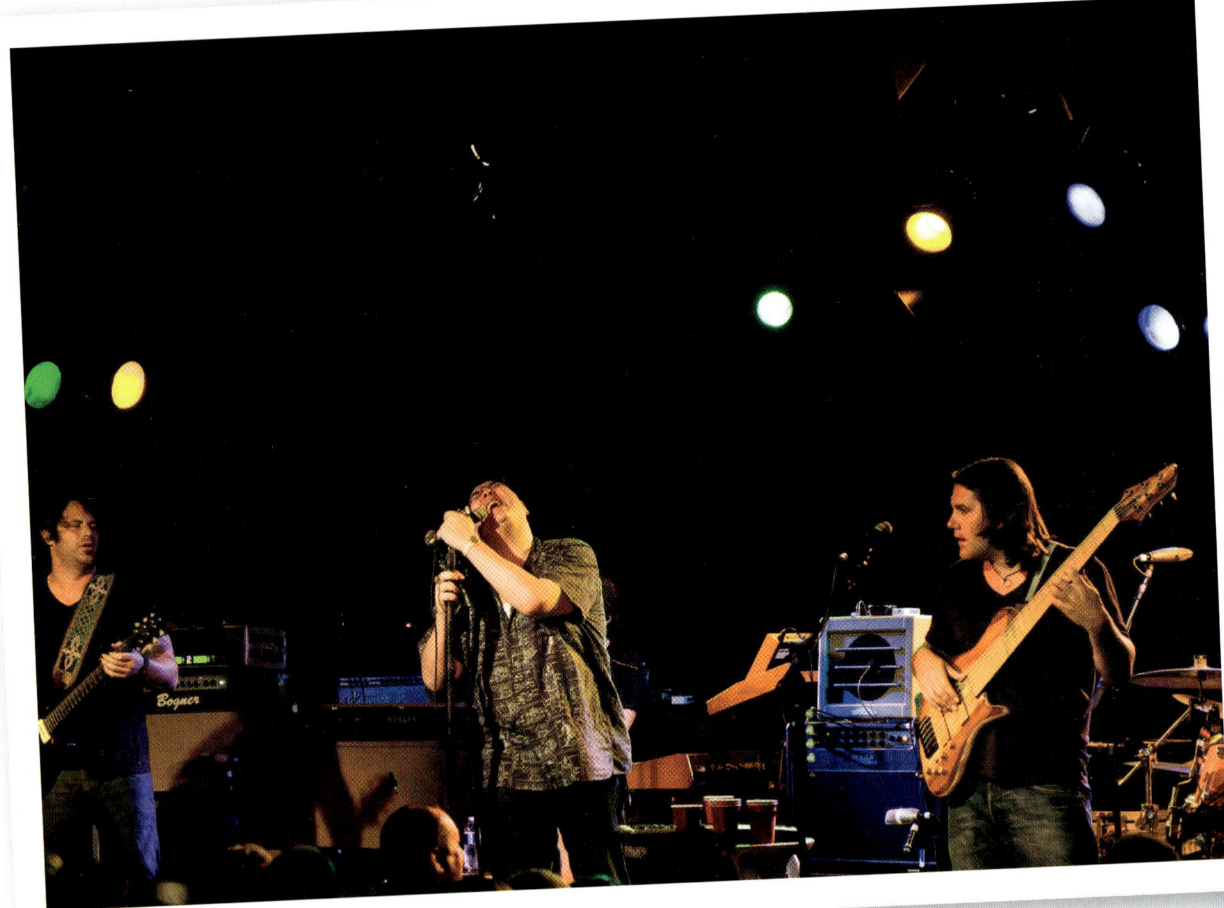

Bruce Hornsby is sitting at his piano during an intimate show with his band at the Belly Up Tavern in Solana Beach, CA. There was one light hitting the stage, and it was aimed at him. I first got the exposure right, and then I waited until the moment was right to take the photo.

Taken at 1/250 second, f/2.2, and ISO 1600

MY PHOTO BAG: BAR

What I take to a bar shoot

Photographing in a bar usually means tight quarters and no place to leave your gear ... or coat. That's why I go lean and mean for bar shoots. I usually take the following gear with me in a small Domke bag:

- 1x dSLR body (a Nikon D700 with or without the battery grip)
- 1x 50mm f/1.8 prime lens (under $200)
- 1x 35mm f/2 prime lens (under $300)

This two-lens setup allows me to capture most of the action in small bars and it's a great way to start your concert photography work without costing a prohibitive amount of money.

I also take a 85mm f/1.4 prime lens (over $1000), which allows me to get in close to my subject(s) ... even in really low light. This is a great lens, but it's rather expensive and can be purchased later in your career.

Also in my bag:

- Extra CompactFlash cards (You never know how many images you might take.)
- Earplugs (Always use earplugs, always. And carry spares.)
- Extra battery (...just in case)
- Business cards
- Lens cloth
- Small flashlight
- Flash (This is for shoots when it's possible to meet the band and maybe do a quick portrait.)

WORKING WITH BAD LIGHT

When I talk about bad bar lighting, I am talking about stage setups that include a couple of lights placed on the ceiling that seem to all be red or green and not well-aimed. These are the kind of lights that can really make you rethink the whole concert photography thing. At the very least, they'll have you wondering if using a flash is maybe a decent idea. (It's not. But there's more on using a flash a little later.)

My favorite (note sarcasm) is what I call *traffic-stop lighting*—one green, one orange, and one red light illuminating the stage. And if you're really lucky, the band you're shooting will use all three of the lights at the same time, but that's really rare. Traffic-stop lighting makes it tough to shoot good photographs, because the light is dim and tends to have a severe color cast.

Now for the positive side! That kind of lighting can actually be fun to shoot under, especially if you don't expect much. The trick is to make sure you understand where the light is coming from and how to place it in your image for good effects. For example, try to get the lights in the background to produce halos around the subject(s) or become part of the image.

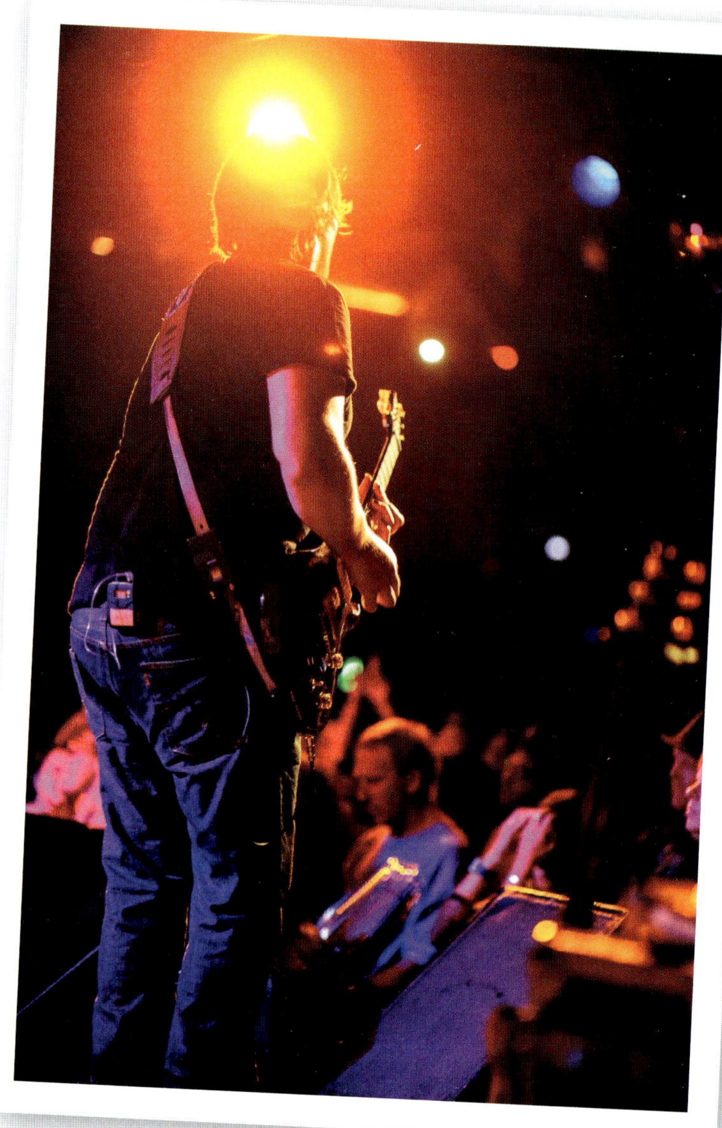

Shooting from the side of the stage is a lot easier in bars than it is in larger venues. And this angle allowed me to place the light in my photo right around the head of the guitar player.

Taken at 1/80 second, f/1.4, and ISO 3200

Watch the lighting and determine if there's a pattern to its usage. Try to time your photographs to capture the scene when the lights are at their brightest. In other words, to get a great shot, you need to get the timing of the lights down and hope for a "Kodak moment" from the musicians to coincide with good lighting. When bright lights and interesting action come together, you can get a great bar concert shot.

To ensure you're ready when the moment is right, check the exposure settings on your camera beforehand. With those correct, all you have to do is watch for a great moment. So let's talk about proper exposure for a bar show.

CHOOSING EXPOSURE SETTINGS

Exposure is covered in Chapter 5, but here's a refresher: Only three camera settings affect exposure. They are shutter speed, aperture, and ISO. Together, these settings control how much light reaches the sensor of your camera and how that light is handled.

When shooting large concerts, fast glass is a must. Zoom lenses with a constant widest aperture of f/2.8 work great for that environment. But when it comes to shooting in bars, *really* fast glass—that is, prime lenses with very wide apertures, such as f/1.8—will save the day. So leave the zoom lenses at home when heading out for a bar shoot and use the primes.

One advantage of this, especially for those starting out, is gear cost. A 50mm f/1.8 prime lens is relatively inexpensive, and it does a great job in really low light. Of course if you have the budget, then buy a 50mm f/1.4. It opens even wider but costs more. And consider the 35mm f/2 lens. I've been a fan of this one because it gives a wider view and opens to f/2—for less than $300. Check Chapter 4 for more details on gear.

Initial Camera Setting for Bar Shoots: 1/80 second, f/1.4, ISO 1600

To get my exposure settings right, I start by setting the camera to manual. This ensures that I control all the settings and that the camera can't change anything no matter what the lights do. Then I set the aperture to the widest setting allowed by the lens I'm using. Next I set the shutter speed to 1/80 second and the ISO to 1600.

With the camera's metering mode set to spot metering, make sure that the lighting being read by the camera is in the critical area of the scene. For example, if focusing on a face, then spot meter on the face. If focusing on someone's hands or instrument, then spot meter for that area.

Many cameras make this really easy, because the spot-metering area is based on the focus point being used. Just keep in mind that the meter reading is not going to be perfect; it will usually show that the scene is still underexposed. But it'll provide better information

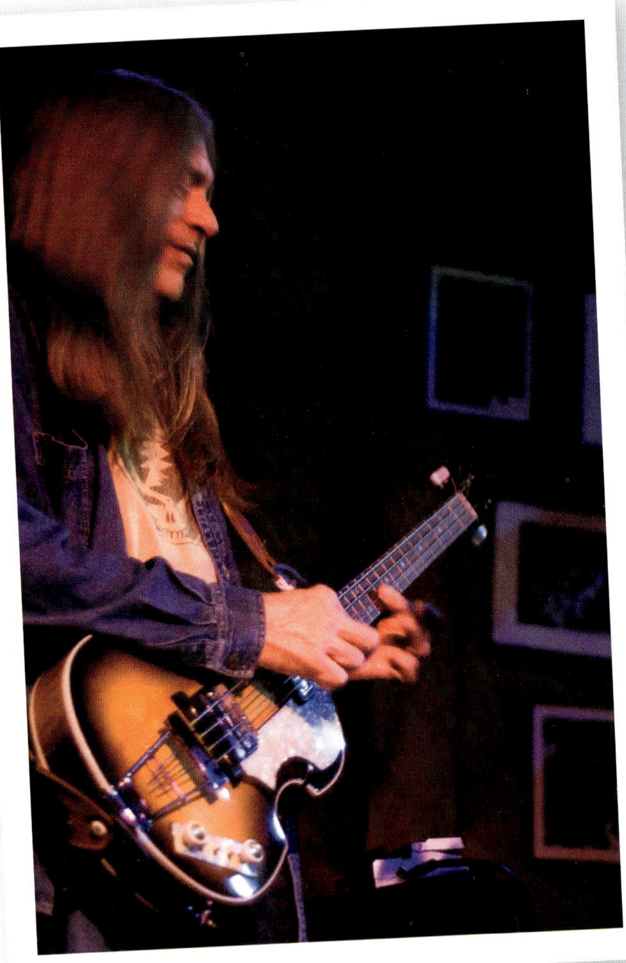

Using the 50mm in a bar setting can produce shots that would take a much longer lens at bigger shows. This photograph shows bass player Robin Sylvester at the Sweetwater Saloon. It was shot with the 50mm f/1.8, a great little lens.

Taken at 1/50 second, f/1.8, and ISO 640

than any of the other metering modes (covered in Chapter 5).

The real test when shooting in a bar though is looking at some actual images. So take a few test photos and review them on the LCD screen on the back of your camera. Your results will be best if you wait to take a shot until you think the most light is on the musician. Then look at the preview. If the scene seems too dark, then you need to decrease the shutter speed or raise the ISO.

Make adjustments based on how fast the musician is moving and how you want to portray that movement. To freeze the action, keep the shutter speed high and push the ISO higher. If the band is mellow and not moving very fast, you can reduce the shutter speed. You can also reduce the shutter speed if you want to show some blur. Just remember that the blur needs to be planned. It's not cool when you have blurry pictures just because you didn't get the camera settings right. And this just takes practice.

If, on the other hand, the image is too light, or *overexposed*, then you can increase the shutter speed, use a smaller aperture to get a deeper depth of field, or lower the ISO.

PUSHING THE ISO: WHAT'S TOO HIGH?

I know how high the ISO goes in my camera, and I also know how high I'm willing to push it. These two numbers are not the same. I only go so far with ISO, because higher ISO settings mean more digital noise in my photos. Remember, the sensor's light sensitivity is amplified as ISO increases. At some point, the level of noise becomes too much.

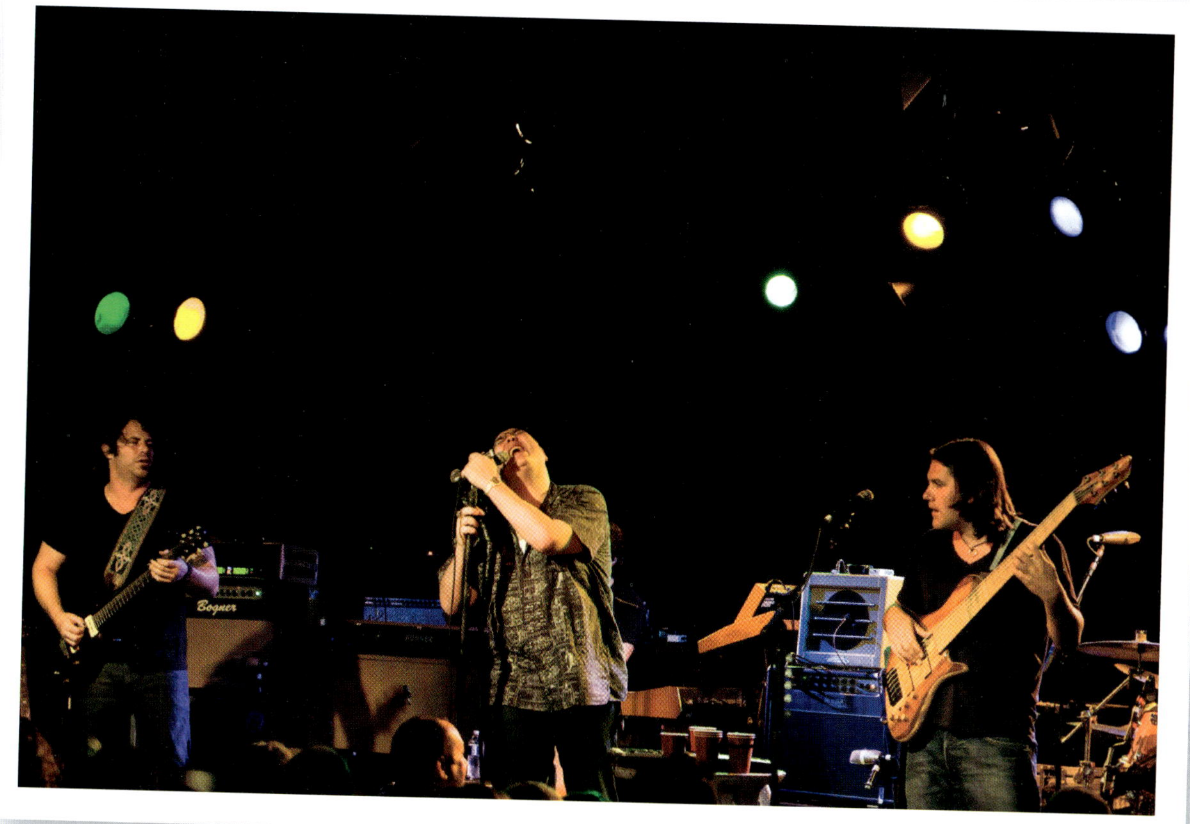

For this photo of Blues Traveler, I needed to push the ISO to 3200. Because the shutter speed needed to be set at 1/200 second to freeze the action—the always-moving Chan Kinchla on guitar, in particular—it wasn't possible to get a properly exposed shot at a lower ISO.

Taken at 1/200 second, f/2.8, and ISO 3200

For instance, my D700 has an ISO range of 200–6400 along with an option to shoot at Hi-1 (ISO 12,800) and Hi-2 (ISO 25,600). But I'm only willing to push the camera to 6400. In fact, my true comfort zone really only extends to about ISO 3200.

These are not arbitrary numbers. Rather, they come from testing my camera and seeing the results. I'm only willing to live with so much digital noise in my images. I recommend that you do this exercise with your cameras, too. It's not hard. All you need is a dimly lit room and a subject to photograph.

Start at ISO 800 and take a photo. Then go to 1600, 3200, 6400, and so on—all the way to the top ISO setting available on your camera. Check the images on your computer and you'll see where the digital noise becomes unbearable. Voilà! Now you know your true ISO range.

USING THE FLASH

The light at a show is sometimes so low that using a flash seems like the only option. And while this is the case in some situations, I try at (almost) all costs to avoid using a flash for stage shots. Here's why:

- The white light from a flash will ruin any ambient lighting.
- A flash is distracting to the band.
- Using a flash can make you lazy. That is, if you start to rely on a flash, you won't be prepared for shoots involving bands that don't allow them. And most bands don't allow them.

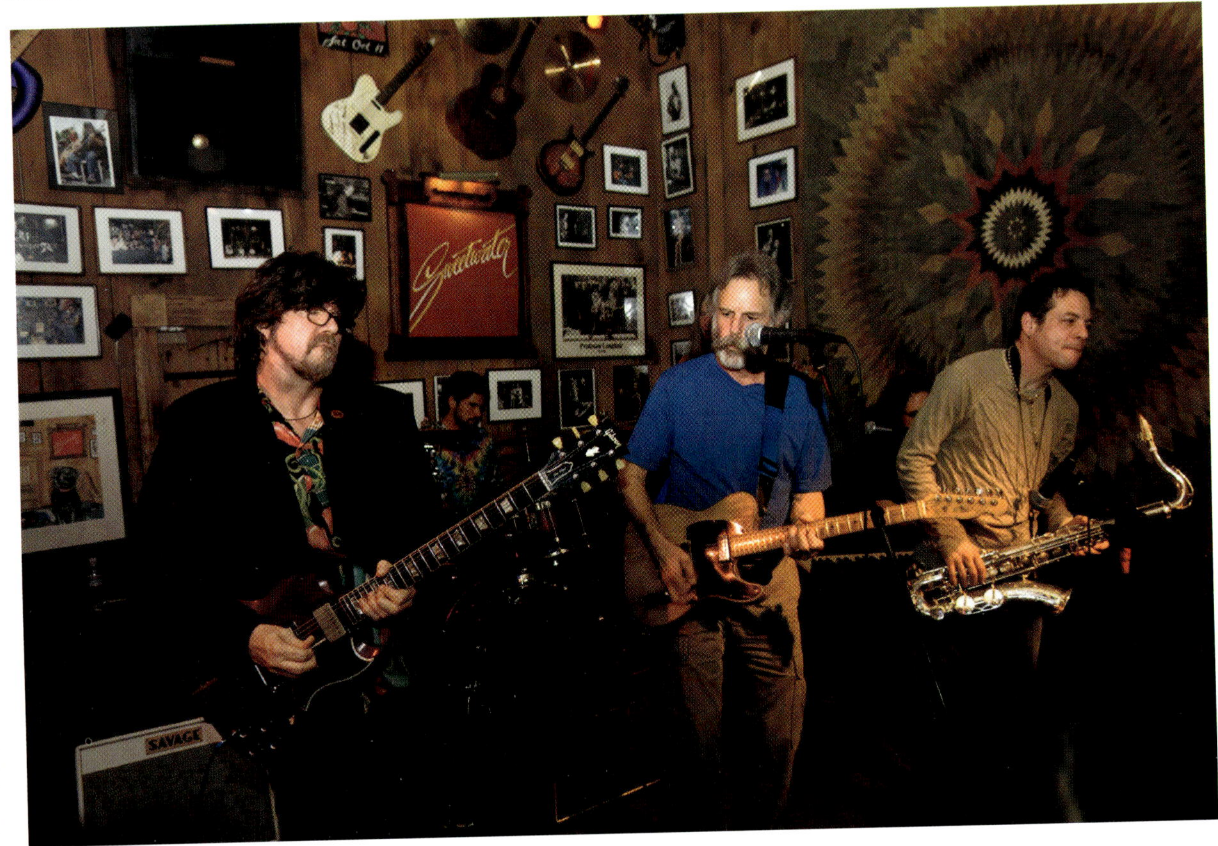

I used a flash for this photo of Mark Karan, Bob Weir, and RatDog during a fundraiser at the Sweetwater Saloon.

Taken at 1/40 second, f/2.8, and ISO 125

All that being said, I have used a flash in a few situations, when a scene just had to be better lit. I mean, you need to have *some* light to take a photograph. So if you must use a flash, there are a few things you can do to make your image(s) not *look* like they are flash-lit.

- **Bounce:** Aim the flash toward the ceiling and bounce the light down onto the stage. This makes the direction of the light look a little more natural.
- **Power Down:** Lower the flash power so it isn't the only light source in the image. By trying to match the flash light to the ambient light, you create a more natural-looking photo.
- **Stay Open:** Use a long shutter speed to allow the ambient light to be present in the image. This could 1/30 of second or 5 seconds; it depends on the amount of ambient light present.
- **Fire Late:** Use rear curtain sync, so that the flash fires at the end of the exposure. This freezes the subject and any motion, which looks a lot better than when the motion is frozen at the beginning of the exposure.

If possible, try to set up a wireless flash high up near the ceiling and trigger it remotely. This will look the most natural. A few years ago, when I was working with a band on a tour of small clubs, a sound engineer at one of the clubs was also a photographer. He had set up a flash in the lighting rig and had it controlled by a Pocket Wizard remote. This flash was aimed at the center of the stage and added just enough light to allow for slightly lower ISO settings. It was really useful to add a little burst of light when needed. The trick to getting this to work correctly is placing the flash at the same angle as the regular stage lights.

COMPOSITION

There are a lot of advantages to shooting in a bar, especially compared to bigger clubs and halls. And nearly all of these advantages involve getting a more diverse array of images and better composition. Here are some of the most important perks of shooting a bar show.

MOBILITY

Most bars don't have a photo pit, and photography is usually allowed from anywhere in the venue … as long as you don't get in the way of the band and service staff. This means you can shoot from a variety of locations and get a diverse collection of shots. So try out different angles of the performance and use your feet to get closer or farther away from the show. This mobility is especially handy when using prime lenses that can't zoom.

EXTREME ACCESS

The high level of access—to the performance, people, and venue overall—that you can get when photographing in a bar is unmatched. It even surpasses an All Access pass at a larger venue. True, the stage might not be very high and the lights might not be great; but there is usually no barricade, and you can get great shots from the front and sides of the stage.

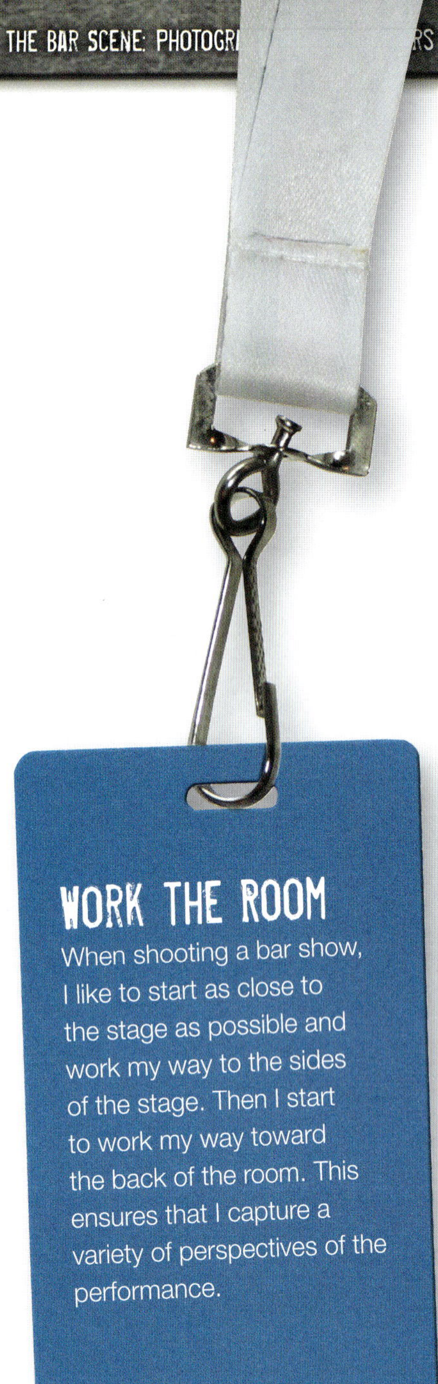

For example, at the Sweetwater Saloon in Northern California, the stage was set up at the back of the room. Anyone could walk down the side of the stage area to the back door of the saloon, and this allowed great angles for capturing the band, especially drummer photos.

PLAYTIME

When you're shooting a local band in a local bar, it's a great time to experiment with your composition techniques and exposure settings. Take advantage of the mobility and access benefits described earlier by shooting at different angles. And use the extended shooting time to try some slower shutter speeds.

Another composition technique to try is getting close—really close—and photographing just parts of the story. I really love to do this. It's cool to get a musician's hands on his/her instrument. It can be hands on a guitar or fingers on keyboards or even a hand on a microphone. Close-ups allow a viewer's imagination to fill in the rest of the story.

CROWD

When photographing in a bar, it's actually difficult *not* to get some of the audience in your photos, especially when shooting from the back and sides of the room, because there is no photo pit. So make the crowd a part of the image and have them add to the scene being captured without detracting from it. I suggest taking advantage of the shallow depth of field that the wide apertures give to keep the crowd blurred.

THE BAND

Photographing in bars is one of the most intimate settings available for concert photographers—and

Make sure that you respect the rules of the bar and listen to security.

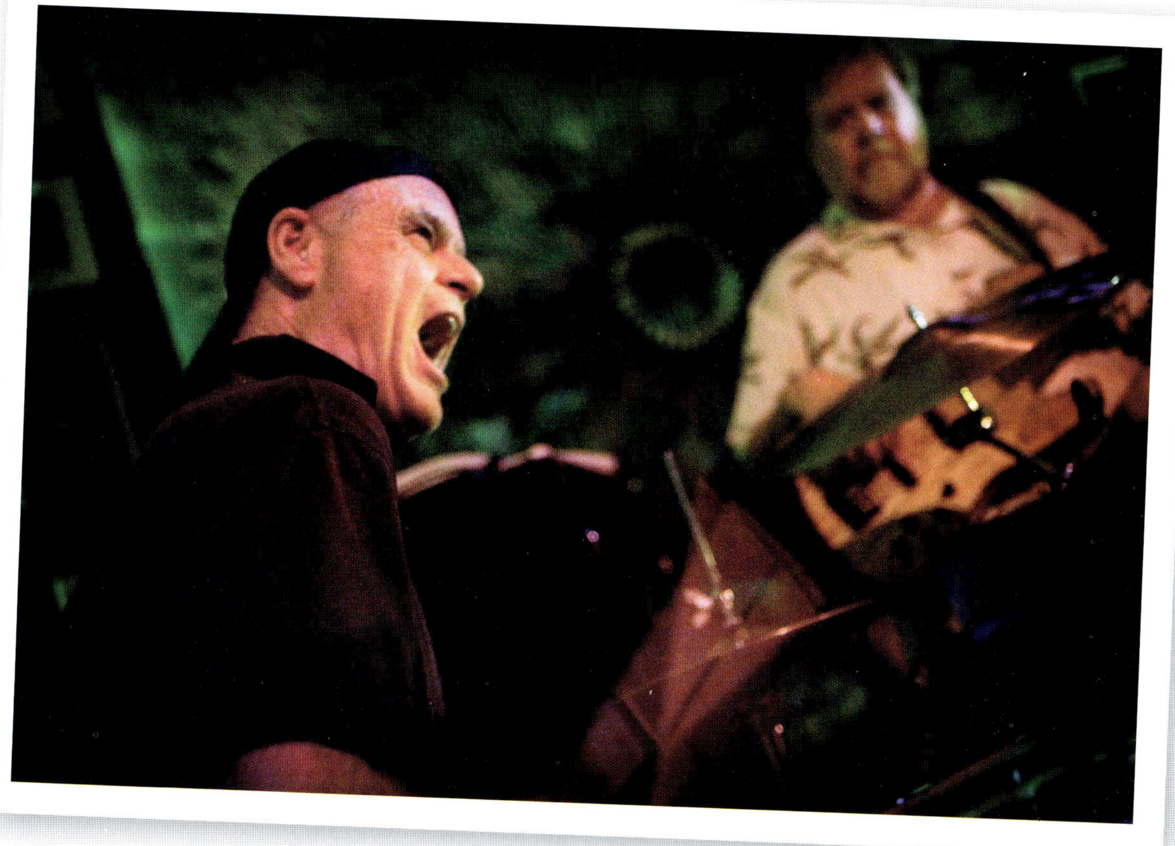

Because I was shooting in a bar, I was able to get up close and personal with drummer John Molo. Notice that the drumsticks are just a blur. This is due to the relatively low (1/40 second) shutter speed.

Taken at 1/40 second, f/2, and ISO 1000

audiences. And because of the cozy nature of this venue, it's usually possible to meet the band. This is an opportunity to seize. There's just no way to know who will eventually make it big.

Here are three things I try to do every time I shoot a band in a bar:

- Give the band my business card.
- Get one of the band's cards or email address, so I can send sample images.
- Convince the band to pose for a quick shot.

Many times I'll try to get the band to pose before they play, because they usually look better before the show—definitely more clean and alert. After playing a long set in a bar, bands tend to look a bit sweaty and tired. But any time you get the opportunity to capture a portrait of a band, take it.

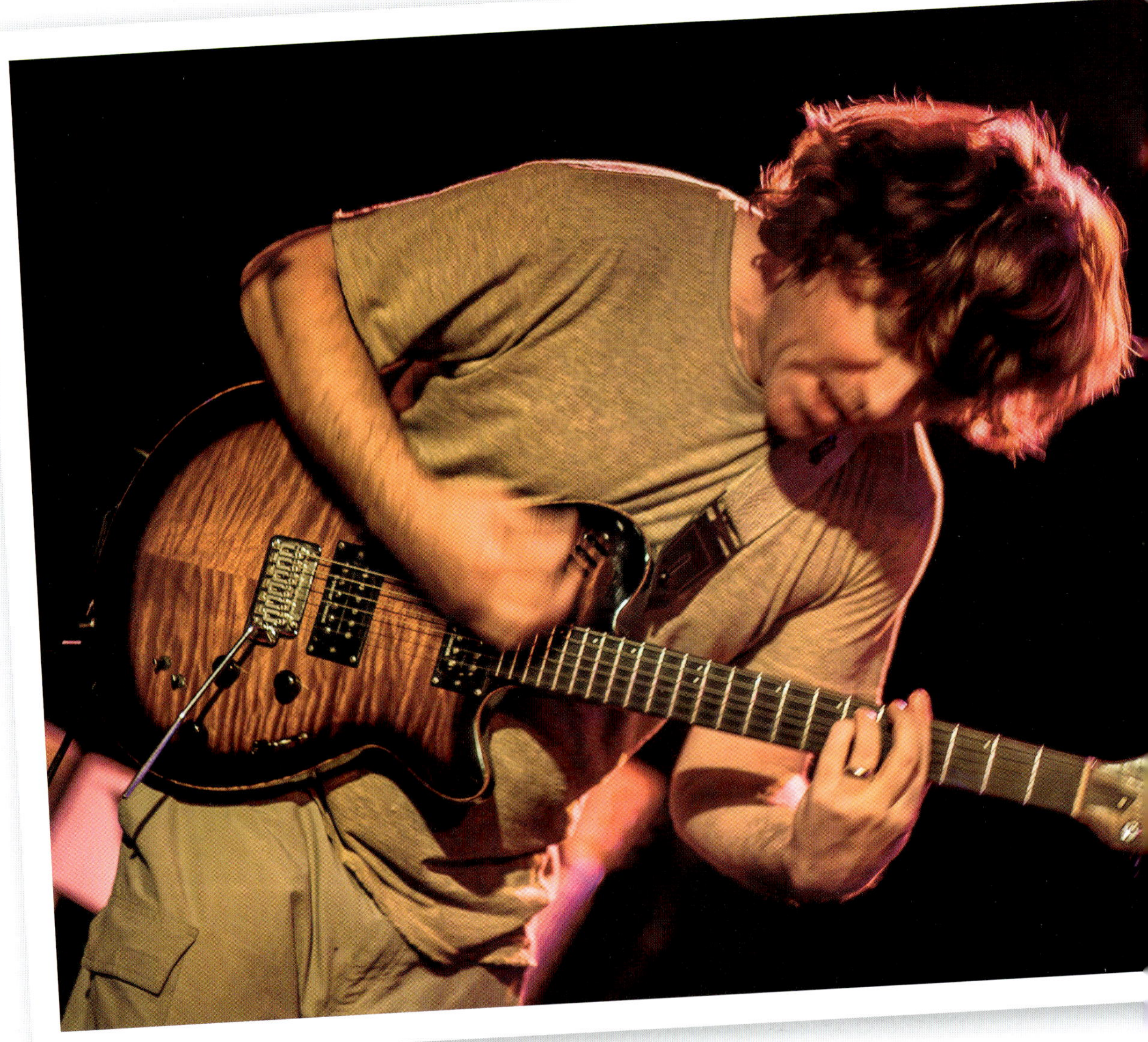

Photographing guitarist, singer, songwriter Keller Williams in a low-light bar situation motivated me to try capturing a certain balance between freezing the action and showing a little motion. I wanted the hand that was strumming the guitar to be a little blurred. And after experimenting a little, a shutter speed of 1/60 second seemed to work best.

Taken at 1/60 second, f/1.4, and ISO 1250

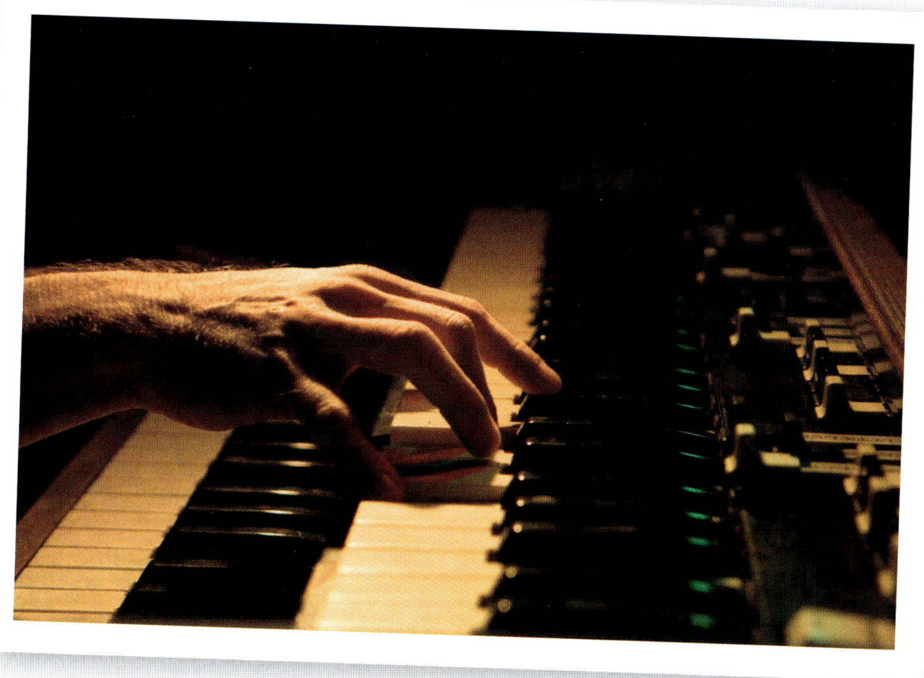

I photographed this hand on the keys while on tour with a band in 2005. I've always loved the simplicity of this shot and the way the fingers bend over the keys.

Taken at 1/60 second, f/3.2, and ISO 500

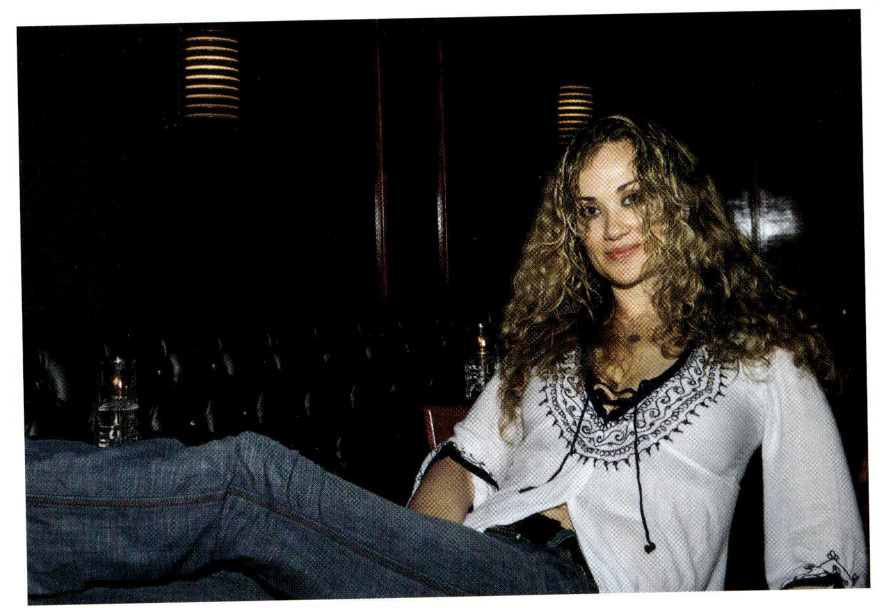

I got this shot of Dana Fuchs after her show in Los Angeles in 2008. A single flash bounced off the ceiling is all it took. I asked politely if she would pose after signing autographs, and I took a total of three frames.

Taken at 1/25 second, f/5.6, and ISO 100

Bob Minkin

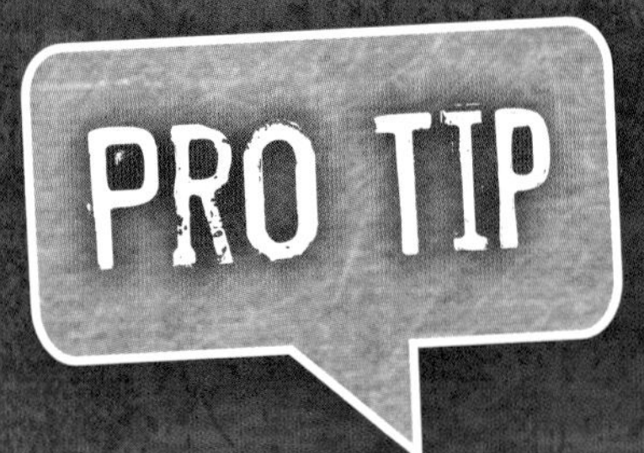

www.minkindesign.com/photo

What's your gear for shooting in bars?

Currently I use:

- Nikon D300
- 17–55mm f/2.8 Nikkor
- 50mm f/1.4 Nikkor
- 85mm f/1.8 Nikkor
- 80–200 f/2.8 Nikkor
- 10.5mm f/2.8 Nikkor
- SB800 Speedlight

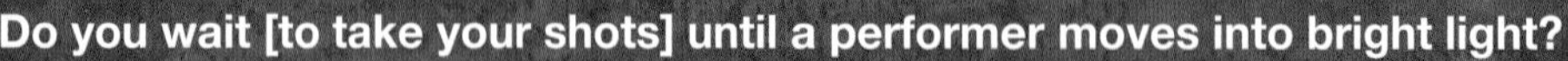

Do you wait [to take your shots] until a performer moves into bright light?

It's all about timing and being ready for when the good light comes on. Knowing the music will help you anticipate these often-fleeting moments.

What camera settings do you start with to deal with low light? And how do you set the white balance?

I try to use the lowest ISO I can get away with. That said, sometimes I bump it up if I feel that I need extra shutter speed or a smaller aperture. Typically I begin with 800–1000 ISO, 1/30 second, wide open (f/2.8 usually) in manual [mode]. I leave the [white balance] WB on Auto and make adjustments in Lightroom. Having great Lightroom chops can dramatically improve your photos.

What was your first concert shoot?

First concert I shot was New Riders Of The Purple Sage, Academy Of Music, NYC, 11/28/74. At the time, I was a fan trying to get shots for souvenirs. The first concert I shot with a 35mm SLR was the Grateful Dead, Winterland, San Francisco, 12/29/77. These were some of my first published shots in *Relix* magazine.

What was your first bar shoot?

Robert Hunter at "My Father's Place" Roslyn, Long Island, 3/10/78.

How do you deal with getting around in the crowd?

Get there early and claim your space is the only sure way to get a good spot. Otherwise I ask people if I can stay in their spot for part of a song, and then I move on. People are usually obliging if you're polite. Be respectful of the people that got there before you though. Introduce yourself and they'll most likely let you hang in their spot for awhile.

Do you have a tip for photographers trying to get started in the concert photography business?
It's all about access. You need to align yourself with a publication, so you can get that access, a credential that allows you to shoot in the venue and a forum to publish your photographs. That said, I shot for years without that access, just determination; but things were a lot looser when I was starting out.

Giving away your photos for a photo credit won't get you far. You'll never be taken seriously by giving away your work for free. That said, in some rare cases, it pays to make an exception when it will have a real, immediate, benefit for you.

Almost anyone get a decent live shot; that's the low-hanging fruit. To stand out, you need to be able to get off-stage, intimate shots of the artist—maybe in the studio, during rehearsals, at home. Of course, it helps to have a good eye and good equipment; and above all, know how to behave yourself, so you'll be invited back.

Shoot local bands, become a regular at the venues in your area. Be nice to the people you meet along the way: club owners, security, roadies, fans. They can all help you down the road. Learn your craft and become a Photoshop or Lightroom expert. Shooting a photo is only the beginning. Knowing how to process that photo into a show stopper is quite another.

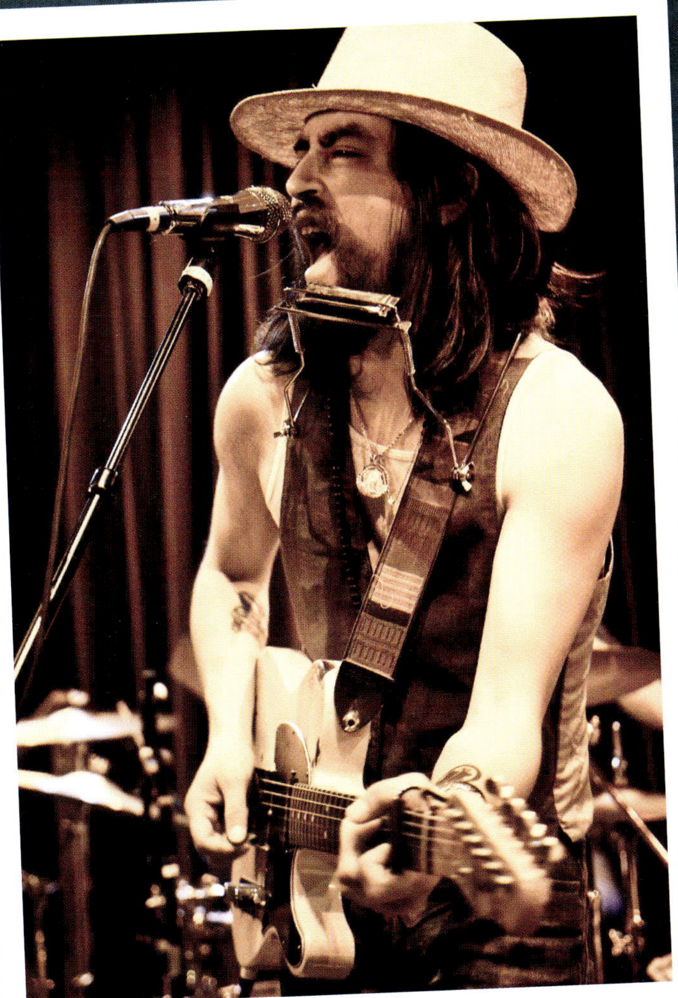

Jackie Greene was photographed by Bob Minkin at the Palm Room in San Rafael, CA, 4/15/2011.

Taken at 1/40 second, f/2.8, and ISO 1600.

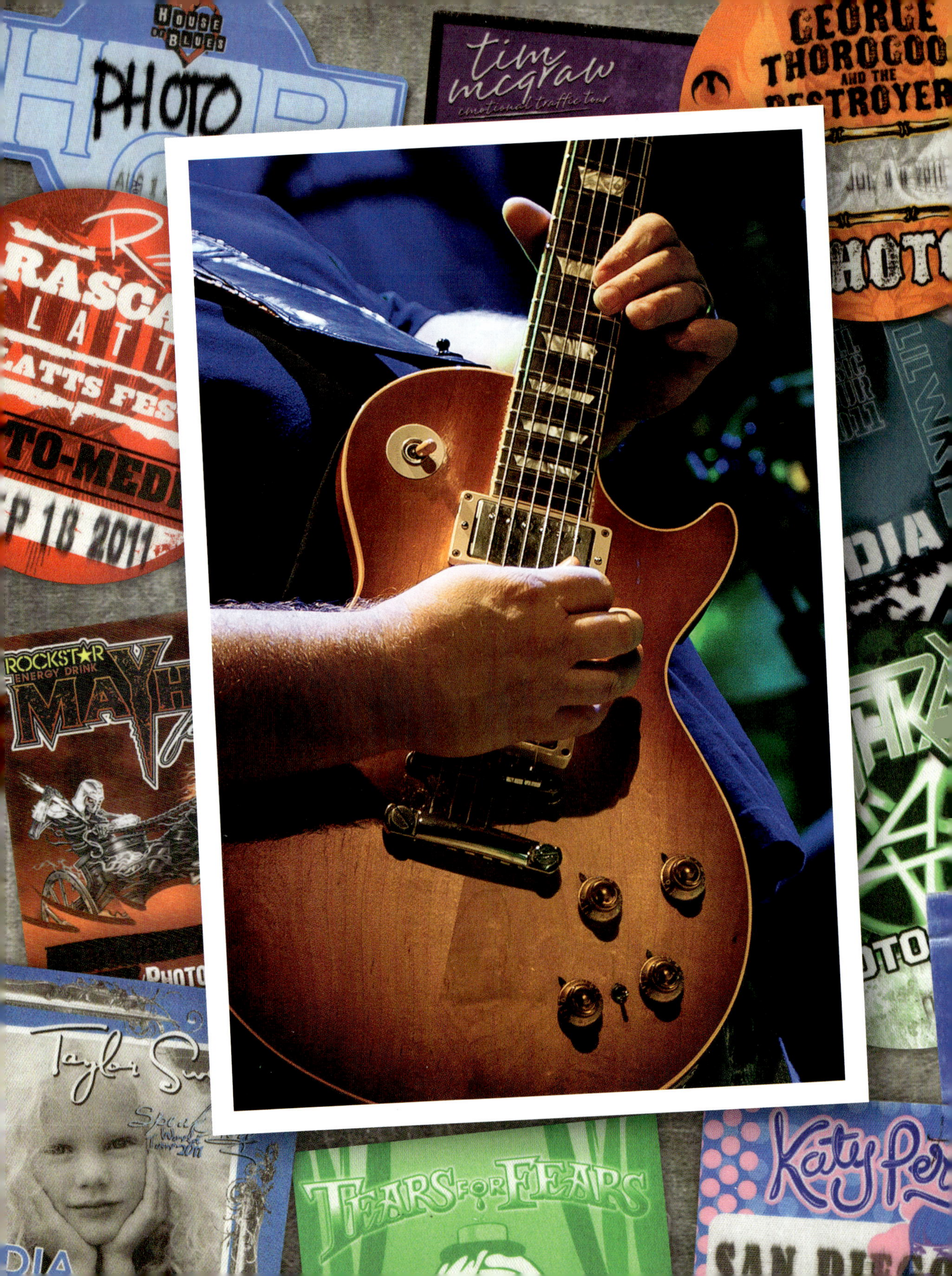
HOUSE OF BLUES
PHOTO
tim mcgraw
emotional traffic tour
AND THE
ROCKSTAR
ENERGY DRINK
TEARS FOR FEARS

8 CLUB LEVEL: SHOOTING AT LARGER LOCAL VENUES

Most concert photographers start out at the local level in bars and clubs. I know I did! And since we already covered how to photograph shows in bars, we'll move on to the local club scene now.

Clubs are venues larger than bars, and they're usually set up for regularly scheduled live performances. It can be a little tougher to get into shows at a club than it is at a bar, especially with a pro-level camera. And unlike bars, you will usually need credentials to shoot at a club, but not always.

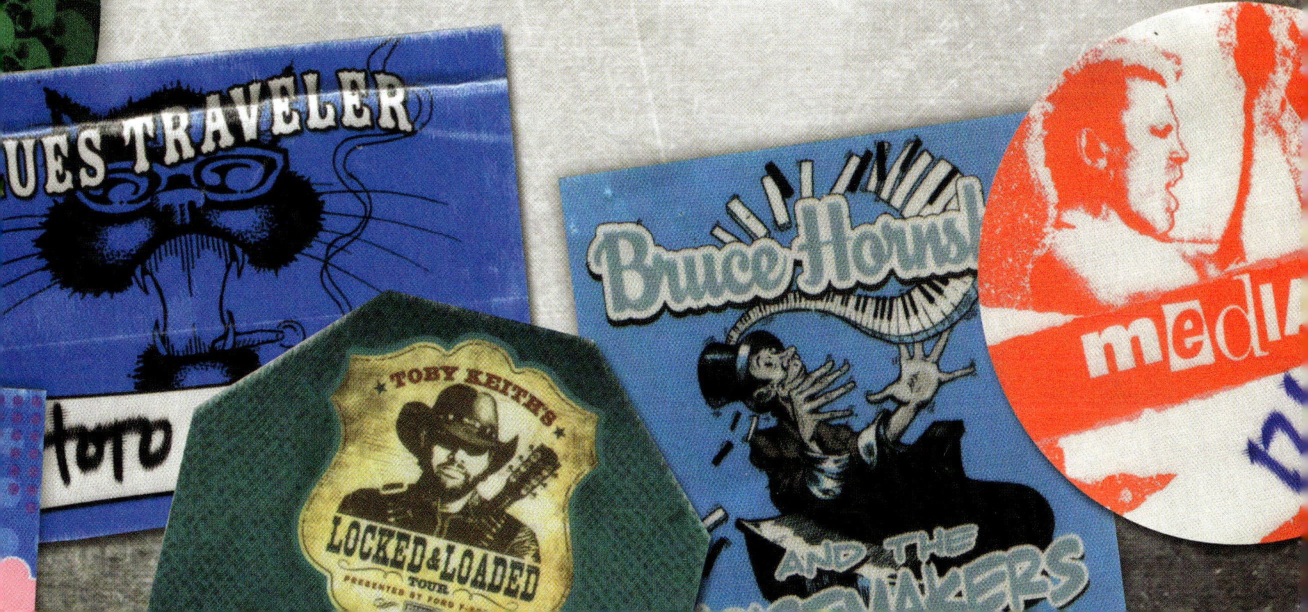

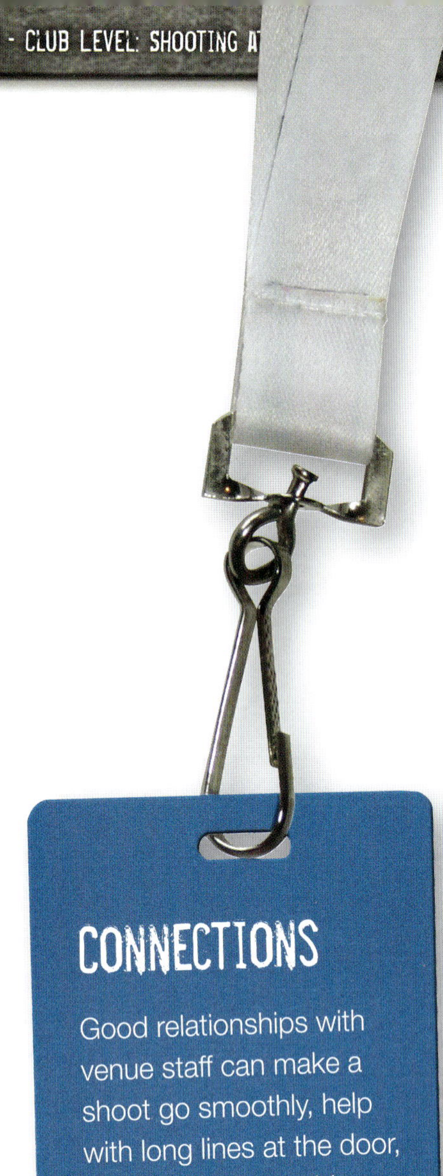

CONNECTIONS

Good relationships with venue staff can make a shoot go smoothly, help with long lines at the door, and even solve problems with missing credentials.

An example of the type of club I'm talking about is the House of Blues chain, which has thirteen venues across the country. There's a House of Blues in San Diego, one in Anaheim, and one in Los Angeles. That's three different House of Blues clubs within 120 miles of my home, making it place I go often to photograph music.

There are also performance venues that are a little bigger than what most people would consider a club, but these places are still not considered *halls* (covered in the next chapter). These performance venues hold roughly 1,500 patrons and are also covered in this chapter, because the restrictions, sight lines, photo pits, and other factors of shooting in them are the same.

In most cases, clubs of all sizes have better lights than bars, and many have photo pits. Some clubs allow photographers to shoot from the floor or anywhere in the venue … just like a bar. Many, like the House of Blues, even go as far as having their own credentials for photographers, and these passes override the credentials issued by a band. This means, when shooting at the House of Blues or another club with this policy, you need the venue's photo pass to do your work.

PROFESSIONAL BEHAVIOR

When you start to shoot concerts at clubs, you'll notice a few important things. One of them is that club staff doesn't change much over time, so the same people will probably be working the door and the stage for all the shows you want to shoot over the course of several years. That's why it really pays off to act professionally right from the start. If you act like a jerk, then the staff will treat you like a jerk, which can make it tough for you to do your best work. Understand that these people are doing their jobs … just like you're doing your job.

MY PHOTO BAG: LOCAL CLUB

What I take to a club shoot

Photographing in a club can mean tight quarters--no place to leave anything--as well as short shooting times and a stage that's larger than those often found in a bar. Depending on the venue, I either go lean and mean for a club shoot or I use a two-body setup with two zoom lenses and a few primes in my bag.

Here's my list:

- 2x dSLR body (a Nikon D3 and Nikon D700)
- 24-70mm f/2.8 lens
- 70-200mm f/2.8 lens
- 50mm f/1.8 prime lens
- 16mm Fisheye lens

This setup allows me to capture most of the action in any club from just about anywhere in the room. And I always pack the following essentials:

- Earplugs
- Extra battery
- Business cards
- Lens cloth
- Small flashlight

Here's an example: I shoot at the San Diego House of Blues a lot, and the same great staff work the door for every show. I see them once a week or more, and they ask to check my bag every time. So I have it ready to be checked every time. They know me … and know that I'm not trying to bring anything illegal into the club, but they need to do their job and check the bag. I understand that it isn't personal and I make sure that my bag is ready to be checked so we can all get through the process quickly and without issues. But I've seen photographers who acted like jerks in the past being thoroughly searched and held up at the door, which made them late for the shoot.

LIGHTING

The lighting and stage setups at clubs are usually better than at bars. And this makes life marginally easier for concert photographers, but it doesn't mean that the lights will be super bright or that any given band will use all the available lights. I've shot at a specific club multiple times in the same week, and the lighting was really different at each show. The lighting situation depends a lot on what the band wants and how they perform.

Many clubs have a follow spot or two, and this adds a lot of light in a small room. To prepare for your shoot, look to see if the club has a spotlight set up at the rear of the room or in the balcony, and find out if there's a spotlight operator. I've been fooled in the past by seeing the spotlight. I assumed that the band would be well lit, but found out later that the spotlights were not being used.

If spotlights are used, the difference in the amount of light is big—usually at least a full stop different. That means if the stage lighting gives you exposure settings of 1/160 second, f/2.8, and ISO 1600, then you can use 1/160 second, f/2.8, and ISO 800 when the spotlight is on.

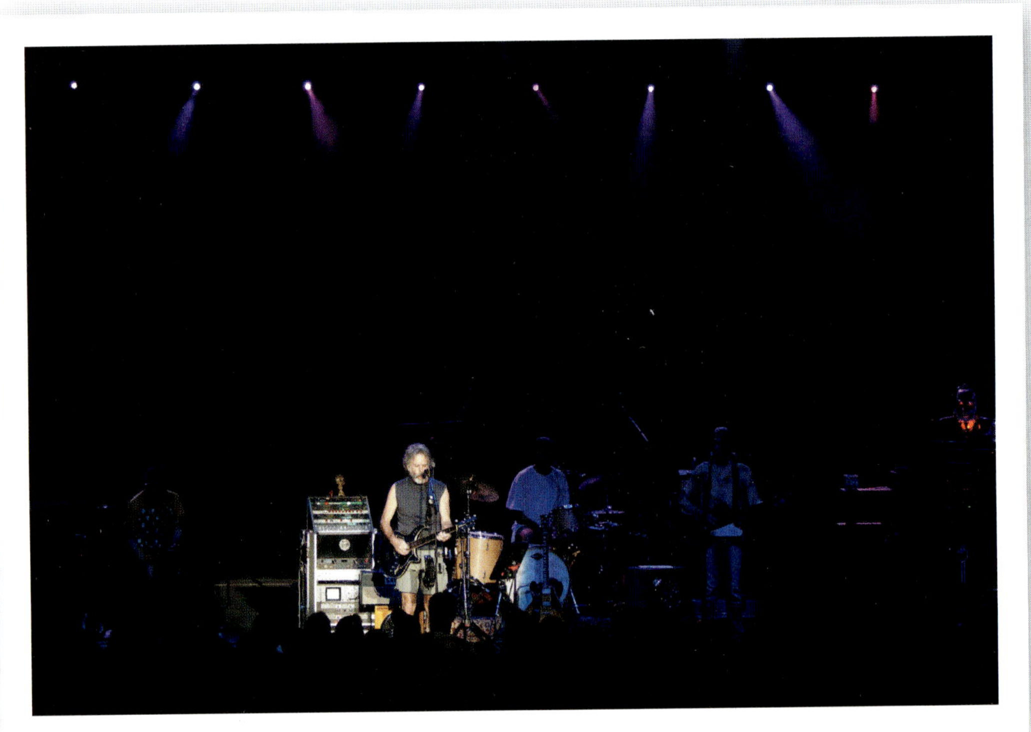

Having a spotlight illuminating a musician gives you plenty of light to capture him. For example, I was able to use an ISO as low as 400 at the Bob Weir and RatDog show, but it can leave the rest of the stage looking very dark. *Taken 1/100 second, f/2.8, and ISO 400*

The one problem with spotlights is that the person in the spotlight is noticeably brighter than the rest of the stage … and the other band members. This makes it very difficult to get a proper exposure for a group shot. But there's little you can do to fix this. The *contrast*, or difference in the amount of light, is just too much to allow details in the dark areas and the light areas to be visible.

What happens is that if you expose for the person in the spotlight, then the rest of the stage is underexposed. And if you expose for the band, then the person in the spotlight will be overexposed. You need to choose a subject for your image and photograph according to how the light works to show it well.

If you're hoping for a group shot, then keep an eye out for when the spotlight might be turned off or band members cluster together in the spotlight.

PHOTO PIT

One of the nice things about shooting in a club is that there's usually a photo pit. Not always, but most of the time. When there is a photo pit, here are some things to keep in mind. (The next section will offer some tips for shooting at a club that doesn't offer a photo pit.)

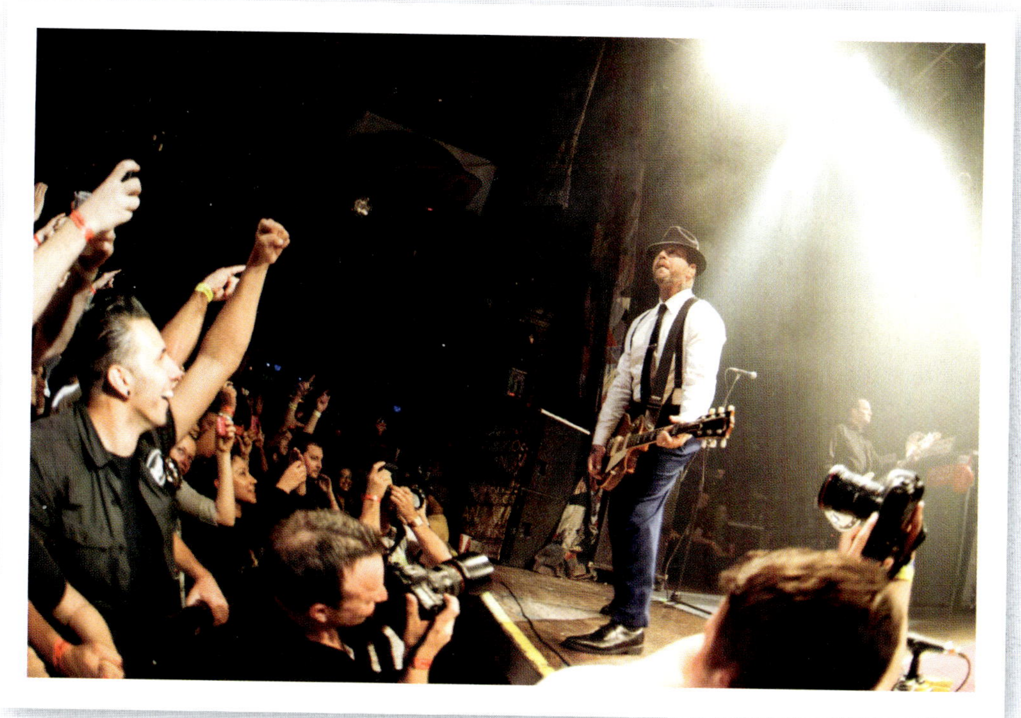

The photo pit was crowded for the Social Distortion show, so I started off to the side to avoid blocking the fans' view.

Taken at 1/250 second, f/2.8, and ISO 2500

The following tips apply to all photo pits—no matter what type or size of venue. Some were covered in Chapter 3, but they're important enough to repeat here.

- **Respect the fans.**
  The fans are the most important element at any show. And in most clubs, the stage is low; so if you stand up straight in the middle of the photo pit, you will most likely block the view of fans. Try to stay off to the sides. If shooting from the middle, then stay low.
- **Respect the band.**
  One very important way to respect the band in a small and crowded club photo pit is to not lean onto the stage. The stage is the band's workplace—not yours. When you lean onto the stage, you end up being a distraction to the band, the fans, the security staff, and the other photographers. Don't do it. Respect this space by staying out of it.
- **Respect security.**
  Security has a tough job. These people are busy making sure that everything runs smoothly at the show and that there are no problems in the club. Do not become a problem. Instead, make sure you stay out of the way and behave so that security doesn't need to worry about you.
- **Respect the other photographers.**
  At times, the pit will be yours alone. At other times, it will be really crowded. When working in the pit with other photographers, be polite and respectful. You never know who's working next to you and what (s)he might mean to your career.
- **Do what it takes.**
  While you definitely need to follow the rules of the venue, you also need to put yourself in the right position to get great images of the concert. This might mean kneeling down or being in awkward positions, but you probably only have three songs to do your work. Make them count. Many times, I try to shoot from a low angle to make the performers seem larger on the stage. This also makes the images look as if they were taken at a larger venue. Wide angle lenses are great for this because they make the stage look bigger.
- **Keep it compact.**
  As I've mentioned, the photo pit can be a small and cramped space, so pack light and make sure that your gear doesn't get in the way of other people trying to work or enjoy the show.
- **Be aware of your surroundings.**
  Airborne beer, water, and even spit from the stage seems to be more prevalent in club shows than other venues. Crowd surfers can also be more of an issue in clubs, due in part to less security (compared to large venues and festivals) to deal with issues that may involve the pit.

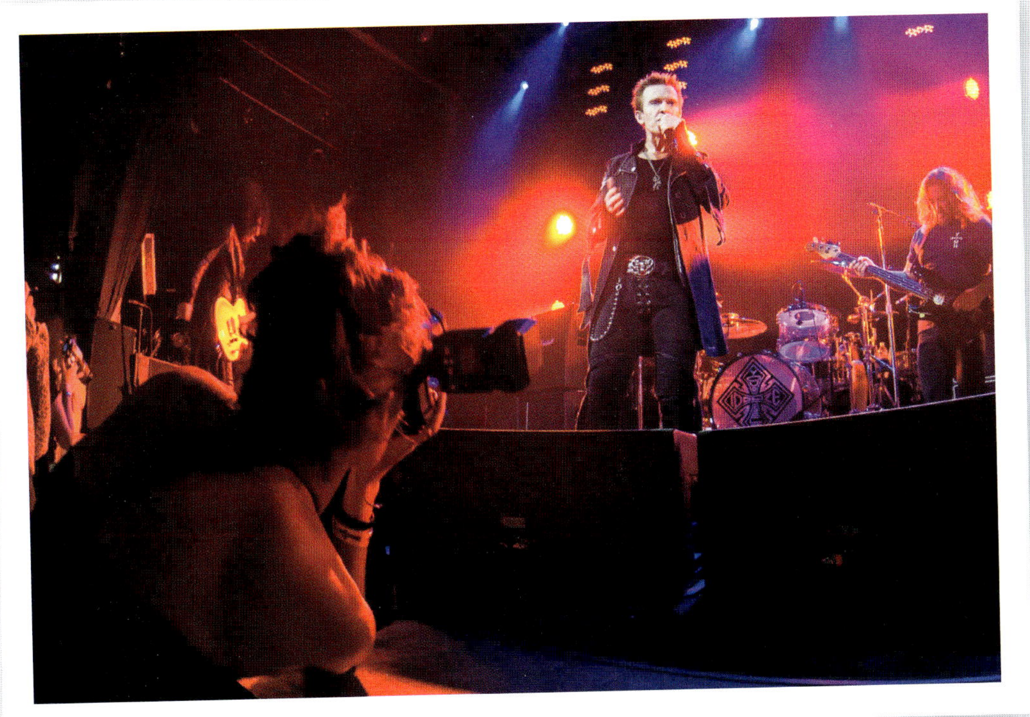

When working in the photo pit, flash photography is usually not allowed. It's also a no-no to lean over the stage. This blocks other photographers from getting their shots, especially when the photo pit is narrow and movement restricted ... as it was in this venue.

Taken at 1/60 second, f/2.8, and ISO 640

Oh, and a word on positioning yourself: When working in a full photo pit, be aware that it will be close to impossible sometimes to move from one side to the other. So it helps to be on time to the show and secure your position as soon as you can. I like to be on the left or right of the main performer or at the middle of the stage. And if I know that the pit is going to be full, I'll make sure that I'm ready to enter as soon as it opens. It helps to know where you want to go as soon as you can get inside.

ROOM WORK

There are two different scenarios that require you to shoot from the audience. The first is that the venue has no photo pit. The second is that you're allowed to shoot the whole night, but you need to leave the photo pit after the first three songs and work from the room.

In a perfect world, getting to a venue early should allow you plenty of opportunity to get a spot up close. But there are times when you'll get to the venue and the credentials list from

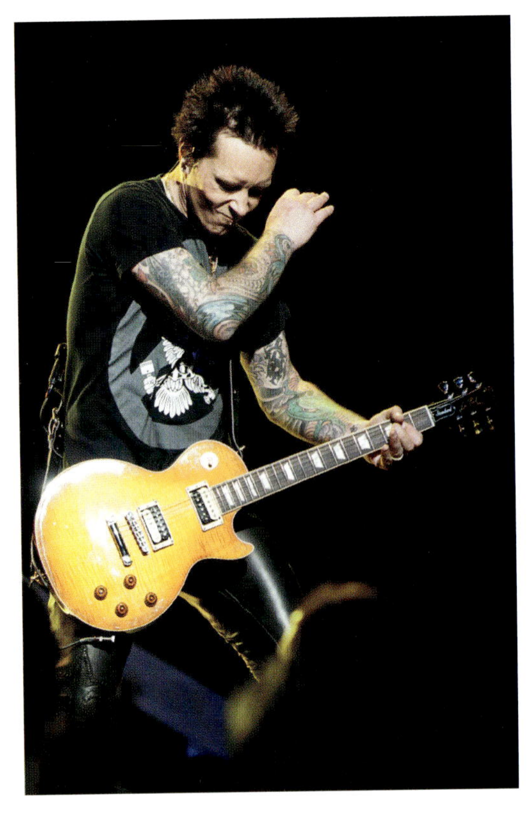

the band isn't at the box office. So the doors open and you stand there waiting to be admitted until the list finally shows up. And then you walk in to a packed room with no photo pit.

Of course, when the list is already there, you can walk in and get a great spot on the floor. But be prepared to alter you plans if that doesn't happen.

The first thing you'll notice when there are people between you and the stage is that you need a longer lens. This helps you to shoot through the crowd and still get close up images of the performers. The shallow depth of field offered by a longer lens will keep the crowd out of focus and attention on the performer. The 70–200mm f/2.8 lens is perfect for this and it gets a huge workout from me at club shows when I'm shooting from the crowd.

One of my favorite shots of Billy Morrison was taken with a long lens from behind the fans. The photograph was taken late in the show, when photography was no longer allowed in the pit.

Taken at 1/500 second, f/2.8, and ISO 1000

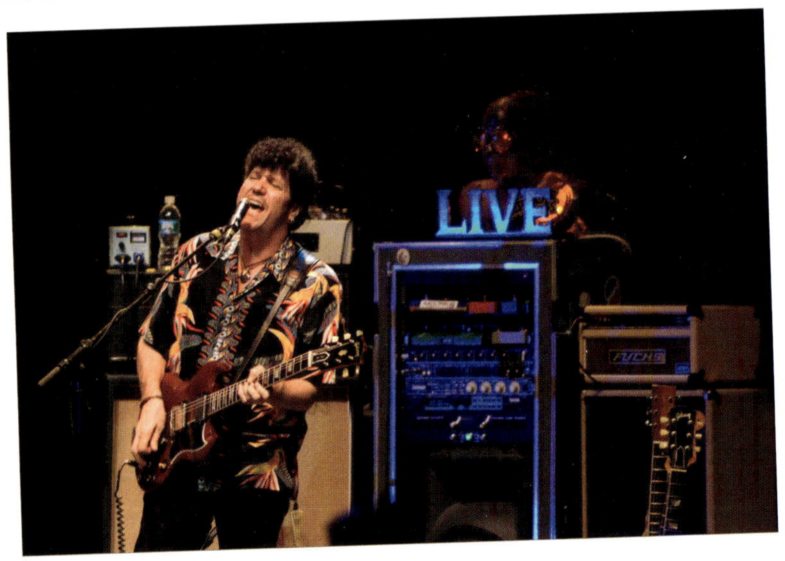

Guitarist Mark Karan was back on tour after beating neck cancer—hence the LIVE sign on his gear. This photo was taken at a club without a photo pit. To get this shot, I used a 70–200mm lens at the 200mm focal length.

Taken at 1/100 second, f/2.8, and ISO 400

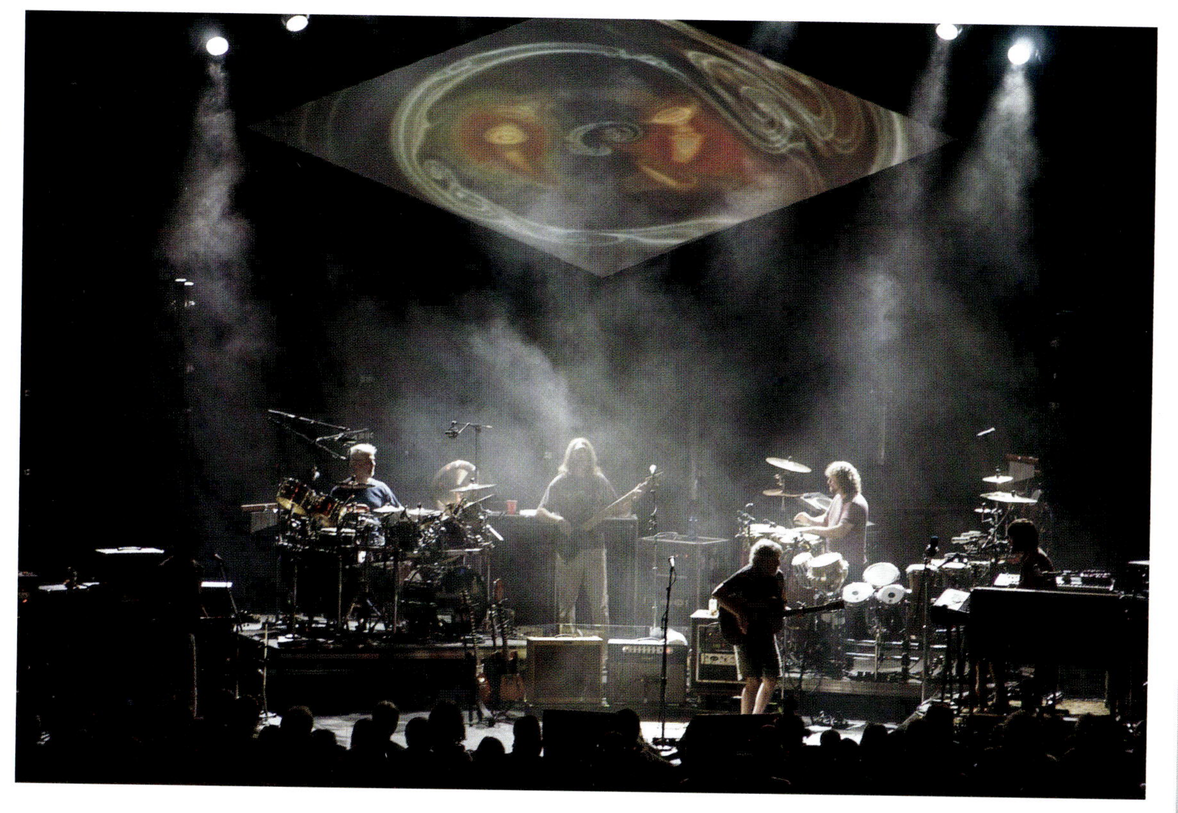

String Cheese Incident was photographed from the crowd during the 2006 tour.
Taken at 1/80 second, f/2.8, and ISO 320

The shooting plan I use when photographing from the crowd is to spend the first song getting the shots I need. Then I try to move either left or right, depending on the stage and band, to get shots from a different angle. If the club has an accessible balcony, then I like to head there for the last song. The overhead perspective is great for drummer and keyboard shots, so I try to focus on those when I'm in this position.

If allowed to shoot from the crowd after the first three songs, then the plan is different. I shoot from the photo pit during the first three songs, and I make sure to spend that time getting the close ups that I want. I'll leave the wide-angle stuff for when shooting from the room.

When you leave the photo pit, try to use the edges of the room to get overall band photos. Use the longer lens to get in as close as possible to the performers. If there's a balcony, try to use it to get shots of the keyboards and drums. And since there's more time to shoot in this scenario, also work on getting shots of the rest of the band. Use the extra time to experiment.

EXPERIMENT

Experimenting with your photography in a club is a lot easier when you have all night and can shoot from the photo pit and the rest of the house. The only time I experiment with my concert photography is when I know I already have the shots that a client wants. So if shooting for the band, make sure you have photos of all the band members and an overall band shot before trying anything wacky or untested. If shooting for the venue, make sure you have the standard shots and some wide angle captures that show the room or venue.

But once the requisite stuff is done, play! One way to experiment is to shoot close-ups, or detail shots, of the instruments; ignore the faces. Look for details that will still be identifiable to fan of the band, like a signature guitar or microphone.

Also try using extreme wide angles and fisheye lenses up close. And instead of shooting in landscape orientation, shoot the fisheye in portrait mode.

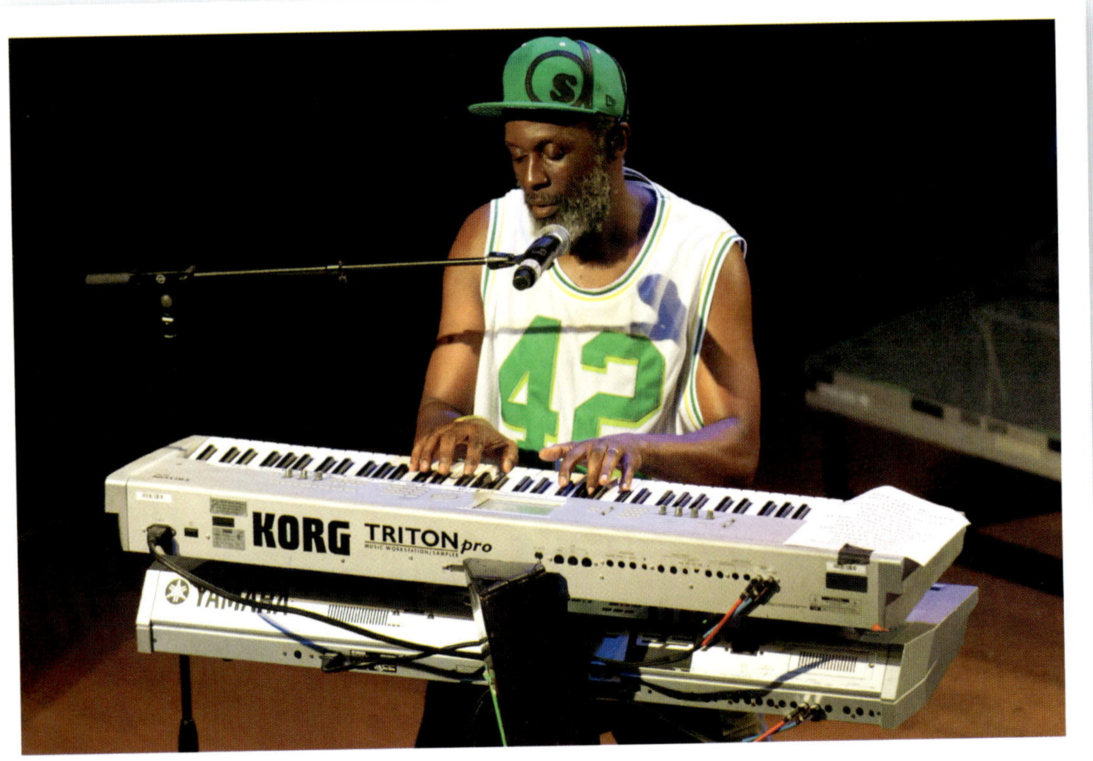

One of the hardest things to capture when shooting a concert are the keyboards. Using the balcony and a zoom lens allowed me to capture not only the keyboards but also the hands on the keys.
Taken at 1/250 second, f/2.8, and ISO 3200

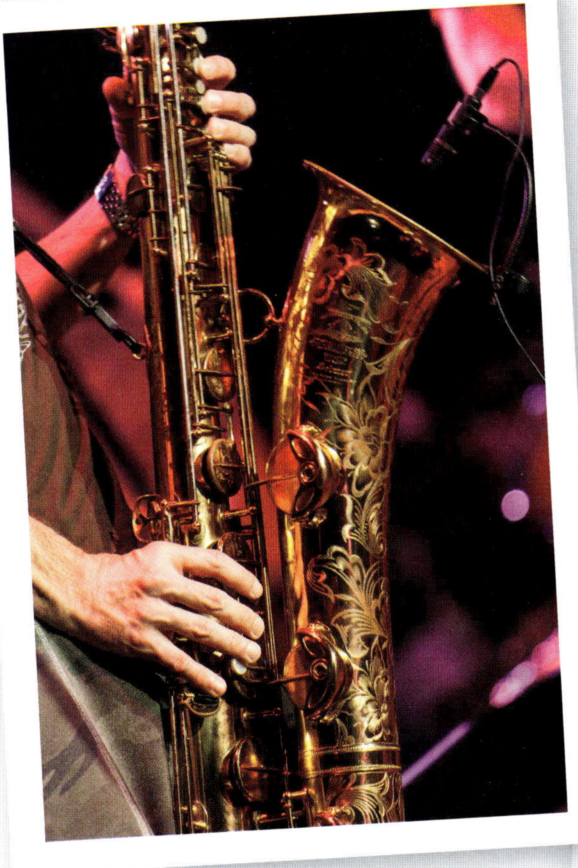

Getting in close on this saxophone allowed me to capture the details that are just not seen in most photos.

Taken at 1/60 second, f/2.8, and ISO 400

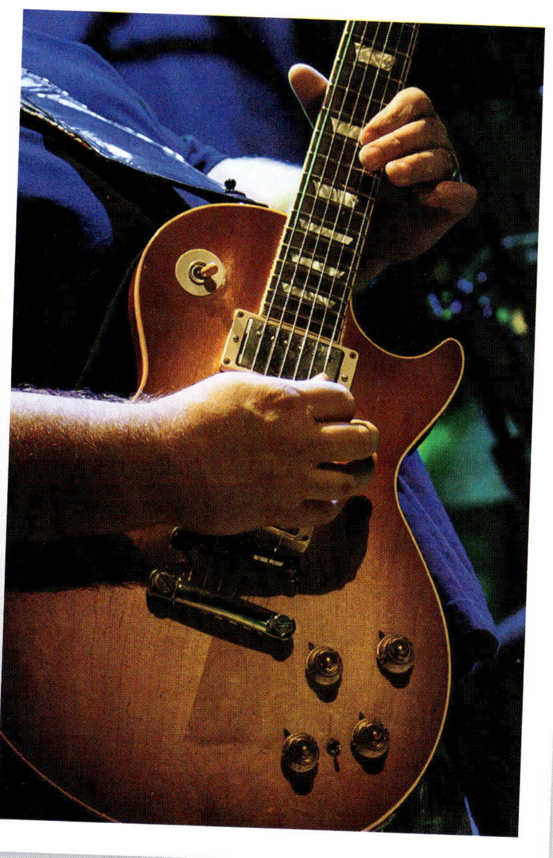

Photographing guitars up close is actually pretty easy. Just wait until the hand on the guitar neck is low enough to act as an anchor point for the composition.

Taken at 1/200, f/2.8, and ISO 1600

EXPOSURE SETTINGS

The exposure settings you want to use in a club, as with any other setting, depends on the available light. Nevertheless, I start every show with my cameras set to the same settings:

- The shutter speed is set to 1/160 of a second.
- The aperture is set to f/2.8.
- The ISO is set to 1600.

When I started to write this book, I went back through thousands of images. And due to the neat way that programs like Lightroom and Bridge allow you to look at your images' metadata, I was able to see how many of my images were actually taken with these settings.

There weren't too many, but this is the starting point I use. The actual settings were based on the lights on the given night along with the speed of the action I was capturing and the lenses I was using. When I shot Anthrax with Testament and Death Angle at the San Diego House of Blues, for instance, I took a total of zero photos with my start settings … not because the settings were wrong but because they weren't right for those bands under the light that was present.

It's important to know what settings you can change during a show and how to best change them to accommodate quickly fluctuating stage lights. For a band like Anthrax, a photographer wants to keep the shutter speed fairly high due to the fast action on the stage. This means you'll up the ISO a full stop (to ISO 3200) if the shutter speed is set so low that the action is blurred. That allows you to use a faster shutter speed. Keep the aperture as wide open as possible. You'll need to time the lights—wait for the bright lights—to get a proper exposure.

So with the ISO set at 3200, the shutter speed set at 1/160, and the aperture set to f/2.8, I took 166 photos. All it took to get there was to push the ISO one full stop. And once that new baseline was set, I was able to adjust the shutter speed as needed. I even pushed it to 1/500 second for a few shots to freeze hair flying around. But most of the images I took that night had a shutter speed of 1/200, 1/250, or 1/320—all at f/2.8 and ISO 3200.

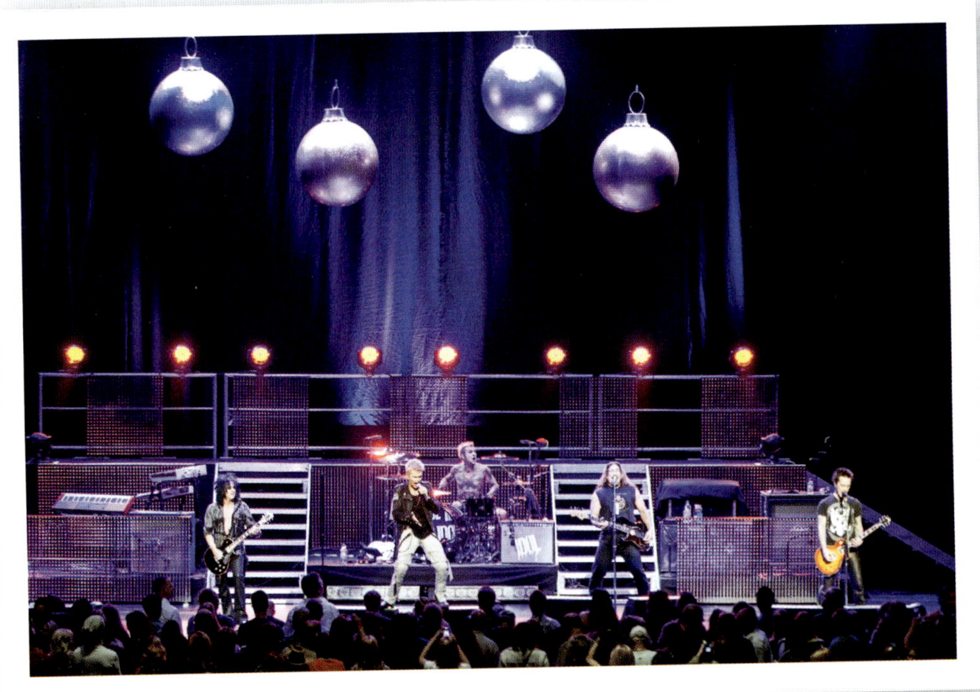

I used the 70–200mm f/2.8 zoom lens to get this shot of the whole stage. Shooting from behind the soundboard, I was able to freeze the action.

Taken at 1/200 second, f/2.8, and ISO 1600

FAST GLASS

One of the real differences between shooting in clubs and in bars is the lenses you can use. Since the light is usually better in a club, there's no reason to use prime lenses. You can get away with using zoom lenses as long as they have a constant aperture of f/2.8 wide open.

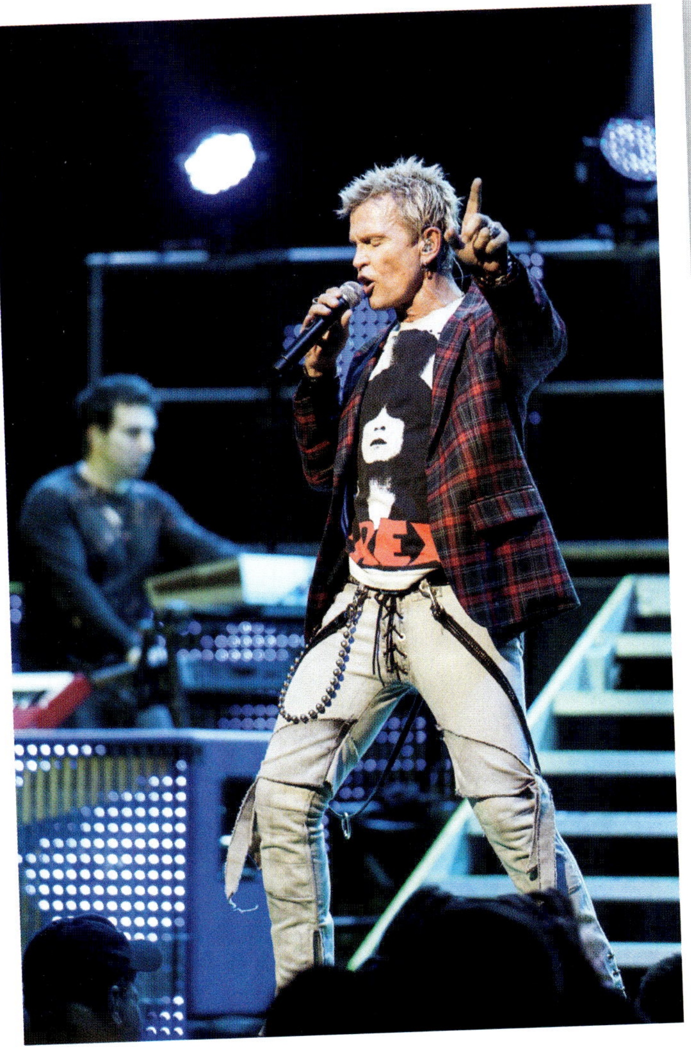

Using the same lens as the previous photo, I was able to get in close, too, and freeze the action.

Taken at 1/400 second, f/2.8, and ISO 1000

Three zoom lenses are used in concert photography today:

- 14–24mm f/2.8
- 24–70mm f/2.8
- 70–200m f/2.8

These lenses cover a huge range of focal lengths, and they can all shoot at f/2.8 … at all focal lengths. But these lenses are expensive. Together, they'll set you back more than $6000. I do not own or use a 14–24mm f/2.8 lens … not because I don't want to, but because it doesn't match my style of shooting. I do own and use the other two lenses though at just about every show.

Of course you *can* use prime lenses, and sometimes they will be enough. But if you start to shoot a lot of club shows, I expect that you'll want to invest in a fast zoom lens … or two or three.

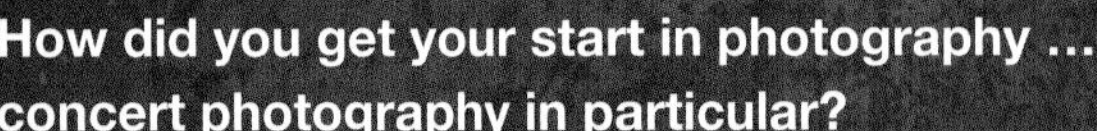

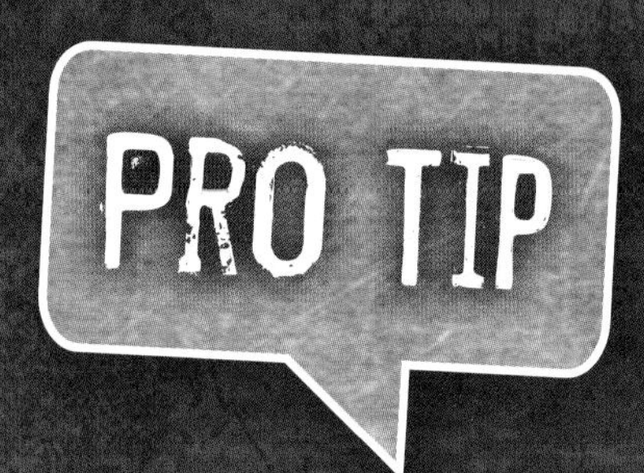

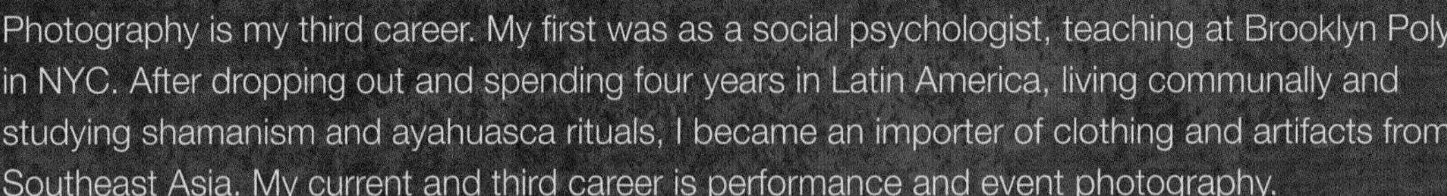

Photography is my third career. My first was as a social psychologist, teaching at Brooklyn Poly in NYC. After dropping out and spending four years in Latin America, living communally and studying shamanism and ayahuasca rituals, I became an importer of clothing and artifacts from Southeast Asia. My current and third career is performance and event photography.

I became a Deadhead in the mid-70s after moving to California. At the 20th anniversary show in 1980 in Boulder, I saw a woman—I never have been able to identify her—walk across the area in front of the stage with a camera and a silver Halliburton case. She snapped a few shots, and I was smitten with the idea of photographing the Grateful Dead.

In the mid-80s, it was no problem to walk into a concert with a camera and edge up to the front and take pictures. The Grateful Dead always allowed cameras (still cameras, not video) into the building … even as other bands got more uptight and the three songs rule became the norm.

How does your dance photography influence your concert photography?

Dance photography allows me to shoot the whole piece (dress rehearsal only) to get all the great moments of moves, expressions, and lighting … which can occur anywhere in the work. I look for these decisive moments in all the performance shooting that I do.

Shooting dance and other entertainment has made the three-songs rule truly distasteful to me, and I honestly don't understand why a band wouldn't want the best possible photos of themselves, which are not necessarily likely to occur in the first three songs.

How do you deal with low light in venues like the Warfield and the Fillmore?

I use the Nikon D3, which is full frame and also meant for low-light rooms. Red light is ugly and should be avoided if possible. But for other lighting situations, it's easy to shoot with ISO of 5000 and, if you nail the exposure, come out with a grain-free exposure. I love shooting digital!

What is your favorite/most crucial piece of gear?

It is a toss-up between the Nikon D3 and the Nikon 70–200 EDIF VR 2.8 lens. In combination, these two pieces of equipment (plus a fast CF card) enable quick focusing, continuous rapid clicks on one subject (or changing quickly from one subject to another), and capturing the whole gamut of a series of expressions or motions.

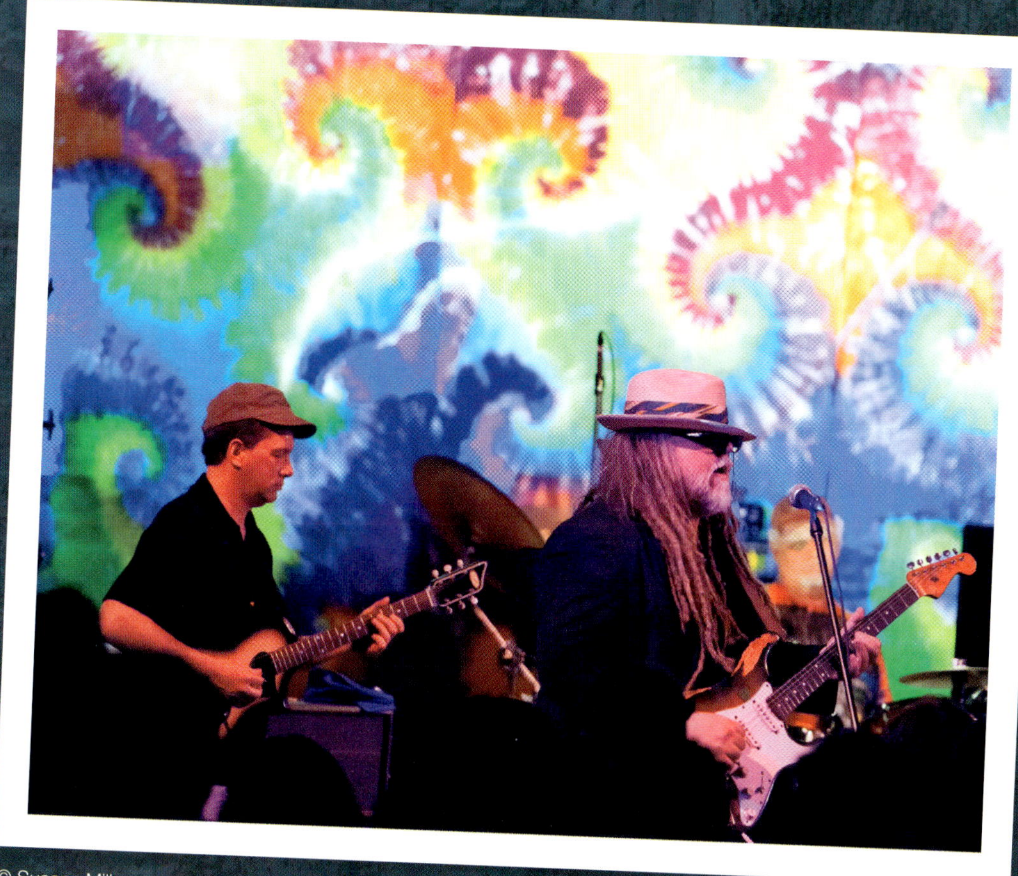

What advice do you have for a photographer wanting to start concert photography?

Get a good publication to represent. Shoot bands whose music you like, and get to know the band members so that you have a chance of shooting more of a show. Feel blessed to have a digital camera, and post your images early and often—with your copyright!

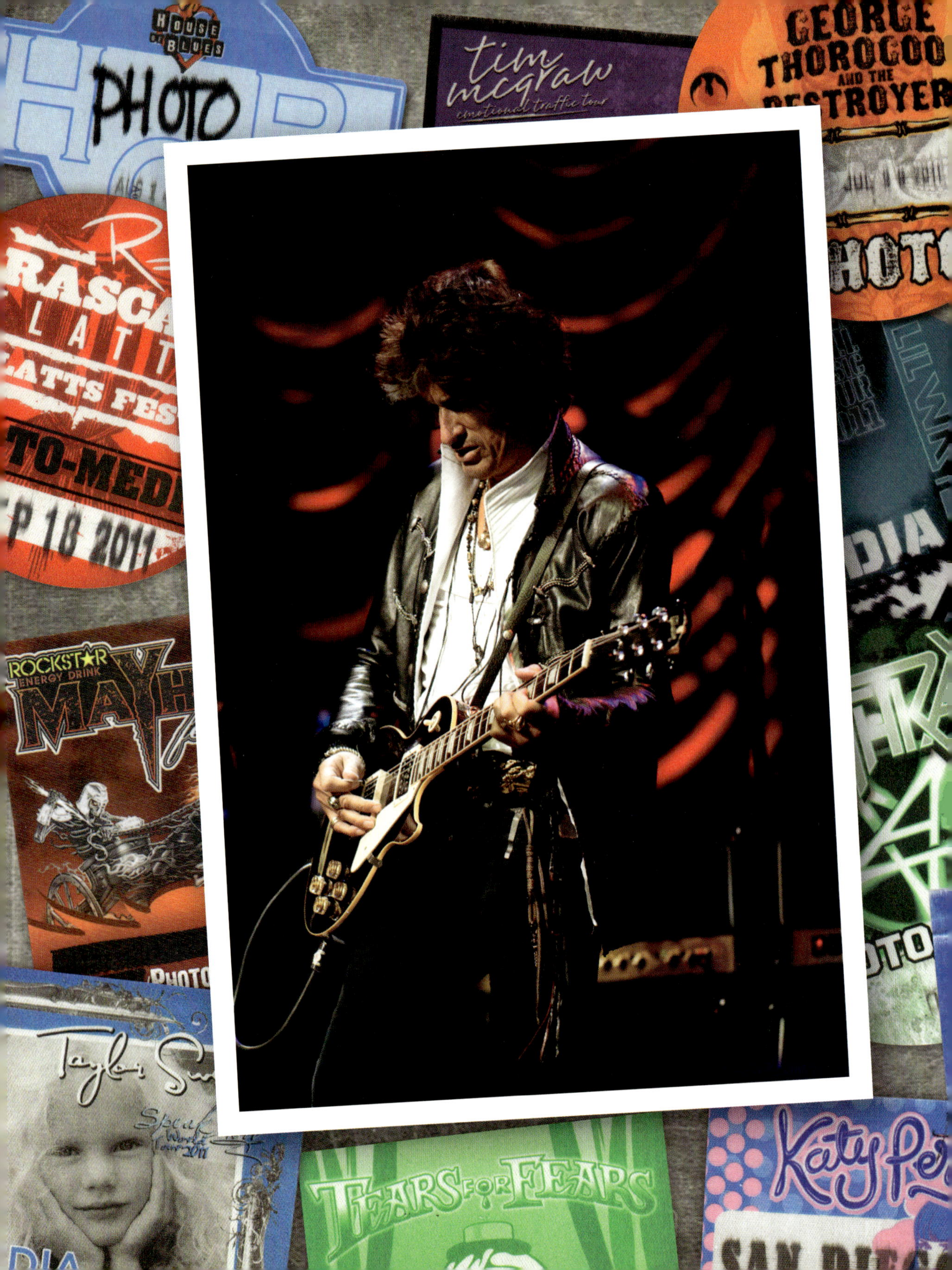
HOUSE OF BLUES
PHOTO
tim mcgraw
emotional traffic tour
GEORGE THOROGOO
AND THE
DESTROYER
RASCA
LATTS FES
TO-MEDI
P 18 2011
ROCKSTAR
ENERGY DRINK
World Tour 2011
TEARS FOR FEARS
PHOTO

9 ROCK THE HALLS: BIGGER AND BRIGHTER VENUES

A lot of venues are bigger than clubs but aren't quite at the arena level to attract big tours. Halls can hold many thousands of people and, depending on the configuration, feel as intimate as a club or as big and open as an amphitheatre. They can be beautiful indoor theaters with row upon row of plush seats, or they can be outdoor areas with folding plastic chairs. The real difference of halls when compared to clubs and bars is size and focus.

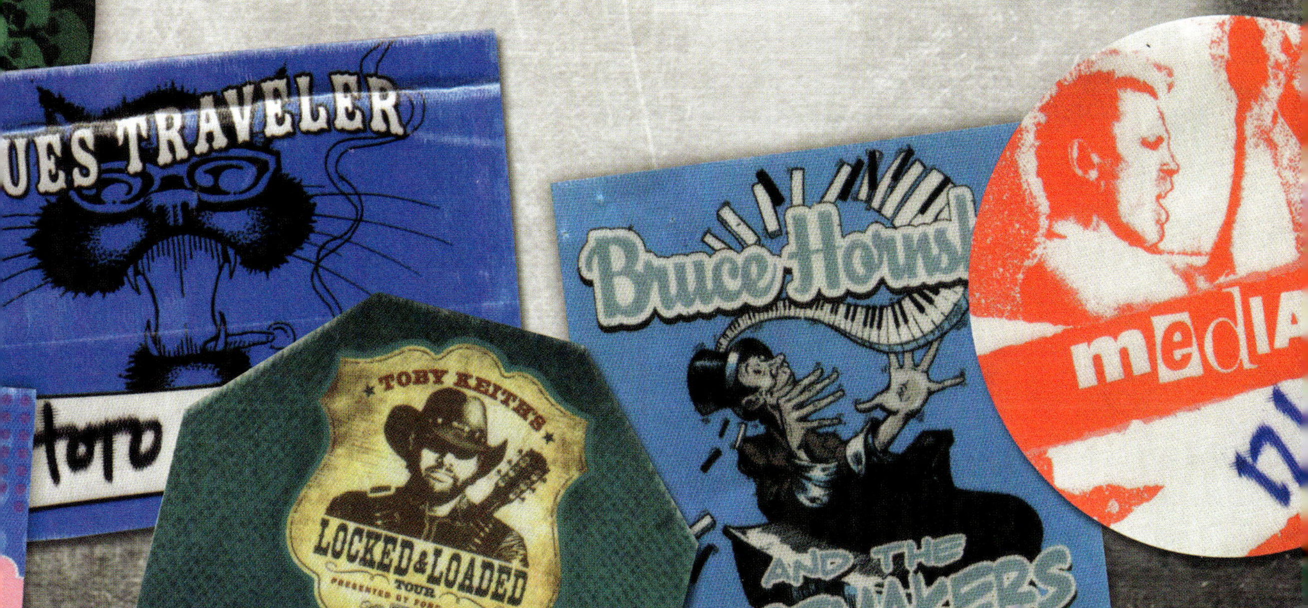

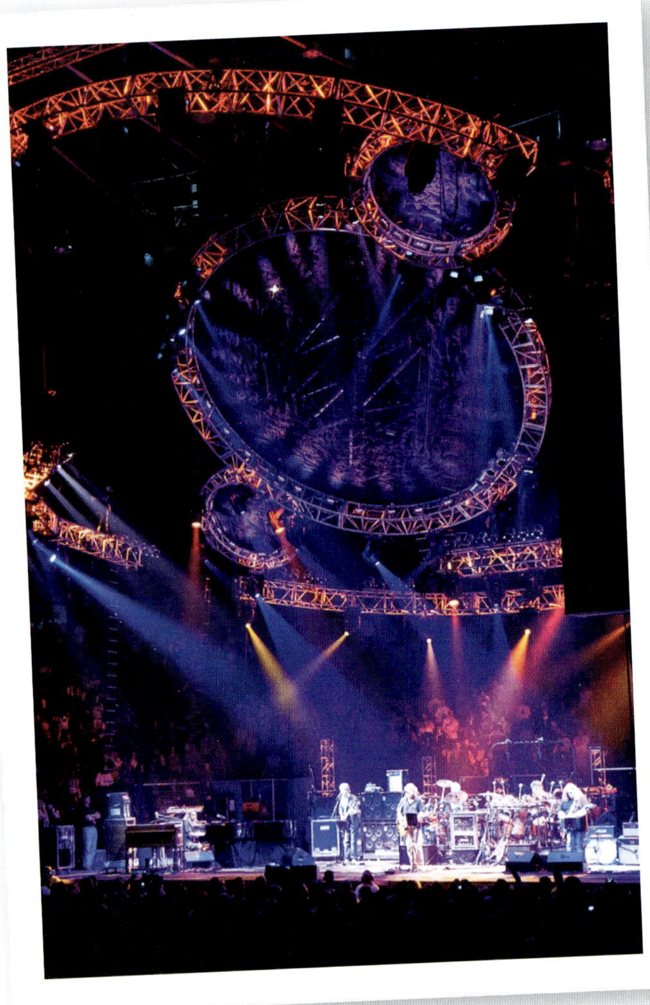

The lighting rig for The Dead tour in 2009 was really impressive. It was so big that it was tough to fully capture.
Taken at 1/50 second, f/2.8, and ISO 1600

These are my favorite venues for concert photography. They are bigger than clubs; they have better light; and they feature larger up-and-coming acts and artists who've sustained a steady fan base. As such, the music is taken seriously in a hall.

Bars and clubs are great in their own ways, but the main purpose in those venues is to sell adult beverages. Live music helps make this happen. At the bigger venues, the focus is on the show; drinks are an added service.

And with more light on the performance in a hall, there are more and different opportunities for terrific photographs, especially if you're given a little extra access.

GREAT LIGHT

When you get to photograph a band in a music hall, the first thing you'll notice is that there is better light. This is great. Because the main purpose of a hall is to host live music and other performance-type events, these venues tend to have their own equipment or rent it for shows … or musicians supply it themselves.

This usually means multiple rows of overhead light as well as side lights, lights on the stage floor, several follow spots, and even big screens on the sides and behind the stage. So there's more light to work with for photography. But this means you need to pay attention to the sides and backgrounds of your scenes. All this great light can illuminate areas you might prefer to be hidden.

MY PHOTO BAG: HALL

What I take to shoot at a performance hall

Photographing in a bigger venue, such as a performance hall, often means more space, short shooting times, and possibly a larger stage. For these shows, I usually use the two-body setup with two zoom lenses, and I take a few primes in my bag, including the 16mm fisheye. If I know it's going to be a soundboard shoot, or even think it might be, then I make sure to have my 300mm f/4 with me, too.

Here's my packing list:

- 2x dSLR body (a Nikon D3 and Nikon D700)
- 24-70mm f/2.8 lens
- 70-200mm f/2.8 lens
- 300mm f/4 prime lens
- 50mm f/1.8 prime lens
- 16mm Fisheye lens

Make sure that the basics are also packed:

- Earplugs
- Extra battery
- Business cards
- Lens cloth
- Small flashlight

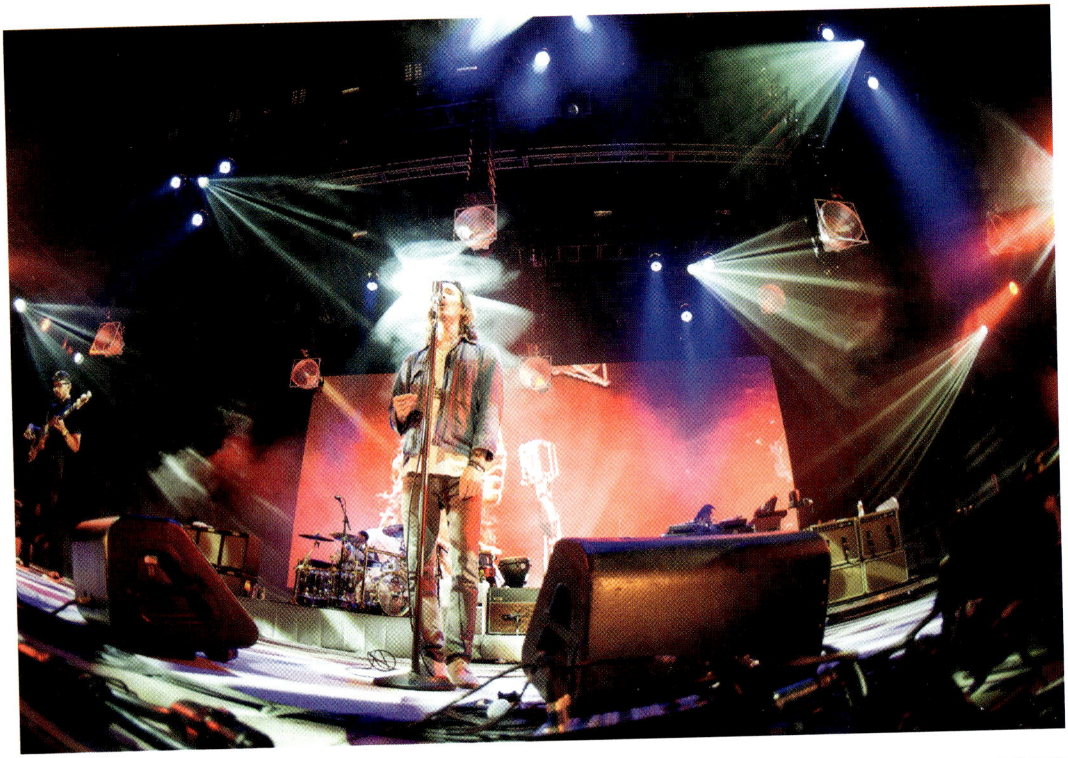

There were lights everywhere during the Incubus show. Even with the main follow spots out of the picture, there was enough light from the side lights to fully illuminate the stage.
Taken at 1/125 second, f/2.8, and ISO 1600

CAMERA SETTINGS

When I started using digital cameras for concert work, one of the biggest limitations I noticed was related to ISO settings. Digital noise was a real problem when shooting in bars and clubs, where I often needed ISO settings higher than 800. So when I started shooting the bigger shows, it was a nice change of pace. The greater amount of ambient light allows for lower ISO settings to be used.

Of course, all this has changed in recent years because newer cameras produce much less noise at higher ISO settings. But if you have an older camera, this is definitely something to consider.

Since you can now use higher ISO settings with low noise, think about freezing action on stage by raising the shutter speed instead of reducing the ISO. This is really useful for shooting bands that tend to move fast during performances. For example, if the settings that give you a proper exposure in a given situation are 1/125 second, f/2.8, and ISO 400, then you can increase the ISO to 1600—a difference of two full stops. Or you can increase the shutter speed two full stops to get an equivalent exposure. This gets you a shutter speed of 1/500 second, enough to freeze the action and get a relatively noise-free image. Of course, this depends on what camera you're using, so make sure you're familiar with the amount of noise your camera produces at the higher ISOs.

So, while I start with my cameras set at 1/160 of a second, f/2.8, and ISO 1600 when I pack my gear at home, I immediately start to increase the shutter speed when shooting under the better lights of the bigger halls. I usually start by increasing the shutter speed to 1/320 of a second and work from there.

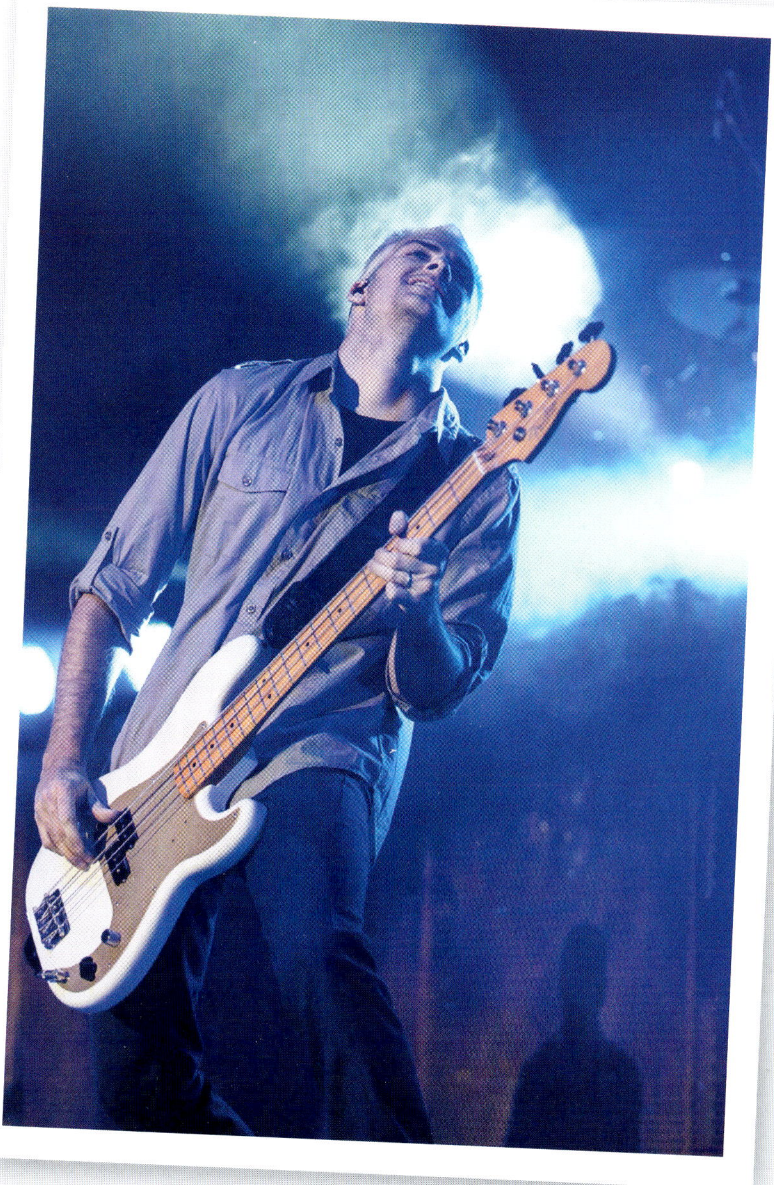

Freezing the action by using 1/500 second shutter speed was easy with the amount of light present at the show. It was also nice to use higher ISO settings with little to no noise in the final image.

Taken at 1/500 second, f/2.8, and ISO 1600

Some habits are tough to break. I still tend to keep my ISO settings lower than 1600 (and play with shutter speed instead to get the exposure right) because of the problem with noise when using the older generation of cameras.

WORK THE ROOM

Working in a performance hall usually comes with more rules and more restrictions than what you typically find in a bar or club. So while the light is great there, it's likely that you'll be restricted to the photo pit or the soundboard for your shooting. It might not seem like a bad thing to be restricted to the photo pit, but at bigger venues, that can mean you never get to shoot any photos of the full stage or settings. You're too close to get a large scene in a single shot … even with a fisheye lens.

Throughout this book, I've stressed the importance of following the rules of a venue … and I'm not going to change that advice here … but I've found that no harm's done if you ask to take a shot or two from the back of the room to get the whole stage and concert scene in a

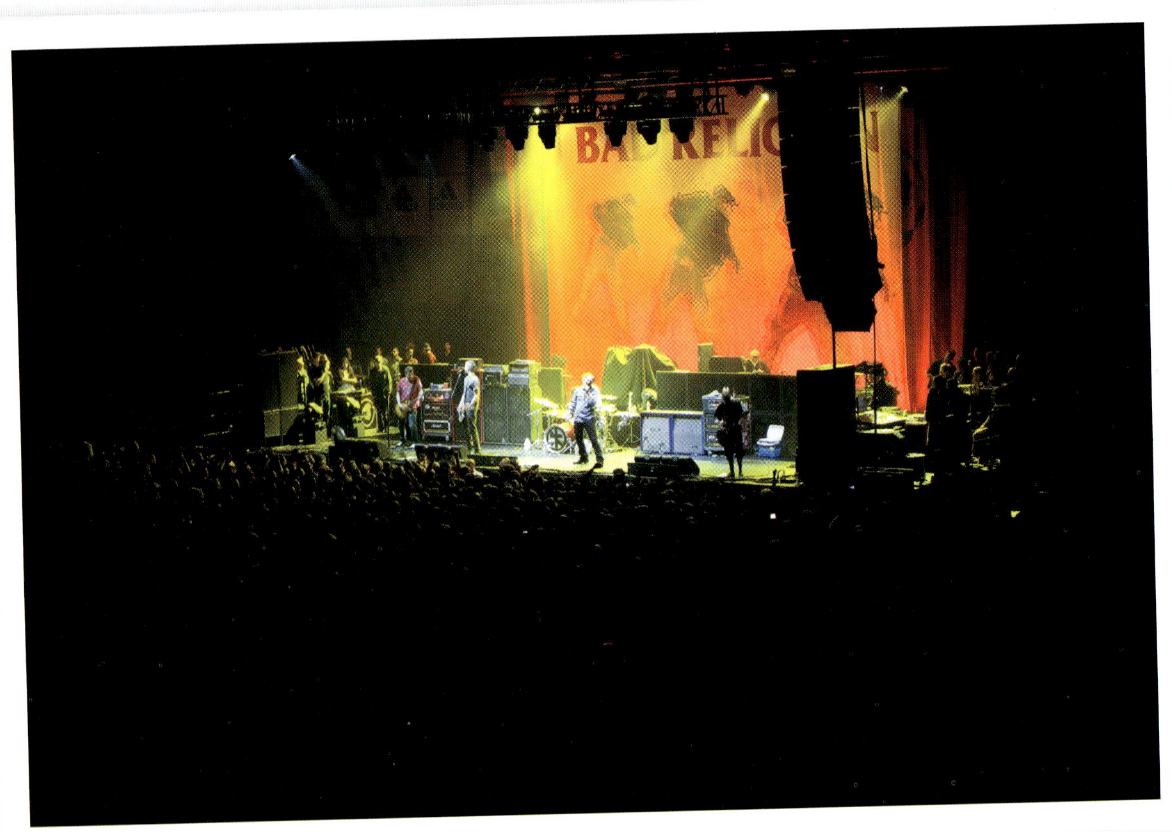

A quick shot on the way out the door can be useful to set the scene. It's best to ask permission to do this.
Taken at 1/30 seconds, f/2.8, and ISO 1600

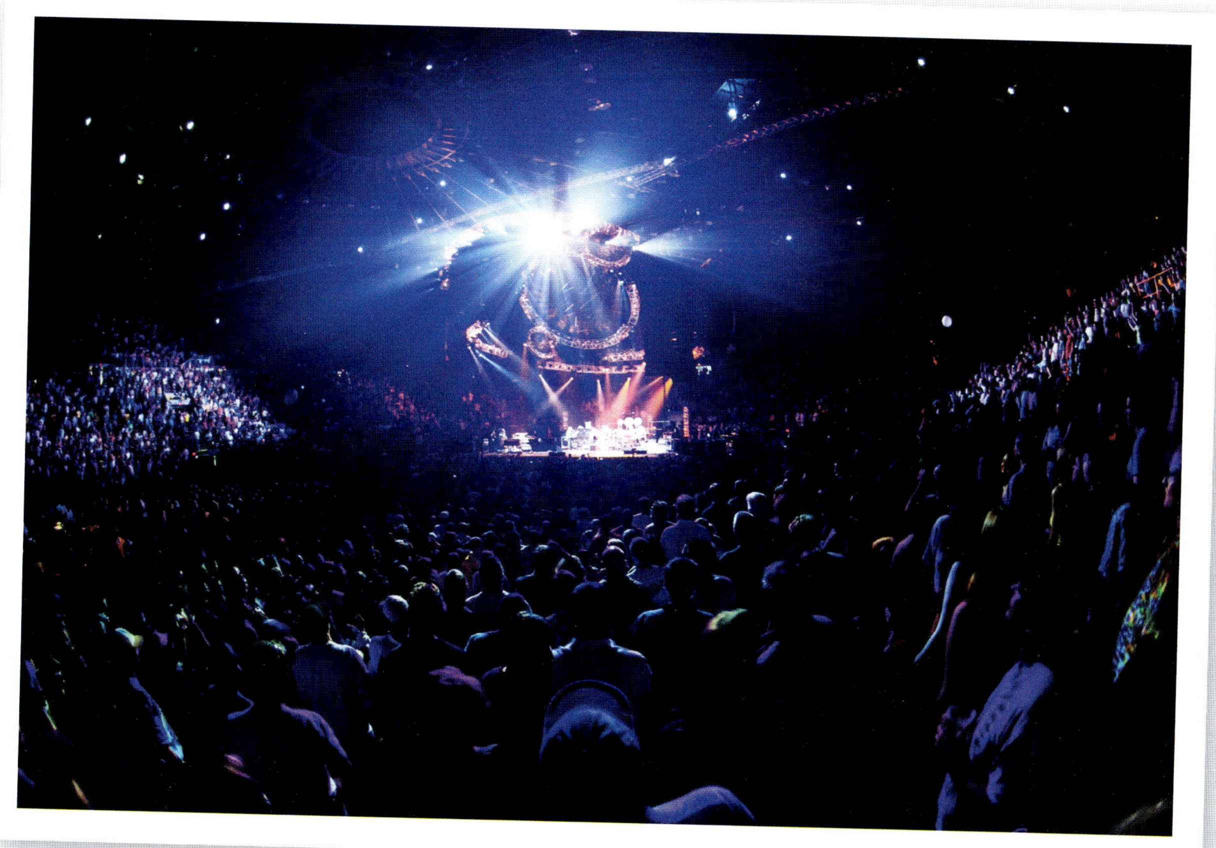

If I think it might be possible to shoot from the back of the room during a show, I'll bring my 16mm fisheye or 10.5mm fisheye lens. These lenses work great from really close or really far away. Here, it's used at the very back of the room, making the crowd look even bigger than it was.

Taken at 1/20 second, f/2.8, and ISO 1600

frame. Many times, I've been told yes and gotten permission to take a few shots on my way out of the building after the first three songs. But sometimes the answer is no. That's okay, too. No hard feelings.

If you are allowed to shoot from the room, a fisheye lens is a great choice to get the whole scene in the image.

Sometimes the bigger shows only allow photos from the soundboard, and you may not get that information until you show up for the shoot. That's why I always pack the 300mm f/4 lens to a hall show. It allows me to get closer to my subject(s) than the 70–200mm f/2.8, and it can work really well with the brighter lights of the bigger venues.

SHOOT OUTSIDE

Part of telling the whole story of a show is to capture everything. And while photographing the outside of the bar isn't always very exciting, getting the outside of a big, beautiful venue is a great idea ... and it's easy.

Look for a view that captures the name of the venue and the name of the band in the same shot. This might take a little effort to find the right angle. Try walking across the street or up the block if the closer positions don't get it right.

Sometimes the signage is easier to get after the show or after the three-song shooting period. Before the show, your time might be devoted to securing your photo credentials and getting into the venue. Just be aware that some venues change the signage during the show; so when you come out, the marquee might be advertising the next show.

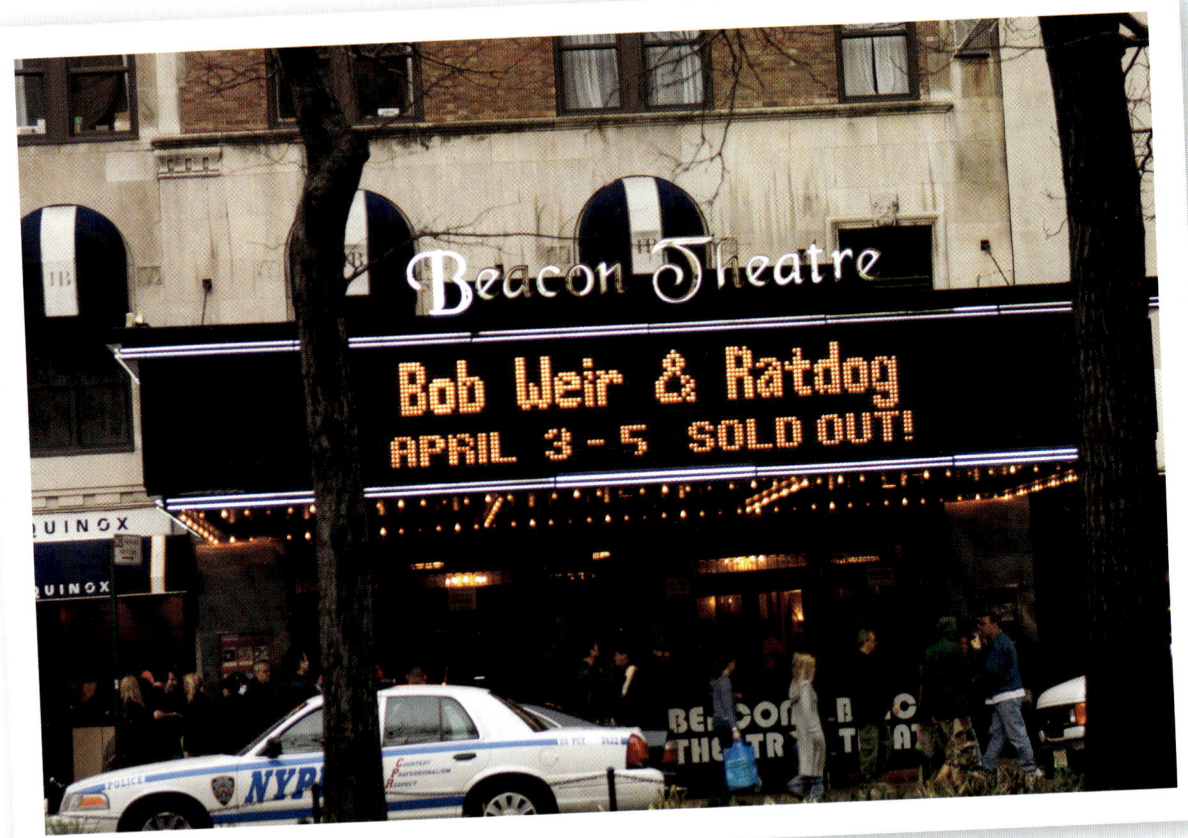

When possible, take a photo of the signage outside. This can take place when you first get to the venue. It can help set the scene when creating a gallery of images.

Taken at 1/40 second, f/2.8, and ISO 100

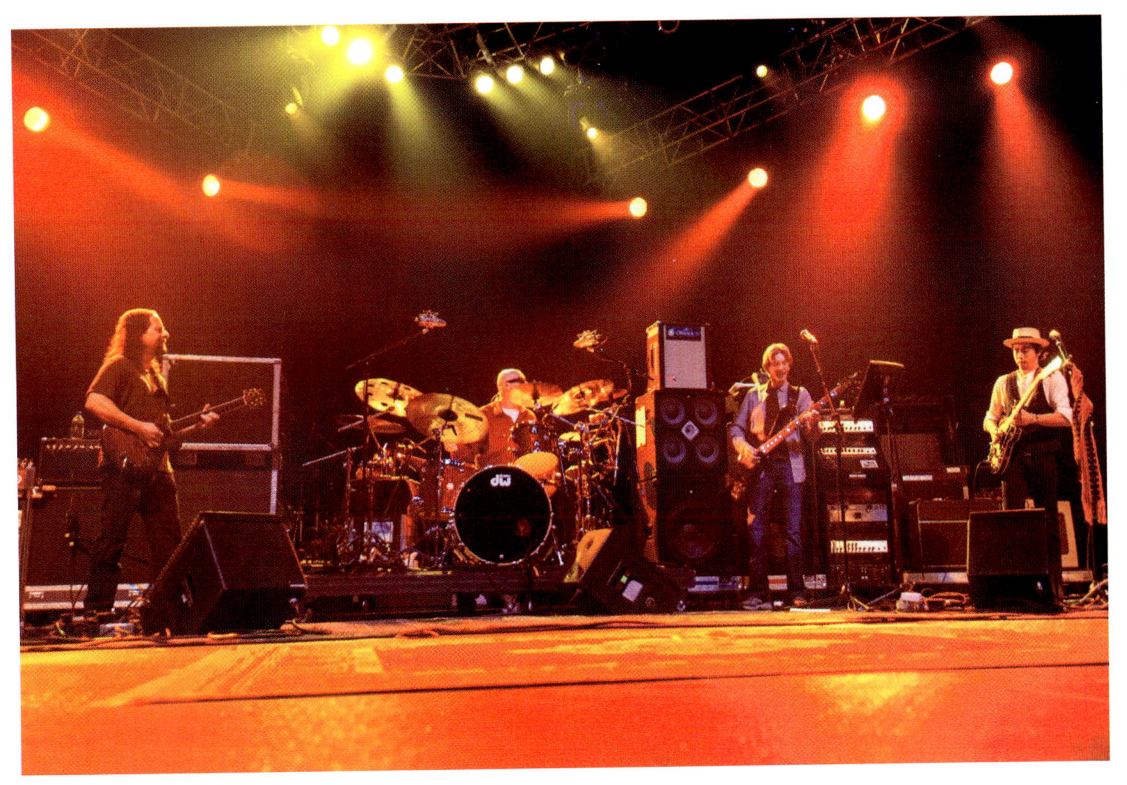

The lighting director is responsible for the visual feel of a show. Here, the reds and yellows create a very warm feel to the stage.

Taken at 1/100 second, f/2.8, and ISO 800

THE LIGHTING DIRECTOR

When it comes to the specific elements of a live show that make it different from sitting at home listening to an album, there are two people handling it, and they usually work from a spot in the middle of the audience. These guys are the front of house crew. At minimum, they're in charge of the sound and the lights.

To a concert-goer, these individuals are equally important; but to a photographer, the lighting director rules the world, because (s)he control the lights.

Some shows have the same songs, choreography, and lights every night at every performance. At others, the lighting director has much more control and can match the lights to the sounds differently every night. One thing to keep in mind is that a good lighting director will do his/her best to make sure that the action is illuminated. So the most important person on the stage at any given time will be the one that's lit the best. This is a good way to choose your shots at a performance hall show and other venues, too.

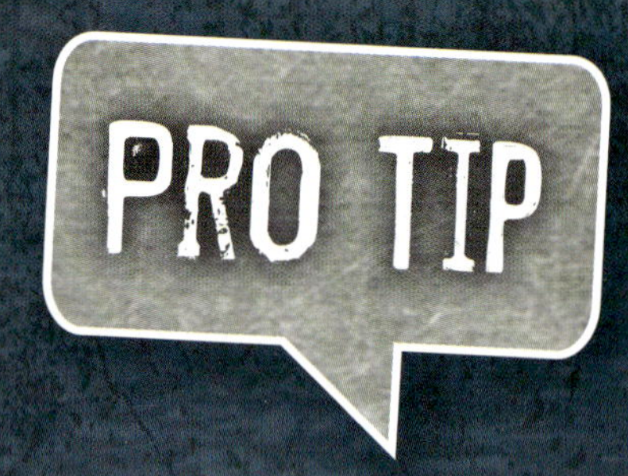

Anthony "GROOVE" Pirrone

Lighting Director

What is your background as a lighting director?

I came to Baltimore in fall of 1995 to go to Radio School and I was an On Air Personality for a year and a half. Wanting to promote local bands, I started going out to clubs to see live shows. One band I saw in late 1996, a seven-piece acid jazz band named Jay Jay, sparked my lighting director fire. So on Valentine's Day 1997, my career as a lighting director began.

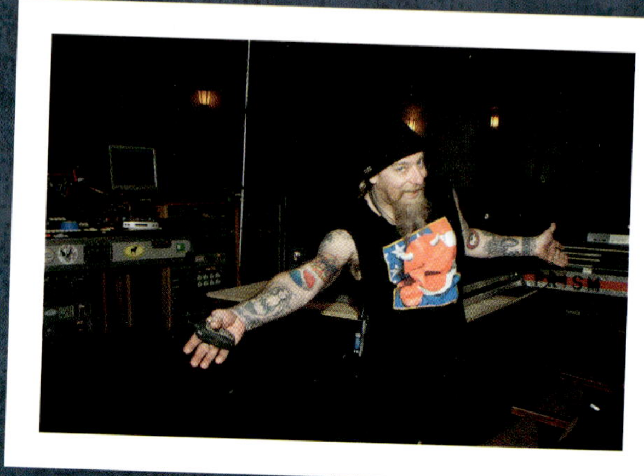

Groove

In 1998 I got tapped by Tim Walther (All Good) to start lighting the shows he was promoting. In September 1999 I filled in on lights for Ziggy Marley and was picked up as the house lighting director for IMP (930 Club). In 2002 I left 930 to start building stages again, but I kept my foot in the door at the 930 Club and mostly worked the sold-out shows or when a band requested me.

This led me to RatDog. After lighting a show for them at 930 Club in 2004, Jay Lane got my info, and two years later I was on the road for The Fall 2006 Tour. I was back on the road with Gogol Bordello in March 2011. I spent that whole summer traveling Europe with Gogol, so I'm now in the International LD Club!

When you light a show, what is the most important thing for you?

When I light a show, I love to make people see what they're hearing.

Do you care about the photographers or the images produced from your shows?

Having many close friends in the picture-takin' biz, I am always concerned that my shows provide lots of depth and textures for them to capture. That way I can see what I've done. It's impossible to pay attention when I'm doing the work, because I'm constantly thinking three steps ahead, like a pool shooter. What the camera captures helps me appreciate the job I'm doing.

Do you ever change the lighting after the first three songs?

I never change the lighting after first three songs, because my whole show is improvisational. I play it like I hear it. So what I do depends on the vibe onstage.

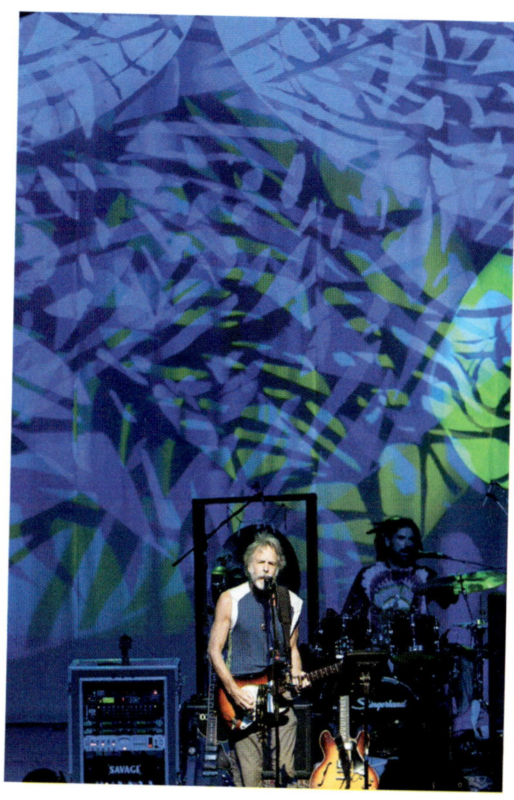

How much input comes from the band compared to what you come up with yourself?

I always invite the band to help me, help them, with suggestions. But due to my reputation, they usually don't keep me on a leash. I've now been at the 930 Club in Baltimore for twelve years, travelled with Bob Weir & RatDog for five years, and I am coming up on my one year anniversary of working with Gogol Bordello. So my career does my talking, and most bands give me the respect I've earned to do my own interpretive dance … with their lights and stage!

Bob Weir
Taken at 1/250 second, f/2.8, and ISO 1600

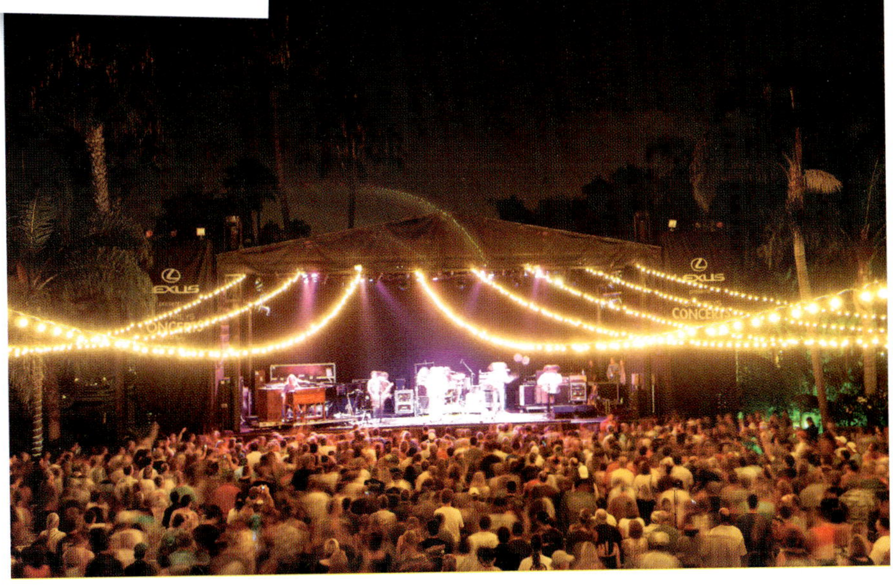

Taken at 3.0 seconds, f/3.2, and ISO 200

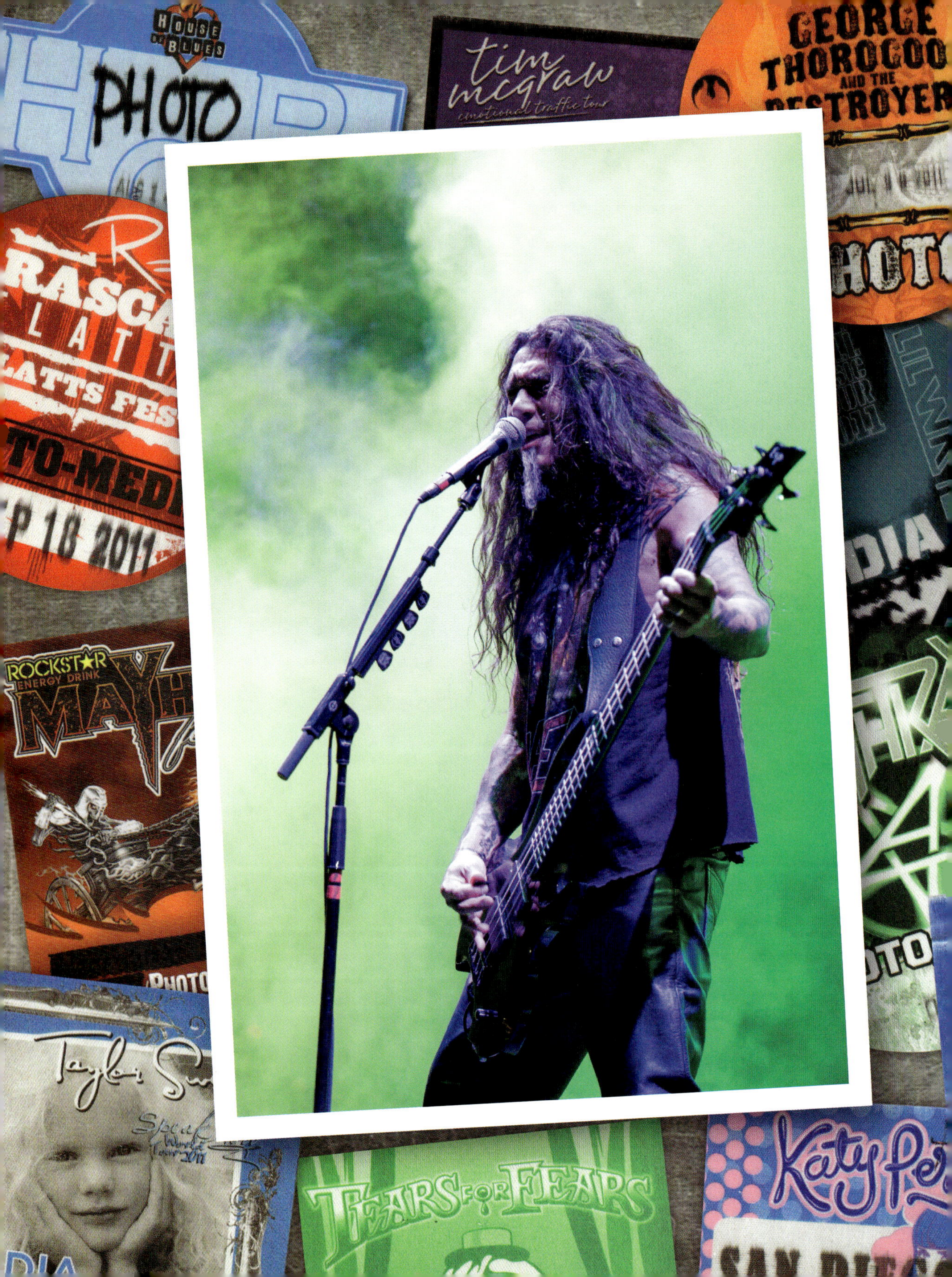

HOUSE OF BLUES
PHOTO
tim mcgraw
emotional traffic tour
GEORGE
AND THE
ROCKSTAR
ENERGY DRINK
PHOTO
TEARS FOR FEARS

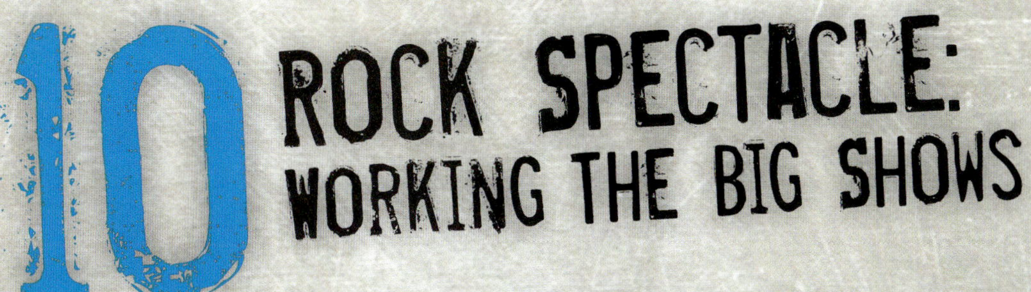

10 ROCK SPECTACLE: WORKING THE BIG SHOWS

Shooting big concerts is what most concert photographers dream about. Great big shows fill amphitheaters and have a buzz about them before the band's tour even starts.

The bigger shows usually come with bigger photo pits, higher profile artists, and a more professional attitude at the shoot. But for a photographer, the best part these shows (technically speaking) is that the lighting is usually really bright; there's no need to push your camera to the higher ISO settings. In fact, you can usually lower the ISO when photographing the big shows.

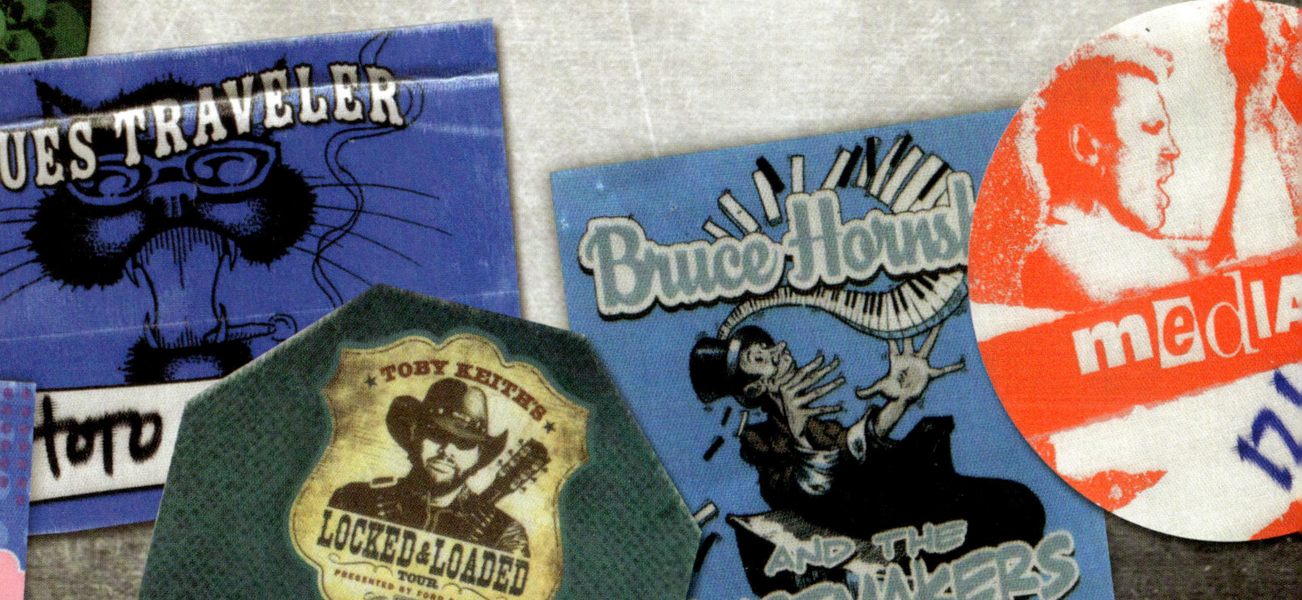

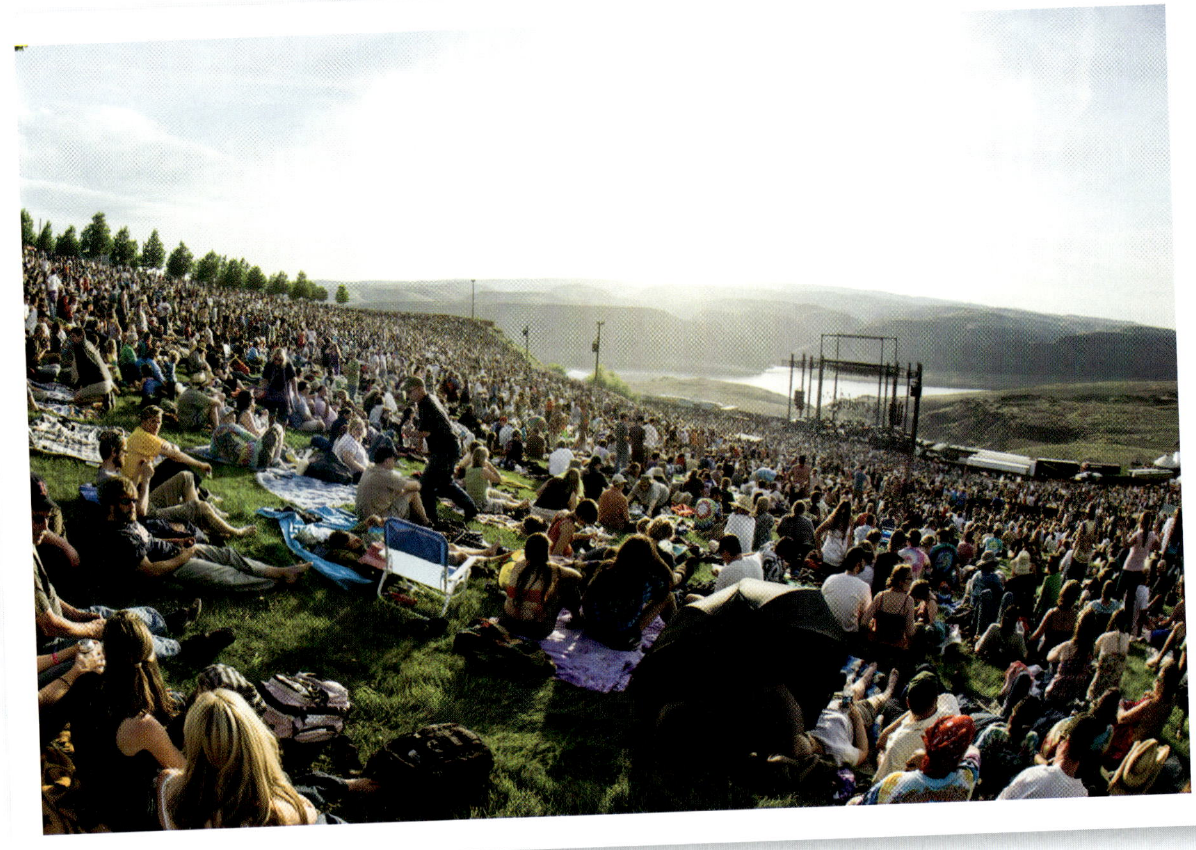

The Dead played its last night of the 2009 tour at The Gorge Amphitheatre, located above the Columbia River in Washington. The 20,000-plus-seat venue is really amazing to see.
Taken at 1/250, f/8.0, and ISO 200

On the downside, it's a lot harder to get permission to photograph these shows if you're not working for one of the bigger news services or magazines. Even once inside, the limited views and the restrictive releases of the big names can make this a tough gig for even the most experienced photographers.

LOVELY LIGHT

After shooting in a bar or a club, you'll feel wholly liberated by the amount of light at a big rock show in an arena or amphitheater. Here, you probably won't need to use the highest ISO settings or try to get the most out of the slowest shutter speed possible. Instead, shooting a big show usually means lots of great light—spotlights, vari-lights, and tons of stage lights.

MY PHOTO BAG: ROCK SPECTACLE

What I take to shoot a big show

Photographing a big show is all about being prepared, because you get only three, maybe two, songs to capture all the shots you need. I usually carry my gear in a large Domke camera bag, because it's easy to get lenses in and out of it. This bag is bigger than my other ones, but the larger venues usually mean larger photo pits and more space.

Here's my packing list for this kind of show:

- 2x dSLR body (a Nikon D700 with the battery grip and a Nikon D3)
- 24-70mm f/2.8 zoom lens
- 70-200mm f/2.8 zoom lens
- 300mm f/4 prime lens
- 16mm f/2.8 fisheye lens

The main gear consists of the 24-70mm f/2.8 lens on one body and the 70-200mm f/2.8 lens on the second body. This provides a wide range of focal lengths without requiring a lens change. And if it looks like the stage is going to be very deep or that the photographers might end up at the soundboard, I pack the 300mm f/4 as well.

I also take along:

- Extra memory cards
- Earplugs
- Extra batteries
- Business cards
- Lens cloth
- Small flashlight

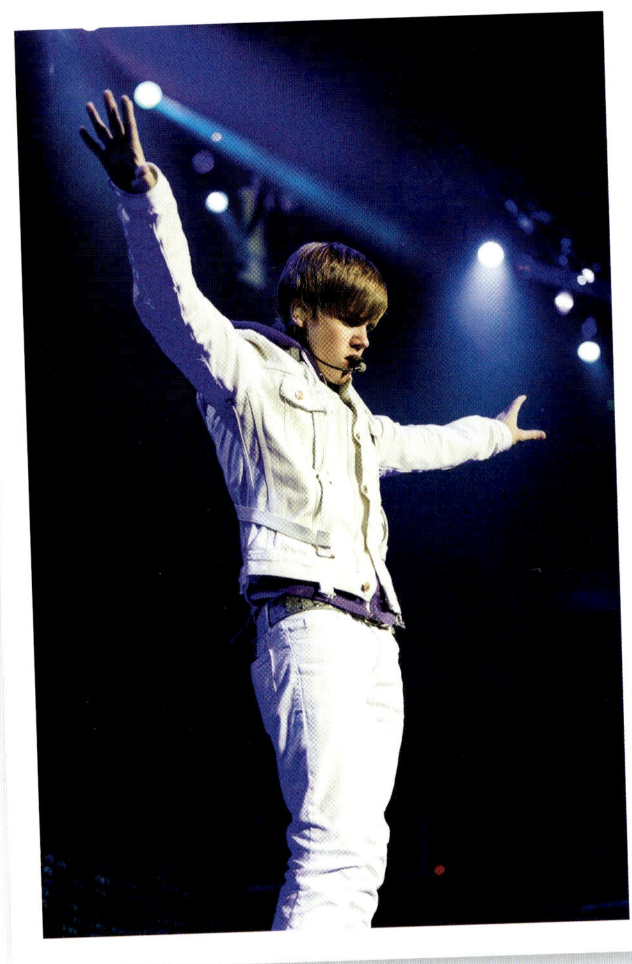

There was enough light to use a 1/400 second shutter speed for this photo of Justin Bieber. Also, I was able to drop the ISO from 1600 to 800 and still get a good exposure.

Taken at 1/400 second, f/2.8, and ISO 800

One reason for all this light at big shows is that they're usually filmed for projection onto screens in the venue, and those cameras need light. Another reason is that more people sit farther away from the action on stage at big venues. Sometimes these fans can only see the light show; the performers are tiny specs in the distance.

Because the light show can be such an integral part of a well-known band's performance, it usually doesn't change much from night to night. And there is very little room for ad-libbing, which means that the light show stays the same throughout a tour. Granted, there are still some bands that change things overnight, but this takes a lot of work, so few groups do this.

LIMITS!

One of the more recent developments I've noticed at the bigger shows is a reduction of shooting time from three songs to two. Another is that photographers can no longer count on a photo pit. Instead, photographers are directed to work from the soundboard. And sometimes it's the worst of both worlds; there are shows at which only two songs (or less) can be photographed … from the soundboard.

The obvious downside of having such a limited time to shoot is that you get less time to get the basic shots. For example, if you're shooting for a guitar magazine, you need to get photos of the guitar player(s). If you're shooting for the venue, then you need photos of the main star and everyone in the band. This can be tough to do in two songs.

But even if you do manage to capture the images you need, it leaves very little time to experiment or try for unique shots. Three songs equals roughly fifteen minutes at a big concert. Each song lasts about five minutes, including any banter. So two songs isn't much time.

At The Dead shows, the actual shooting time for press photographers was a timed fifteen minutes. And those minutes can fly by at the best of times, but when you reduce it to ten minutes or less, the stress can really build. You need to be able to get the most from every second you're allowed to shoot. Here are some tips for maximizing this time.

KNOW YOUR CAMERA.

When you lift your camera to your eye, you need to know how to change the shutter speed and the aperture and even the ISO without looking at the controls. Most dSLR cameras now allow you to customize the controls to suit your needs. So I try to make both cameras I use act the same way … even though they're different models. What I mean is that I set the front dials on each camera to function the same way. Both are set for spot metering; each time I rotate a dial, it adjusts that setting by one-third of a step.

I also set the dial on the back of the camera—the one under my right thumb— to control the shutter speed. If I rotate this dial to the left, the shutter speed decreases. If I rotate it to the right, the shutter speed increases. Easy enough.

Being quick on your feet during a shoot also requires you to understand all the symbols in the viewfinder. You'll work smarter if you know what your camera is doing without taking your eye away from the eyepiece. The information varies from camera to camera, but the basics are shutter speed, aperture, and ISO along with the exposure value, metering mode, shooting mode, and the number of frames left until the buffer and memory card are full. Get very familiar with these symbols before you shoot a big concert, and know what they're telling you.

SET YOUR EXPOSURE IN 30 SECONDS.

Acquiring an instinctual response to exposure takes a bit of practice, but it helps to use the right settings on your camera's LCD screen. When I check the exposure on the back of my camera, I'm looking to make sure that the important elements of a scene are properly exposed. That is, I don't worry about the background exposure or the composition at this point. No time.

The quickest way to see if an area is overexposed is to turn on the Highlight Warning. This will cause the areas of pure white to blink on and off at the back of the screen, so you can see if important areas are overexposed. Also be sure to preview your images at 100% when checking your LCD, because every image looks great at three inches on the back of a camera. On the back of my camera is a button that, with one push, provides a full-size preview of an image, so I can quickly look at the critical areas and adjust exposure settings if necessary.

If the image looks too bright, then use a faster shutter speed. If it's too dark, use a longer shutter speed … unless that will introduce blurring. If blurring is likely at a long shutter speed, then increase the ISO or open up the lens, if possible. But again, if you're shooting a big-name show, there will probably be enough light and your exposure problem will be overexposure. So be sure to dial in the right shutter speed and ISO to get the shot you envision.

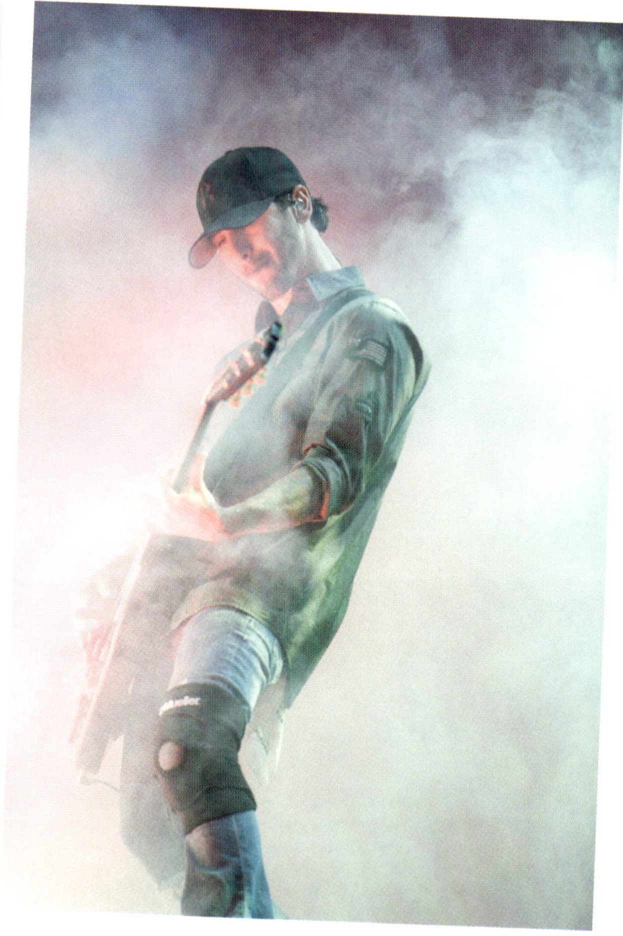

The heavy smoke used at the beginning of the Godsmack set made it tough to get the proper exposure. But when I looked at the image on the back of my camera, none of the important parts were blinking, so I knew I was good.
Taken at 1/500, f/2.8, and ISO 1600

STUDY THE BAND.

The upside to shooting a band that has been photographed a lot is that images are available to study. Take time to look at existing photos and use the information to determine the best position for capturing the action right from the start.

If the act is a band, you can probably figure out where the members will stand. If the act is a solo musician, then try to determine where (s)he'll be standing, based on a typical setup. Some acts put large instruments, like pianos, up front; being on the wrong side of that can be detrimental. So, if possible, look at the current tour set lists to see if the same songs are being played in the same order every night. This can help you figure out where to stand in order to capture the best shots.

HAVE A PLAN.

As mentioned, it really helps to step into a photo pit with a plan of what you want to shoot. Of course, that plan needs to be simple and flexible, but it needs to be well considered and top of mind. Think about who you're shooting for and what image(s) they need. This usually means getting a shot of the main performers, starting with the most famous and working your way through the band.

If the concert is single-person act (like Ricky Martin, Katy Perry, or Justin Bieber), then stay focused on the main performer while you shoot. But try to change angles so that all your shots don't look the same. If the act is a band, try to get in position to capture all the members. If the

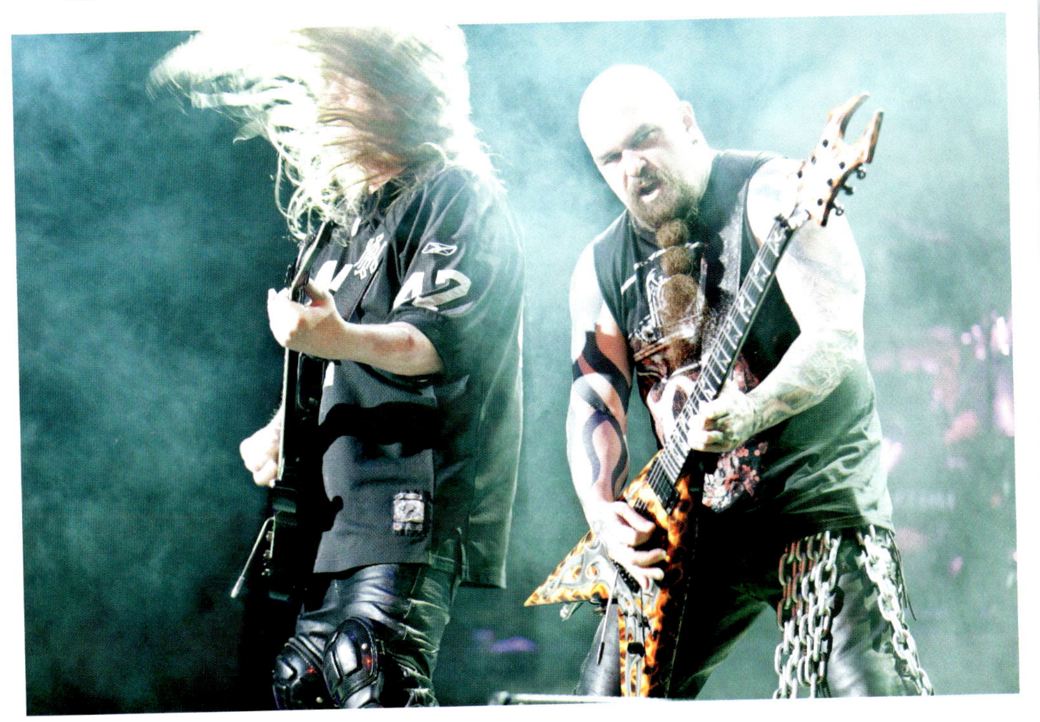

I was shooting Slayer from Kerry King's side of the stage with no way to get over to the other side when Jeff Hanneman walked over, allowing me to get both guitarists in the same frame. This is when it pays to be ready to take the shot no matter how frustrated you might be about your position.

Taken 1/80 second, f/2.8, and ISO 1600

available angles from your position don't allow for that, then focus on the members that you can see. The point is to get as many different kinds of great shots as you can.

Having limited time to shoot in a photo pit is better, in my opinion, than unlimited shooting from the soundboard or some other designated location farther back from the stage. Unfortunate positioning for photographers seems to be getting more common though … unfortunately. For instance, Lady Gaga restricts photographers to the back of the floor; Lil Wayne puts us at the soundboard; and Ricky Martin positions photographers on a platform behind the soundboard.

A longer lens will get you in close, but that's only part of the problem. The bigger deal is that photographers can't move, so all the images of a show look the same. It's much harder to get a great, unique shot when you're standing in the exact same position as everyone else. But this is when it pays to have a great sense of timing. Keep your eye to the camera, follow the action through the lens, and take as many shots as possible to capture a great shot that no one else will get.

CAMERA SETTINGS

As I've mentioned, the initial camera settings for my cameras are shutter speed 1/160 second, f/2.8, and ISO 1600. For many of the larger shows, these settings will cause images to be overexposed due to the brighter lights and use of follow spots.

The easiest way to adjust the exposure is to use a faster shutter speed. This means one adjustment. This also works great for capturing faster-moving subjects and, since digital noise at

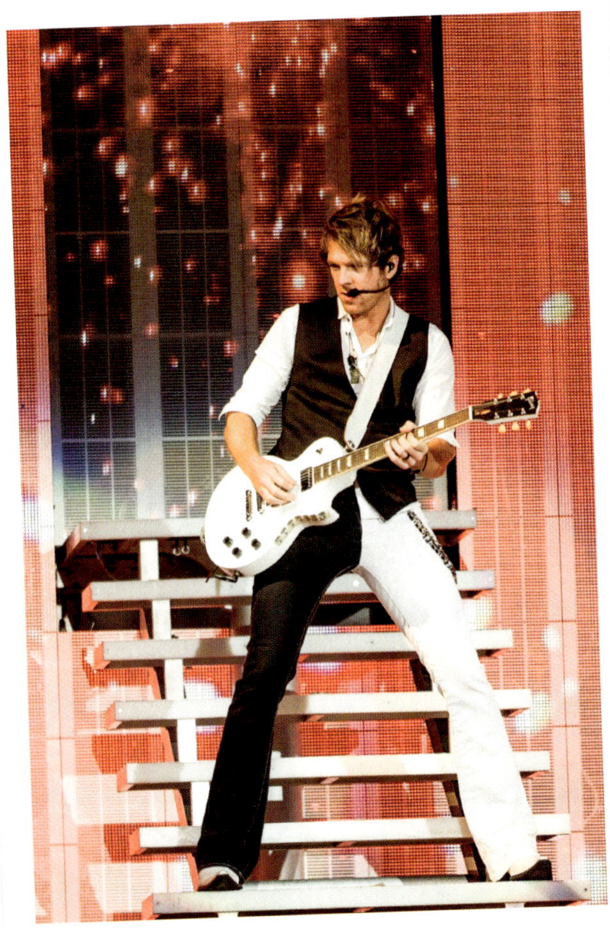

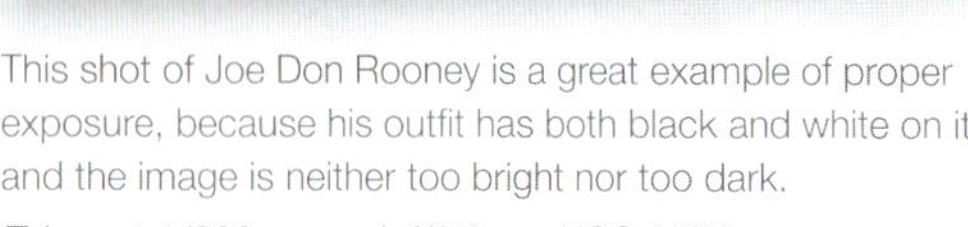

This shot of Joe Don Rooney is a great example of proper exposure, because his outfit has both black and white on it and the image is neither too bright nor too dark.

Taken at 1/800 second, f/2.8, and ISO 1600

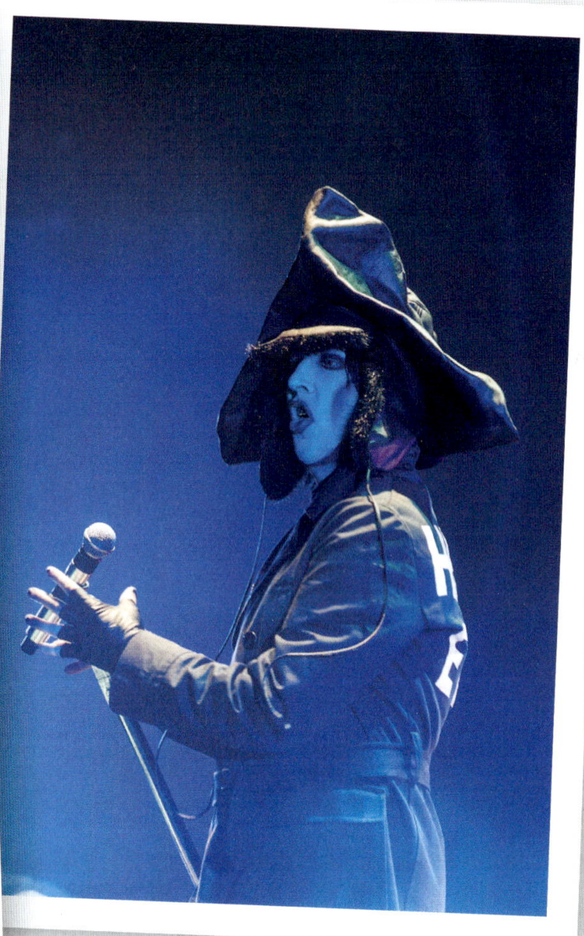

Moments before the curtain fell to open the show, Marilyn Manson gets ready to rock the crowd. I adjusted the aperture and then the shutter speed to get the right exposure for this shot.

Taken at 1/320 second, f/3.5, and ISO 1600

higher ISO settings is so much less visible in newer cameras than in older models, the use of ISO 1600 should not be a problem if you have a camera that was made after 2010 or thereabouts.

The image of Joe Don Rooney is a great example of this technique. There was plenty of light at the Rascal Flatts show, so instead of using a smaller aperture or a lower ISO to get the shots, I kept using faster shutter speeds … until I was shooting at 1/800 of a second. This allowed in the right amount of light and froze the action for crisp shots.

But sometimes you want to use a smaller aperture to get a deeper depth of field. In this case, just set the aperture you want and then find the shutter speed you need to freeze the action. Finally, adjust the ISO to get a proper exposure. The brighter lights of the big shows makes this possible.

For the Marilyn Manson photo, I started at 1/160 second and then decreased the aperture to f/3.5. I increased the shutter speed to 1/320 second and left the ISO alone.

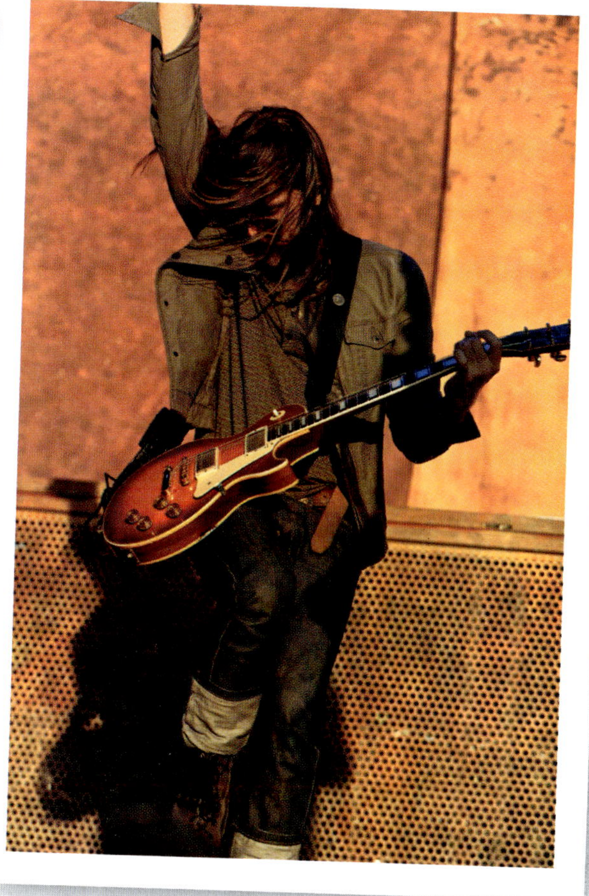

Photographing a big show that starts in the afternoon can result in some very bright lights. This is Chris Traynor from the band Bush.
Taken at 1/2000 second, f/3.5, and ISO 320

When there's a lot of light—and I mean a ton of bright, late afternoon light—you can increase the shutter speed, decrease the ISO, and use smaller apertures. The basics are the same: Get the aperture right, and then increase the shutter speed and decrease the ISO until the three settings are right to give you a proper exposure.

From my starter settings (1/160 second, f/2.8, and ISO 1600), when shooting in bright light, the first thing I do is to change the aperture a little (usually to f/3.5). I then increase the shutter speed to 1/500 second and begin decreasing the ISO (to 400). Finally, I increase the shutter speed until I get the proper exposure. If I get to 1/2000 second shutter speed, I'll decrease the ISO even more. Try to keep the lens wide open to have a background that's nicely blurred.

It gets easier to judge the lights as you get more experience. But when starting out, use the spot meter focused on the critical area to get an idea of the correct exposure. Take a look back at Chapter 5 for a refresher on exposure tools and settings.

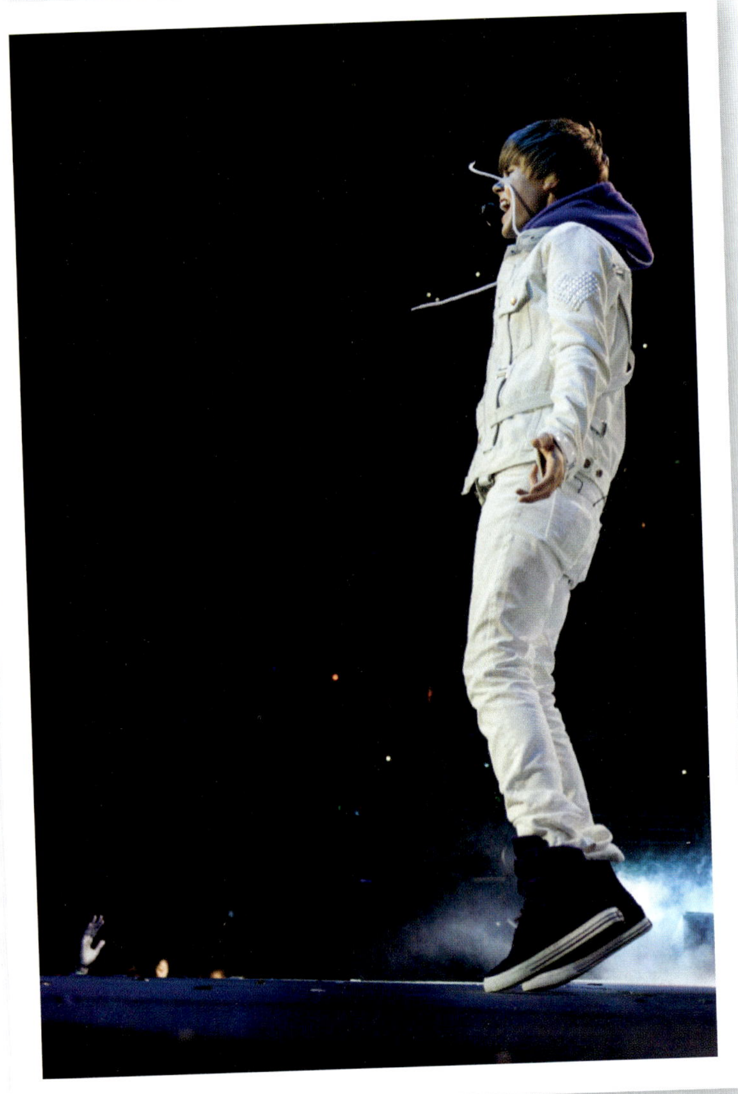

Earlier in this chapter is a photo of Justin Bieber in concert. It was taken from close to the center of the stage, and I'm pretty sure that every photographer there got the same shot. Well, this image was taken at the same show but at a very different shooting position. I moved all the way to the side and tried to get a different angle on the same performer.

Taken at 1/500 second, f/3.5, and ISO 800

STAND-OUT SHOTS

One of the problems you can have when shooting a big concert is that so many photographs of the act have already been taken over the years. Getting a unique shot is difficult. In fact, it's often difficult to get a shot that's much different from the other photographers at the same show ... or those who shot the previous night's show or the ones who will shoot the next night. Everyone's capturing the same songs with the same lighting and the same stage antics as you are on a given night.

When I photographed Toby Keith on his last tour, for instance, the intro to the show was the same night after night. The fireworks show was the same, and the video screens showed the same images. The performance was so predictable that one of the crew members warned me about a few loud bangs and told me when they would occur. This is not necessarily a bad thing for a performance, but it can make it difficult to get a unique shot.

Here are some things you can do to increase the chance of getting a shot that's different from other photographers.

DISTANCE YOURSELF FROM THE PACK.

I cannot tell you how many times I've been in the photo pit and seen a clump of photographers in the same area, working on the same shot. If you're trying to get a different shot, you need to take some risks and shoot from different angles.

Depending on who you're shooting for, it's not always possible to ignore the standard shots though. You may be expected to deliver these. But once you have them, look to use as much of the photo pit area as you can. Go to the left or the right and shoot across the stage. If you've been shooting from the sides, work your way into the middle to get a different perspective on the action.

CHANGE YOUR FOCAL LENGTH.

If you usually shoot in tight, try to go wide angle. If you usually shoot wide, crop in tight. The idea is to change the way you typically shoot and to try different focal lengths. When right up close, a fisheye lens comes in handy.

When you're shooting big shows, it's not the time to try new things for the first time. That's what your gigs in bars and clubs are for. When shooting a big show, you need to know what you're doing from the minute you arrive and act professionally the whole time. This is the big time, so be ready and do your thing.

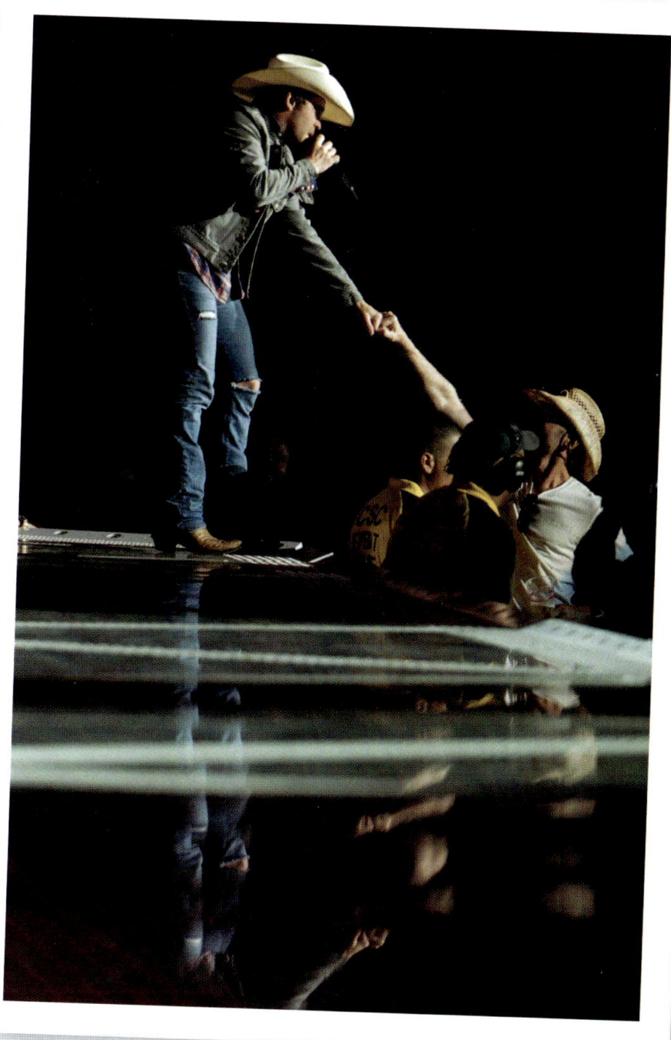

Instead of zooming all the way in and filling the frame with the performer, I chose to stay zoomed out and worked on capturing a mirror image of the action on the reflective stage.

Taken at 1/250 second, f/2.8, and ISO 1600

Charles Jischke

www.cfjphoto.com

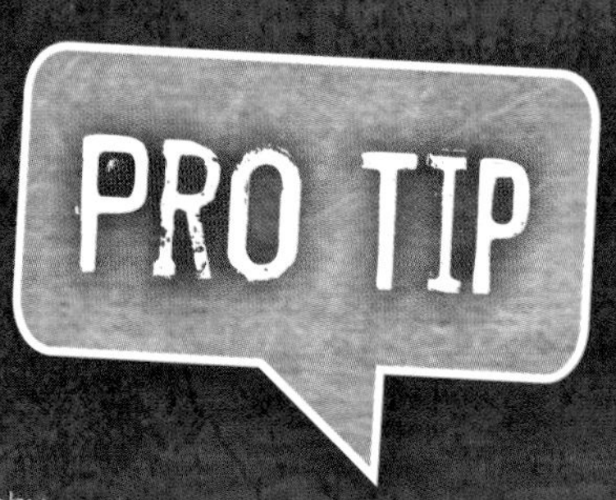

How did you get started in this business?

I fell in love with photography in high school, where I somehow convinced our art teacher, Ms. Gugel, to extend the original four-semester curriculum into seven semesters of black and white photography.

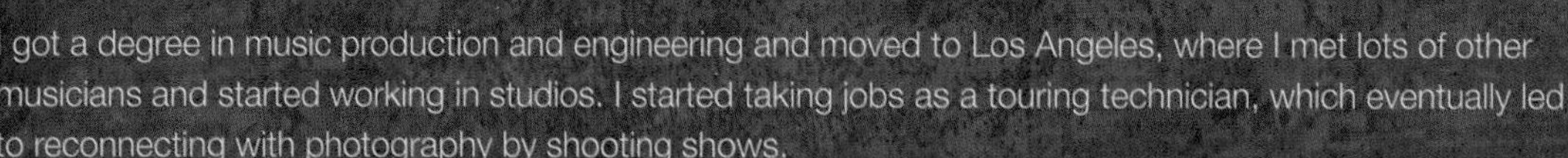

I got a degree in music production and engineering and moved to Los Angeles, where I met lots of other musicians and started working in studios. I started taking jobs as a touring technician, which eventually led to reconnecting with photography by shooting shows.

How long have you been shooting concerts and what was your first show?

The first shows that I shot were for a band called The Flying Tigers, in 2002. I landed a job as a tech/stage manager, and I thought it would be cool to shoot pics during the shows. Coming from a background in music, the combination of the two art forms was perfect for me. And the immediacy of digital photography gave me the near-instant gratification that working with music didn't always provide.

What are your starting settings? Exposure modes and metering mode?

I shoot with a fully manual exposure 99.9% of the time. I typically start with settings at ISO 1250 and f/2.8 at 1/200 second. I then adjust them based on what I'm getting from the lighting rig by checking my LCD screen and histograms. I'm currently shooting a Nikon D3s, and high-ISO noise is not really an issue. It is an incredible camera for shooting shows. I use the camera's auto focus system and only use manual focus when the lens is really having issues finding its target. Some of the time I use all 51 points of the auto focus system, but when I can see the exact composition I'm looking for in advance, I'll go down to a single focus point and position it in the viewfinder.

How many shots do you take during an average show?

For a typical show, I'll end up with anywhere from 500 to 1000 exposures. Because musicians are really active on stage and their expressions/positions can change very quickly, I give myself more opportunities to get that perfect moment by shooting high-speed bursts. I also come a bit from Moose Peterson's school of thinking, which is: hard drive space is cheap. The first frame of a burst often has slight blur from pressing the shutter button, and it's sort of like giving yourself an instant backup of a pic (on the off-chance a file gets corrupted).

What is your post production workflow?

I almost exclusively work within Adobe Lightroom and only turn to Photoshop when an image really needs to be altered. But this is a very rare occurrence.

After importing the photos into Lightroom, my process starts by quickly going through all of the shots and selecting the good ones (including possible duplicates) by flagging them as a pick (P key). I then create a collection within the Lightroom library for that individual show and add the flagged shots. After that, I go through the picks and develop the ones I feel are best. I give the fully developed pics a rating of 1 to 3 stars and deliver these to the client.

Once the band or its management picks photos, I rate those files as 4 stars and output them for whatever use they need. This allows me to quickly go back and find what pics they used and still provide further options if they want to revisit the photos at a later time. My entire process takes 1–2 hours per show.

What tip can you give a photographer starting out in the concert photography business?

Developing trust is the single greatest thing you can do with an artist. Artists, bands, and managers are quite conscious of image, so demonstrating to them that you are 100% on their side is critical. This means delivering good photos that show the artists in their best light, and also not being intrusive or getting in the way of the concert's production. You need to create a dialog that allows you to find out what the band (or your client) wants and needs.

A more practical tip I'd give someone who's getting started is to always be conscious of the venue. As a touring photographer, you're given new venues every day. Some halls have huge, amazing lighting rigs, while others offer virtually nothing but a cavern of black. Some old theaters have beautiful, ornate walls; others are filled with eyesores like bright signs advertising beer, the exits, etc. Sometimes you're shooting at sunset, broad daylight, or with a beautiful city in the background. And occasionally, you'll find yourself shooting an event with 100,000-plus people. See what advantages and disadvantages the venue has and approach your shoot accordingly.

Here are a few suggestions:

- **Big lighting rig with fog:** Shoot wide-angle shots that show the leading lines and colors of the lights.
- **Small lighting rig or no fog:** Shoot tighter, cropped shots. Look for detail shots.
- **Daylight or sunset shoot:** Shoot from behind and create silhouettes of the most recognizable band members
- **Giant festival crowds:** Shoot from the sides with a wide lens to show the artist in command of the massive crowd.

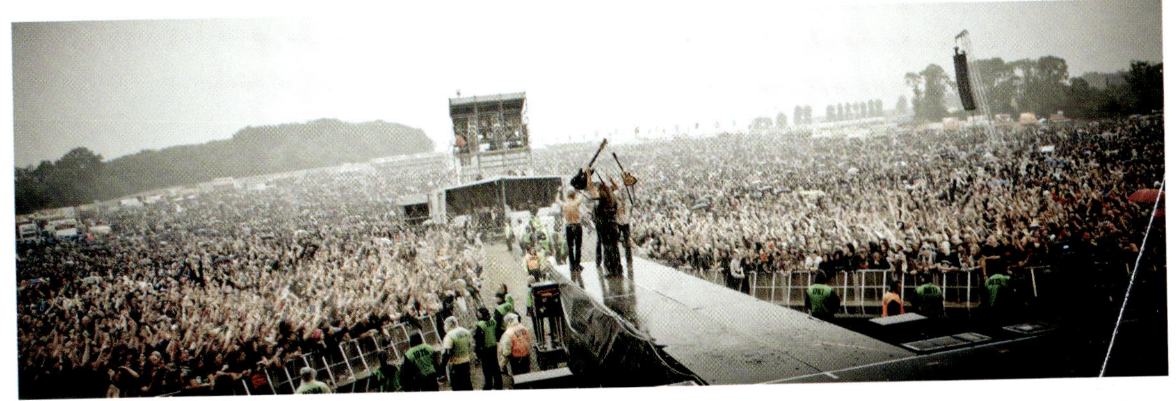

© Charles Jischke

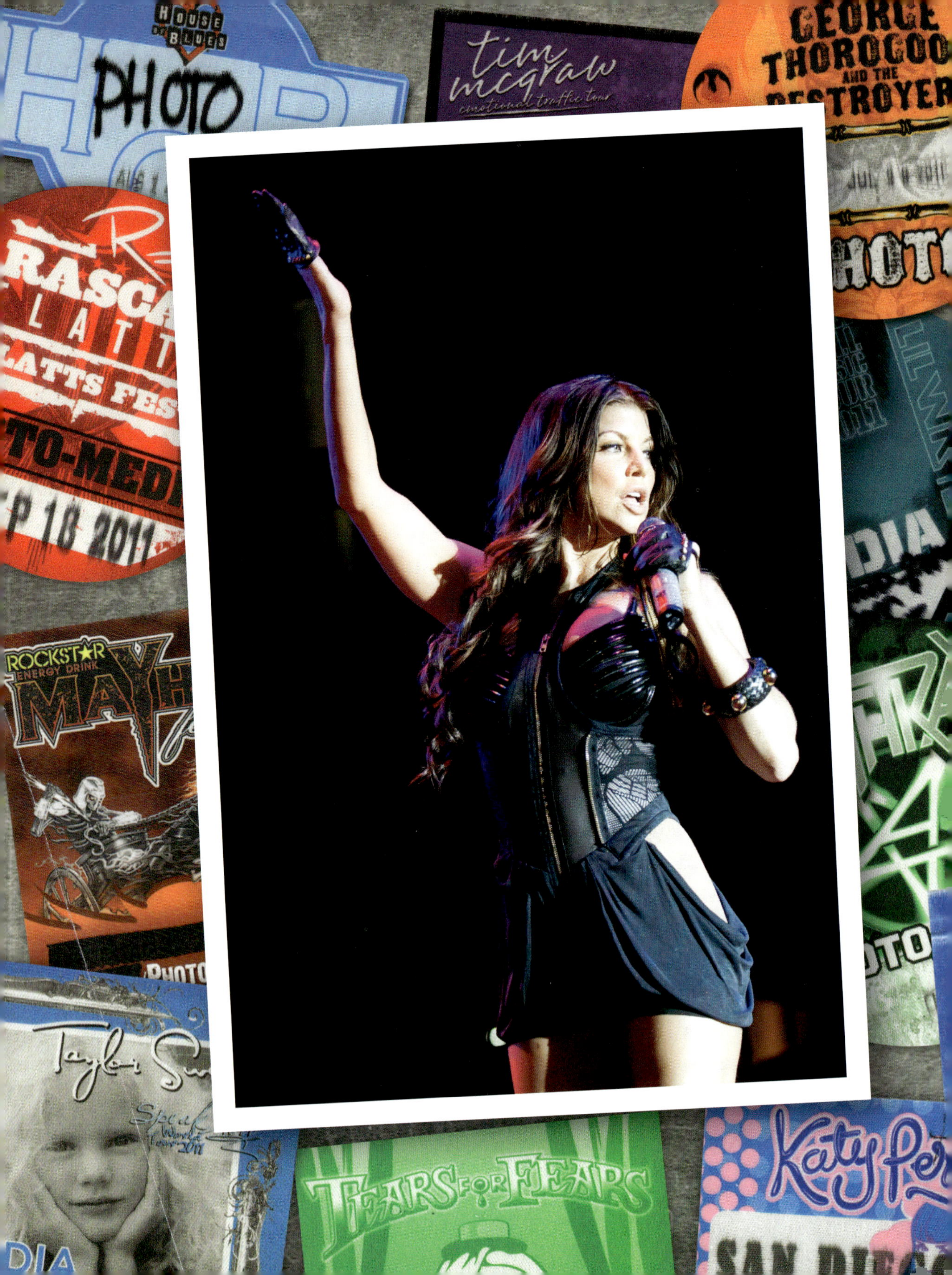
HOUSE OF BLUES
PHOTO
tim mcgraw
emotional traffic tour
THOROGOO
AND THE
ROCKSTAR ENERGY DRINK
TEARS FOR FEARS

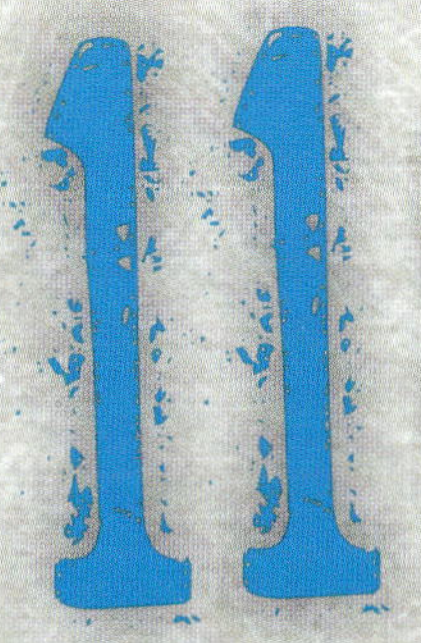

AN ALL-DAY PARTY: SHOOTING FESTIVALS

My favorite type of concert shoot is a multi-band, all-day festival. The reason is really simple: I get to photograph many different bands in a relatively short period of time. At a recent festival, I got to photograph ten different bands in about eight hours. That's a lot of concert shooting in a compressed amount of time.

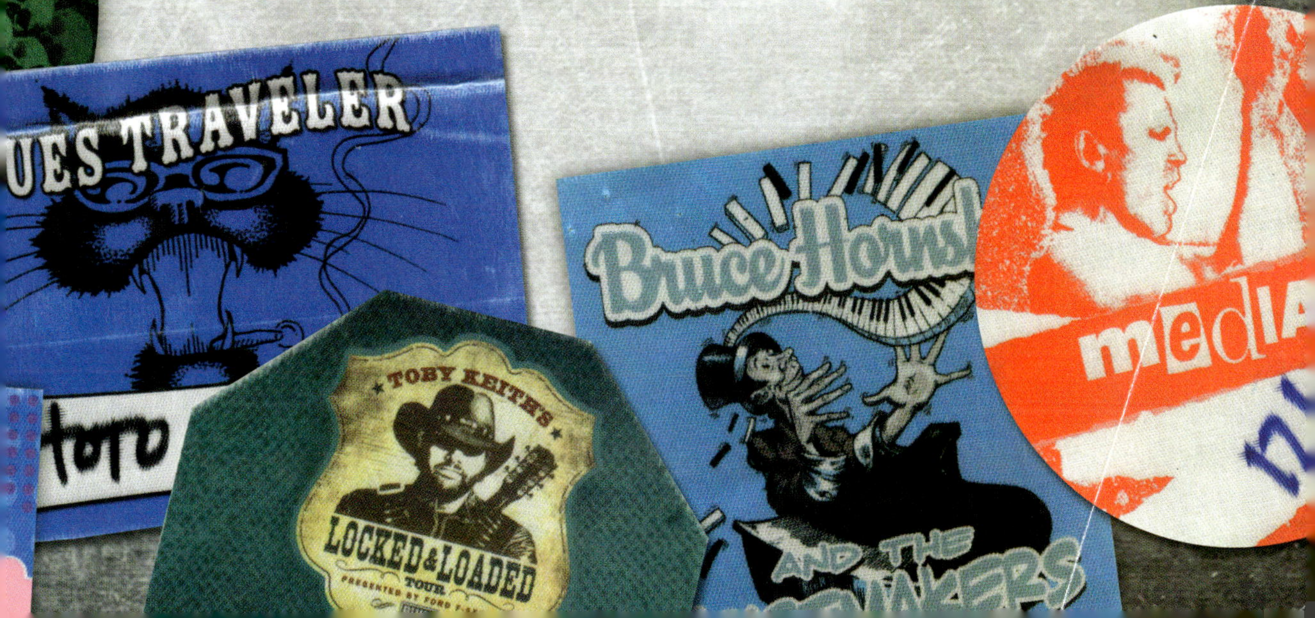

The lighting can be problematic at these events, and there are usually a lot of other photographers working the same show, but being able to shoot a bunch of bands in a single day is just plain awesome. So the lighting thing is not *that* big of an issue, especially considering the terrific access to musicians.

Festivals come in all shapes and sizes. The smaller local festivals can be a great place to shoot ... even if you're not a credentialed photographer. Many of the smaller festivals allow photography from the audience, which means you can get in a lot of shooting practice without being affiliated with a publication.

And don't overlook the music component to other types of festivals, too, including neighborhood street fairs and county fairs. These photo opportunities might not be on the same level of excitement and prestige as a large touring festival, but the approach to photographing them is similar.

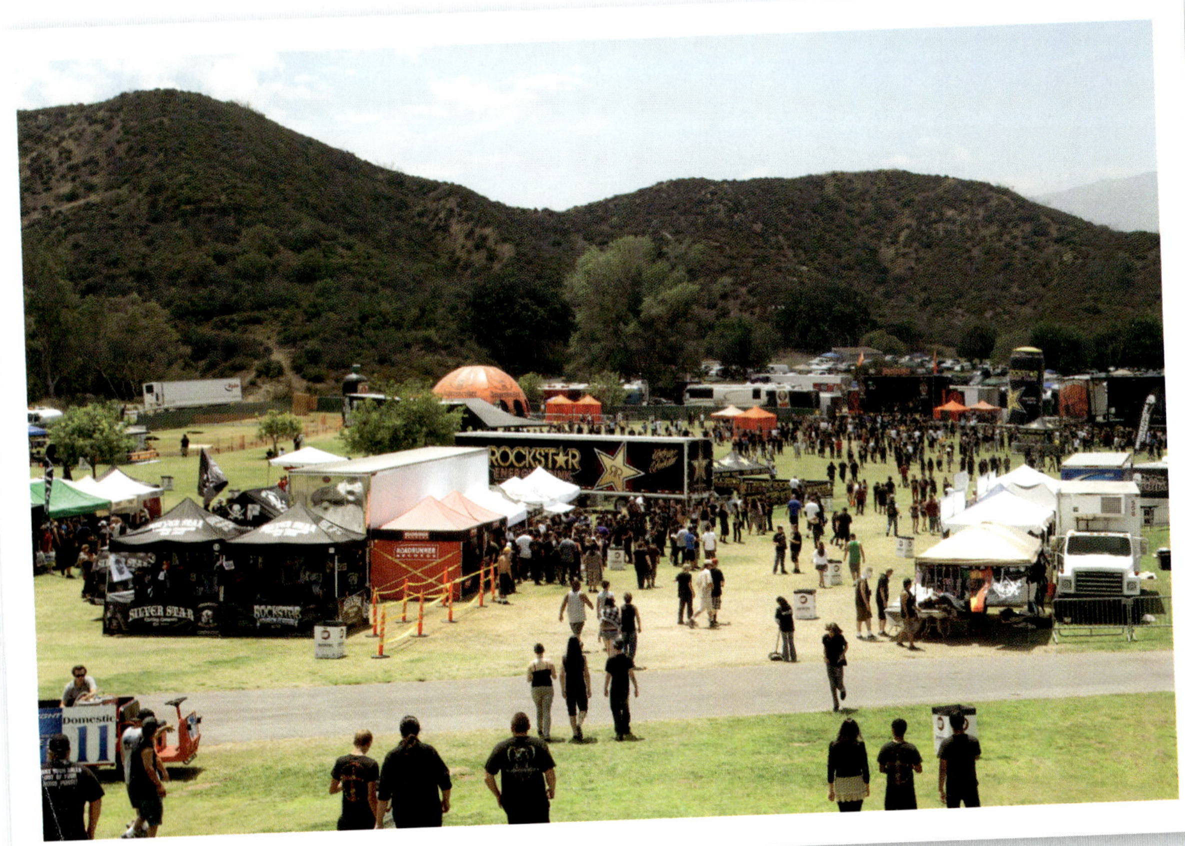

The Rockstar Mayhem Festival is a huge show that I have the privilege to shoot every year for PR Photo wire service. There are usually three stages, and getting to them all can be a hike. If you look at the distance, you can see the two side stages.

Taken at 1/320 second, f/8.5, and ISO 200

MY PHOTO BAG: FESTIVALS

What I take to shoot an all-day festival

Photographing a festival means a lot of gear. Not only do I carry the camera gear needed to shoot the event, but I also usually carry a laptop to begin the importing, editing, and uploading process while on location.

I carry all the gear in a ThinkTankPhoto Shape Shifter bag, which seems to be just about perfect for this type of shooting. It holds two dSLR bodies, three lenses, a laptop, and a whole bunch of extra gear.

Here's the list:

- 2x dSLR body (a Nikon D700 with the battery grip and a Nikon D3)
- 24-70mm f/2.8 zoom lens
- 70-200mm f/2.8 zoom lens
- 16mm Fisheye lens
- 300mm f/4 prime lens
- Extra memory cards
- Earplugs
- Extra batteries
- Business cards
- Lens cloth
- Small flashlight
- Flash
  * This is packed when I think it will be possible to meet the band and maybe do a quick portrait:
  - Apple MacBook Pro 15"
  - Power cord
  - Firewire 800 card reader
  - Portable hardrive for backups
  - Security cable to lock laptop to table
  - Small Monster cable powerstrip
  - Couple of protein bars

COMFORTABLE SHOES

All-day festivals involve a lot of walking and standing ... and more walking ... and more standing. A good pair of shoes is an absolute necessity. I'm a fan of Merrell hiking boots, and I wear a pair of the company's lightweight boots at all festival shoots. When combined with a pair of good hiking socks, my feet are usually tired (but not sore) after a long day of walking between stages and the press area.

It's important to know that you'll be doing a lot of walking at these events, even if it's just between the photo pit and a press tent. And if there are multiple stages spread out with acts you want to photograph on all of them, you might walk miles carrying your gear at a festival, which sometimes extend multiple days!

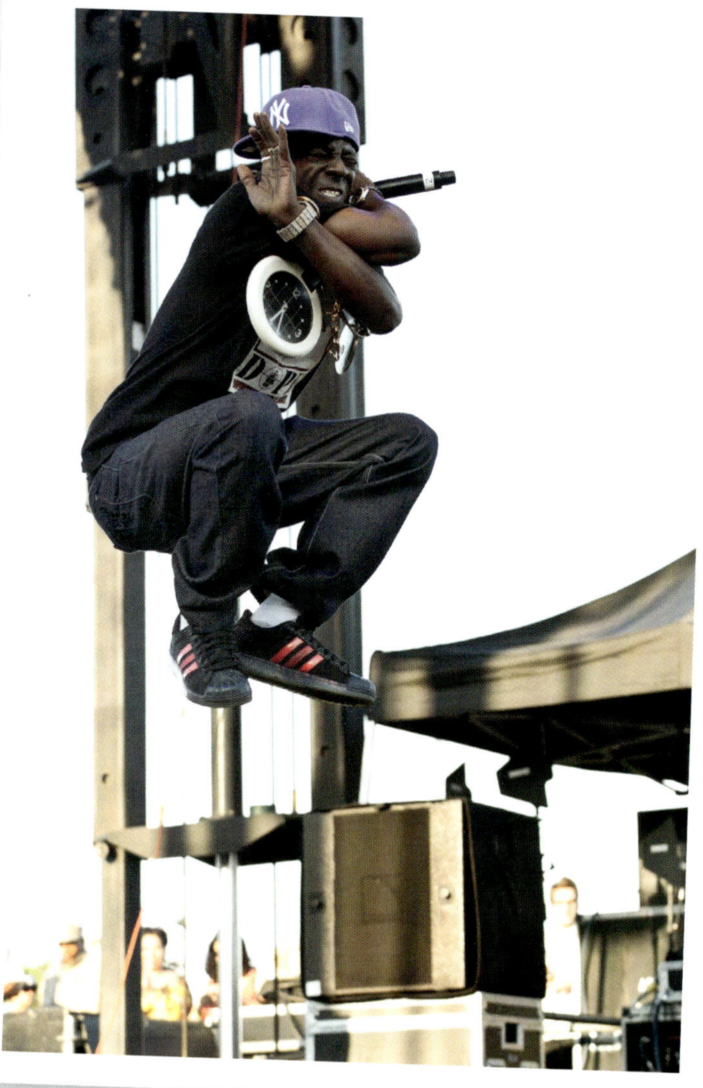

When Public Enemy finally took the stage at the San Diego Street Scene in 2009, the photographers had been standing in a crowded pit for 45 minutes or so without moving. I can't tell you how happy I was to have comfortable shoes on my feet during the wait. Here, Flavor Flav gets a little air during the performance. To me, this shot made the wait worthwhile.

Taken at 1/320 second, f/4.0, and ISO 400

PICKS

Many of the all-day festivals have multiple bands playing at the same time on different stages. Sometimes the performance areas are really far apart, making it impossible to photograph all the bands at a festival. This means you need to pick the bands you want to photograph—and the ones you're alright with missing. Quite a lot goes into deciding which bands to photograph and which to skip.

The following list of considerations helps me decide what to cover:

- **Who am I shooting for?**
  If covering an event for the wire service, then make sure you cover the bands that are most popular or in the news. If shooting for a specific band, then you obviously need to be sure to cover that performance. If shooting for a magazine or other type of publication, check with the assignment editor to find out what (s)he needs.
- **Am I the first or second shooter?**
  Sometimes more than one photographer from a single outlet will be working a festival, and the shooters divide the bands to be covered. Usually the first (or main) photographer gets to pick the bands (s)he wants to photograph, and the second shooter makes sure that the other acts are covered. The second also acts as a backup on the main acts. When working as a second shooter, it's a good idea to check in periodically with the main photographer to make sure you both know what to cover.
- **Which bands do I like/want to shoot?**
  I started photographing concerts because I'm a huge fan of live music. So when I get to choose which band(s) to shoot, I will always try to pick the one(s) I like best or have always wanted to shoot. Photographing bands you like usually results in better images, too, because you're familiar with the music and musicians, which helps you better time your shots.

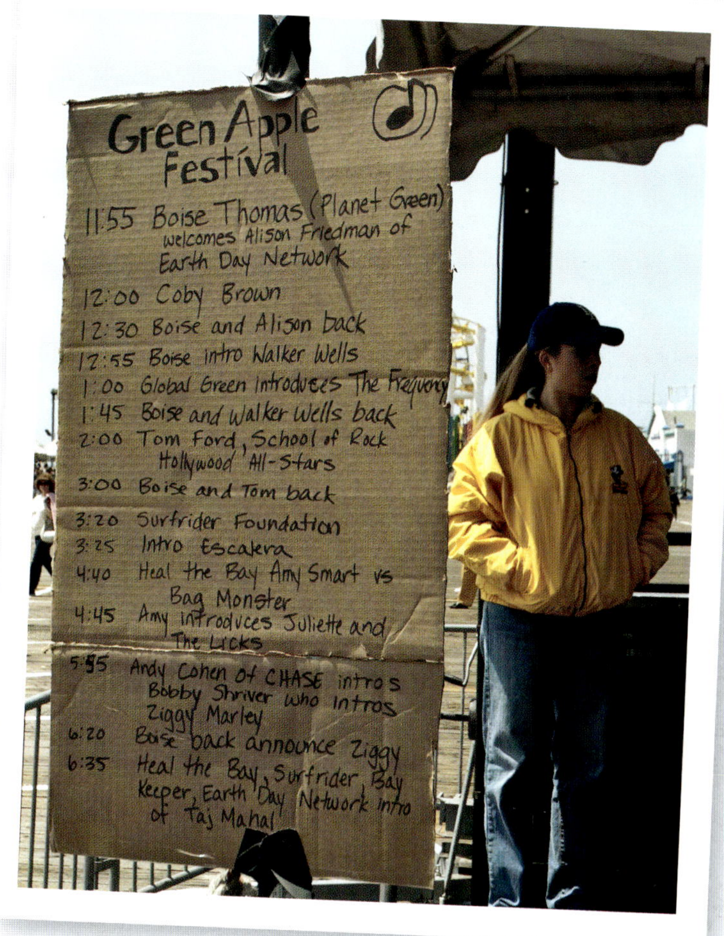

Not every festival has a nice printed schedule, but you can usually find one posted at the main soundboard. Take a quick photo of it with your cell phone so you'll have access to it all day. At the Green Apple Music Festival in 2008, the engineers got tired of answering questions about the schedule, so they posted a handwritten copy of it at the soundboard.

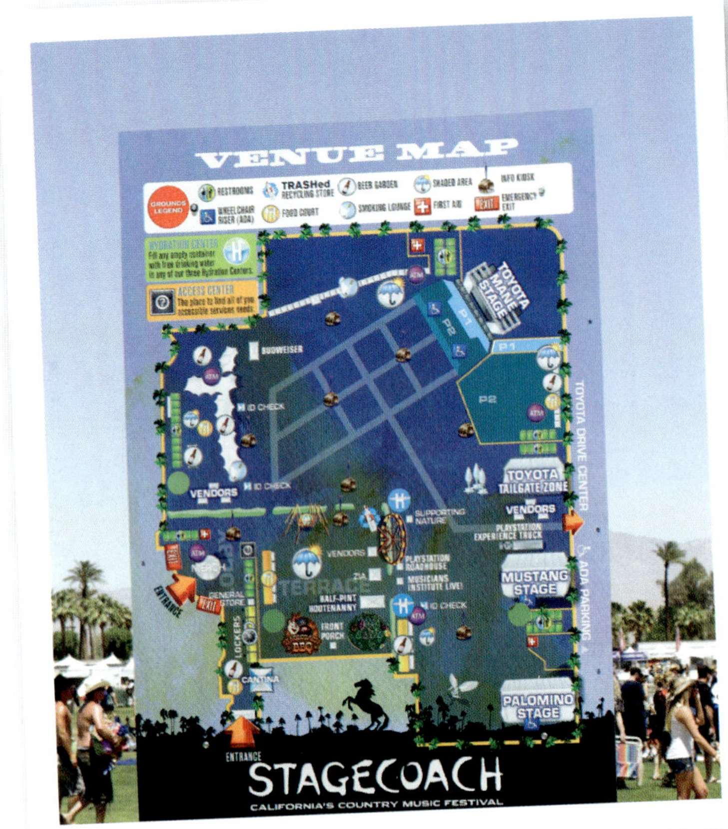

Here's the map to Stagecoach: California's Country Music Festival in 2011. There were three different stages to find. I took a photo of this map on my cell phone, so I could access it at any time.

- **What will result in the best images?** If a group of bands are playing and I'm free to choose which to photograph, I tend to pick the ones I think will give me the best shots. A little time spent looking at images on a band's website can help you know what to expect.

A key piece of information you need when shooting a festival and deciding what bands to photograph is the performance schedule, which usually includes a map to tell you which stage is which. Use this information to plan out where to be at any given time.

Some festivals are easier to navigate than others. At a recent festival, for example, the stage was set up on a rotating device that allowed a second stage to be prepared while the first stage was being used. This allowed changes between bands to clock in at less than ten minutes. For me, this meant no long treks; but the moment a band ended, I needed to be ready to enter the photo pit for the start of the next band.

For festivals that do require long walks between stages, keep in mind that as the day goes on, and more festival goers arrive on the scene, it will take longer for you to get around. This can be a hard lesson to learn, so make sure that you leave enough time to get from one stage to another. The routes you take early in the day might not be available as the crowd grows.

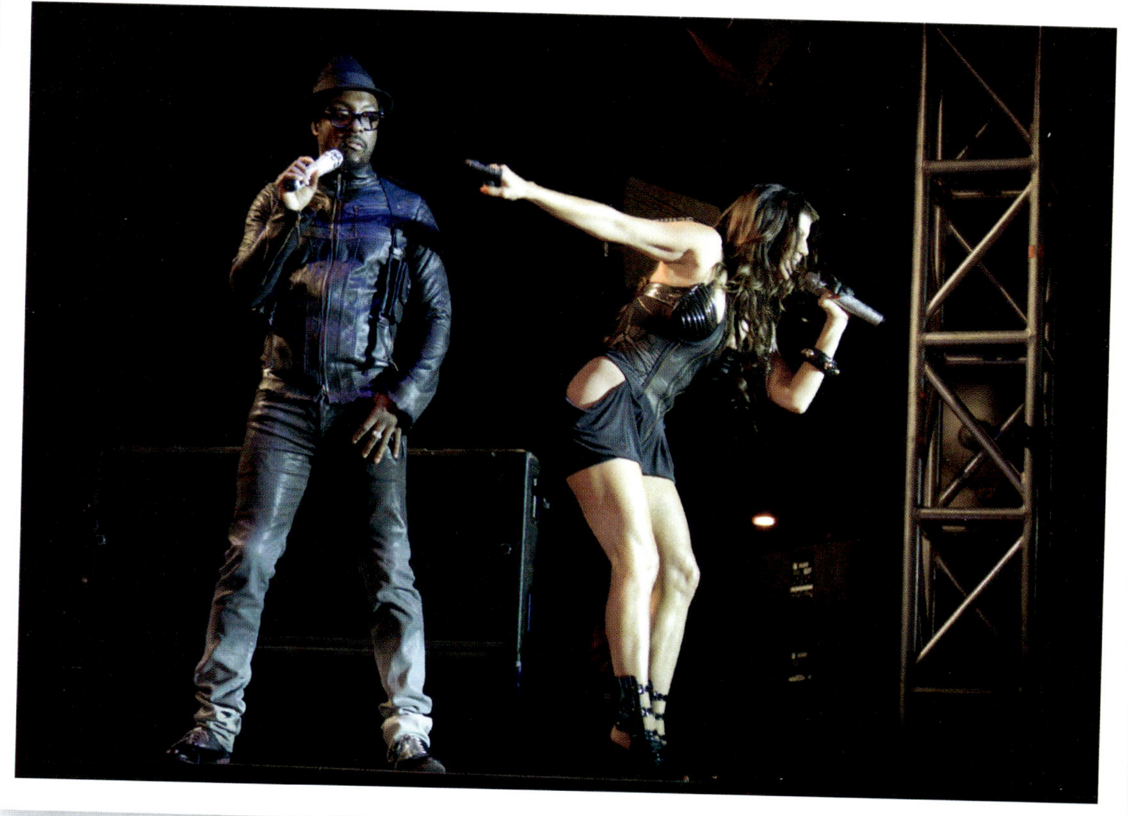

By the time the festival headliners, The Black Eyed Peas, took the stage at the San Diego Street Scene, the crowd was at its biggest. It took awhile for me to get out of the venue.
Taken at 1/125 second, f/2.8, and ISO 2500

CHANGING EXPOSURES

Photographing all day means that the lighting situation is going to change—usually from predominantly sunlight to fully artificial stage light. So your exposure settings and the look of the performers will differ as the event progresses.

The key to getting great concert images, no matter what the lighting does, is to shoot in manual mode ... even during the day. There are a few reasons for this. The main one is that it gives you consistent exposure results. The second is that it helps you control the depth of field. I suggest that you keep it pretty shallow for most of the time.

The tough part about photographing concerts during the day is that you can see the backgrounds really well in your images, and they can be distracting. Composition is covered in Chapter 5, including what to watch for on stage backgrounds. But when shooting bands

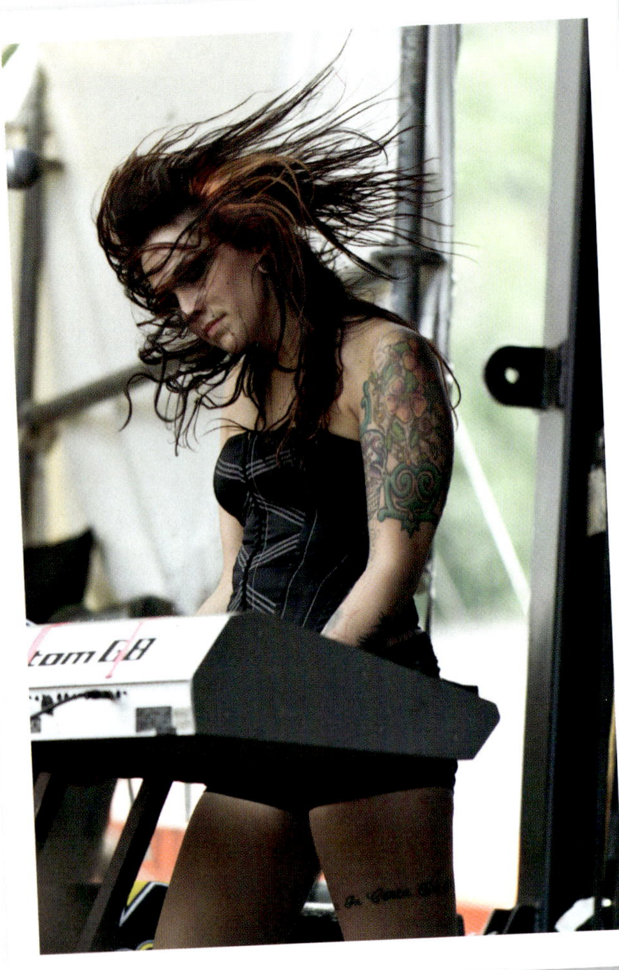

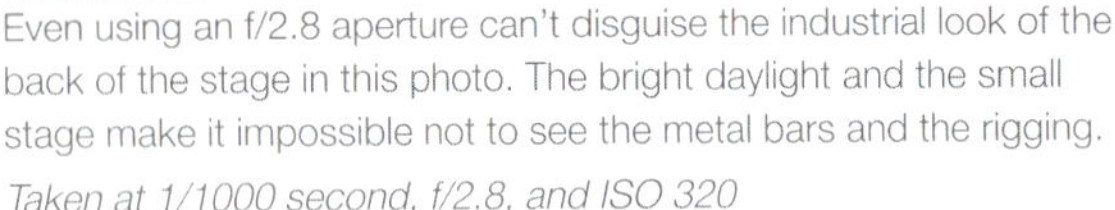

Even using an f/2.8 aperture can't disguise the industrial look of the back of the stage in this photo. The bright daylight and the small stage make it impossible not to see the metal bars and the rigging.
Taken at 1/1000 second, f/2.8, and ISO 320

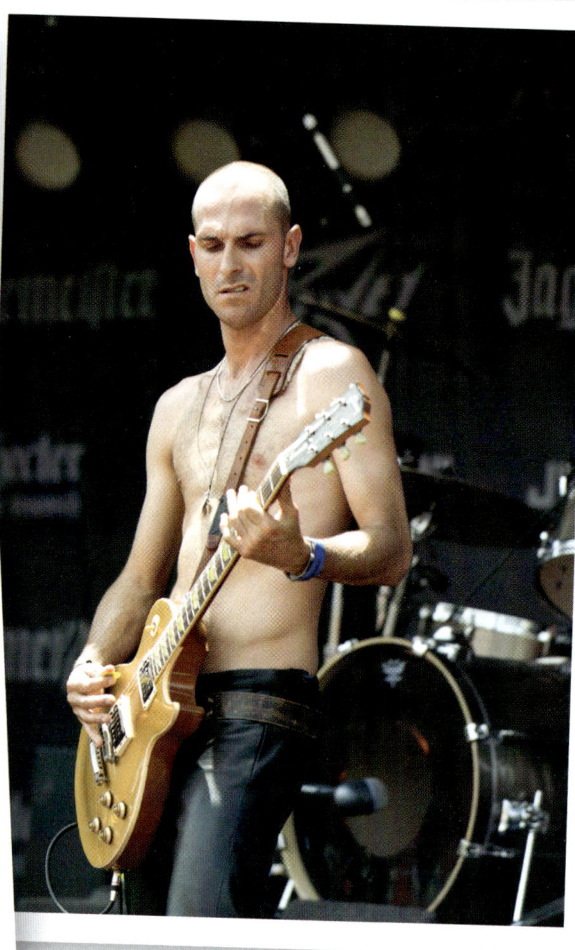

Changing the angle and using a slightly smaller aperture can make for a pretty good background. Here you can see the sponsors behind the guitar player. They're just enough in focus to be useable for marketing purposes.
Taken at 1/640 second, f/3.2, and ISO 200

during the day, the backgrounds will be viable. The best way to minimize the distracting elements is to shoot wide open and use a shallow depth of field to blur the background.

To make sure that the depth of field is shallow for scenes in this lighting situation, drop the ISO and increase the shutter speed. Keep the f-stop at f/2.8 to preserve the shallow depth of field. But if the shutter speed is pushing close to the upper limits of the camera (usually at 1/8000 or less), then keep dropping the ISO.

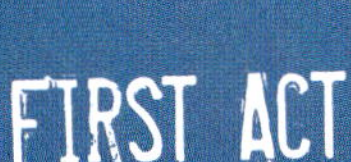

FIRST ACT

The first act that takes the stage during an all-day festival has a tough job. It's usually a band at the start of its members' careers, and not many of the fans are there to see them. They also have the worst lighting—often very bright, full sun.

But on the up side, many photographers don't show up for the opening acts, so the photo pit is less crowded. That alone can make up for the light. But it's also a good opportunity to capture images of a relatively unknown band. If they make it big, you'll have those rare shots of its tender years.

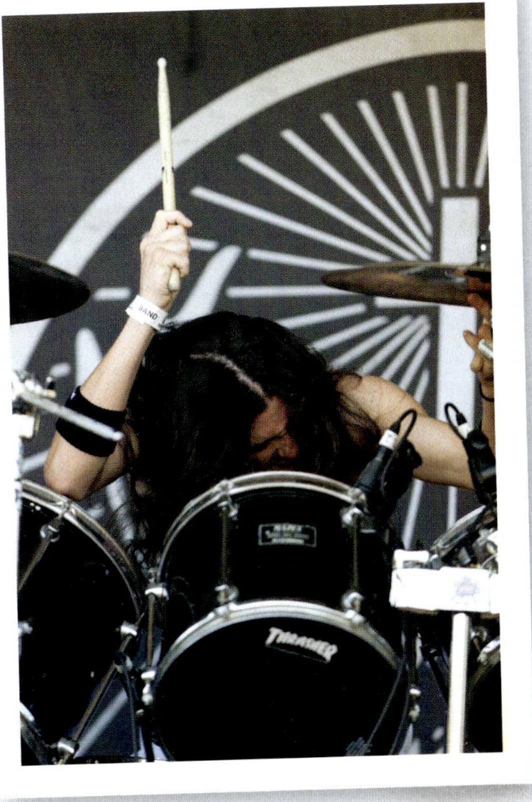

Shooting the opening acts allows you to get shots that are impossible later on in the day due to the light and the size of the stage. For this shot, I was able to freeze the drumstick in the air using a shutter speed of 1/500 second. You can even see the word *band* on the musician's wristband.

Taken 1/500 second, f/2.8, and ISO 400

For an opening band at an all-day festival, I suggest starting at 1/250 second, f/2.8, and ISO 200 to deal with the harsh sunlight. From there, adjust the shutter speed as needed. If the light starts to soften (due maybe to cloud cover or the passing of time), reduce the shutter speed until you're back to a movement-stopping setting. If it drops to 1/160 second, think about raising the ISO.

As the day progresses, use the spot meter as a basic guide for exposures. Place the spot metering area on the face of the subject and use that meter reading as a basis for your exposures. Bear with me here.

The spot meter reading might not give you the proper exposure, but knowing it can be a good guide for making your adjustments. It helps to know the previous exposure reading and the actual exposure. This is important; it can really help with your images and exposure consistency. So let's walk through this.

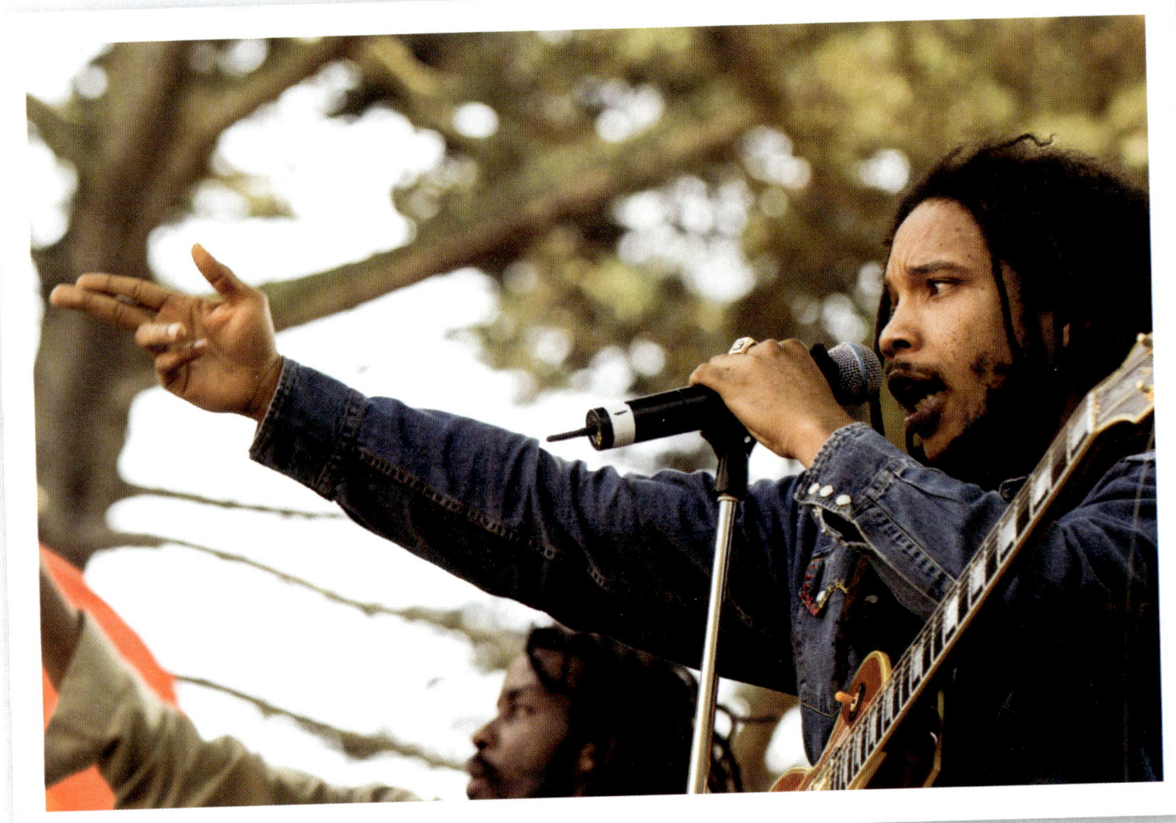

When shooting Stephen Marley at the Green Apple Music Festival in 2007, I used the spot meter on his face to get a starting exposure point.
Taken at 1/160 second, f/4.5, and ISO 160

In the viewfinder, there's an exposure meter that tells you if an image is exposed and if the camera thinks the image is over- or underexposed … and by how many stops. The key is to know the difference between what the camera thinks is a properly exposed shot (based on the built-in light meter) and what you want to capture.

For example, say I put the spot metering area on the face of the performer and the camera thinks the settings that I have manually set will underexpose the image the image by a full stop (not an uncommon meter reading). When I take the photo at my manual setting, despite the camera's warning, and find that the exposure on the back of the camera looks good to me, I know that the camera is off by about a stop. So later, in similar lighting conditions, I can take a meter reading from the performer's face and dial in exposure settings that look to underexpose the image by a full stop. I'll know I'm in the ballpark for a proper exposure.

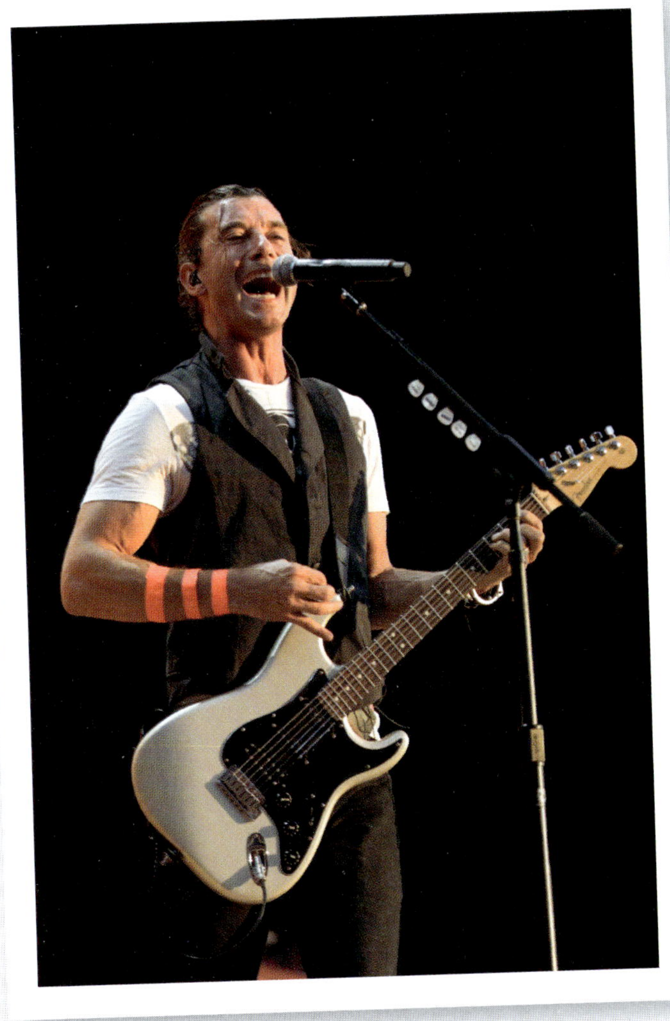

At the Epicenter TwentyTen show, the pit was jammed with photographers. This made it difficult to change positions. I used a longer lens and an off-center position to capture each member of the band, but I made sure that I got a shot of lead singer Gavin Rossdale.
Taken at 1/1250 second, f/2.8, and ISO 320

CROWDED HOUSE

Being a photographer at a festival can be really tough. This is especially so at the biggest festivals, where it seems that everyone's credentialed. You might find yourself in a photo pit with seventy-plus photographers. All-day festivals provide opportunity to photograph many bands in the same place, so a lot of photographers want to shoot the same show(s), and they're probably all approved to do it.

No photographer likes to be stuck in a single spot for the allotted shooting time, and no photographer wants to be jammed up against other photographers in a photo pit. But it happens. Here are some things you can try in order to make the most of this situation.

BE PREPARED.

Attach the lens you want to your camera and dial in the right settings, so you can spend more time trying to get great shots and less time dealing with your camera settings.

STORE YOUR BAG.

When the photo pit is really packed, every inch counts, so try to pack your gear in the smallest bag for the occasion. I carry two cameras with lenses attached and extra lenses in a lens bag. But I leave the ThinkTankPhoto backpack locked to my laptop and a desk in the press tent. If there's no press tent, then carry the cameras and compress the backpack to its tiniest size, so it takes up less space than a traditional shoulder bag.

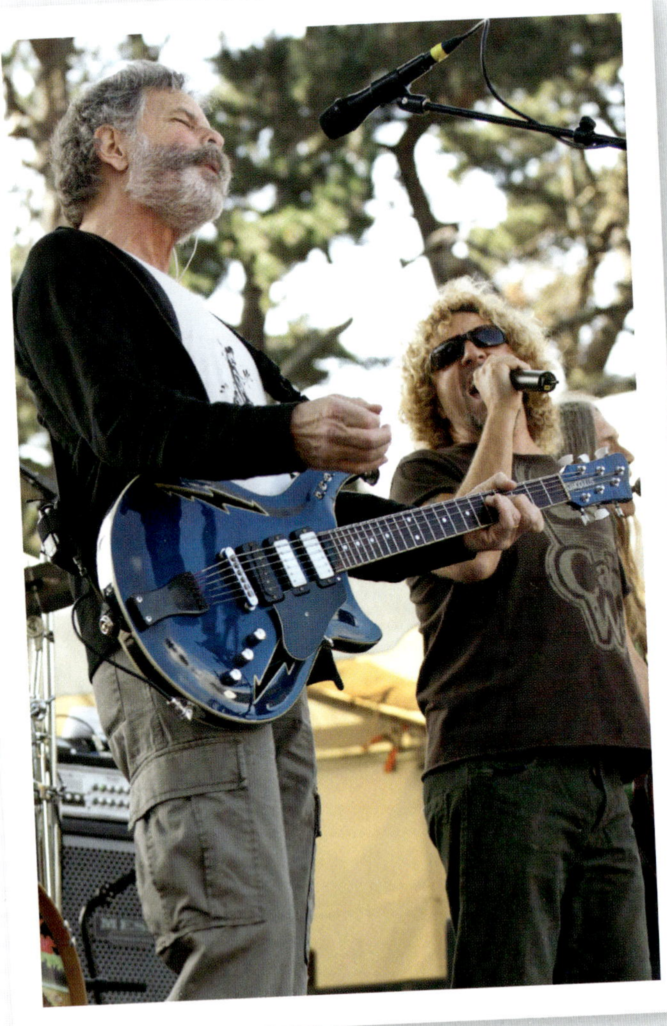

Bob Weir and Sammy Hagar played together during the Green Apple Music festival in Golden Gate Park in 2007. I could not get to the other side of the stage; I had to stay and shoot from where I was. As frustrating as it was, I still managed to salvage a shot or two of the pairing.

Taken at 1/160 second, f/4, and ISO 200

SHOOT FROM AN ANGLE.

I tend to photograph from the left or right sides of a stage and use the longer lenses. At times this gives me more working room. Other photographers work in the center with wider angle lenses. If one position isn't working, try another.

HAVE A PLAN.

Not all plans work, so it pays to be flexible. But every time I walk into a photo pit, even when it's really crowded, I have a plan for what I want to shoot. For example, at a recent shoot I was going to be photographing Papa Roach, and I know that the guitar player Jerry Horton is usually positioned stage right. I wanted to make sure I captured him playing, so I started out on that side of the photo pit.

KNOW THE BAND.

Information is the name of the game. Knowing where the band members set up and where they play is the golden ticket to getting great shots. Check out the band's website and live photos from Flickr or the wire services before a show to prepare your plan. This way you can know where to start and get the important shots first.

Even with all the planning, it's sometimes impossible to move in the photo pit. In these cases, just make the best of the view you have. Try to capture the scene you can access instead of being concerned with the areas you can't.

THE PRESS TENT

An oasis in the chaos of an all-day festival is the press tent. Of course, that's not to say that every festival has a press tent, but many of the bigger ones do. And this is a spot that allows photographers to set up laptops and then download and submit photos to their editors during the event. The press area usually has a power outlet or two along with wireless Internet access, a few tables, and maybe some water and snacks.

Many times the press tent looks like it's a secure area, but it isn't. Anyone with a photo or media pass, a guest pass, a backstage pass, a working pass, or any kind of pass can access the area. It's even accessible to the general concert-going public at some places. So do not leave your gear unattended and unlocked … ever.

When shooting a festival for a wire service, when I need to download and edit images as I go, I make sure that my laptop is either in my bag or locked to a sturdy table. I use a

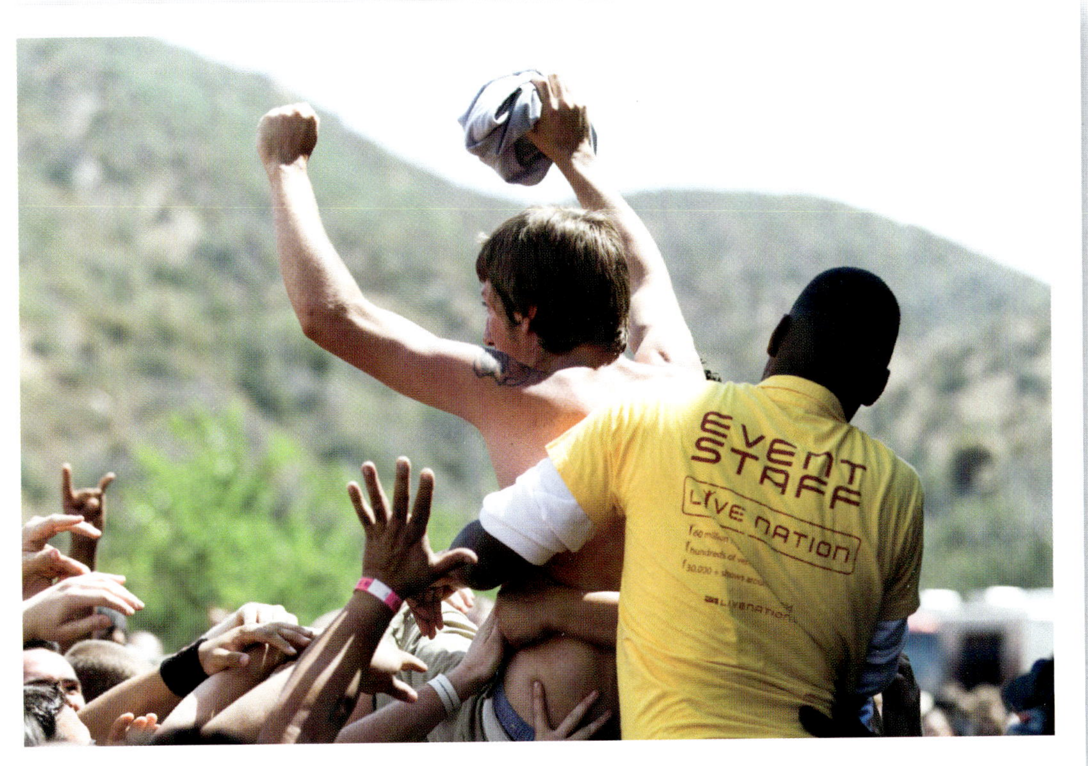

Personal safety is important. Watch your back when working in the photo pit, as some shows can have crazy fans. This is one of the reasons that I really like and respect the security in the photo pit. *Taken at 1/3200 second, f/3.2, and ISO 320*

security cable that attaches to my laptop using the Kensington lock slot. The laptop lock runs about $30 and is well worth it. Losing your equipment would be devastating.

Keep in mind that the press tent is a place where people are trying to get work done—usually under a time deadline. So it's important to respect the workspace and the people working. If you're disruptive, people will remember you. Also, because you never know when and where you might meet someone who can help you out later, it's a good idea to have a business card or two with you in the press tent. And, terrific professional etiquette is helpful.

SURVIVING THE DAY

Working an all-day festival or a multi-day festival can take its toll. Earlier in this chapter, we covered the importance of good, comfortable shoes. Well, now it's time to go over the other stuff that can make the day a breeze ... or a nightmare.

PACING

It's important to pace yourself throughout your day; don't use all your energy early. Unless you're working specifically for one of the early bands or your assignment is to cover one of the early bands, save yourself to be on your game for the headliners. These acts are usually scheduled toward the end of the day, so if you fail to pace yourself appropriately, you could find yourself wiped out and unable to do your best work at an important time. Part of the trick to pacing is having a plan. Figure out which bands you want to photograph and give yourself plenty of time to get between the stages if needed. It's no fun to run while trying to carry a bunch of camera gear.

HYDRATION

Many of the festivals I shoot take place under the blazing summer sun. At these events especially, it's important to stay hydrated. Drink plenty of water, even if you'd prefer Diet Coke. Water keeps you hydrated; sodas don't. And on a serious note: It's a very bad idea to drink beer or any other alcoholic beverage when you're working at a festival or any other place. Don't drink and shoot.

PROTEIN

Don't forget to eat! This one can actually be a problem at an all-day festival, because food lines can be long. I recommend packing a protein bar or two in a side pocket of your camera bag to give yourself some nourishment when needed.

SUNSCREEN/HAT

A full day outside under the sun can cause real damage to your skin. Use a sunscreen that's not greasy and won't get on your camera gear. If you're not a fan of sunscreen, then you need to wear a hat. This is my favorite method of keeping the sun off my face during a festival shoot. I have a favorite crushable hat that goes with me to every outdoor show. When it's time to shoot, I can easily stuff it into my camera bag.

RAIN GEAR

I'm based in southern California, so I don't get too many rainy days. But the rest of the world isn't so lucky. The chance of shooting in the rain at some point is high, so you'll need rain gear. A good, inexpensive option is the OpTech Rainsleeve. You've got to keep your camera and lens dry without putting anything in front of the lens to reduce image quality.

If there's a chance of rain, remember to pack a small towel into your bag as well. Use this to wipe dry your gear between bands. And be sure to decide which lens to use before leaving cover; you never want to change a lens in the rain.

PEN AND PAPER

Shooting a full-day or multi-day festival is a lot of work, make no mistake. In addition to shooting great images, you need to keep notes. Document the bands you shoot, the schedule of the day, and anything that you might need to know when it comes to processing the images later. Sometimes there are lots of bands at a festival that you've never seen, and trying to match names to images can be problematic without a list.

Mayhem Fest line up 2011

Jager Band - 2:10
Red Fang - 3:10
Kingdom of Sorrow - 4:10
Unearth - 5:10
Trivium - 6:15

Straight Line Stitch - 2:40
All Shall Perish - 3:40
Suicide Silence - 4:40
Testament- 5:40

Machine Head - 7:10
Godsmack - 8:15
Disturbed - 9:45
Dethklok - 11:10

This is the list of bands that played the opening day of Rockstar Energy Drink Mayhem Festival. I had this saved on my iPhone so I could keep track of where I was supposed to be and who I was going to shoot. It also helped me after the event as I tried to match images to the names of performers.

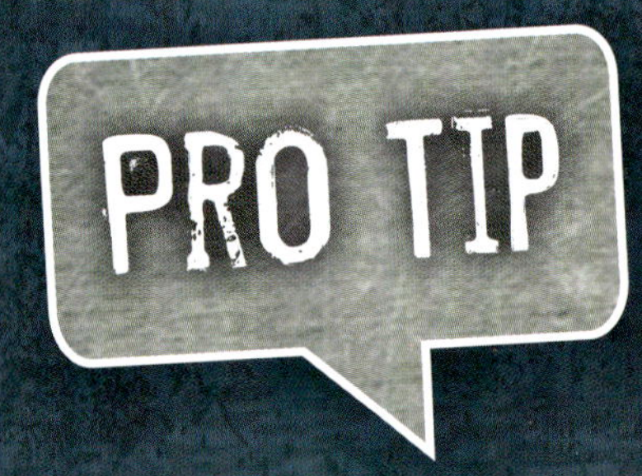

Chelsea Lauren

Contributing photographer for Getty Images, WireImage, Film Magic

Chelsea@chelsealauren.com

www.chelsealauren.com

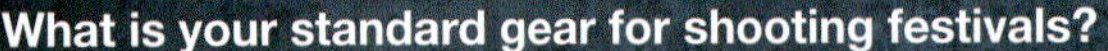

What is your standard gear for shooting festivals?

- Canon 5dMKII
- 24–70mm f/2.8 L Canon lens
- 70–200mm f/2.8L Canon lens
- 15mm Fisheye and 16–35 Wide Angle

What's the most important piece of gear (other than camera or lens) that you make sure is in your camera bag?

A stool!!

How do you deal with very crowded photo pits?

I scoot my way up as close as I can to the stage, or I put my stool up in the rear and shoot over someone relatively short.

Is there competition in the pit? If so, how do you deal with it?

Of course there is. I am pretty much always able to squeeze my way into whatever location I need to be in. In the rare instance I cannot, I will find another angle ... or shoot another member of the band and come back to the challenging one.

How many photos per band?

Depends. If it's a solo act that doesn't move a lot or have expressive faces, maybe 50. If it's a band with a few interesting/more noteworthy members that happens to have very challenging lighting, like Rob Zombie, it's closer to 500. Or.... if the band has strobes, like Prodigy, I probably fire 750 shots for three songs; only 150 of them will come out with any light at all. Of those 150, maybe 20 will be usable.

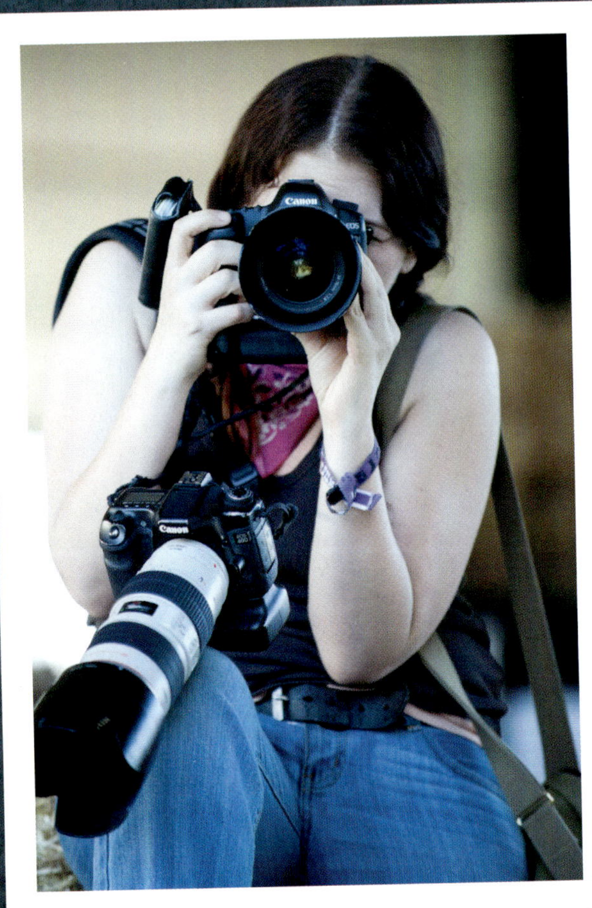

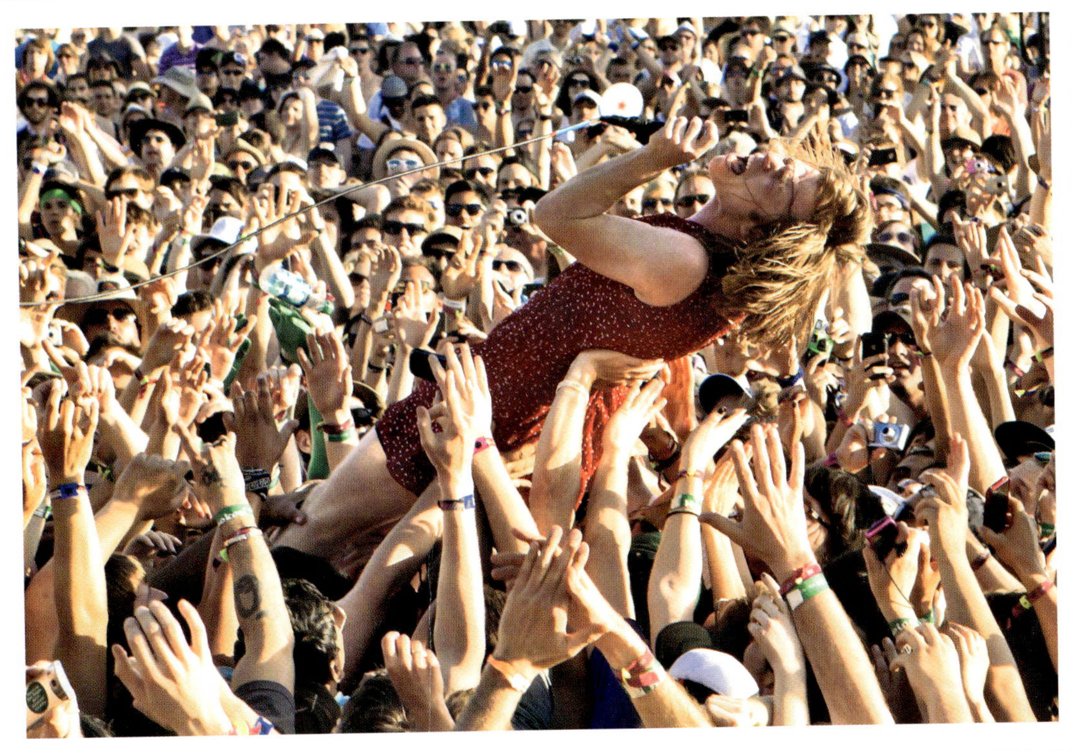

© Chelsea Lauren

How do you edit your images?
I load them all into Lightroom and make my selects in there. I go through three times or so to narrow them down. After that, I'll do a batch adjustment for sharpness, contrast, clarity, and noise reduction, and then hand adjust each image from there.

How long do you spend on an edit?
I spend longer than most. For a normal concert, I think two to three hours. If it's a festival, like Warped Tour, VooDoo, Mayhem… I'm looking at a full day of editing.

What advice can you give a photographer starting out in the concert business?
Be kind to everybody. You never know who someone is or knows. People want to help people who are kind and genuine. Pretension gets you nowhere in this industry.

Don't do it for money or notoriety. Because, more likely than not, those things will not come to you. The most successful people I know in this business love photography, love music, and love the art they

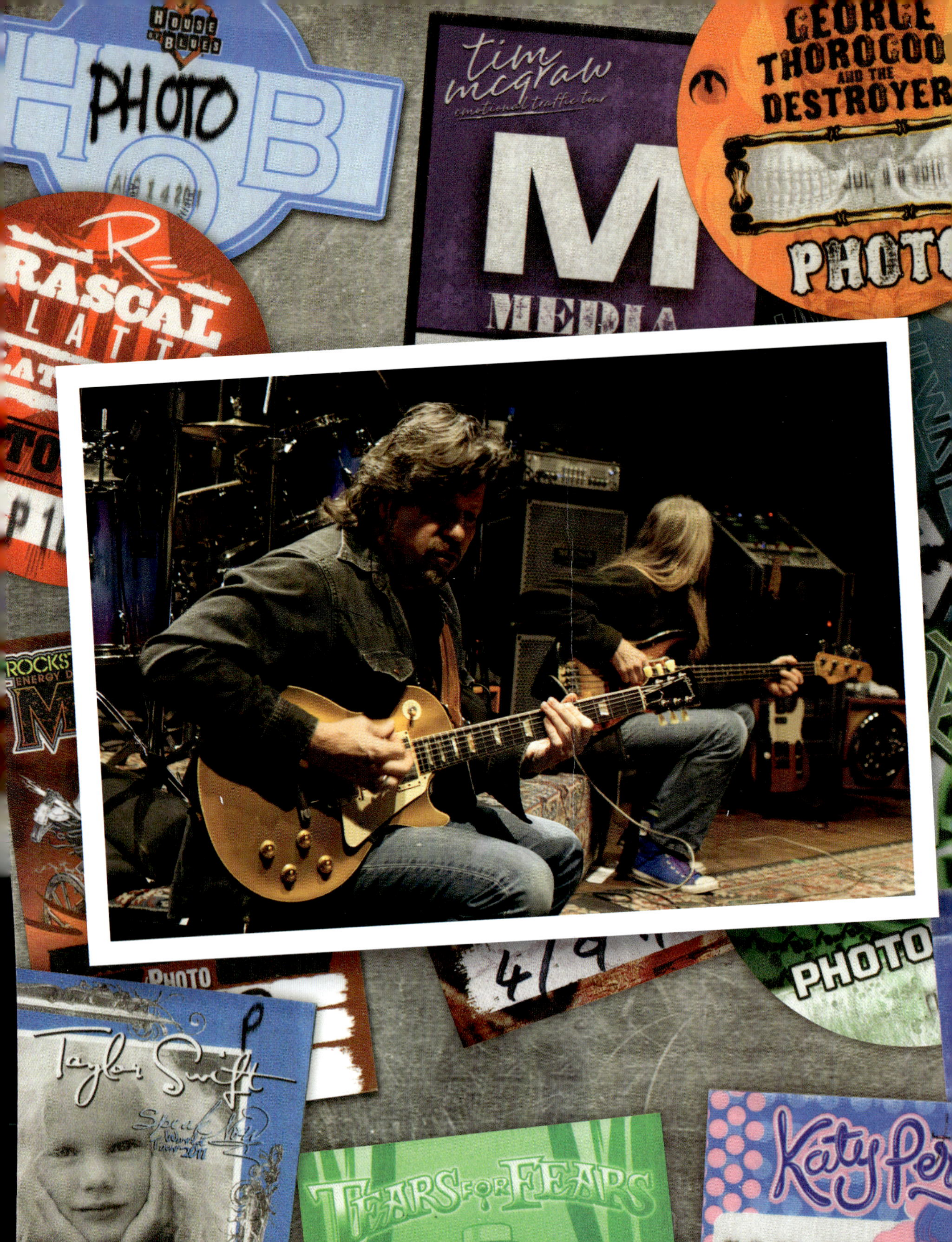
HOUSE OF BLUES
PHOTO
HOB
tim mcgraw
emotional traffic tour
M
GEORGE
AND THE
RASCAL
PHOTO
PHOTO
Taylor Swift
Speak Now
World Tour 2011
TEARS FOR FEARS

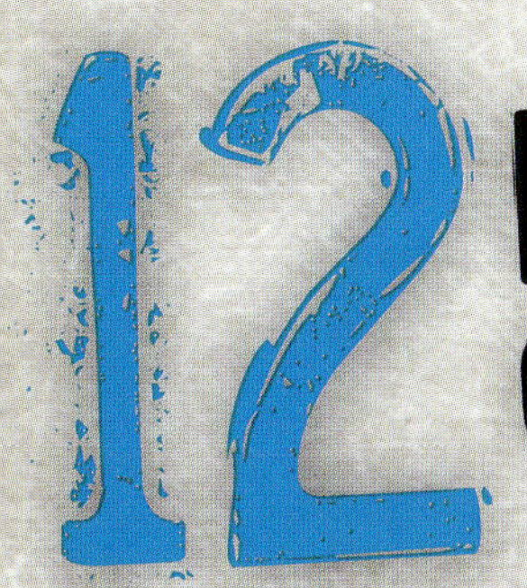

BACKSTAGE PASS: GETTING BEHIND THE SCENES

It seemed that the minute I started getting photo passes on a regular basis, I wanted more access. And what I *really* wanted was to be the photographer who got to shoot backstage and on the stage. Well, it's not something that happens a lot, and it takes a special relationship; but I've been there. Let me tell you, it's amazing!

There are some special things to consider here though. So let's talk about the pros and cons of shooting on the stage ... and backstage.

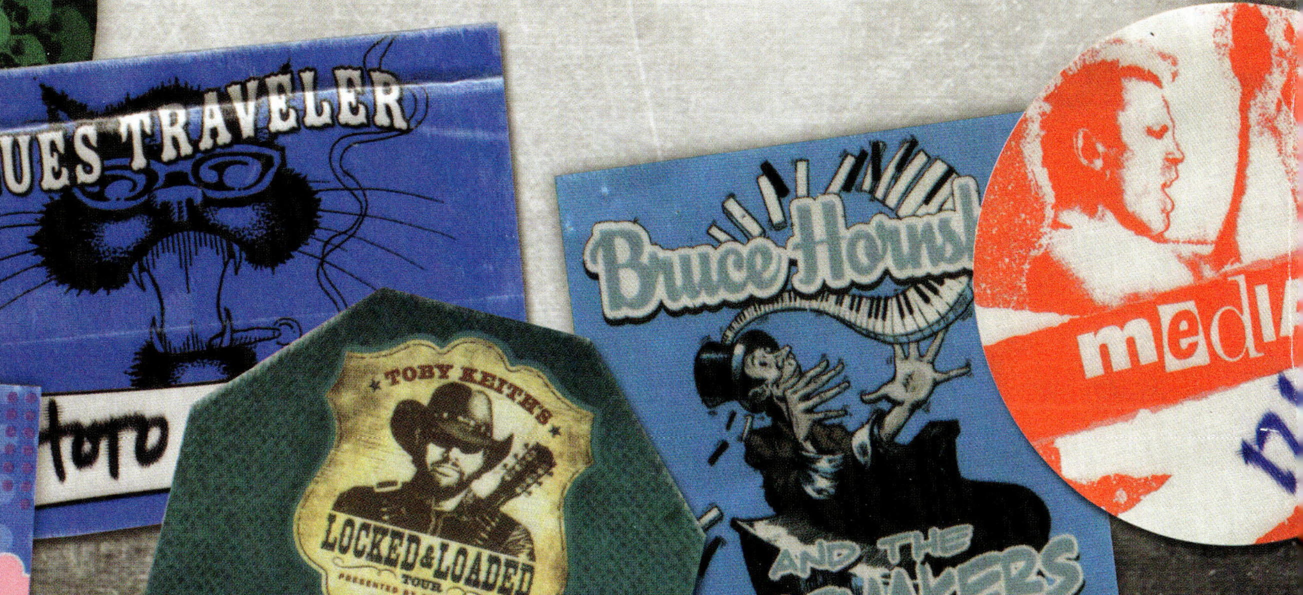

SHOOTING FROM THE STAGE

Shooting from the stage can be a real thrill for a photographer, but it can also be one of the most frustrating things to do. I mean, think about it. The stage is not set up to be viewed from the side or back; the performance on stage is designed to be viewed from the front. So good angles for capturing images of a band on stage from a position at the side of the stage are extremely limited.

If you get invited to shoot from the stage during a performance, here are some things to keep in mind.

BE AWARE OF YOUR SURROUNDINGS.

There is a lot of stuff on a stage—power lines and cables, cords, etc.—and it's all usually on the ground, not easily seen. Just imagine for a moment that you inadvertently unplug the band. Not a good scenario. Indeed, I cannot stress this enough: you must make sure that you know what is around you at all times, and be prepared to move your position if needed.

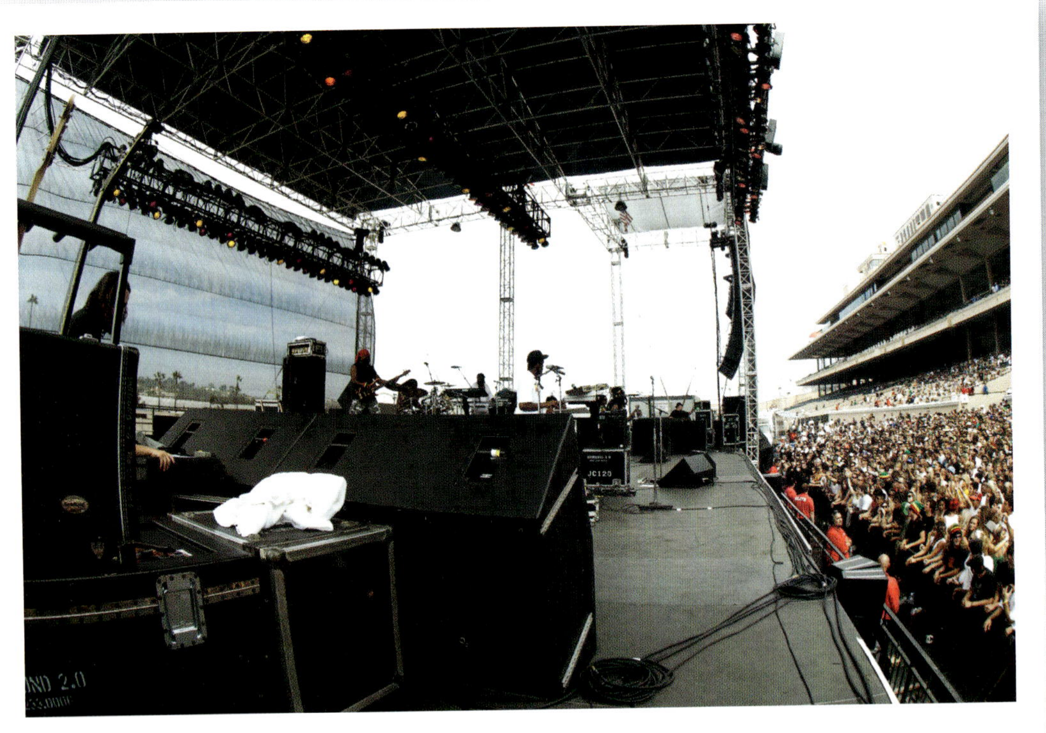

A big stage and large crowds are great, but this can also mean that the action is far away from where a photographer is standing. And if you're at side stage, the musicians are probably facing the wrong way.

MY PHOTO BAG: SIDE STAGE AND BACKSTAGE

Photographing from the side stage and backstage usually means two things:

- You will need a flash.
- Your gear will need to be compact and out of the way.

I carry all my gear for these shoots in a ThinkTankPhoto Shape Shifter bag. It holds two dSLR bodies, three lenses, my flash, and light modifiers. The important thing about this bag is that it compresses when the cameras are unloaded, so I can wear it without taking up much space.

Here's my list of gear for a shoot that includes side- and backstage photography:

- 2x dSLR body (a Nikon D700 with a battery grip and a Nikon D3)
- 24-70mm f/2.8 zoom lens
- 70-200mm f/2.8 zoom lens
- 16mm Fisheye lens
- Extra memory cards
- Earplugs
- Extra batteries
- Business cards
- Lens cloth
- Small flashlight
- Flash
- Flash batteries
- Rouge flash bender light modifiers (in the laptop pocket)

STAY OUT OF THE WAY.

You are not part of the show, and you need to stay out of the way of people working. The excitement of a live show is unmatched. But to pull it off, a lot of people do a lot of work, and many of them are on the stage. Doing their job requires that you stay out of their sight line and away from their equipment. These people include:

- **Guitar Tech**

  Depending on the band, there may be one or two or three guitar techs working at a particular show. Each one has a spot on the side of the stage where (s)he keeps the band's guitars in working order. Guitar techs need to get to the musicians on stage as quickly as possible to trade, fix, tune, and otherwise handle their guitars.

- **Drum Tech**

  This is the person who keeps the drums working and the drummer happy. The drum tech is usually stationed toward the back of the stage, so (s)he can get to the drum kit quickly.

- **Other Tech**

  Other side-stage staff may include a keyboard tech, vocal tech, and others working on the stage to make sure that the band's instruments are working and that the performers have what they need. As a photographer in this area, know where these people are and make sure you are not in their line of sight.

- **Sound Guy**

  One of the most important people on the stage is the guy who mixes the stage sound, which is the sound that the band hears as they play. This person is usually on the side of the stage behind a mixing board. (S)he needs to be able to see the band, and the band needs to be able to see the sound guy. So never stand between the monitor board and the band.

  Let me repeat that, because it's so important, Never get between the band and the monitor mix. The sound that the fans hear is not the same as what the band hears. And for the show to sound good to the fans, the band needs to be able to hear the music around them. I got in the way once—only once. And I somehow lived to tell about it. It'll never happen again though.

- **Stage Manager**

  The stage manager does exactly what the job title describes. (S)he manages the stage. This includes making sure that guests (photographers included) don't get in the way of working staff. The stage manager is the boss, and if (s)he tells you to do something, do it. Otherwise you may find yourself barred from backstage.

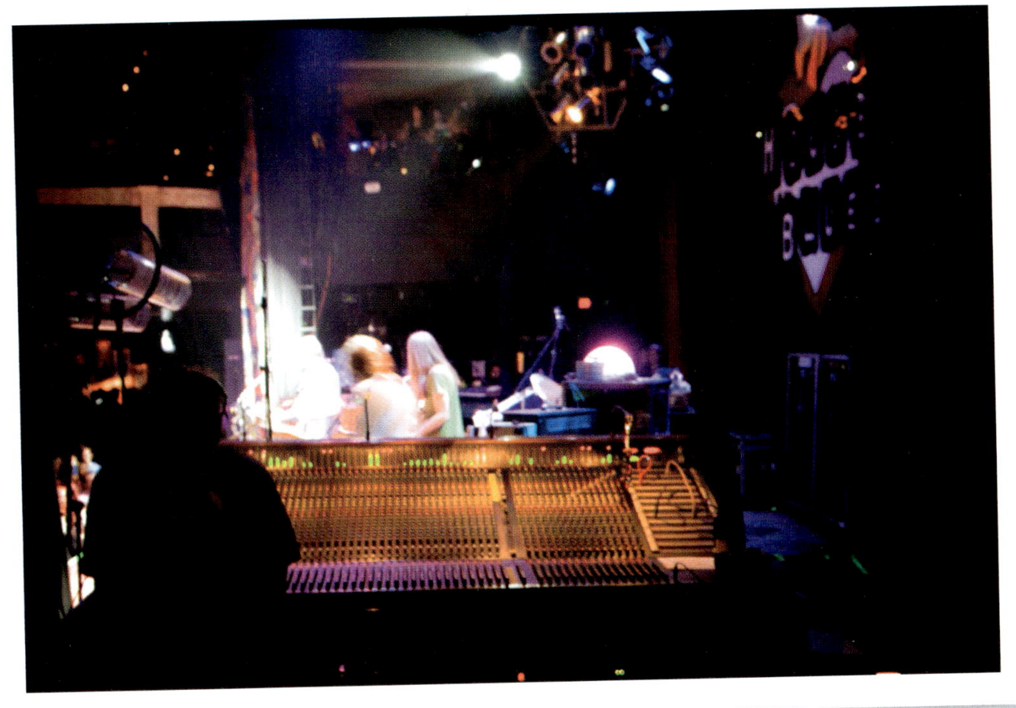

The monitor mixing board is usually set up on one side of the stage. And while it may seem like a great place from which to shoot, you need to make sure that you are not in the sound tech's way. (S)he is mixing the monitor sound.
Taken at 1/3 second, f/3.2, and ISO 400

- **Guests**
  Every band has guests with stage access, and chances are they mean more to the performers than you do. These people are usually wives or girlfriends of band members as well as managers, business partners, family members, and good friends. In other words, they are people who have close relationships with the band, and it's important that you do not get in their way.

  Keep in mind that these people might really want photos of the show, so don't be afraid to hand out a business card or two if the opportunity presents itself. Just don't do it while the band is playing. Wait for a set break or after the show if possible.

- **Security**
  There will probably be some type of security controlling access to the backstage. I've found that it helps to introduce yourself to these people early on and explain what you're doing. Make sure they know you're allowed to be there. And do this before you actually need to shoot, because you might need the stage manager or tour manager to come over and confirm with security that you are indeed allowed to shoot from the stage.

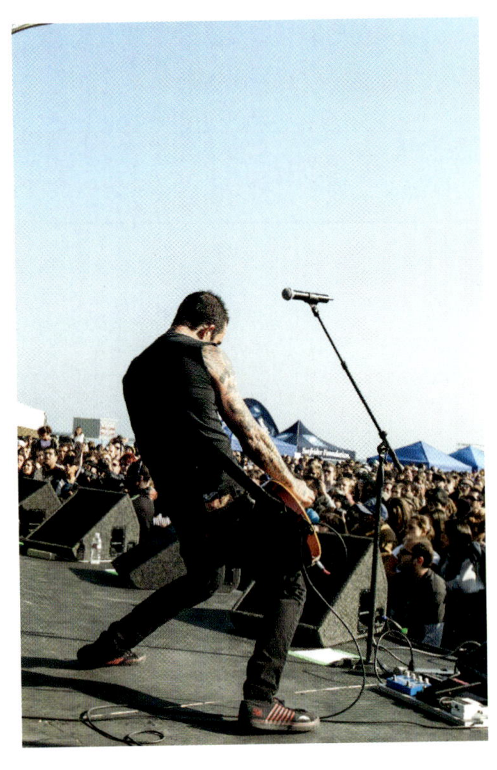

You can't even see the musician's face in this shot, but that doesn't matter. It's all about the point of view.

Taken at 1/320 second, f/5.6, and ISO 100

BE PREPARED TO MOVE.

Always make sure that you can quickly get out of the way … from wherever you're shooting. This means not positioning yourself in a place with no exit. I'm saying, it might look like a great spot, but getting between a guitar tech and the band is a bad idea. It can lead to a situation in which you're stuck in the way if the tech needs to switch guitars with a musician or get on the stage to fix something.

KNOW YOUR BOUNDARIES.

Being allowed to shoot on stage during a show *doesn't* mean that you can walk around on stage during the performance. When in doubt, don't do it … or ask before doing it. For example, the spot right next to the drum set might look like a great place to position yourself for a shot, but you might be visible to the audience or distract the band, so it's probably not a good idea to go there. The best thing to do is check with the stage manager as to where you can and cannot go … before the show begins.

DO NOT TOUCH ANYTHING.

This one is self explanatory. Do Not Touch Anything. Just don't do it. It isn't your job. Personally, I know cameras and camera settings, and I can change a lens in the dark very quickly. But I have no idea how to plug in a guitar rig or how to deal with microphones and speaker cables, so I don't touch them—ever.

Sometimes a band member will turn and look at you, as Jeff Chimenti did in this photo from the 2007 Green Apple Music Festival in Golden Gate Park. It's a great shot of Jeff and the crowd.

Taken at 1/200 second, f/7.1, and ISO 200

BE PROFESSIONAL.

I've said it before and I'll say it again: Always behave as a professional. You are there to do a job, so be sure that you act like it … all the time. You never want to give anyone the impression that you are anything but a professional photographer.

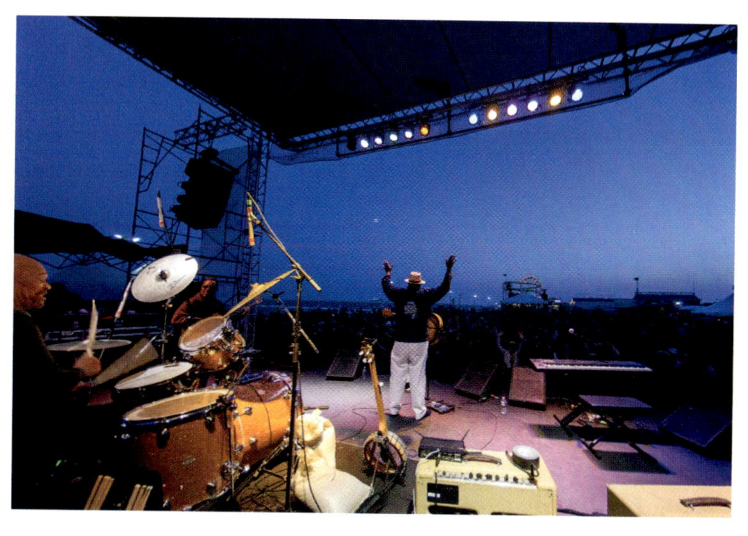

At the end of the Taj Mahal show at the 2008 Green Apple Music Festival on the Santa Monica Pier, the sun had just set. The band had just finished playing, and it was time for one last shot.
Taken at 1/60 second, f/2.8, and ISO 125

When it comes to professionally capturing images from the stage, there is one photo in particular that should be attempted if possible. That shot is of the band or musician in the foreground with the crowd in the background.

The bigger the crowd, the better the shot; but for this to work, you need to be able to see the crowd. This means that the crowd can probably see you. So work quickly when you're visible and then get out of view.

If the stage is deep, you can shoot from behind the drum kit or off to the side of it. If the stage is shallow, try to get as close to the center as possible … without getting in the way. This is one of the only times that I use a deep depth of field. You don't want the crowd to turn into a blurry blotch of color in this situation.

When shooting outdoors during the day, this is easy. When shooting indoors or during a night show, this shot works best when the lights are aimed at the crowd. Check with the lighting director to find out what songs will have lights aimed to illuminate the crowd. And be sure to get in position so you can get the shot during that song.

SOUND CHECK

When I started to really get to know bands, I was hanging around during the sound check and thought it might be a perfect time to get great behind-the-scenes concert photographs. It turns out that I was wrong.

You can get some great photographs during the sound check, but since there is no audience, there's a real lack of energy. This is when the band a nd crew make sure that any wrinkles in the performance are ironed out before the show starts. They want to be sure that paying fans get the best musical experience possible. It's unlikely they're worrying about giving you good material for images.

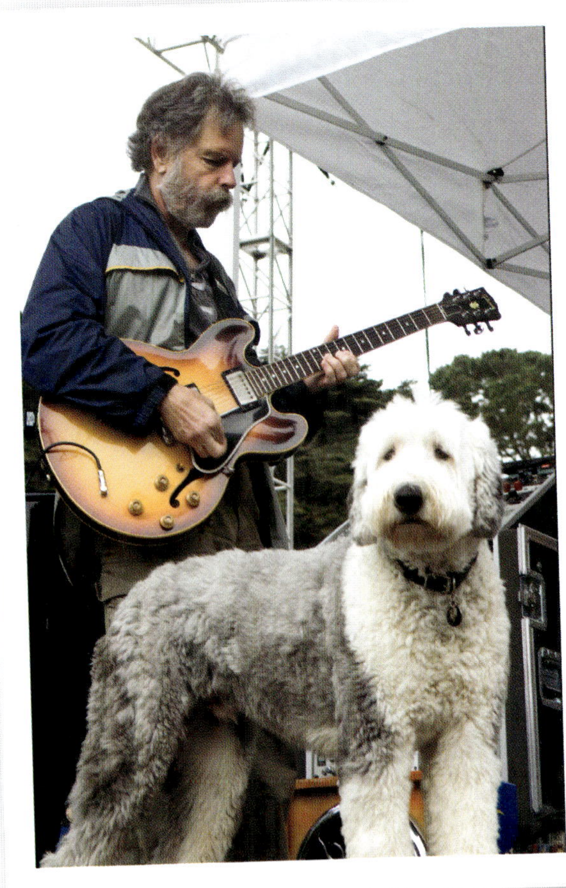

You never know what type of photos you might get at a sound check. In April of 2007, the Green Apple Music Festival in Golden Gate Park's sound check had Bob Weir bringing his dog along for the ride.
Taken at 1/160 second, f/5.6 and ISO 160

The sound check is an opportunity for the front of house sound engineer and lighting director to work out details of the sound and light systems. It's also a time for the band to practice a new song or fine-tune a number they've been working on. So from a musical point of view, it can be a real treat. But it can also be really boring, because the lights are usually off, the band is not performing, and shooting opportunities are limited.

As the photographer, you need to be very aware of how the band members look, because a sound check does not constitute a public performance; it's a private rehearsal. Many times the musicians have not yet showered or dressed for the show and they don't want that look to be public. So be sure to check with the band or the band's management to find out what can be used or shown publicly and what needs to stay private. This is all part of building trust with the band, and we'll dive deeper into this a little later in this chapter.

Sound checks are a great time to shoot specific gear photos if needed. And if you set it up with the band member and tech beforehand, you can get some angles that are not possible during the show. You can get in much closer during a sound check, for instance, than you can during a show.

But since the sound check is when the band and crew get everything ready, make sure you stay out of the way. Again, don't touch *anything*. This includes putting your camera bag down where it might get in the way. I learned that the hard way.

Here's the story: Backstage during a sound check in Arizona a few years ago, I thought it would be a good idea to stash my camera bag on the top of a gear case that was sitting off to the side of the stage. What I didn't know was that the spot I had chosen was where the standup bass guitar case went during the show. Needless to say, the guitar tech was not happy with my choice and I vowed never to do that again. If AJ is reading this, I want you to know that I have never done anything like that again!

SHOOTING BACKSTAGE

Backstage at a concert can be broken down into two different types of photography: posed portraits and candids. But the first thing to understand is that being allowed backstage with a camera is a huge privilege that can be revoked at any time. Even with this access, there are areas that are off limits and should be respected. Some of the areas and scenes that you will find backstage are described below.

TOUR BUS

This is the band's home away from home, and it's usually the only place where the performers are free of crowds and fans and everyone else. It's unlikely that you will be allowed on the tour bus unless a band member specifically invites you. But if

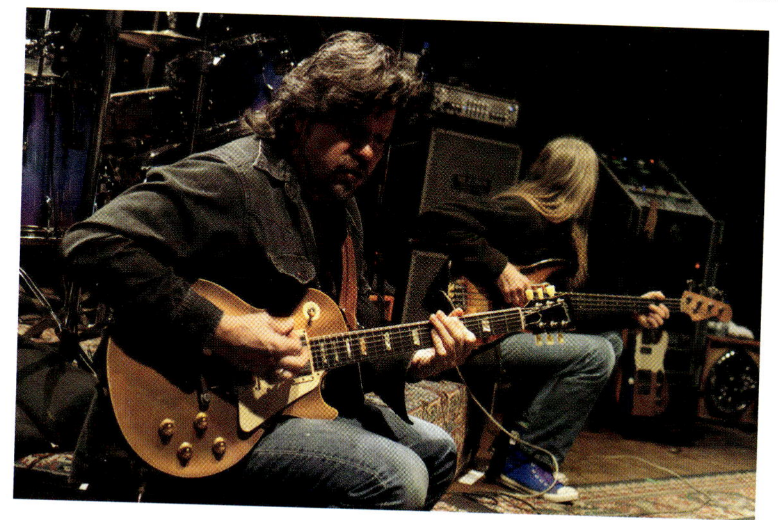

Mark Karan and Robin Sylvester tune up before the show in New York.

Taken at 1/40 second, f/3.2, and ISO 320

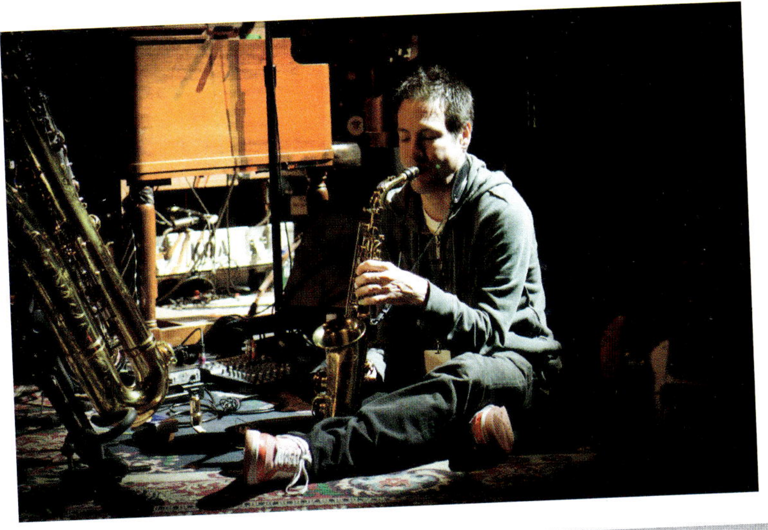

Kenny Brooks takes a few moments to get his gear working right before the sound check at the Ventura Theater. I used the available light to take this shot. There was enough to allow me to use a relatively low shutter speed of 1/40 second and still keep Kenny looking sharp. This photo was taken back when the high ISO settings still produced a lot of digital noise, so I tried to keep the ISO down at 400 to 800.

Taken at1/20 second, f/3.2, and ISO 400

you're lucky enough to get such an invitation, treat the space as you would their home. Make sure that taking photos is allowed before you bring the camera up to your eye. If you're on the bus, then you are close enough to just ask. These images are usually not candids, but rather posed or semi-posed shots.

The shooting area is small enough that a single dedicated flash unit on the camera aimed at the ceiling will bounce enough light into the scene to allow you to use a lower ISO and deeper depth of field.

DRESSING ROOMS

The band usually has a dressing room that's accessible to only the band and those with All Access laminates. Even with this kind of pass though, the tour manager might restrict access to make sure that the band has private time before or after a show.

Photos taken in dressing rooms can be posed or candid, depending on the images you want and the relationship you have with the subjects. I've done portraits using an off-camera flash and candids using available light. And I love it when a musician motions me over and asks for a photograph or (s)he poses with friends and family for a quick shot.

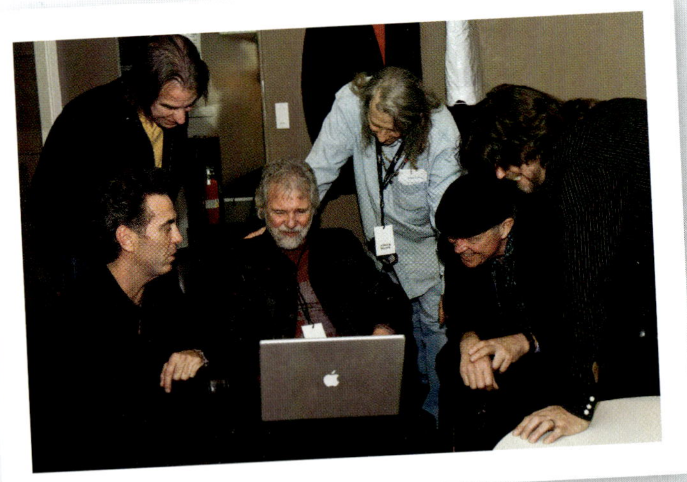

Being in a performer's dressing room allows you to see moments that later on will stand out in your memory. Be ready to capture them. This impromptu gathering of the musicians around Chuck Leavell's computer after the sound check made for a great shot, and it is totally candid. By this time of the day, I was part of the scenery and they didn't even notice when I snapped this shot with a dedicated flash unit aimed at the ceiling to get a nice natural-looking light.

Taken at 1/30 second, f/4.2, and ISO 125

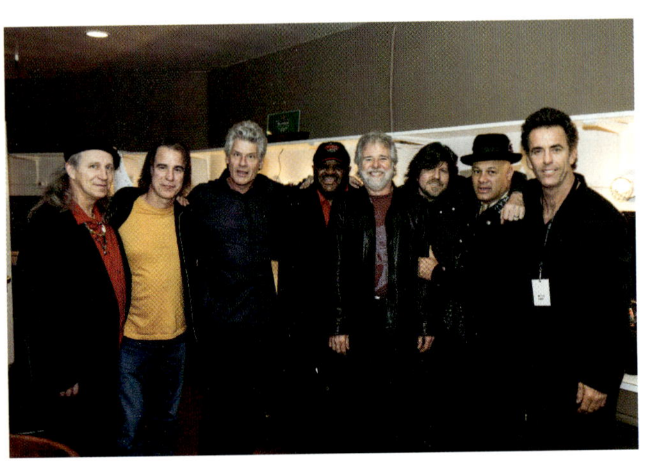

Moments before the band was going to take the stage, they gathered for a quick shot. Be ready, because there is no second chance for a shot like this. There's no way that this group would be together again soon. From left: Norton Buffalo, Dewayne Pate, Ozzie Ohlers, Larry Batiste, Chuck Leavell, Mark Karan, Narada Michael Walden, and Jimmy Dillon.

Taken at 1/60 second, f/4 and ISO 100 with on-camera flash aimed at the ceiling

ONE OF THOSE MOMENTS

Back in 2006 I was backstage at the Greek Theater in Los Angeles—Yes, the same Greek Theater that was the in the movie, *Get Him To The Greek*—with Bob Weir and RatDog when I saw lead guitarist Mark Karan talking to his good friend Delaney Bramlett. The opportunity was too good to pass up. I got Mark, Delaney and Delaney's wife Susan to pose for a quick shot together using the dressings room's lighted mirrors as a background. Delaney passed away a few years after this shot was taken; but when I look at this image, I remember that night in 2006 when he came to see his friend play guitar.

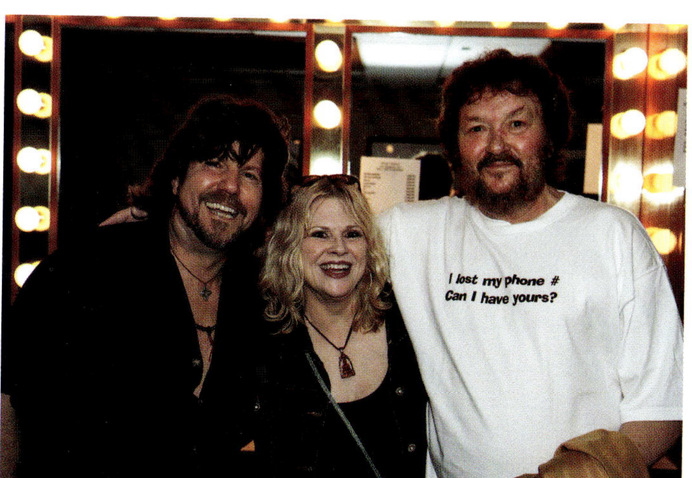

Mark Karan, Susan Lanier-Bramlett, and Delaney Bramlett were backstage at the Greek in 2006.
Taken at 1/45 second, f/4.5 and ISO 160

MEET AND GREETS

Bands sometimes have meet-and-greet events with fans before or after a show. These little gatherings are a good place to get photos of the performers with their fans. As a professional photographer, you can also help keep things moving along. Get fans posed with the musicians, take the photo, and then get the next fan to pose. The fans will appreciate the professional photos. Just be sure to have business cards to give to fans and follow up promptly when they contact you.

The band will appreciate having good photos of themselves with their fans instead of fuzzy, out of focus, point-and-shoot camera images taken by a friend or stranger. It's a great way to make yourself useful and get invited back.

Just be aware of who you're photographing and when it's appropriate to put the camera down. Not everyone backstage wants to have his/her photo taken, and it's likely that some people there will not know who you are. So make sure that the subjects of your posed and candid photos know who you are and for whom you're working. When you're unsure if you should take a photo, ask.

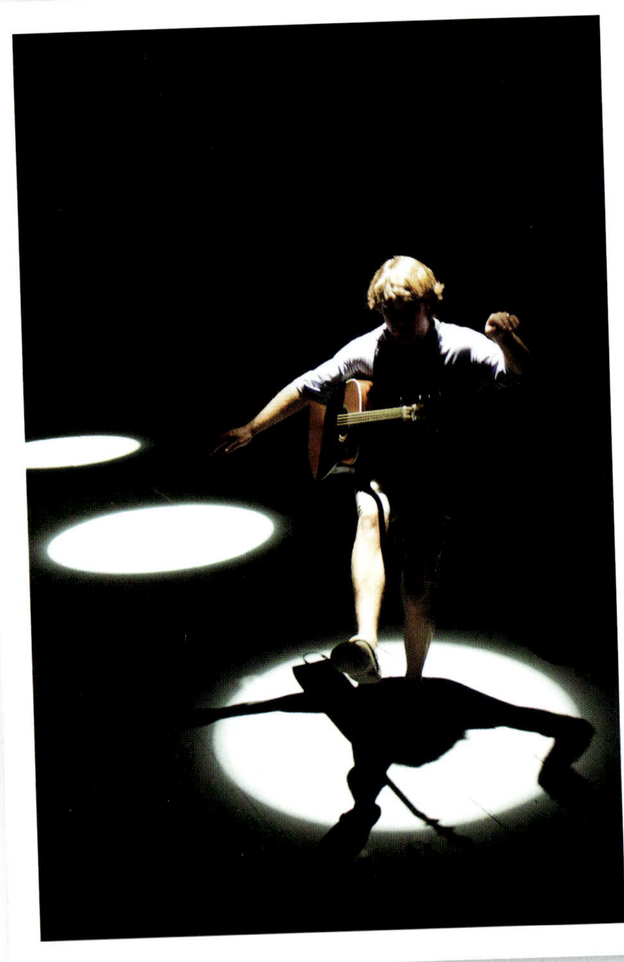

Standing backstage at the Greek Theatre, Keller Williams noticed how the spotlights in the ceiling were creating distinct shadows on the stage, and he started fooling around in the light. It's one of my favorite shots of him. And I only got it because trust had been built between us over the course of the tour.

Taken at 1/40 second, f/2.8, and ISO 250

TRUST

Successful photographers earn the trust of their subjects. I believe this is true for all types of photography, but it's especially true for backstage concert photography of a band. Musicians grant access to a photographer if they trust him/her. They trust that (s)he will act professionally at all times.

I believe that I've gotten certain access with musicians because they trust that I'll show only the best images of them—work that I think is good and worth showing. They also trust … even in this day and age of paparazzi trying to capture the next tabloid cover … that I'll hold myself to certain standards.

This kind of relationship is built with bands, publicists, crew, promoters, and everyone I work with. So when a publicist grants me permission to photograph a band, they know that I'll follow the rules. They can trust that the access they grant me is not going to be abused. Proof of a job well done is that I'm invited back for another show.

When you do your job well, you eventually become part of the regular scene backstage. You become almost invisible to the performers and their crew, and that's a good thing, because it gives you freedom to capture the real moments and not just posed shots.

But I'll say it again: The most important thing you can do for your career is to always act professionally. You just never know who is around at any given moment. One of the reasons

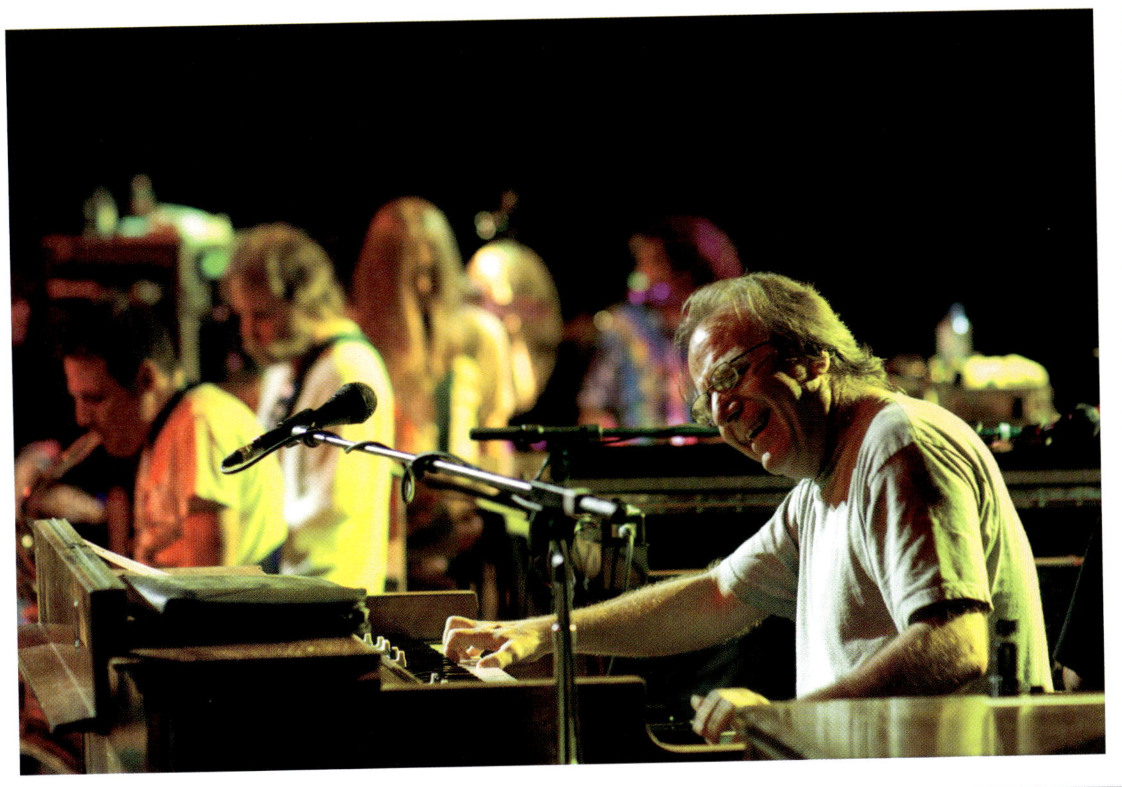

I was allowed all access during many of the Bob Weir and RatDog tours in part because they trusted me to get the shots. This photo of keyboard player JT Thomas was shot from the side of the stage during a RatDog performance. There would have been no way to get this without the access I had.
Taken at 1/60 second, f/2.0, and ISO 400

I'm allowed to shoot some bands with full access is that a band manager saw me working backstage with another band. My behavior at that show spoke more about me as a photographer than anything I could have said and shown him. So behave!

Jay Blakesberg

Jay Blakesberg is a San Francisco-based commercial photographer and video director whose work appears regularly in magazines, including Rolling Stone *and* Guitar Player. *Over the last 32 years, his photographic rock and roll journey has allowed him to work with many legendary artists, including the Grateful Dead, Carlos Santana, Tom Waits, Neil Young, Joni Mitchell, Radiohead, Phish, Dave Matthews, and John Lee Hooker … to name just a few.*

www.blakesberg.com

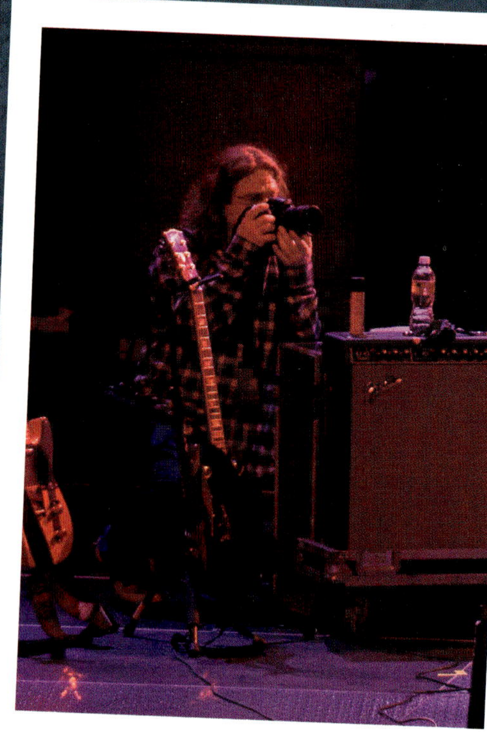

What is the one piece of photography gear you just couldn't live without?

I'm a Nikon guy. I love wide lenses. My new fav is 14–24mm f/2.8, so that would be the *can't live without* item. You also HAVE to have a wide lens if you're shooting backstage, as the rooms can be small. Also, the fast lenses let you shoot available light. MacPro is another essential piece of gear. Lightroom and Photoshop, too.

When shooting backstage/on stage, what are the rules you follow?

I've made my career by breaking the rules! That's how I got backstage! Be polite; be invisible. Don't GEEK out on your subjects. Take brilliant pictures and maybe they will invite you back!

When shooting on stage, you need eyes in the back of your head. You need to be aware of where every mic stand is, every electrical box on the floor, every cable. You never want to put yourself somewhere you can't get out of quickly. Never touch the band's equipment. Never rest a camera on an amp or speaker, and be aware of sight lines for crew/guitar techs, sound engineers, stage managers. Don't ever piss off someone! It's their stage; you are just visiting. You're a guest. Act that way!

How important is the trust between you and the band?

It's the most important thing.

How do you build that trust?

Over time. You build a reputation by working with artists, having a purpose, and not being a hanger-on … unless you're already friends with the band. You don't release compromising photos without permission.

How do you market yourself and stay current in a field that seems to change all the time?

Keep shooting really good work and stay relevant. Transitioning to digital was not easy for many shooters. It took me a few years, and it's not the same as shooting film. You have to bend with the technology and use the tools available to create brilliant images. You're only as good as your last shoot. Marketing is important. Blogs, Facebook, word of mouth, promo email blasts … use anything that keeps your work in front of people who hire photogs!

What advice do you give a photographer just starting out in the concert photography field?

If you want to make a living shooting pictures, then be professional. You actually have to be a business person to be in business! You must put a value on your work. You MUST make a profit and not just pay yourself $6 an hour and hope for the best. Digital gear, accessories, computers, hard drives … it all costs money. Digital is not free.

Creatively, you must be better and different from everyone else out there, or else no one will notice or care about you. There is a GLUT of mediocre concert photography out there, so if you are not original and creative and occasionally brilliant, then forget it.

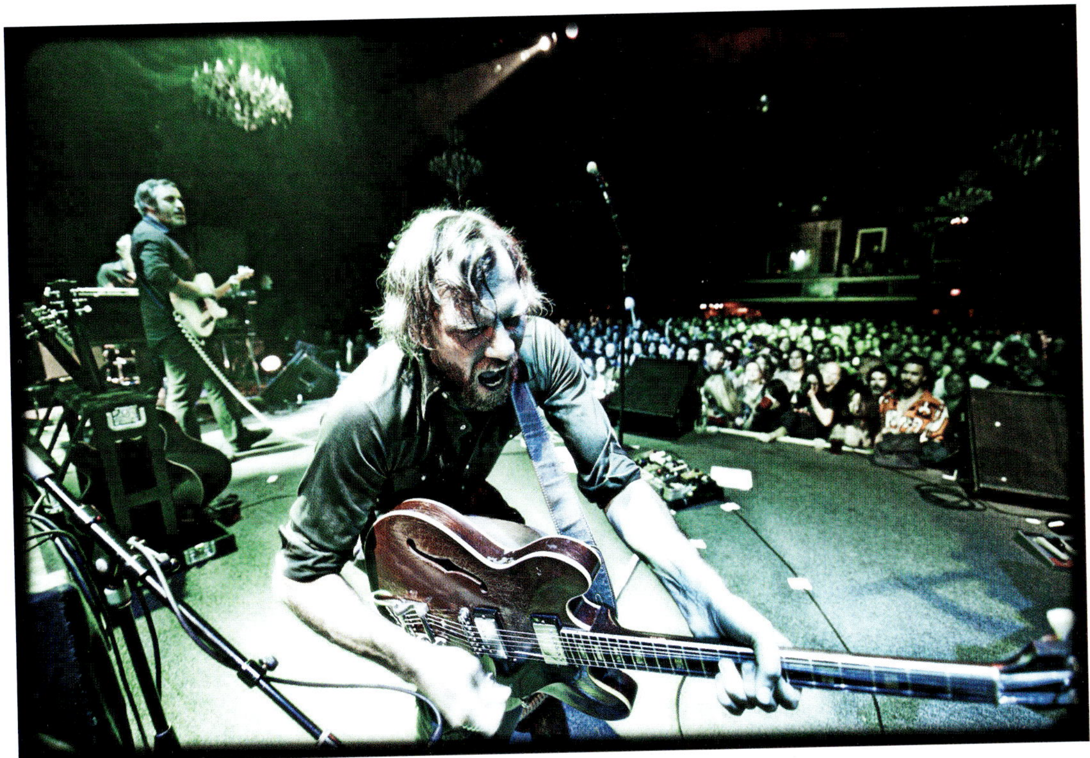

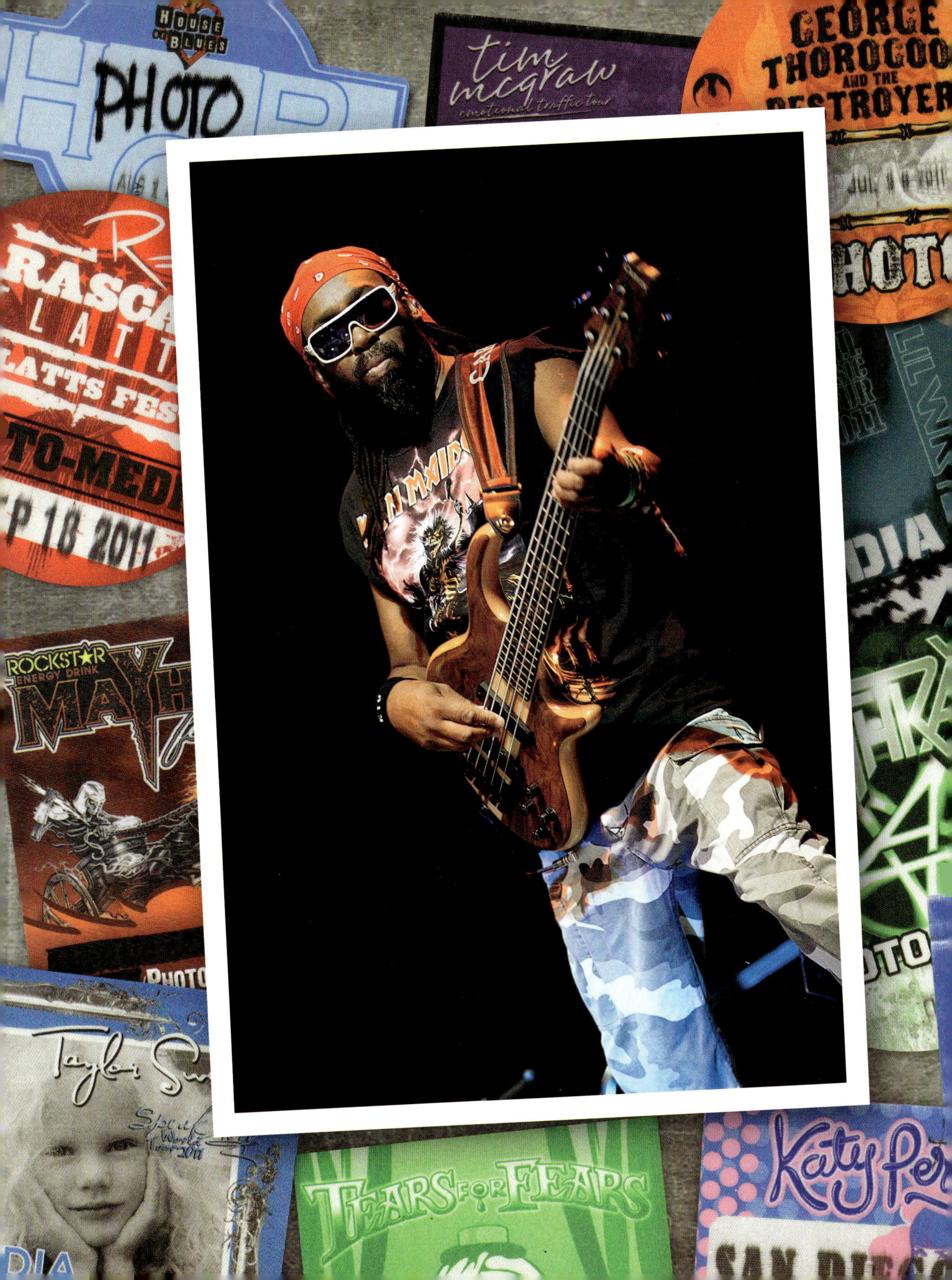

HOUSE OF BLUES
PHOTO
tim mcgraw
emotional traffic tour
GEORGE
THOROGOO
AND THE
ROCKSTAR
ENERGY DRINK
PHOTO
TEARS FOR FEARS

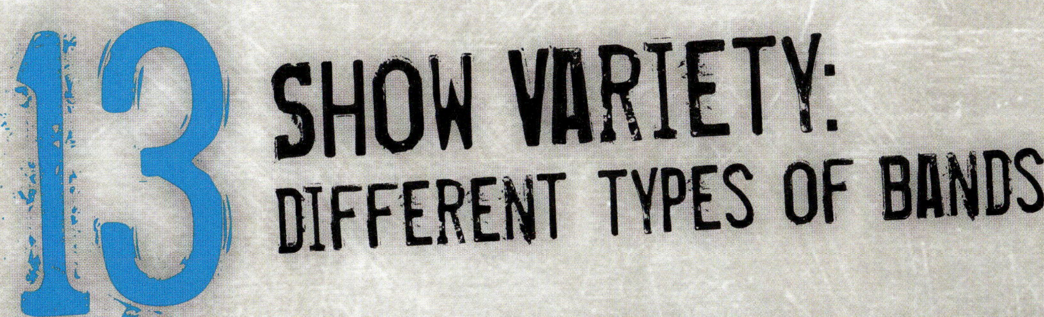

13 SHOW VARIETY: DIFFERENT TYPES OF BANDS

As a concert photographer, you can decide to shoot only the bands you like, or you can shoot any and every show you can . . . regardless of the band or musical genre. And there's everything in between as well. It doesn't really matter what your approach is to choosing shoots, but most of us start out as a fan of a certain band or type of music. And it's likely that this first inspiration will remain your favorite kind of show(s) to shoot.

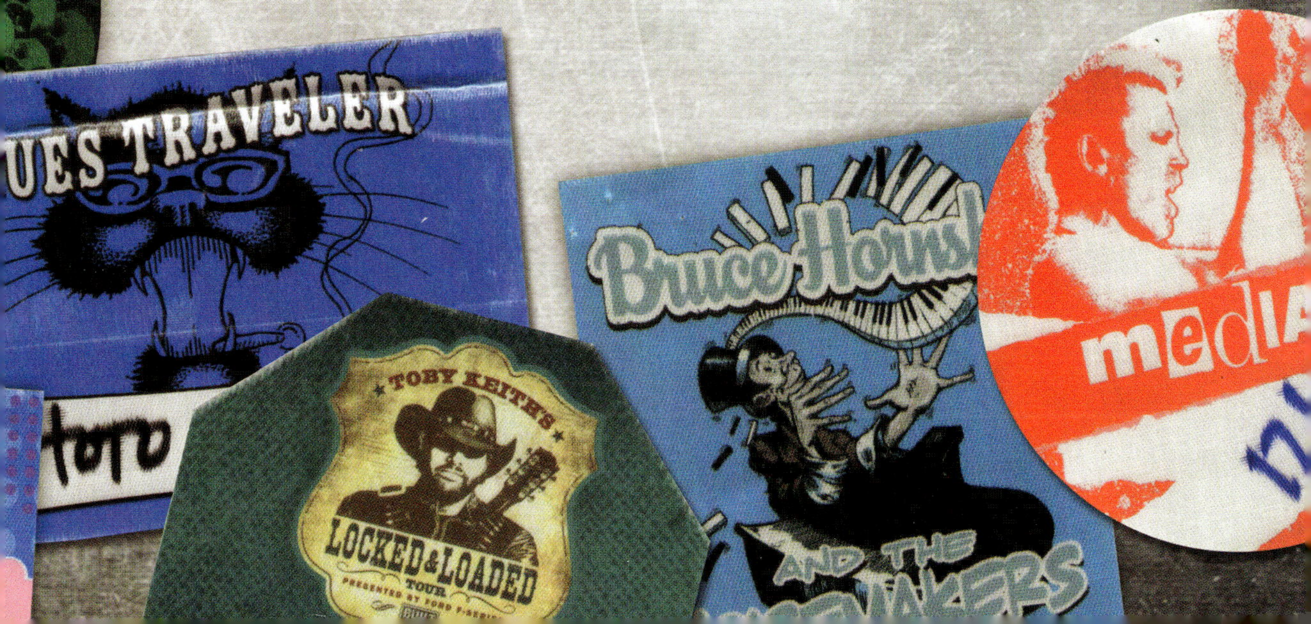

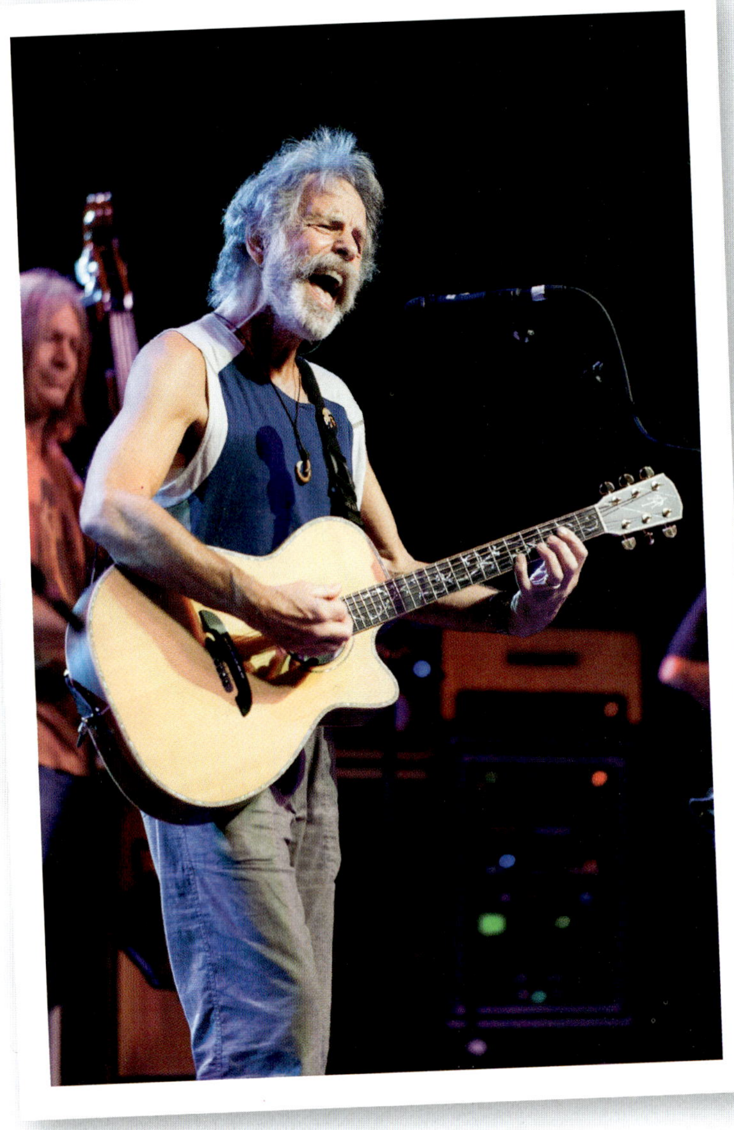

One of the founding members of the Grateful Dead, Bob Weir, formed his band RatDog and continued touring after the death of Jerry Garcia.
Taken at 1/200 second, f/2.8, and ISO 1600

For me it was the psychedelic rock bands (now called *jam bands*) that first inspired my concert photography. One band in particular set my concert photography on this course: the Grateful Dead. And this was fortunate for me, because the Grateful Dead had a very liberal camera policy. The band allowed fans to take photos anytime and from nearly any spot in the audience … as long as no one ruined the concert experience for other fans.

Other bands welcomed photography, too. In 2009, the band Nine Inch Nails relaxed its camera policy. Trent Reznor made a public announcement on the Nine Inch Nails message board outlining what was and was not allowed. The whole message is posted at http://forum.nin.com/bb/read.php?59,641167.

The gist of the message is that dSLR cameras would be allowed, but images could be used only for non-commercial purposes. And photographers could not interfere with anyone else's enjoyment of the show, cause a safety hazard, or sell the images for profit. This sounds very much like the Grateful Dead's policy, right? So it just goes to show that some bands, record labels, and publicity companies are not afraid of fans taking photos.

Every concert is different though. And when it comes to the different genres, I've noticed some similarities. This chapter outlines some tips and guidelines about what to look for when it comes to photographing, say, jam bands versus country or jazz musicians. And we explore how to deal with the fast-moving rock and roll musicians and their head-banging hair flips.

JAM BANDS

The term *jam band* was used to describe the Grateful Dead and other bands that played an improvisational type of music. The Grateful Dead was known to improvise on stage and not necessarily follow a set list. This allowed for a different concert experience every night; no two shows were ever the same.

Now, many bands have embraced the jam band label, while others have tried to distance themselves from it. But for photographers, jam bands can be really fun to shoot. They can also be very frustrating.

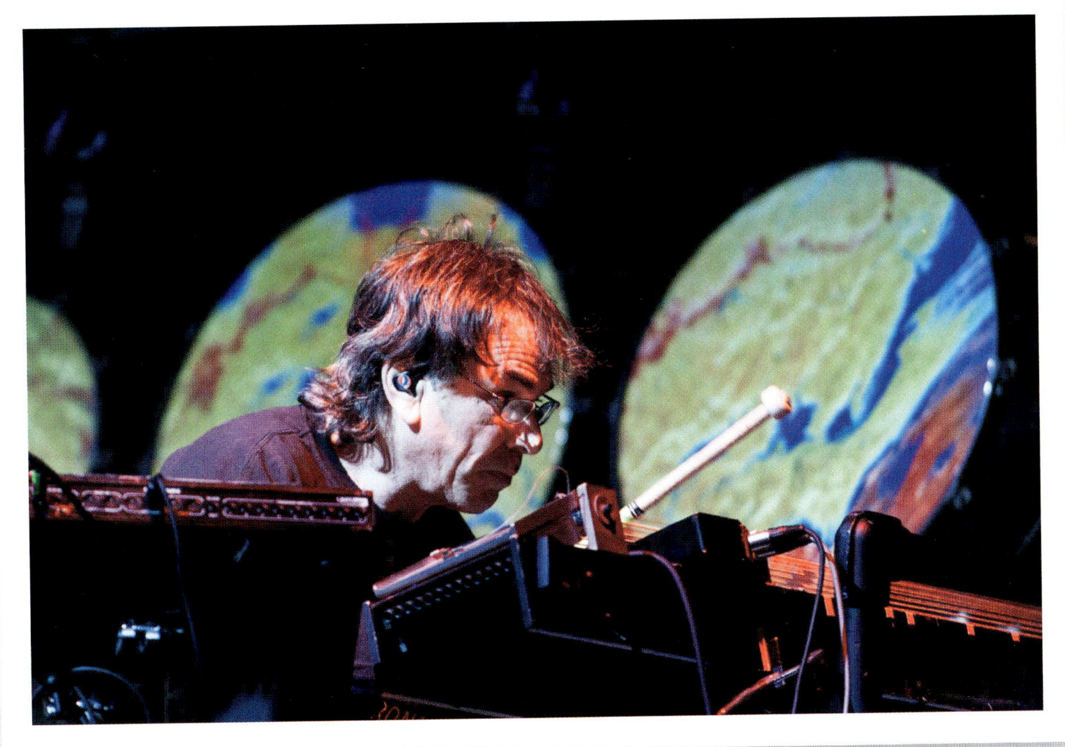

Mickey Hart, half of the Grateful Dead drum duo that was known as the Rhythm Devils, was photographed playing during The Dead tour in 2009.
Taken at 1/100 second, f/2.8, and ISO 1250

On the plus side, jam bands usually have songs that last longer than the usual four minutes that characterize most concert tunes. This means longer shooting times. And unless a band puts a time limit on the shooting, three songs at a jam band's concert can last for a half hour. So when The Dead went on tour in 2008, instead of a three-song limit, the band had a fifteen-minute shooting limit for the photographers in the photo pit. On some nights, this was only a song and a half!

So, at the very least, there were fifteen minutes to take photos, and that can be an eternity in the photo pit. Think of it this way: If a band has six members, then fifteen minutes equals two and a half minutes per musician. Just count out 150 seconds and think of all the photos you can take in that time. It's actually quite a long time to be photographing a single band member, and it's considered gracious by the increasingly stricter limitations and shorter shooting times being implemented by other bands.

There is a downside to the way jam bands stretch out songs, too, and it's that the improvisational music can result in extended periods of the band just standing around, playing ... with the lights pretty low or moody. I'll never forget being in the photo pit for the first post-Grateful Dead band—the Other Ones. The publicist walked up to the photographers and told us not to freak out but the band was going to start the show with the song *Dark Star*. There would be very little light, and this is often a very, very, very long song.

Indeed, we stood there in near dark with just a few blue lights bathing the stage for a 15:30 (fifteen and a half minutes!) version of *Dark Star* before the band went into *Big Railroad Blues*. It was a good thing that the fifteen-minute time limit didn't apply back then, because the lighting for that first song was really dark and all my photos would have been almost identical.

COUNTRY

It seems that the longer I shoot concerts, the more country shows I photograph ... and the more I appreciate how today's country music stars of treat their fans. These shows all seem to have great production values and the stages are often built to extend out into the audience. The only problem with this is that there's no real photo pit, which means no dedicated space for photographers.

In 2011 I photographed Tim McGraw, Toby Keith, and Rascal Flats on their separate tours, and the one thing they all had in common was a lack of a photo pit ... oh, and a two song photo limit!

A growing trend in concert photography (that's especially prevalent in country music) is to reduce the three-song shooting time to two songs. So photographers absolutely must be ready to shoot from the moment the band takes the stage. Another trend, since photo pits are disappearing, is that photographers are positioned at the back of the floor or from the soundboard. Even when shooting at Stagecoach, California's largest country music festival, the main acts on the main stage were soundboard shoots.

But there's something that the country acts seem to do really well, and that is interact with the crowd. With no barrier between the stage and fans, a lot of very up-close-and-personal time happens, and it makes for great performance images. Capturing a moment between a performer and fans makes for a terrific concert shot.

Another thing to watch for when shooting a country show are shadows. Microphones and cowboy hats can cast distracting shadows on a performer's face. With some luck and good timing, you can avoid shadows from the microphone by snapping the shot when the performer moves away from the microphone. But when it comes to cowboy hats, the shadow can be there the whole time. And this can really make it tough to capture the whole face, particularly the eyes.

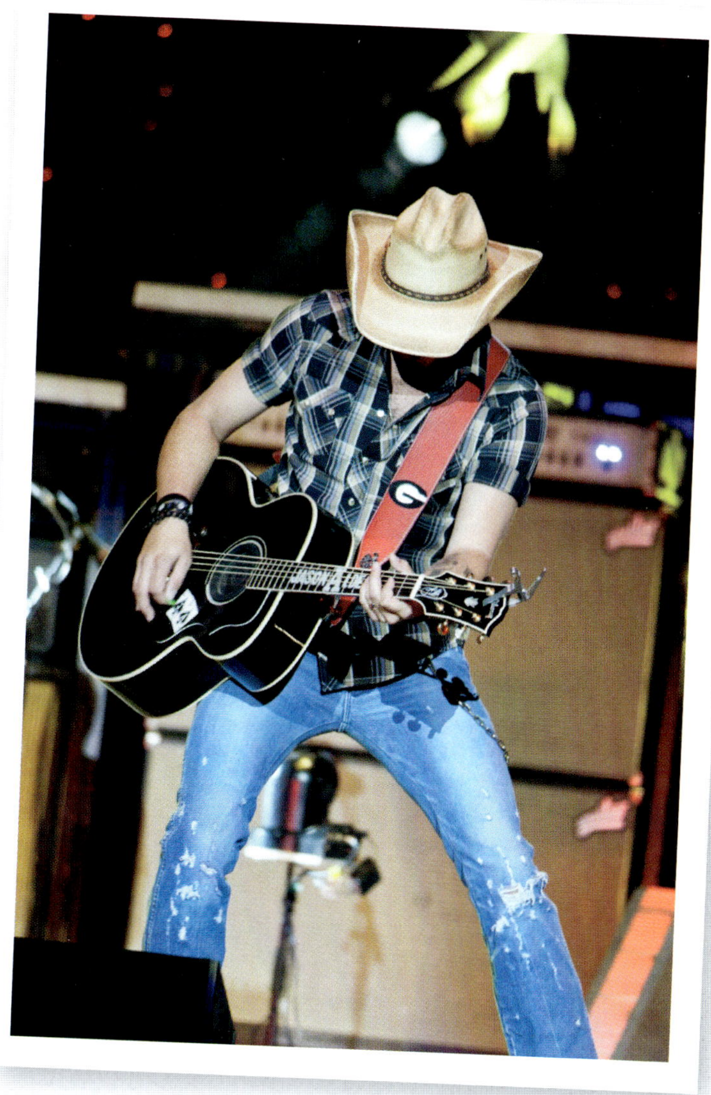

Nothing says country music quite like the cowboy hat and an acoustic guitar.
Taken at 1/320 second, f/4.0, and ISO 1600

A shadow from a hat can be negated if there's a follow spot and the performer looks up, but many times the hat and the shadow will just be there, and it's frustrating. Watch for the subject to look up at the back of the venue or to walk to a position with better up light from the front of the stage. Take those opportunities to focus on the performer's eyes. But keep in mind that sometimes the hat can make the shot.

JAZZ

I don't get many opportunities to shoot jazz shows, but I jump at the chances that do come my way. Photographing jazz is not easy, because these shows tend to take place in moody, dark venues; that's all part of the mystique of this kind of music. It helps that the action isn't very fast moving, so you can use a slower shutter speed to get a proper exposure. But even with the slower shutter speeds, you still need to be prepared to really push the ISO on your camera.

One thing to try when shooting jazz is to shoot in black and white or convert your color images to black and white later. I've found that this can give the images a more timeless feel that harkens back to an earlier era.

The thing with jazz is that it's subtle—the movements and the music. And there's something about jazz musicians that defines cool. But when I photographed a small jazz show and then looked through the images at home, I was shocked to see that they were all very similar … and a little underwhelming. It surprised me because I remember the music being so interesting. The images seemed to miss that.

When I looked closer at the facial expressions of the players, I realized that I had captured the moments but in a more subtle way. This was not the windmilling arm of Pete Townshend or the guitar bashing of Jimi Hendricks; it was the cool jazz cat doing his thing.

ROCK AND ROLL

The term *rock and roll* covers a lot of different sounds and many different looks. Its look has definitely changed with the times. The hair gets longer and then shorter; the style goes from a skinny tie and a flannel shirt and back to suits … or just your favorite jeans and t-shirt.

The sound, the music itself, changes with the times, too, but it always seems to match the generation. The angry protest songs of the 1960s by Bob Dylan, for instance, do not sound the same as the angry songs by Korn. But in essence they are the same. And really, the basics of rock and roll have not changed much since the Beatles took the stage back in the 1960s and launched the genre. It's all about guitars, drums, and vocals … and sometimes a keyboard or a saxophone … oh, and attitude—plenty of attitude.

When photographing rock bands, it's that certain attitude that I want to capture. Rock and roll has always been about rebellion … from when Elvis Presley first gyrated on the Ed Sullivan show to the rise of the grunge movement in Seattle. With that in mind, there are three things I look for when shooting rock and roll:

- **Posture and Poses**
  From alarming hip gyrations to the madness of screaming fans, rock and rollers have been posing for the crowds for decades. Watch for this and capture it. Check the Internet to see if the band you're shooting has a signature move. This will help you know what to watch for.

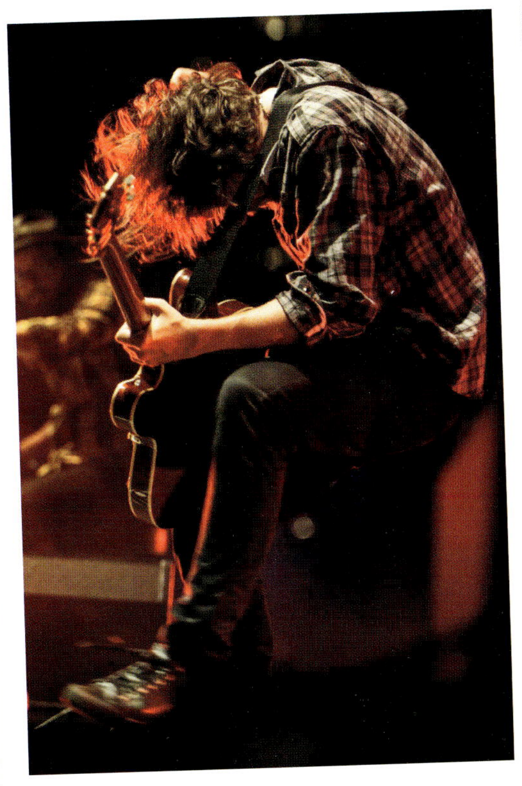

The body position makes this shot. There is no doubt that the guitar player is just rocking out.

Taken at 1/160 seconds, f/2.8, and ISO 1600

- **The Guitar**
  We covered how to photograph the guitar back in Chapter 6, and here's where that info gets put to use. In my opinion, the guitar *is* rock and roll. And when I think of the famous rock and roll shots that inspire me, it always comes back to photographs of musicians with their guitars. The photograph by the great Jim Marshal of Jimi Hendricks at Woodstock with his hat in the air and the guitar hanging across his body just screams rock and roll to me.
- **Facial Expressions**
  The emotion on a performer's face is really important for these images. Watch the expressions, the moments of a pause, and the peak moments of a sustained note. Pay attention to the eyes, especially during a particularly heartfelt lyric. Capture emotion and you'll create photos that people want to look at. Emotion is compelling.

HEAVY METAL

I'm drawn to action, and photographing heavy metal concerts and hard rock bands are definitely action-packed. The thing with the metal bands though is that they move around … a lot, and you need to freeze this action. That's why the

Rock and Roll is all about attitude, and there is no doubt that there is attitude on the bass player's face. Indeed, Ted Russell Kamp has plenty of attitude.

Taken at 1/640 second, f/5.6, and ISO 200

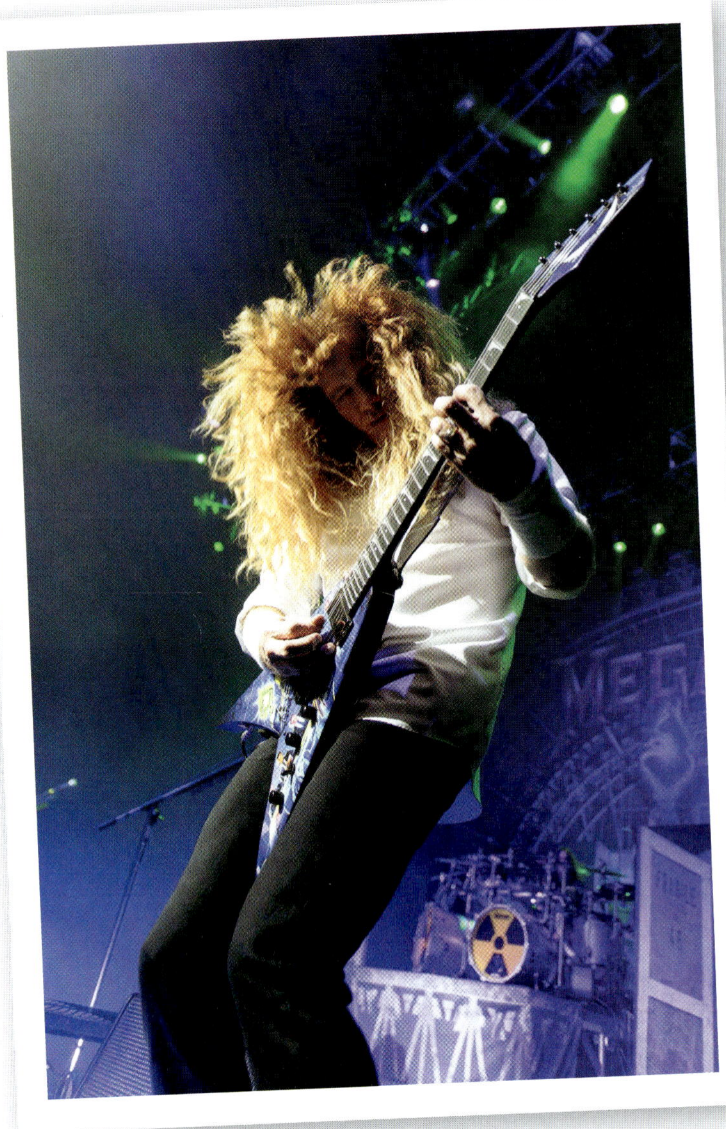

Here's a shot of the hair flying and guitar shredding Dave Mustaine of the band Megadeth. This is a great band to photograph, but be prepared for fast action, which calls for high shutter speeds.
Taken at 1/250 second, f/2.8, and ISO 800

shutter speed for a heavy metal show needs to be a lot higher than what's needed for jazz or jam band concert photos. Of course, each show is different, but I suggest maintaining a shutter speed of about 1/250 or faster for a heavy metal show.

These concerts also tend to have very fast-moving light shows. Getting the timing right, so you can get a shot that captures the band at interesting moments and with good light, can be a challenge. That's why I don't move much at these shows. Instead, I pick a spot that gives me a good view of the stage from about a 45-degree angle. This position minimizes photos in which the microphone is blocking the performer's face.

And the thing with heavy metal is hair. Like attitude, hair has always been a big part of rock and roll. And while times and styles change, flying hair is still very much a part of the hard rock scene, which is good and bad. It's great to photograph flying hair, but it's really annoying when it covers the face of a performer you're trying to shoot.

To capture the exact right moment of the hair fling, high speed advance and a little luck are really helpful. Frame the shot and take a sequence of images, then cross your fingers and hope to get a good one as the hair flies around.

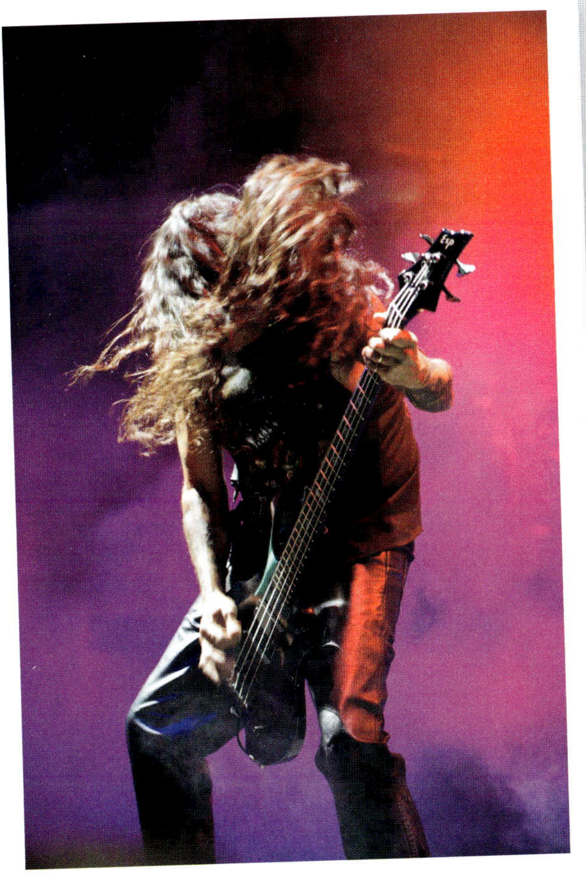

It's not always important to see the face of the musician through all the hair. And with a slightly slower shutter speed, the hair can seem to be in motion with a slight blur.

Taken at 1/100 second, f/2.8, and ISO 1600

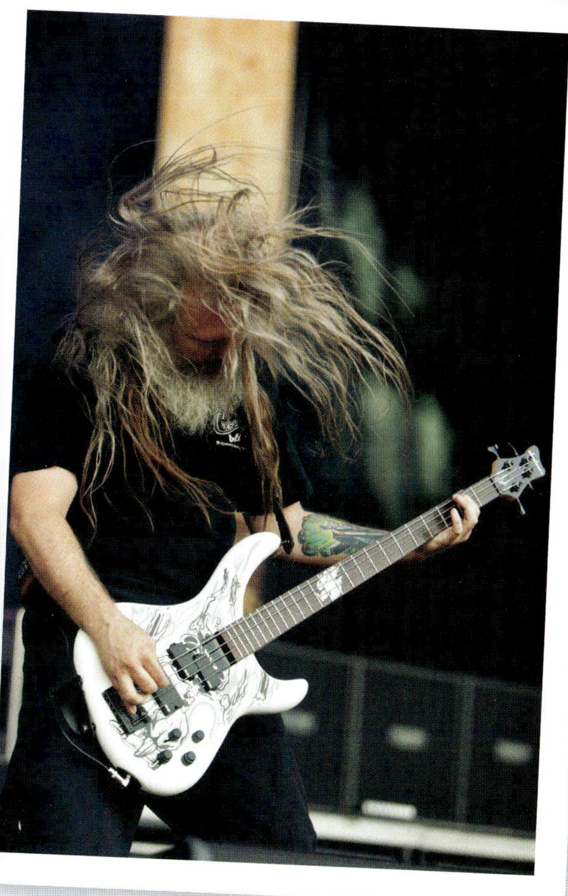

Pushing the shutter speed up to 1/400 freezes the guitar action but still leaves a little motion in the hair. The difference between this and the previous photo is that you can actually see some of the face here.

Taken at 1/400 second, f/2.8, and ISO 800

RAP/DJ

When it comes to photographing rap and DJ shows, you don't usually need to worry about capturing instruments in photos. What you *do* need to show though is the microphone. But this shouldn't be too much of a challenge; any musicians are usually at the back of the stage and the rapper is up front and center.

One of the more disappointing and scary concerts I've worked was the show of a very popular rapper who was the headliner at an all-day show. It turned out that my photo pass wasn't good for his set, so I wasn't able to shoot all of the performance. When I was

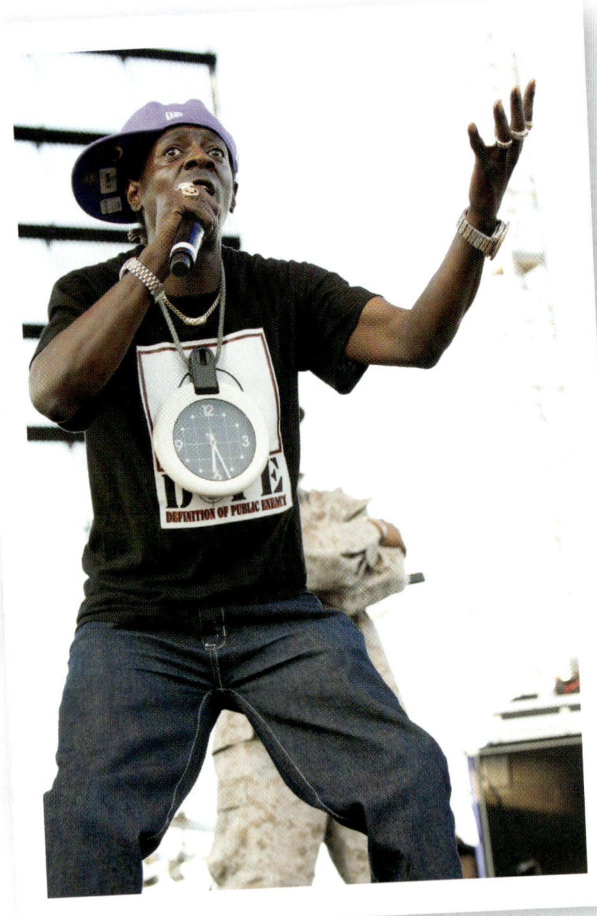

Flavor Flav, part of the group Public Enemy, is shown here in concert in 2009. Getting a shot where the microphone wasn't in the image was tough, so I focused on the face and made sure the eyes and the trademark clock were both visible. *Taken at 1/250 second, f/4.0, and ISO 400*

walking from the front of the stage to the press area at the back of the venue, the aisles had disappeared. And for the first time in my career as a photographer, I was genuinely afraid that I was going to end up with broken camera gear.

Keeping a cool head … not panicking, I made my way through the crowd slowly and carefully. That's the way things go sometime. Crowds can get rowdy—especially rap fans. They are so enthusiastic that they've been known to push into the photo pit. And this makes it tough for photographers to work. When trying to photograph the incredibly popular DJ Girl Talk, for instance, we were removed from the photo pit before the show even started due to a history of the crowd trying to get on the stage.

But the real problem with photographing this and any other DJ, in my experience, is that you really want to capture the turntables in a cool way from a spot in the photo pit. If the angle isn't right though, it's almost impossible. Try to get a side angle on the stage and focus on the hands (if you can see them).

When photographing DJs, notice that most of them use computers now. The light from the screen can be used to illuminate the DJ's face as (s)he leans down into the mix. Watch for this brighter light and use it.

Instead of shooting from the front of the photo pit, I stood off to the side and used a longer lens to get in close.
Taken at 1/250 second, f/4.0, and ISO 400

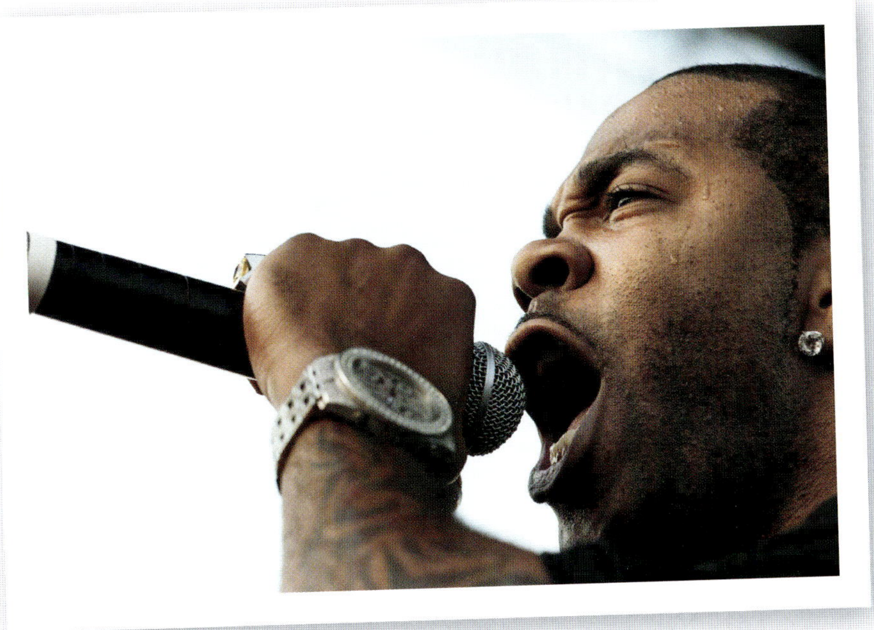

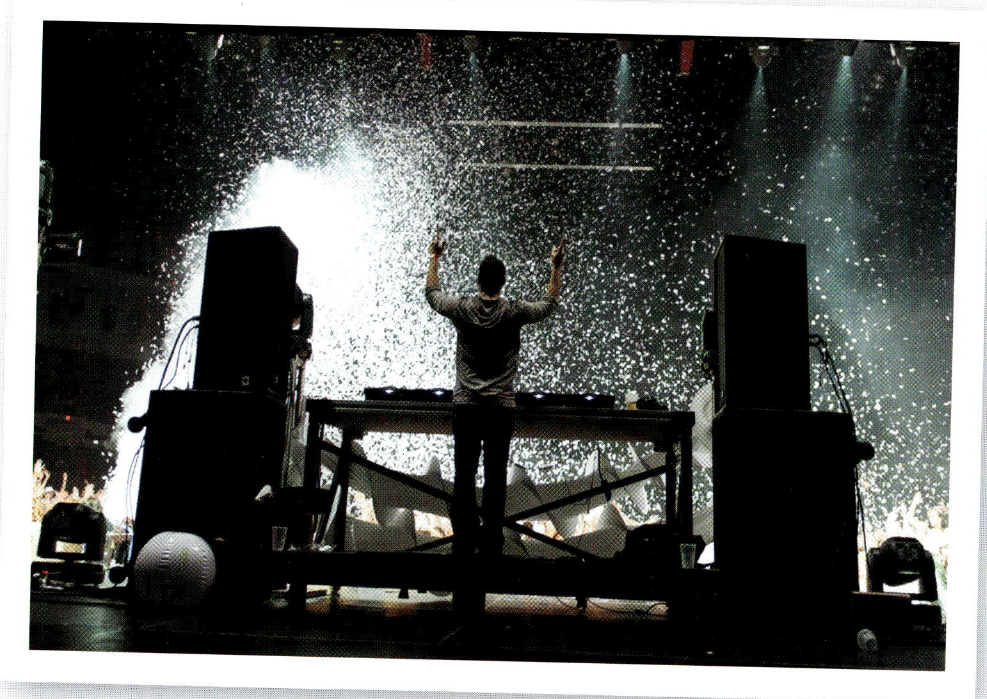

Being able to shoot from behind the DJ allowed me to capture the action … even though I couldn't see the hands on the turntables. There was no angle that allowed that, so I improvised.
Taken at 1/60 second, f/2.8, and ISO 2000

Brad Moore

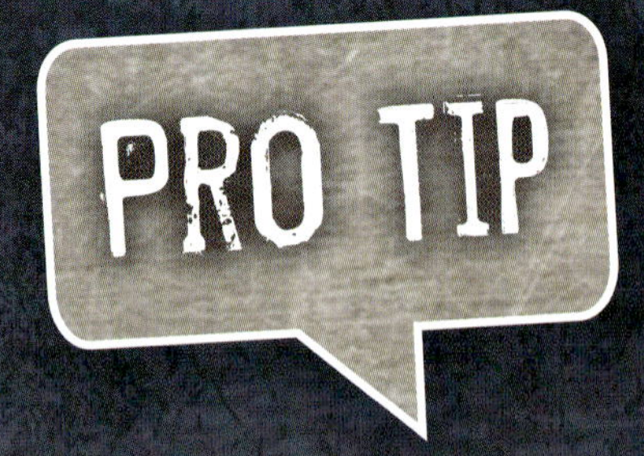

Brad is an entertainment photographer based in Tampa, Florida. He loves being able to combine music and photography to capture the best moments of shows from a unique perspective.

bmoorevisuals.com
twitter.com/bmoorevisuals
bit.ly/bradgplus

What is your favorite type of music to shoot?

My favorite type of music to shoot is anything that's energetic. If the music is energetic, then the performance is going to be energetic, and that makes for great photos.

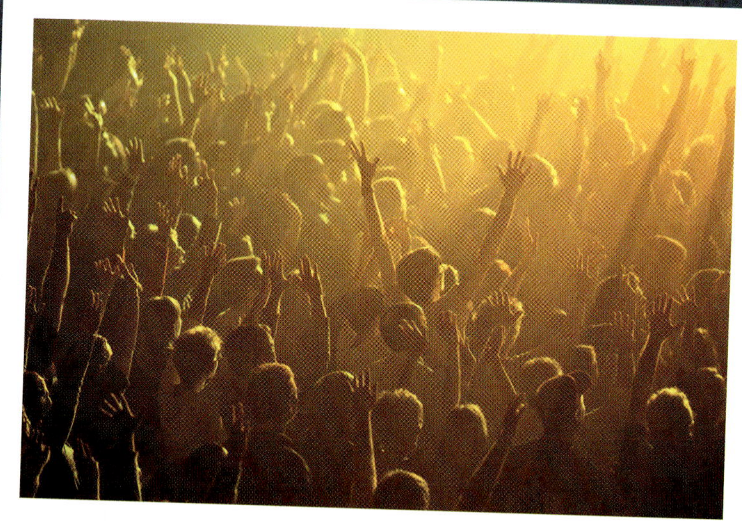

© Brad Moore

Do you approach the different types of shows differently?

I always try to capture tight, medium, and wide shots—no matter type of show I'm shooting. The two things that affect my shooting strategy are shortened shooting times (reduced song limits) and my feelings about the artist. Here's why: If you don't pay attention to your time clock (song limit), then you'll be kicked out of the pit before you have all the shots you need. And when I'm a big fan of the music, it's easy for me to get caught up in enjoying the performance and not realize I'm almost out of time before getting all my shots. I say always go in with a mental shot list and get through it as quickly as you can. Once you've got everything you need, you can use any extra time to get more creative shots.

Does the type of show or music make any difference in your gear or settings?

Not really. Gear is generally the same: two cameras (Nikon D3 and D700), three lenses (14–24mm f/2.8, 24–70mm f/2.8, and 70–200mm f/2.8). Settings, too: aperture priority at f/2.8, continuous/single point focus, spot metering, and auto ISO (especially in constantly changing light, so I don't have to worry about my shutter speed dropping too low). The only time I bring other lenses is if the venue dictates longer glass because of the shooting position; that's when the 200–400 f/4 comes in handy. I'll usually bring a flash for the unexpected, but I rarely use it.

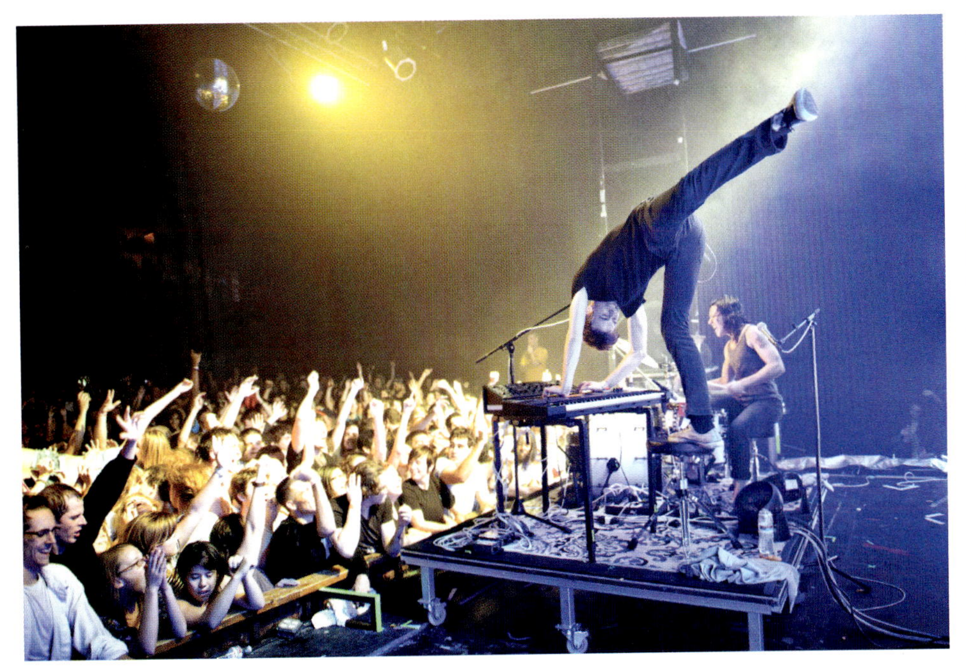

© Brad Moore

Do you only shoot bands you listen to or does it matter? What if the band is not your style?

Because I have a full-time job, concert photography is something I do for fun. This allows me to cover only the shows I would want to go to anyway. The only time I cover shows I wouldn't normally pay to see is when it's a big name and I'm familiar enough with the music to know what I'm getting myself into. That said, I am constantly on the lookout for new music, so I do explore artists I'm not familiar with … just so I don't miss out on a show I'll regret not seeing.

What is one piece of advice you would give a photographer just starting out in the concert photography game?

I'm going to cheat and give three tips. If you want to have any chance whatsoever of making a living doing concert photography, you have to be great at three things:

- The first is a given: Take amazing photos.
- Second: Constantly improve your post-processing skills. Knowing Lightroom and Photoshop inside and out will give you an edge over other concert photographers.
- Third: Learn how to market yourself. If you can't do this, then you have no chance of making any money, because the few people who still have money to spend on concert photography won't know you exist.

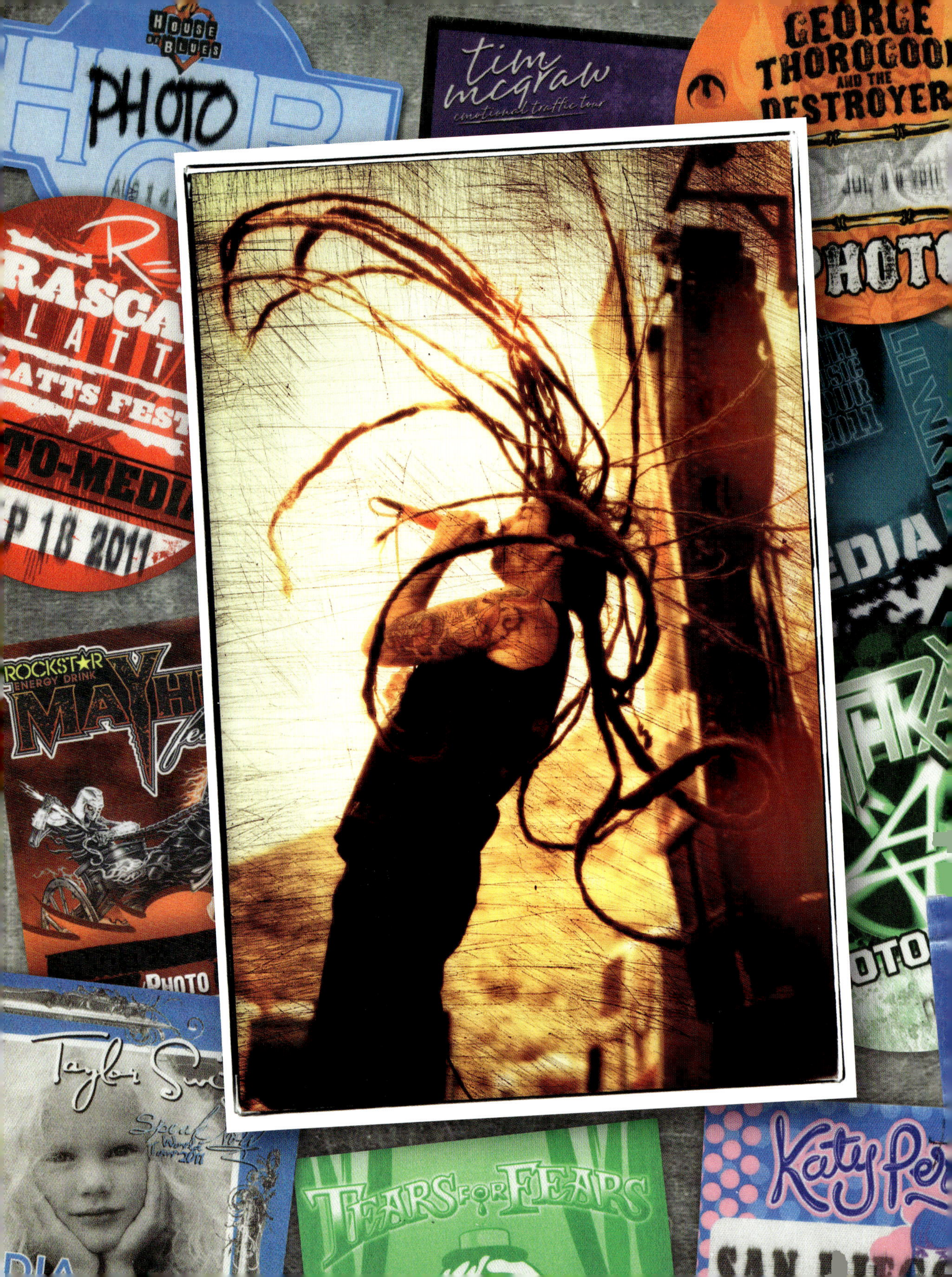
HOUSE OF BLUES
PHOTO
tim mcgraw
emotional traffic tour
GEORGE
AND THE
FLATTS FEST
2011
ROCKSTAR
ENERGY DRINK
PHOTO
TEARS FOR FEARS

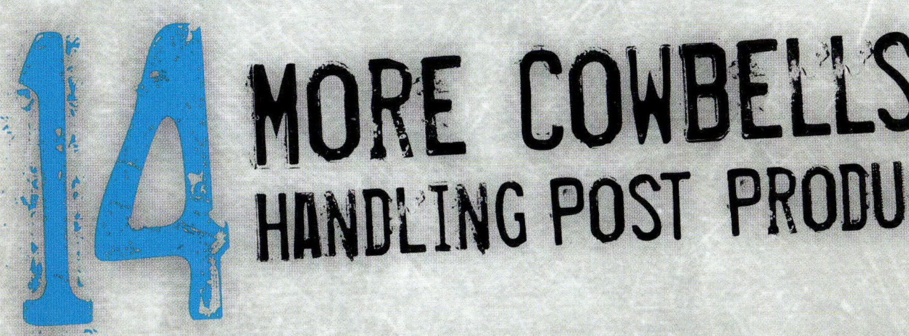

14 More Cowbells: Handling Post Production

When the show is over and you're back home with your memory cards... presumably filled with great concert images, a new kind of work on your photographs begins. It's the post processing. And this part of the gig can actually take longer to complete than shooting the show.

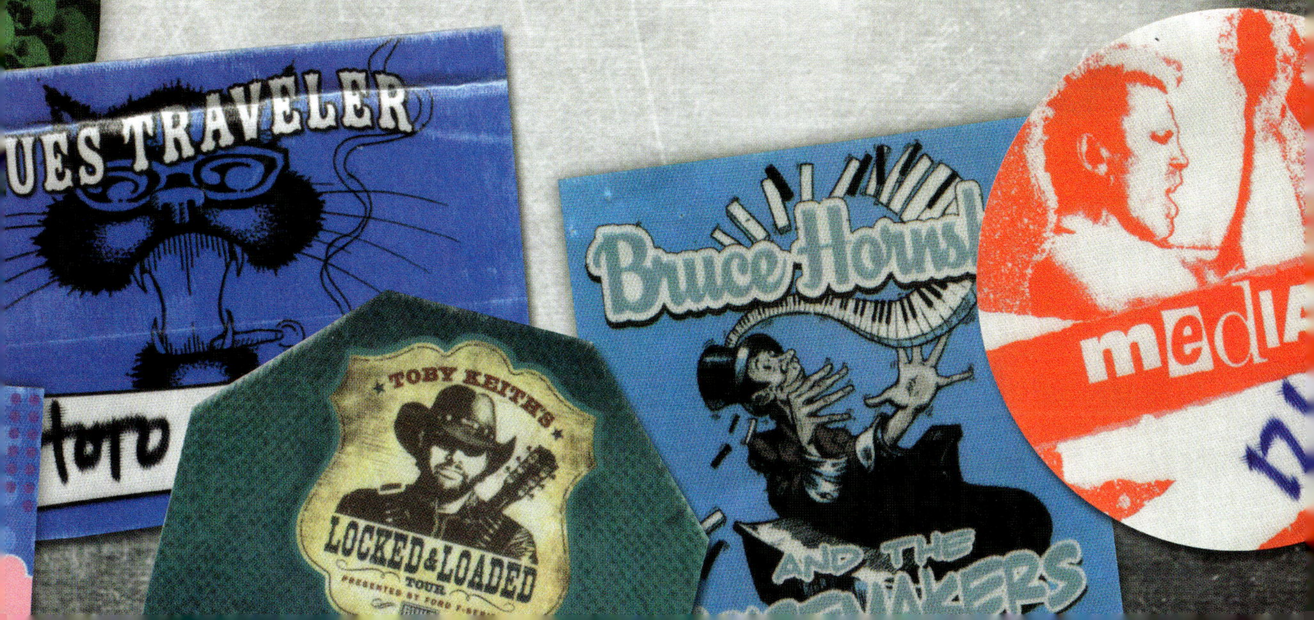

When I started out in this business, I used slide film. I'd bring a box of slides home from processing, spread them out on a big light table, break out the loupe, and study each image. Only the best ones would get printed and scanned. Now, we can download image files to a computer, sort and edit on the screen, and print or export as needed.

Before we get into image sorting and editing though, we need to cover the different file types used in digital photography.

FILE TYPES: JPEG AND RAW

There are two types of image files: those that can be used right out of the camera and those that need to be processed first.

- **JPEG** files are processed as a photo is taken by the camera, and these files are immediately ready to be emailed, printed, or displayed online.
- **RAW** files need to be processed before they can be used. Think of a RAW image as an undeveloped negative.

All dSLR cameras can save images as these two different file types, and most allow you to save a single image as both a RAW and a JPEG at the same time. This can be really useful.

When digital cameras first came out and allowed this dual saving of the same image, I used it all the time, because editing RAW files was a time-consuming process. But the launch of image-editing software programs like Adobe Lightroom changed that. These programs allow images to be edited whether they are RAW or JPEG, so I stopped saving each file in both formats. That requires a lot of digital space!

Remember that if you think you want to capture each image as both file types. Your memory card will fill quickly. RAW files are huge. Shooting images in this format means that fewer images will fit on your card, and your camera will need extra time to process each image. Therefore, it will take longer for your camera to be ready to take the next shot.

JPEG

The JPEG file type is based on a form of image compression that was created by the Joint Photographic Experts Group back in 1992. Some advantages of the JPEG file type are that it can be viewed, printed, and shared just about anywhere.

JPEGs take less space than an uncompressed (RAW) file of the same image. So if you need an image to be emailed, used on the Internet, or printed—and you don't want to edit the file on a computer before doing so—then you need to use the JPEG format. But keep in mind that all the settings you applied to the image in the camera are written into a JPEG file, including the sharpening, color settings, and white balance. This makes it difficult to adjust the image later.

Another downside to using the JPEG file type right out of the camera is that the file is already compressed. This means that if you open and adjust it through editing software, and then save the file again as a JPEG, the image will lose quality. The quality will further degrade with each new cycle of editing.

So if you're going to shoot JPEGs, use the highest quality and size of image available in your camera. This will ensure that your files retain as much image data as possible, so you can edit them without compromising too much quality.

RAW

The RAW file type is a digital negative. And, like a negative, it's not really usable until it's been processed (developed) with software like Photoshop's Adobe Camera Raw module, the Lightroom Develop mode, or the program that came with your camera.

The big advantage to using RAW files is that all the image data captured by the camera sensor is recorded in the file, and this gives you the most latitude when post-processing. Each camera manufacturer has its own version of a RAW file, and it can change among camera models as well. The following file extensions are examples of the different types of RAW files from select manufacturers:

- **NEF, NRW** (Nikon)
- **ARW, SRF, SR2** (Sony)
- **CRW, CR2** (Canon)
- **PTX, PEF** (Pentax)
- **RAW, RW1** (Panasonic)

Since each manufacturer has its own proprietary and often-undocumented RAW format, it can be very difficult to use RAW images. In fact, many times you'll need to wait for the various image-editing software companies to catch up with the newer RAW formats before you can process images with anything other than the software supplied with your camera.

Note that some cameras allow images to be edited right in the camera, including conversion from RAW to JPEG. This makes it pretty darn easy to get a JPEG image from the RAW file. You can create a JPEG file as needed from the RAW file, and both will be downloaded to the computer when the files are imported.

CHOOSING A FORMAT

You need to decide what image format to use before taking any photos, and here's why. Although you can get a JPEG from a RAW file, you cannot turn a JPEG into a RAW file. If you just can't decide, remember that it's possible to capture each image in both formats. This gives you two versions of each of your image files.

My personal choice when it comes to photographing concerts is the RAW file type. As mentioned, a RAW file has more data, which provides a lot more wiggle room when adjustments need to be made using software in post-production. But if you need to use images directly from the camera, choose JPEG.

WORKFLOW OVERVIEW

Make a plan for managing your digital assets. You need to know how you're going to deal with the images you take at concerts. Especially if you shoot a lot of shows, you'll end up with many, many images that need to be organized and managed.

The following workflow is the one I employ based upon years of photography work. Use this as a guideline, an example. Your workflow needs to work for you.

1) **Create a folder** with the shoot name and date. Example: "Steel_Pulse_090511"

2) **Create a subfolder** called "Raw_Files" in that main folder for the shoot.

3) **Import the RAW image files** into the "Raw_Files" folder using Photo Mechanic, and add pertinent information using the International Press Telecommunications Council data fields (IPTC) Stationary Pad.

4) **Quickly cull the images** in Photo Mechanic to get rid of the junk. Select the images that are seriously out of focus or way too underexposed, and delete them. Mark the remaining files with a color label, based on categories like *keepers*, *extras* or *client pick*.

5) **Copy images** labeled as keepers into a new folder called "Picks."

6) **Import the "Picks" folder** into the Adobe Lightroom program to make main sorts and edits.

7) **Use Photoshop** to make any big edits on the images.

8) **Export the images** depending on how the photos are needed. For example, if they are for the wire service, then put them in a new folder for the wire service site.

This process keeps images from a specific shoot in one main folder, which makes it easy to access the files later.

IMPORT IMAGES

There are many different ways to get images from your memory card into a computer, but they all begin with connecting your camera or memory card to the computer. Do this with a USB cable or a card reader (built in or external). Then transfer the files through the computer's operating system or with an image-editing software program. Let's take a closer look at some of these methods.

USB CABLE

It's possible to import your images to your computer by plugging your camera into the computer using the USB cable that came with your camera. The downside of this option is that it uses camera battery power and can be rather slow. The advantage is that you don't need an external card reader—just a small USB cable. That's one less piece of gear to buy and carry.

CARD READER

Another option is to use your computer's built-in card port, if it has one. The Apple MacBook Pro has a built-in SD card slot, but not all computers have this feature. If yours does not, you can use an external card reader, which can be USB or Firewire. Just plug it into an open port on your computer. A real advantage to card readers is that many come with the ability to read a large variety of memory cards. This helps if you're using different kinds of cards in different cameras.

I use an external card reader for the CompactFlash cards that my camera uses, because the built-in port on my camera is for the smaller SD card. When a card is inserted into the card reader, choose which software to use to import the images into the computer.

OS

You can also use your computer's operating system (OS) to transfer image files from a camera to the computer. This method just dumps the images from the card to the computer, and I only go this route if I'm using a computer without Photo Mechanic or Lightroom. It works, but it doesn't allow me to add any data on import.

PHOTO MECHANIC

You can also use the import function that's built into programs like Adobe Lightroom, Apple Aperture, and iPhoto. I like to use a program called Photo Mechanic, which is made by a company called Camera Bits. This program does three things really well:

- It imports image files very quickly.
- It allows you to add your copyright and shoot information to image files when they're being imported.
- It allows you to start sorting images as they are imported.

Photo Mechanic was designed primarily for photo journalists who need to work quickly. And the first thing to know about this program is that you do not *import* images with Photo Mechanic; instead, you *ingest* them.

THE IPTC STATIONARY PAD

The IPTC Stationary Pad is a set of data fields that can be populated and added to your images. This information makes it easier to sort and caption your photo files. Some of this data can be added automatically when an image is taken, but other kinds of information can only be added later.

Photo Mechanic Ingest Window:

1) This is where you select which disks or folders of images to import. If you have two card readers attached, you can select multiple sources and import more than one card at a time. You can also decide to copy just the new images or all images on the card. And if multiple cards are selected, you can merge the files into a single destination. This is really useful if you shoot with two different cameras or fill more than one memory card during a shoot.
2) Here, pick the source directory structure and the structure of the files to copy. You can copy all the images into a single destination (my preference) or you can maintain the file structure that was created on the camera.
3) This is where you pick the destination folder and a secondary backup location—where you want to store the images. My preference is to save the files to a folder called "Raw_Images" inside the main shoot folder that's titled with the band's name and date of the shoot. When I'm on the road or at an all-day festival, I travel with a small external disk that I use as a backup. I copy the files to this external disk as the secondary backup location.
4) You can filter your files here and decide if you want all of them. If you shoot both RAW and JPEG files, this is where you decide which ones to ingest.
5) Here, you can apply the IPTC Stationary Pad to your images.
6) Rename your files on import if you want.
7) Open a contact sheet during import and have the program erase and unmount the source disk after import if this is what you want.

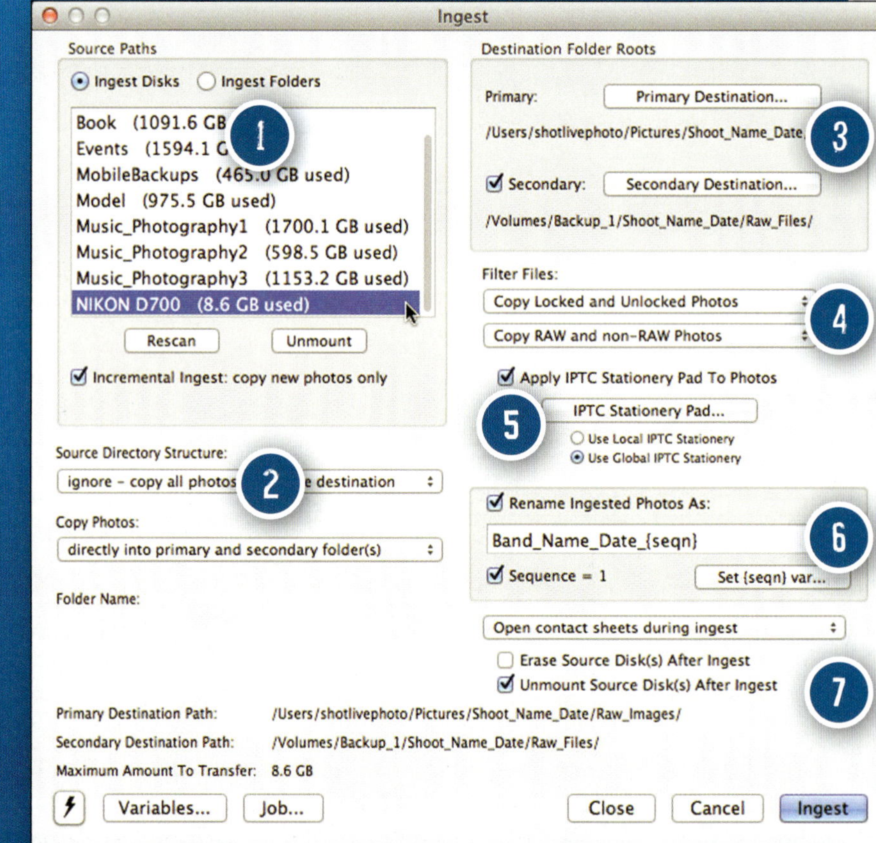

In Photo Mechanic, you can add the following kinds of data using the IPTC Stationary Pad.

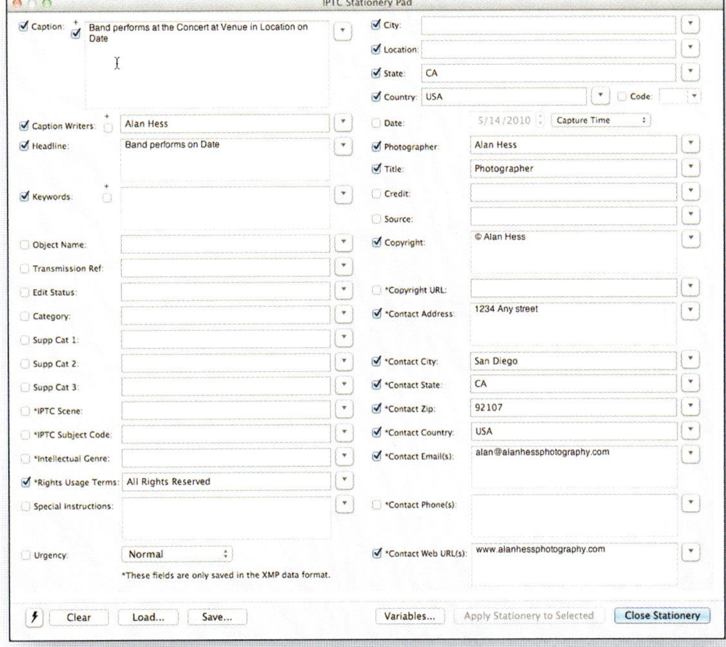

- **Caption:** Use this field to enter a description of the photograph that will stay attached to the file.
- **Caption Writer:** This identifies the person who wrote the caption, which can be helpful for news organizations and other viewers.
- **Headline:** A short data field that's usually very similar to the caption.
- **Keywords:** These words are associated with the image and allow for searching and sorting images.
- **Location:** Specify where the image was taken and when.
- **Photographer Info:** Here, enter info about the photographer, including contact numbers, website address, and copyright information, if available.

This info can be saved to be used again at a later date. For example, I have generic IPTC Stationary Pads for each of the different venues at which I regularly shoot, so the info doesn't need to be entered more than once.

COLOR CALIBRATION

One of the most important parts of editing images is also one of the most overlooked. I'm talking about *color calibration*, which provides consistency and accuracy of colors shown on your computer monitor. Numerous products are available to help photographers calibrate a monitor, and they all work in this same basic way: Just attach the calibrating device to a monitor so it sits flush with the screen. The software displays a series of color boxes that the device reads, and the readings from the device are turned into a custom profile for that monitor.

I use a laptop and an external monitor. Because they're different screens, the colors in my images do not look the same on both. It's tough to edit when you're not sure which (if either) screen is correct. But with both screens calibrated, the images look the same no matter which one they're on.

FIRST SORT

Objectively sorting and rating your own images is difficult. This is because photographers tend to be emotionally invested in all their images—even the not-so-great ones—and have a hard time getting rid of them.

My approach for picking out images that are editing-time worthy and good enough to be shared with others is to go through them fast … and with brutal honesty. It's why I do the first sort as soon as I can and with Photo Mechanic. I start the culling process as soon as the images start to ingest.

When I ingest images, I set Photo Mechanic to automatically open a contact sheet to show me the images being imported. This means I can start to weed out any out-of-focus images, badly composed shots, and mistakes—all of which are a part of every shoot. And as I go through the images, I select the ones that will be thrown away. These are the shots with no redeeming qualities at all; they will never be used for anything.

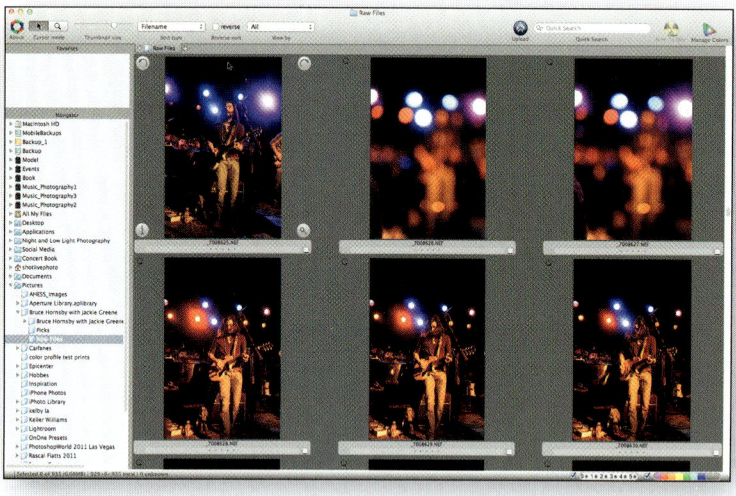

As you can see, two of these photos are seriously out-of-focus. They are selected during the first sort and deleted.

The next step is to go through the remaining images and pick out those that are worth a closer look. They don't have to be great, but they need to be good. And the images that survive this sort are imported into Lightroom and further sorted and edited. I mark these with the red label, making them easy to find.

If I'm working for a client who wants a lot of images, then this sort is fairly relaxed. But if I'm trying to cull images down to just a few great ones, then it's more intense and I get rid of more images. The key is to go fast and not look back. When I'm in doubt, the image is included, because it can always be removed later.

Below are the steps I follow to do my sort.

1) Double click on the first image in the Photo Mechanic contact sheet to open the preview window.

2) Press the letter F for full view.

3) Press the left and right arrow keys to scroll through the images. Select winners by pressing the 2 key. This labels the image "red."

4) When all the keeper images color tagged red, close the preview window to return to the contact sheet.

5) Change the sort to Color Class. This groups the winner images together.

6) Select all the winner images and click File > Copy/Move Photos to open the Copy Option dialog menu.

7) Choose the "Picks" folder inside the "BandName_Date" folder.

8) Make sure that the images are being copied and not moved. The originals should stay in the "RAW_Files" folder, because that is backed up separately. Consider these to be the negatives that can be accessed later if needed.

9) Click Copy to copy the images to the "Picks" folder.

This process creates a folder of images that are worth editing. With that done, it's time to move over to Lightroom for sorting and editing the images.

LIGHTROOM

Lightroom (or, Adobe Photoshop Lightroom, as it is officially named) is in its third version as I write this. But the basics of the program have been the same since the first version. Lightroom is a program that allows photographers to import, edit, and export photographs. It also makes it easy to create slideshows, prints, and web galleries. Lightroom is divided into five distinct modules and separate import and export menus. The five modules are:

- **Library**
- **Develop**
- **Slideshow**
- **Print**
- **Web**

But before we can start working our way through the different modules, you need to get your images into Lightroom. The program's import module has improved greatly with each new version, so now it can import your images and also add IPTC information.

IMPORT

The import menu is divided into four parts.

- On the left, pick the source for the images to be imported—either a memory card or someplace on your computer. In the workflow described earlier, the source is the directory of Picks in the band folder that was created in Photo Mechanic.
- The center top of the screen allows you to choose how you want to Copy/ Move/ Add the files.
- In the middle area, users can select the images to import.
- In the area on the right, tell Lightroom where to save the imported images.

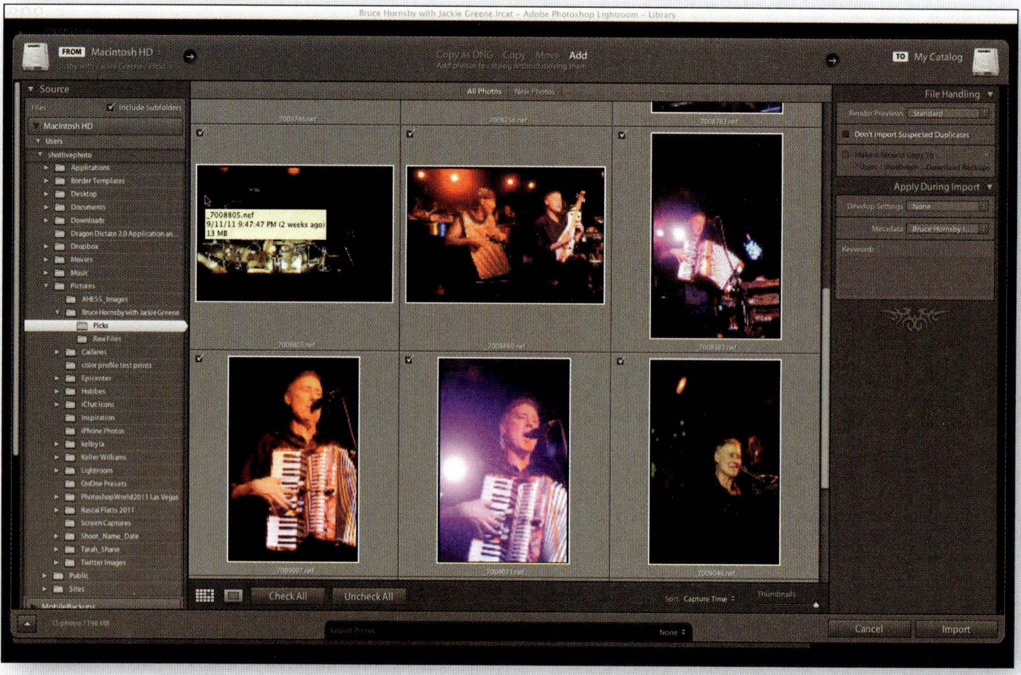

If you've already imported the images to your computer, just add the files to Lightroom. This doesn't take much time.

One of the more powerful features of Lightroom is its ability to add Develop settings to images being imported. Develop presets are just settings from the develop mode that you can apply to the images automatically on import. So if you have a certain develop setting that you want to apply to every image being imported, you can. Just pick the setting from the drop-down list on the right side of the screen.

You can also add a metadata preset to all the images on import. This allows you to add information about each image to the file without entering it each time; it's saved as a preset. To create a metadata preset:

1. Click on the Metadata drop-down list and pick New to open the New Metadata Preset.
2. The New Metadata Preset window allows you to enter a vast amount of information, which is broken down into the following sections:
   - **Basic Info:** Add the Copy Name, Rating, Label, and Caption.
   - **IPTC Content:** Enter a Headline, IPTC Subject Code, Description Writer, Category, and Other Categories.
   - **IPTC Copyright:** Add the Copyright, the Copyright Status, the Rights Usage Terms, and the Copyright Info URL.
   - **IPTC Creator:** Enter the creator's name, address, city, state/ providence, postal code, country, phone number, email, website, and job title.

- **IPTC Image:** Add the Date Created, Intellectual Genre, the IPTC Scene Code, Sublocation, City, State/ Providence, Country, and ISO Country Code.
- **IPTC Status:** Enter the Title, Job Identifier, Instructions, Credit line, and Source.
- You can also add the **IPTC extended** information, which is usually only used by news photographers. Here are the options:
  - IPTC Extension Administrative
  - IPTC Extension Artwork
  - IPTC Extension Description
  - IPTC Extension Models
  - IPTC Extension Rights
- **Keywords:** Add any keywords to the images on import.

3. After entering the information you want attached to each image on import, pick a name for the preset and click the Create button (located in the bottom right corner).

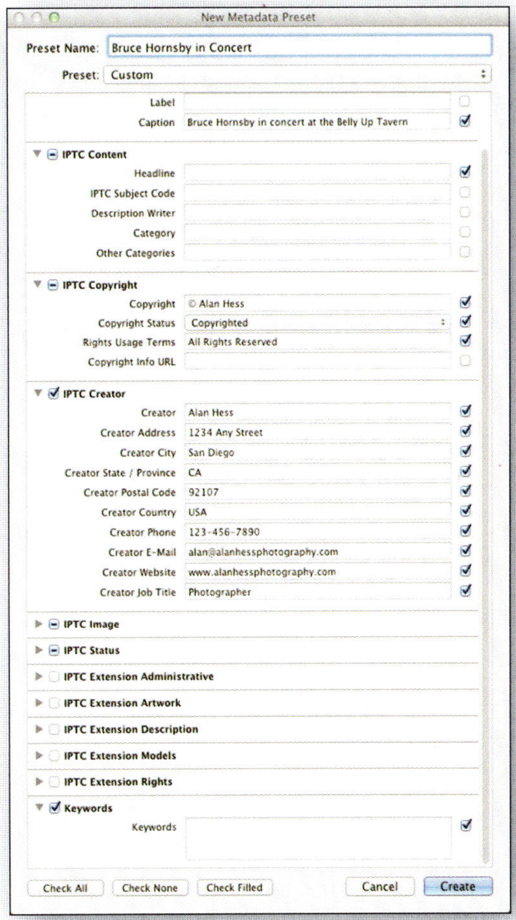

You can enter all of this image information when importing your images with Photo Mechanic, or you can do it here.

When your images are in Lightroom, the real fun can begin. The two most important modules in my workflow are the Library module and the Develop module. After those, we'll be ready for the Export menu. But first things first. Let's find out what the Library module does.

THE LIBRARY MODULE

The Library module allows you to sort your images and rate you images. You can also add keywords, change metadata, and even to do some quick editing. Each image can be rated by using a star system that ranges from no stars to five stars. And you can give each image a color label, too.

But I think the most important thing here is that you can flag your images. This is the one-step rating system that I use when sorting my images. Either they are good enough to be a pick, or they're not. Remember, we already did an initial sort in Photo Mechanic, so this is when it becomes a little tougher. Study each image to make sure it really is one of the best. If it is, mark it as a pick.

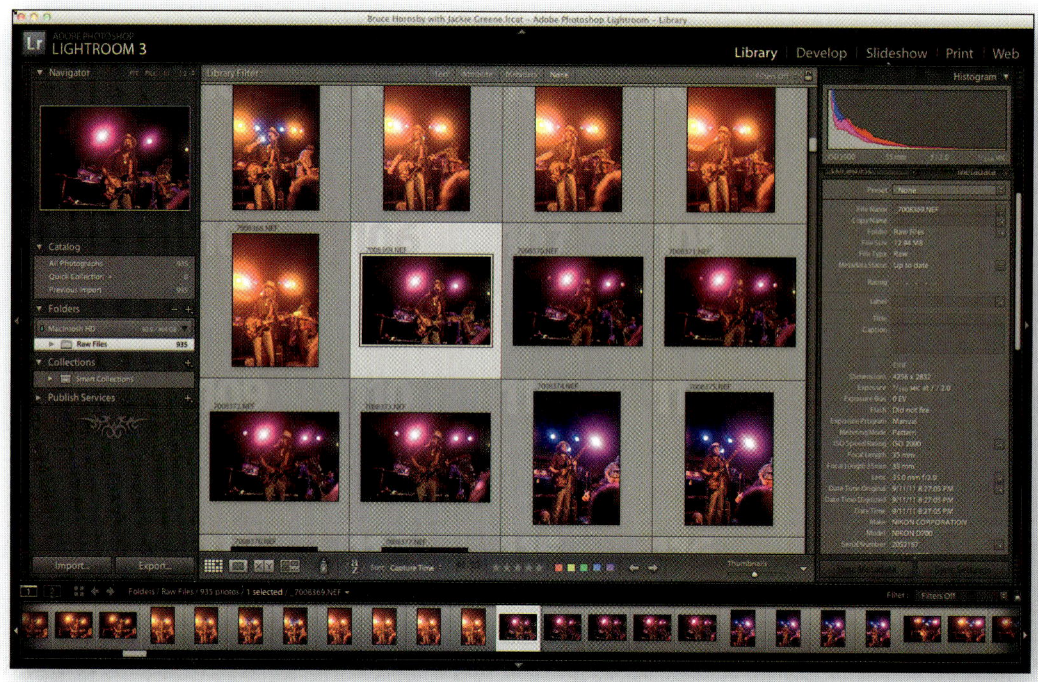

The Library module is where all the sorting, tagging, and keywording is done.

The main thing here is to make sure that the selected photo shows the performer in the best light and the best pose. Be sure it's an image that the band will like. That is, always assume that the performers will see your images, even if they don't. The reality is that sometimes they do, and it can lead to more work (or less) for you, depending on what they think of your images.

THE DEVELOP MODULE

This is where you make edits on your images. The cool part of this is that edits are not set in stone until a photo is actually exported. And even then, you can go back to the original version and change the edits without losing any image data.

The develop module in Lightroom is the same as the Adobe Camera Raw module in Photoshop. My workflow steps do not follow the order that the tools are listed in the application, and I don't use all the tools available. Here's my process:

1. Crop
2. Lens Corrections
3. Camera Calibration
4. Basic Exposure Adjustments
5. Sharpening

The develop module in Lightroom is the same as the Adobe Camera Raw module in Photoshop.

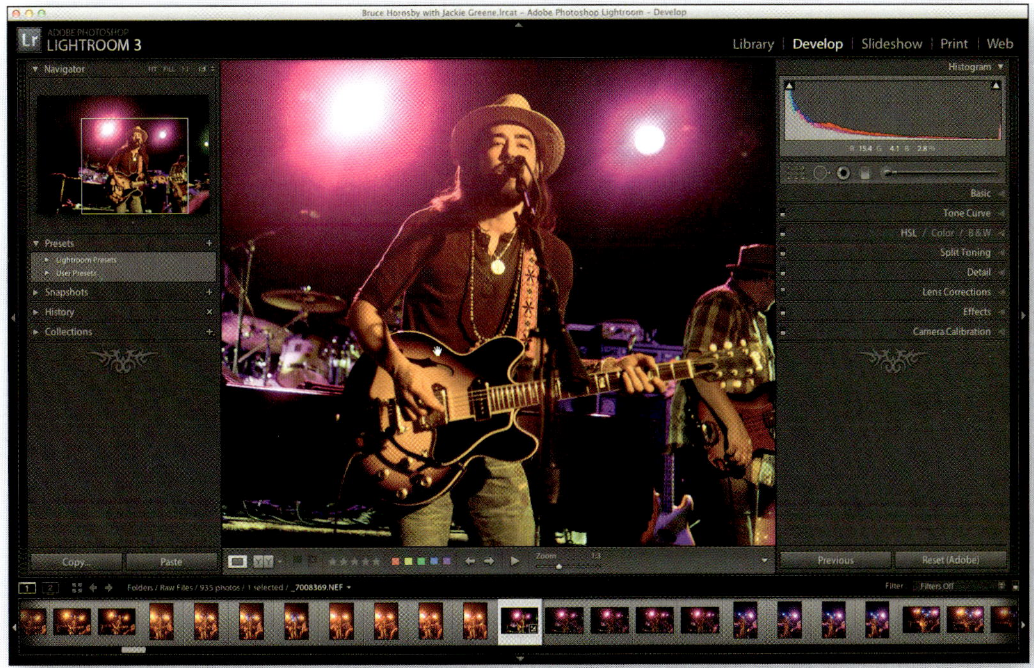

Image editing is done in the Lightroom Develop module.

6. Noise Reduction
7. Effects (if needed)

As I mentioned earlier, these tools can be used in any order you want. But the main tools are divided into eight tabs. Before that though, there are five different editing tools you should know about. The first is the crop overlay, and this is where I start.

The **crop overlay tool** allows you to crop and straighten your images. I use this on just about every image I take. Not by mistake, I shoot a little wide. I do this to make sure that every image can be used with a border or some other type of effect. So when the images are being used without any adornments, they usually need to be cropped a little.

To do this, click on the crop overlay tool, A grid will appear on the screen of the image. Adjust the crop by grabbing any of the points on the image and moving them in and out. You can change the ratio and even the direction of the crop by pressing the letter x.

When you move the crop, you don't move the crop overlay but the image under it. This can take a few minutes to get used to, but it will seem quite natural with time. Then, when the crop is done, click Done.

Remember, the edits to your images are not permanent. They can always be adjusted later. And when you press the shutter release button on your camera, remember that you can always crop, but you can never add content later.

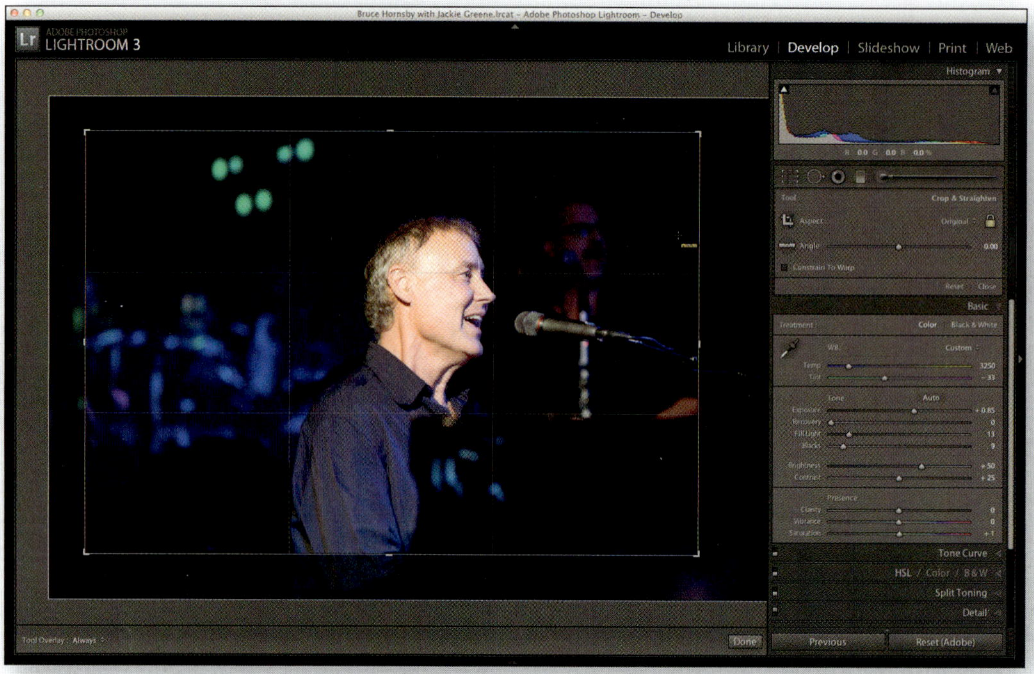

The Lightroom crop overlay allows you to quickly crop your images. And the best part is that the tool is non-destructive, so you can come back later and crop the same image differently if needed.

The other four editing tools include spot overlay, red eye correction, graduated filter, and adjustment brush. I rarely use these tools, but they're available if you want to try them.

- **The Spot Overlay** tool allows you to get rid of little spots in your images. You can either clone or heal the spots.
- **Red Eye Correction** is used to correct red eye in your images. As a concert photographer, you'll probably never use this, because you don't use a flash.
- **Graduated Filter** is a neat tool that can mimic a graduated filter, which goes from dark to light, allowing you to darken an area of the image and still have it look natural.
- **Adjustment Brush** allows you to paint on adjustments to various parts of an image. Used sparingly, it can really help some images. I prefer to use Photoshop for these adjustments though … and do it later in the process. But if you don't have Photoshop, this tool can help with local adjustments.

After cropping, the real image editing begins. Here are the eight editing tabs referenced earlier (Basic, Detail, Lens Correction, Effects, and Camera Calibration). They are described below in the order that they appear on the Lightroom screen, but keep in mind that you can work in any order you want.

Basic

Lightroom's basic exposure adjustments panel is broken into three distinct parts. The first deals with the image's white balance; the second covers the tone of an image; and the third handles the presence. Don't worry; we'll cover what these terms mean.

To adjust the white balance of an image, pick a neutral spot of color on the image and use the eye dropper tool to select it. Or you can adjust the temperature and tint sliders until you get the white balance you want. A final option is to pick one of the presets available.

The next set of sliders contain some of the most important tools for editing your images. They adjust the exposure and tone of your image.

- Use **Tone Curve** to adjust the Highlights, Lights, Darks, and Shadows in your image. I rarely ever adjust this and am usually very happy with the default settings.
- The **HSL/ Color/ B&W** tab houses the Hue, Saturation, Luminance/ Color/ Black and White adjustments. I sometimes use these black and white settings, and that's covered a little later.
- The **Split Toning** menu allows you to set a Highlight and Shadow color to create very cool split-toning effects. This is not really part of my workflow unless I'm trying for a special effect.

Detail

This is one of the most important editing panels in my workflow, because it's where noise reduction is applied to an image. As explained throughout this book, digital noise is one of the biggest problems for concert photographers, because it's a result of using high ISO settings, especially in older cameras.

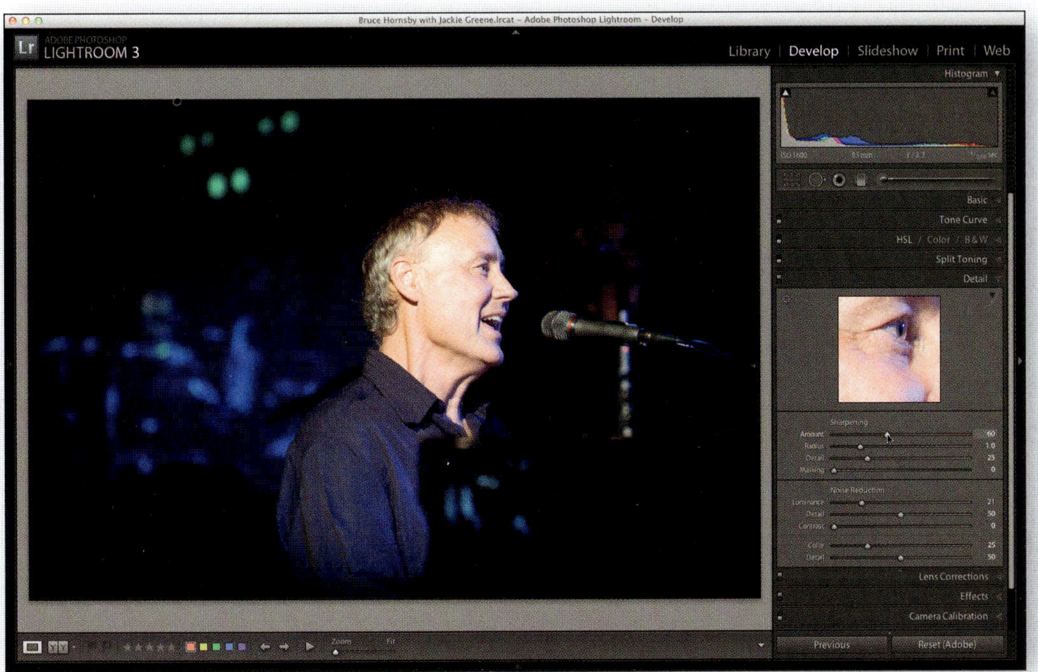

There are a total of nine sliders in the Detail panel. The first deals with sharpening, and the second handles noise reduction. Sharpening and noise reduction are together because applying noise reduction can cause a softening effect on the image, and the sharpening tool can help negate this. Plus, the sharpening effect can increase the visibility of digital noise, which can be minimized with the noise reduction tool. See, these features work in an interconnected way. The key is to get a nice balance between the two settings.

I wish I could give you the perfect settings for your images that will work every time, but the amount of sharpening and noise reduction you need depends on the specific image and the camera that was used to take it. But as a general starting point, I tend to use the following settings. Adjust them to your liking.

Sharpening

Amount: 60

Radius: 1.0

Detail: 25

Masking: 0

Noise Reduction

Luminance: 20

Detail: 50

Contrast: 0

Color: 25

Detail: 50

Lens Corrections

This is one of those tools that can seem like magic when applied. The engineers at Adobe created this tool to compensate for some of the aberrations that are present in any lens. This lens-correction technology uses a database of lenses to fix the problems with Distortion, Chromatic Aberration, and Vignetting. And if your lens isn't in the database, you can adjust the settings manually. Actually, you can adjust the settings manually even if your lens is in the database, but it's usually not needed.

Effects

With a title like *effects*, you might be thinking that this menu holds some really cool effects that you can add to your image. But there are just two options here. They are Post Crop Vignetting and a tool for adding realistic Grain to your images.

I've never added grain to an image, but I have used the vignetting and it works wonders. A little darkening of an image's edges can really help to draw attention to the middle of the scene. The vignetting can also hide parts of a background that's close to the edge of a shot.

Camera Calibration

With the camera calibration menu, you can adjust a Raw file to match the camera profile that's embedded in the JPEG file. There are two parts to this menu. The first allows you to pick a profile that's dependent on the camera used. The second allows you to adjust the shadows tint as well as the hue and saturation of the primary colors: red, green, and blue.

SLIDESHOW MODULE

I'm sure there are thousands of people who use Lightroom and love the slideshow module, but I am not one of them. The slideshow module just doesn't really fit into my workflow. But for those who want to create slideshows and play them for clients, this feature of Lightroom is great.

PRINT MODULE

If you do your own printing, then this module will take care of your printing needs, including creation of custom print packages. The Lightroom print module allows you to pick the images you want to print and lay them out any way you want.

WEB MODULE

You can create entire image galleries right inside of Lightroom in either HTML or Flash. The entire web gallery can then be saved or exported. This tool also allows users to upload images via FTP protocols.

Alright, so now that we've worked our way through the different modules, it's time to get your images out of Lightroom. This is when the Export tools come into play.

EXPORT

Remember, all the editing that is done in Lightroom is non-destructive, which means that none of the changes are permanent ... until you export them. For example, if you import a RAW file, crop the image, adjust the exposure, and reduce the digital noise, then you probably need to actually do something with the image. That is, you eventually need to export the image in a form that can be used (JPEG or TIFF format). The images for this book were all processed in Lightroom and exported as TIFF files. Do this in the Export menu.

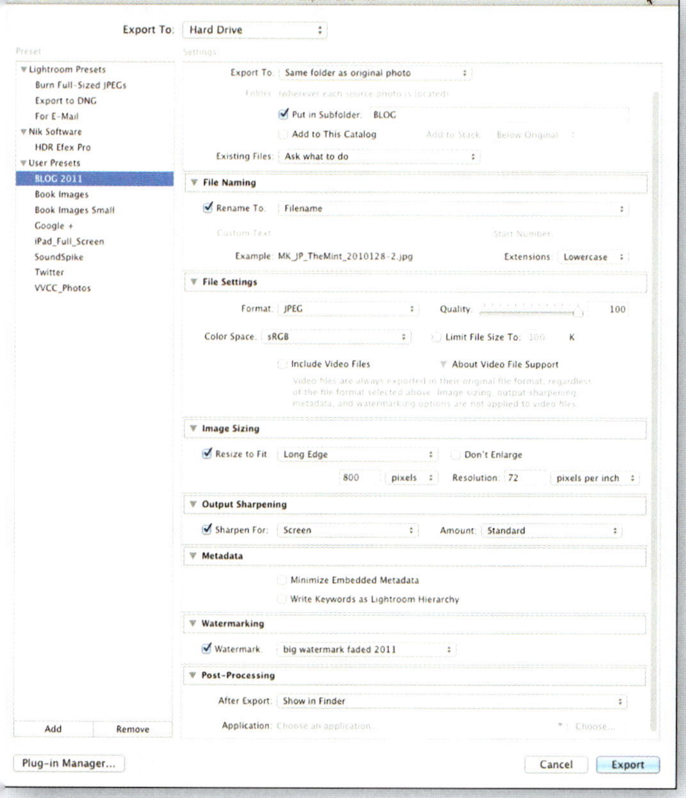

The Lightroom Export window allows you to save the export settings as presets so that you can use them over and over again. This is very useful if you're working for a client who wants images to be the same size and format, and you have images from different shoots.

The Export function in Lightroom is really powerful. And since you can save the set of output parameters as a preset, it's easy to apply consistent settings to different groups of images.

For example, I take photographs for the Valley View Casino Center. The events I cover might change, but the image settings for submission to the Center stay the same. To help me avoid having to manually input the settings for each image or group of images, I created a preset (VVCC_Photos) that allows me to apply those output settings quickly.

The Lightroom export menu contains the following options:

- **Location:** Tell the program where to put the exported files. You can add a subfolder and even have the exported files saved back into the image catalog. It is also possible to pick the "Choose folder later" option to create generic presets.
- **Name:** The file naming menu allows you to rename the files on export.
- **Settings:** Change the file type, file quality, the color space used, and file size limit here.
- **Size:** This menu makes it easy to resize the exported file.
- **Sharpening:** Here, you can add some output sharpening. Depending on the final use of the images, you may or may not need this feature.
- **Metadata:** You can minimize the embedded metadata and write the Keywords as Lightroom Hierarchy. This just tells Lightroom how to embed a keyword into the file for searching.
- **Watermark:** Add a custom watermark, if needed, and tell the application what to do with the exported images (like, open the file in editing software).

Lightroom even makes it easy for users to open an image in an external photo-editing application. And this is handy. There are times when I need to edit a photograph in a way that Lightroom isn't capable of doing. So I open the image in Photoshop from Lightroom directly. Let's look at this process.

PHOTOSHOP

Adobe Photoshop is an amazing program that allows users to edit images on a pixel-by-pixel level. There are a million ways to use this powerful program, but my main use for Photoshop is to remove unwanted elements from photos. I don't do this when photographing for a newspaper or any of the wire services, but I make sure to do it when I'm shooting for a band or creating prints.

Many times, the unwanted thing is a background element that couldn't be avoided during the shoot or cropped out any other way. For example, if a water bottle is sitting on an amplifier, I may or may not remove it. But if that water bottle is being hit by the light and drawing the viewer's eye to the wrong thing in an image, then I remove it.

There are a myriad of ways to remove objects from an image in Photoshop. You can paint over the object or use the clone tool to replace the object with a blank area. The method that works best for one image might not work for another. So it's good to have some options.

BLACK AND WHITE IMAGES

When I started shooting concerts, the highest ISO film available was black and white, and I really enjoyed using it. With the advent of digital photography, the line between color and black and white blurred, because a digital capture in color can be converted easily to a black and white image. You can set the camera to capture in black and white, but I prefer converting a color image to black and white in post production.

Black and white can also help save an image that has bad color, but it's best to start with a good color photograph before the conversion … and not rely on the conversion as a crutch. The best way to convert images to black and white is to use a specialized application, like Nik Software Silver Efex Pro 2. This application works with Adobe Photoshop, Adobe Lightroom, Apple Aperture, and Adobe Photoshop Elements.

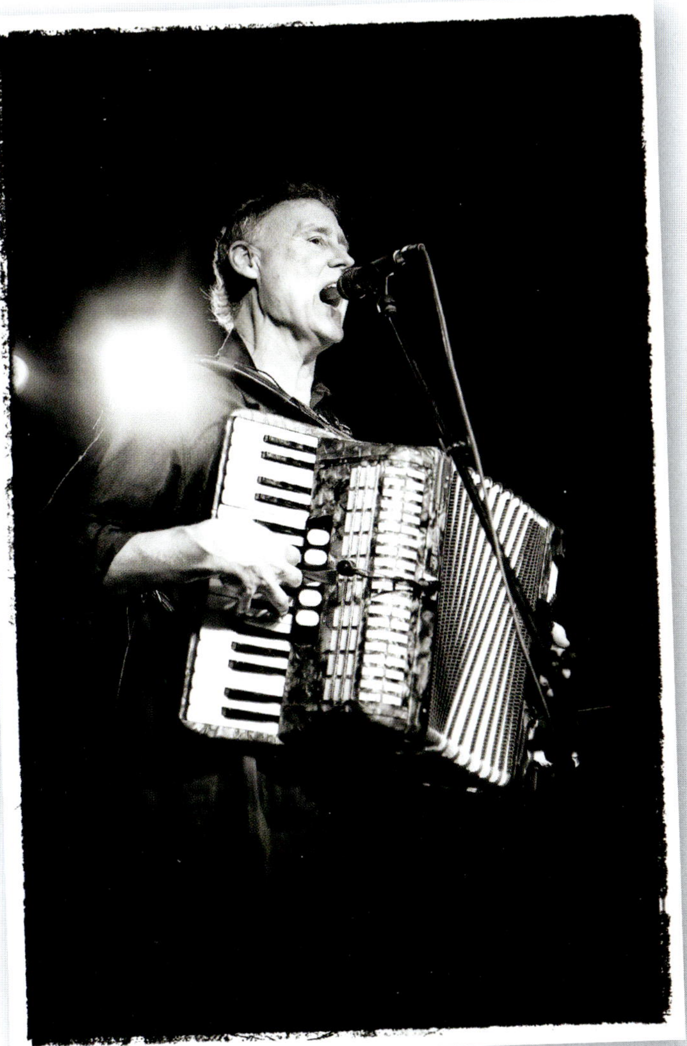

When shooting RAW files, you can capture in black and white in the camera and convert to color later, because all the color information is still there.

Black and white photographs can look really cool. This photo of Bruce Hornsby was taken in a very poorly lit venue. I knew going into the shoot that I would convert the images to black and white, so it wasn't too disappointing.

Taken at 1/200 second, f/2.2, and ISO 1600 converted to black and white using Nik Silver Efex Pro 2

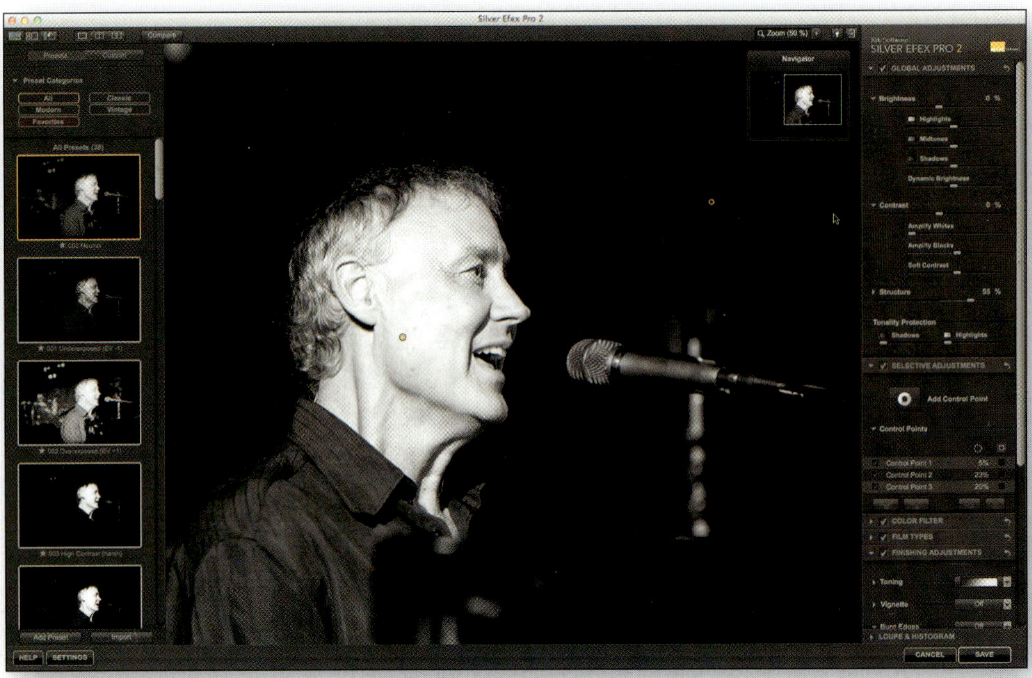

The Nik software Silver Efex Pro 2 interface has the presets on the left and the adjustment tabs on the right. This is a very powerful tool for converting images to black and white.

NIK SILVER EFEX PRO 2

When you edit an image in Silver Efex Pro 2, the image is opened in the Silver Efex Pro 2 (SEP 2) interface. On the left is a menu of presets. The middle of the screen is where you can see the effect of a conversion; the individual controls are on the right. There are five different adjustments tabs on the right. The order of the tabs matches the order that each is used.

The five adjustment tabs are:

- **Global Adjustments** is where you can adjust the Brightness, Contrast, and Structure of an image, and you can protect the tonality of the shadows and highlights.
- Nik software uses control points to make **Selective Adjustments**. Just add a control point on the image to control the Brightness, Contrast, and Structure; to Amplify White or Amplify Black; or to apply Fine Structure and Selective Colorization. These control points can also be combined into groups and adjusted together.
- **Color Filters** allows you to adjust the different colors in an image. You can pick a color or adjust the hue slider. Then you can manipulate the strength of the color.
- **Film Types** matches up to the black and white film types with eighteen different kinds of film, including selections from Agfa, Kodak, Illford, and Fuji. You can also increase the grain and sensitivity, and adjust the levels and curves in your image.

- **Finishing Adjustments** is my favorite panel, because it offers some of the extras that can create great images. Here, you can adjust the Toning, add a Vignette effect, or Burn Edges, and you can add natural-looking borders, too.

Try out Silver Efex Pro 2 for free for 15 days from www.niksoftware.com and get a 15% discount by using the code AHPNIK at checkout.

LIGHTROOM

If you don't have Silver Efex Pro 2, you can create a black and white image very easily by using Lightroom. There are actually two very quick ways to create black and white images in this program, and both are in the develop module.

The first method is to reduce the saturation of the image to -100. This will remove all the color from the image. In the Lightroom develop module, open the Basic tab and find the last slider—Saturation. Slide it all the way to the left to remove all color from the image. This is a very quick way to see what the image will look like in black and white. It can result in a good-looking image, but it doesn't offer much control over the tones in the image.

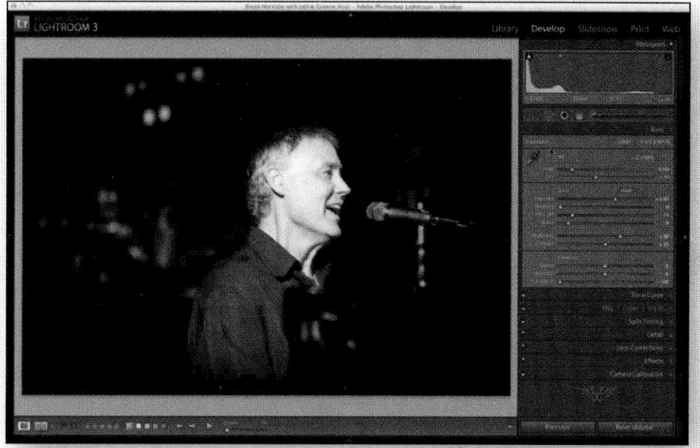

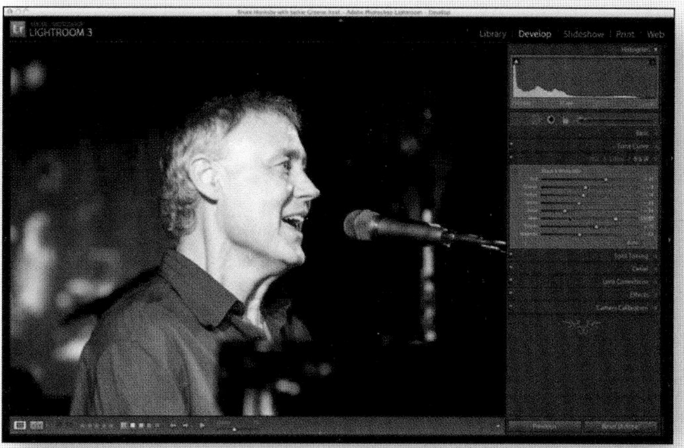

Lightroom offers two different ways to quickly get a black and white version of an image.

The second method is to use the HSL/ Color/ B&W tab (also in the Lightroom develop module). When you open this module, it starts with the HSL (Hue/ Saturation/ Luminance) settings. But when you click on the B&W tab at the top of the tab, it opens the black and white mix, and this lets you fine tune the conversion.

There are eight different color controls here that affect the look of your image. You can either increase or decrease the following tones in your image: Red, Orange, Yellow, Green, Aqua, Blue, Purple, and Magenta. There is also an Auto button, which can provide a good starting point. Each of these controls adjusts how light or dark the tones will be when viewed in black and white.

PHOTOSHOP

There are many different ways to create black and white images in Photoshop, but two of the easiest are to use the B&W adjustment or a Gradient adjustment. Both of these methods are accessed in the Adjustment palette.

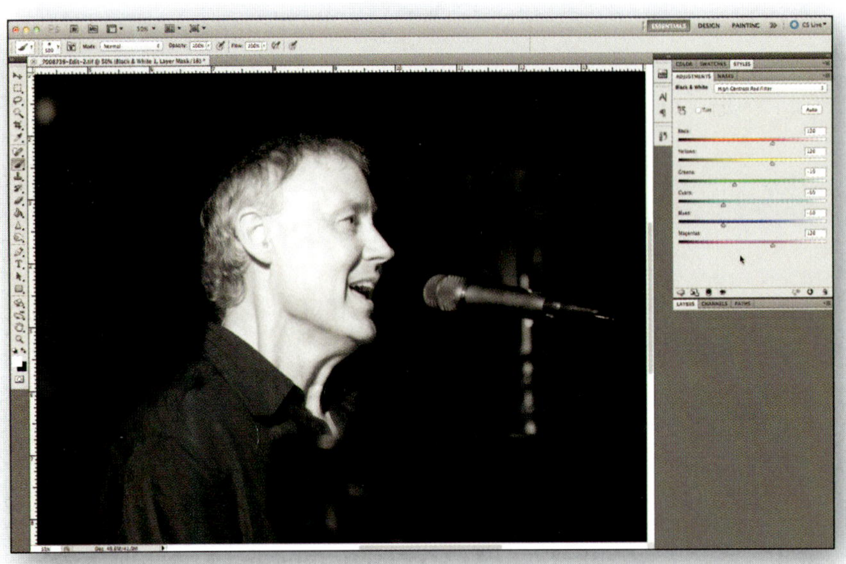

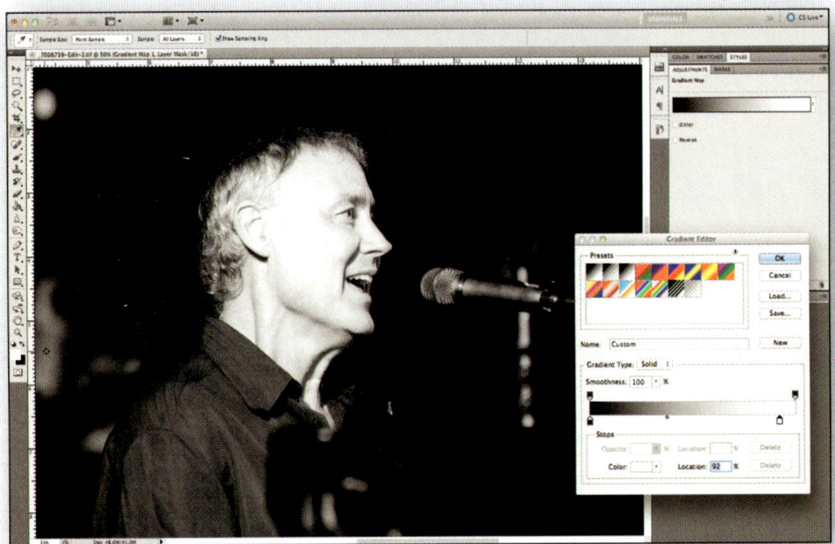

The Photoshop black and white adjustment and the Photoshop gradient adjustment offer two ways to quickly get black and white images in the Photoshop program.

The B&W adjustment allows you to adjust the Reds, Yellows, Greens, Cyans, Blues, and Magentas. Each image is slightly different and you can tweak the look by adjusting how light or dark each of the different colors are rendered in black and white. If you come up with a good recipe that gives you a look you like, then remember to save your settings as a preset. You can also try using one of the standard presets.

The second method, which is one of my favorite ways to convert images to black and white, is to use a gradient map. Click on the Gradient Map adjustment and then pick the gradient that goes from solid black to solid white. You can further adjust the actual gradient to change the way the image looks. You can make it lighter or darker by moving the gradient middle point, but this is all about personal preference. Find a setting that looks good to you.

SHOW YOUR BEST

When I edit my images, the mantra that I repeat to myself over and over again is to show only my best work. This means that despite a desire to post every photo from a show to a website or social media outlet, it's not a good idea. Only post images that are fantastic, unbelievable, stunning.

There are two good reasons for this. The first is that you always want people to be amazed at your photographs. You want to leave them wanting more. A few amazing photos will go a lot further than a few amazing photos diluted by thirty other photos that are just okay. So pick shots that capture the moment, the emotion—photographs that reveal a split second when everything is just ... right. Let the others take a backseat.

MARK KARAN

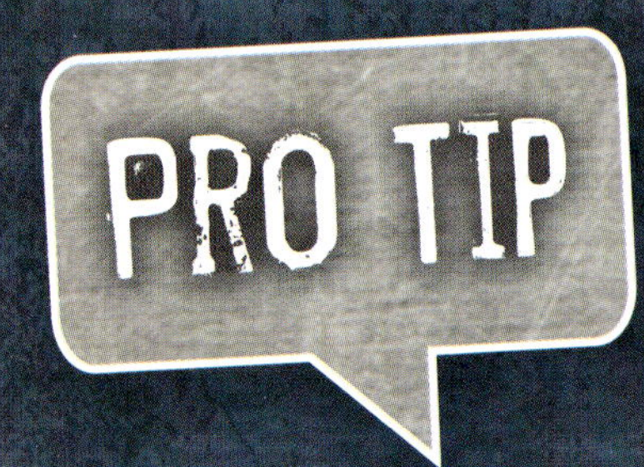

Mark Karan is best known for touring with the extended Grateful Dead family. For twelve years, he was lead guitarist in Bob Weir & RatDog and also worked his guitar and vocal voodoo for the likes of Dave Mason, Delaney Bramlett, the Rembrandts, Paul Carrack, Huey Lewis, Jesse Colin Young, and Sophie B. Hawkins. Mark's debut album, "Walk Through the Fire" was released in 2009 to critical acclaim.

www.markkaran.com

Do you pay any attention to the photographers during a show?

Not generally. I suppose occasionally there's someone that draws attention to him/herself by running around a lot or something, but we've usually got our heads pretty deep in the game. If you let people/events in the audience pull you out of that, it can really screw up your show, so I think most musicians figure out how not to get distracted.

Do you pay much attention to the photos you see of yourself on the Internet?

There are a lot of fan photos out there that can be pretty bad, and I rarely look at those. But yes, I check out shots when I run across them or if someone sends me a file or points out a link. I'm not totally self-obsessed, but I have curiosity and a healthy ego. LOL.

Would you rather see a few great shots or tons of good shots?

That's easy. A few great shots ... always. There are shots we think of as iconic of various rock figures. It's always cool to see something that has that vibe—great composition, cool lighting effects. It's that shot where the subject looks good and it captures an unusual or exciting moment. I don't need to see the equivalent of stop motion photography, capturing every moment of the show. Give me great high lights!

Do you have one piece of advice for someone starting out as a rock and roll photographer?

Edit. Edit. Edit. No one needs to see every shot you take. Out of every song I write, one in ten or more may be good. Maybe. Similarly, out of hundreds (or thousands) of shots will be really good. There are likely only a few truly great ones. I think greatness comes from both seeing a great shot when you take it and recognizing that you captured something special when you see the results.

Also, think in terms of pleasing the artists and fans (and management). Make whoever you're shooting look good. That's flattering angles, exciting poses/moments. If we're happy with your shots, we're gonna use them. And that's good for you, too.

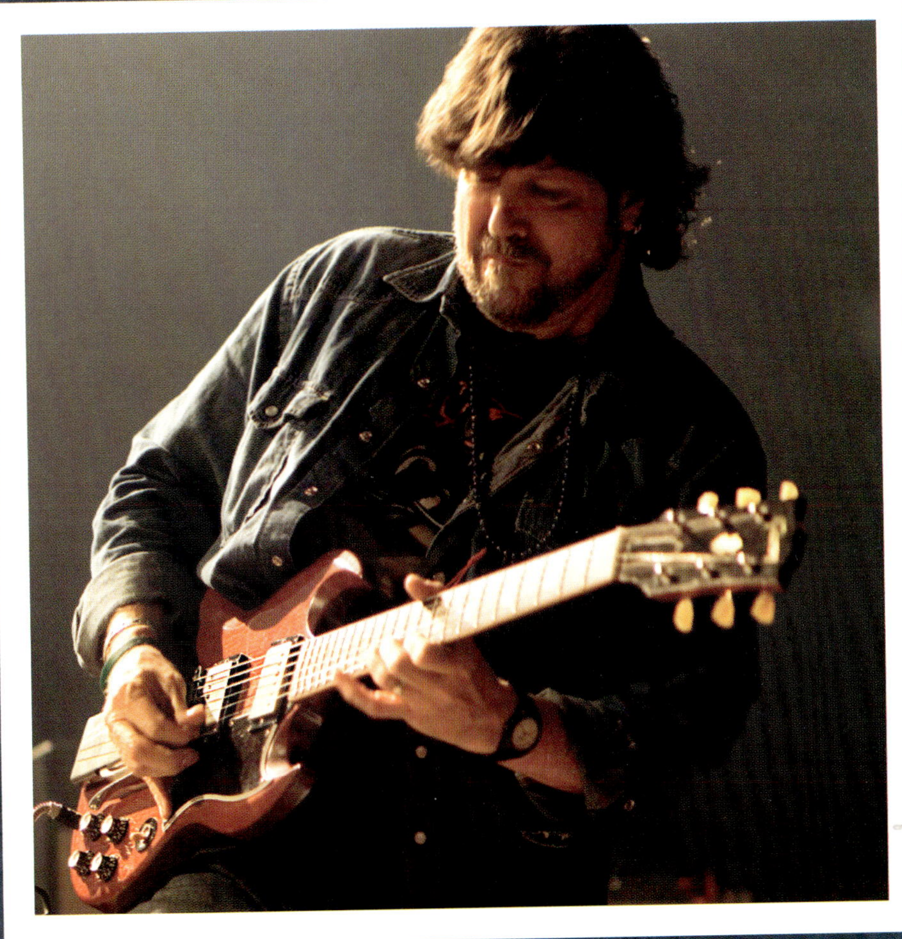

APPENDIX A: ACCESSORIES

While concert photography doesn't necessarily involve buying a lot of photography accessories like lights or studio props, there are things you do need. Some are important, like the memory cards and earplugs, while others just make your life easier in the photo pit … or wherever you're shooting. Here's a rundown of the accessories I find to be most important.

CAMERA BAGS

I've never met a camera bag that I didn't like. I own a variety of camera bags, and each has its special use, which depends on what show or type of concert I'm shooting. Most of the time, I use Domke bags and prefer the regular-style camera bag to a sling bag. But I like to use a ThinkTankPhoto Shape Shifter backpack for the all-day festivals, because of its capacity for carrying a laptop along with two camera bodies and all the lenses I need.

Overall, picking the right camera bag is actually pretty important to your life as a concert photographer. Here are the things I look for when buying a new bag.

SIZE

The first question to ask yourself is whether or not the bag is big enough to hold the gear you need to have with you for the shoot. And this is why you really need more than one bag in your collection. There are times when your bag needs to hold only a single camera and two lenses. But other times you'll need a bag to hold multiple cameras and a variety of lenses. And sometimes your bag needs to help you transport a ton of photo gear … and a laptop and a card reader and power cords and other accessories.

So the first thing to do is to make a pile of the stuff you want the camera bag to hold. And be honest with yourself. If you always take two camera bodies with you, don't make the mistake of getting a bag that holds only one.

Another size factor to keep in mind is that working in a photo pit can be a tight squeeze. Trying to navigate through a small pit with a huge bag will likely earn you more than a few dirty looks … or worse.

PROTECTION

Your go-to camera bag needs to offer a certain level of protection for your gear. Some bags have a ton of padding; others have minimal. I like my camera bag to take up as little space as possible in the photo pit, so I tend to use bags with minimal padding. This really is a personal choice. Know thyself; if you tend to bash your gear around, a bag with a little more padding is probably a good idea.

COMFORT

Your satisfaction with a camera bag will depend a lot on how easy it is to carry and how comfortable it is on your shoulder(s). This is why it's so important to go to a camera store to physically check out a bag. The bag needs to be comfortable to wear when it's full of gear, so load it down and try it on.

I actually take my gear with me to the store when I'm shopping for a new bag. I make sure all the gear fits and that the bag fits *me* when it is full. Some questions to consider when evaluating a new camera bag:

- Are the straps comfortable?
- Are the pockets easily accessible?
- Does the camera fit into the bag with a lens is attached?
- Is this bag going to be comfortable to wear in tight spaces?
- Can this be carried around easily all day?

Make sure that the bag you buy is right for you and your shooting situations.

STYLE

Camera bags come in a variety of styles, ranging from traditional over-the-shoulder bags to backpacks and sling bags. Every photographer works differently, so a bag that works great for me might not work at all for someone else. That said, I've found that the traditional style of bag works really well in most circumstances. I tend to use three different bags that are all the same type … just different sizes.

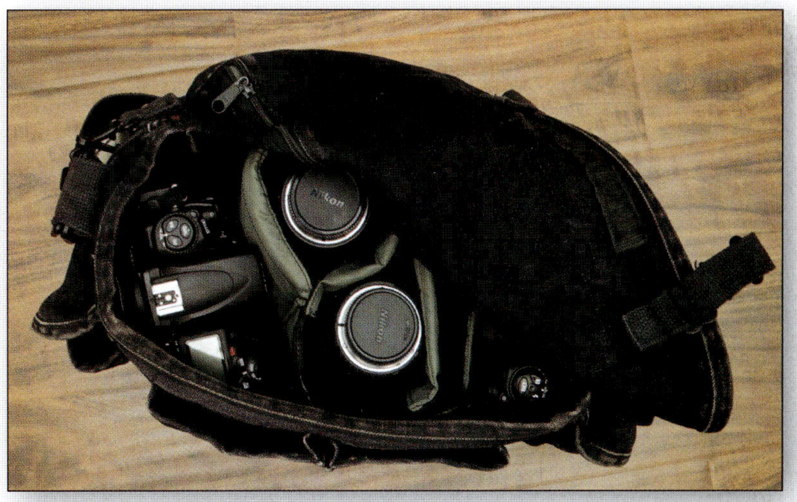

This is the medium-sized Domke bag with a couple of cameras and lenses.

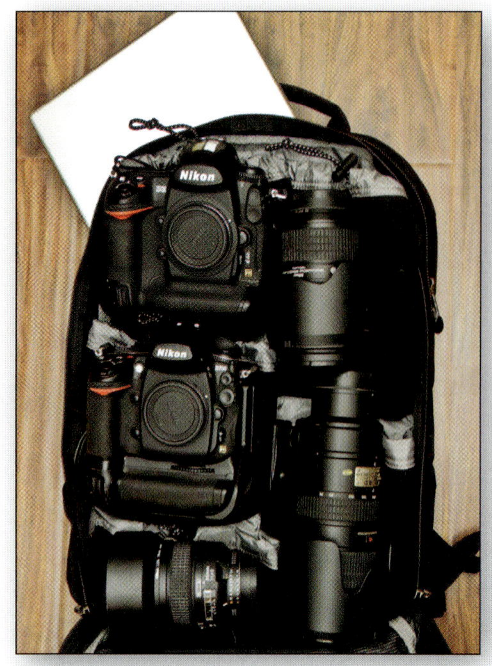

The Shape Shifter bag from ThinkTankPhoto allows me to carry my camera bodies and a laptop easily.

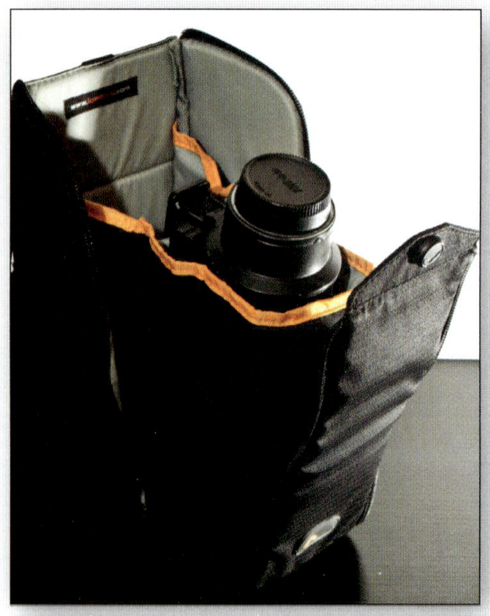

Lowepro Lens Exchange Case 200 AW allows me to carry my 70–200mm lens and to switch it easily.

However, for all-day festivals, I use a backpack, because it's more comfortable and allows me to carry a laptop, which I need for these events.

There are two other categories of bags that are useful to photographers. They are lens bags and harness systems. These options are designed to carry extra lenses while a camera is around your neck or over your shoulder. I use a lens bag all the time, which is especially useful when I'm shooting with one camera and need to change lenses during a shoot.

LENS BAGS

Most lens bags carry just a lens or two. The Lens Case 11x26cm from Lowepro is a great example of a lens bag. It's built using a single piece of foam that provides protection for expensive glass. These lens bags come with detachable shoulder straps to allow for easy carrying.

One of the coolest lens bags I've used is the Lowepro Lens Exchange Case 200 AW. I love it because the bag makes it so easy to exchange lenses. This is due to the patent-pending exchange technology that expands and holds the lens you remove as you attach a new lens right from the bag.

Another great option is the Boda lens bag, which holds a couple of lenses and a whole lot more. These bags are designed to hold lenses and accessories. The one I have can hold two long lenses, memory cards, a cell phone, extra batteries ... basically everything I take to a shoot except the camera.

HARNESS SYSTEMS

This accessory allows you to attach pieces to a harness and/or belt to carry your gear. Harness systems are popular for photographers shooting on the sidelines of pro sports because they keep your gear close and handy. But I've found that they don't work too well in crowded photo pits; they tend to be too bulky. The harness system works best when there's a little more space available.

Whatever bag you end up choosing to use, it helps to remember that the photo pit is usually a very crowded place that's filled with other photographers and their gear. It's an area where every square inch counts. So make sure that you show up requiring the least amount of space possible.

MEMORY CARDS

You never get a second chance to make a first impression, right? Well, you never ever get a second chance to capture images of a specific live concert. That's why I use the best memory cards I can find and afford. It means spending a little more money than what's absolutely necessary, but I believe this investment is well worth it. If you stick to the professional line of cards made by a reputable company, you should have no problems.

In the last few years, the cost of memory cards has decreased while card capacity has increased. This means that there is no excuse for not having enough memory cards to cover a whole event.

Currently, I use 16GB memory cards and carry a couple of 8GB, 4GB, and even 2GB cards … just in case.

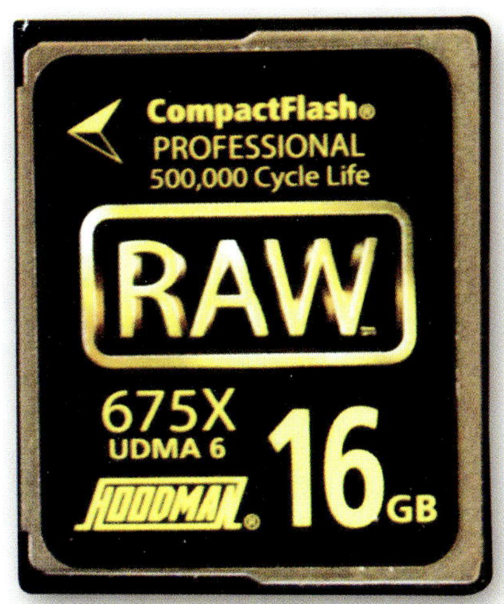

The 16GB Hoodman CompactFlash Cards are my go-to cards right now. On my Nikon D700 and D3 cameras, one of these cards holds more than 600 RAW images.

Memory cards come in a variety of formats. The two most common are the Secure Digital (SD) card and the CompactFlash (CF) card. The ones I trust most with my images are made by Hoodman USA, because I've taken thousands—maybe hundreds of thousands—of images and I've never had one problem with these cards.

Something to think about when transporting your memory cards is keeping them organized and handy. Throwing them in your bag haphazardly is very unhelpful. When you're in the photo pit, you need to find your extra memory cards easily. You don't want to be digging around in your bag for a card—missing great shots. And you really don't want to spend time in this situation trying to figure out if the card you happened to grab is ready to go or if it's loaded with important photos.

Enter the memory card wallet! I have two different types: a soft one made by ThinkTankPhoto and hard one created by Grepe. The hard case is weather-proofed, so I use it when shooting in bad weather or otherwise rough conditions. The thing with the Grepe case is that it only holds four cards, while the ThinkTankPhoto card holder carries twice as many.

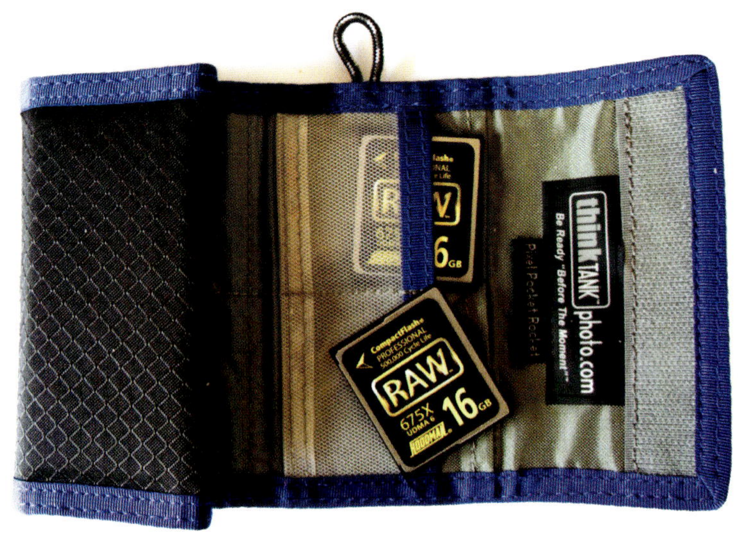

Have a system that makes it easy for you to see which cards are used and which are available for new images.

I use the wallets to organize my memory cards the same way though. Empty formatted cards are placed in the wallet with the label facing outward. A filled card is placed in the wallet with the label facing in. This ensures that I know immediately, as soon as I open the wallet, which cards are ready to use and which ones are already filled with images.

EARPLUGS

If you take away only one thing from this book, I hope that it is to wear earplugs when at a concert—every concert … and for the entire concert. Not only do I carry a set of earplugs with me; I carry extras so that I'm never without a set. I carry a small plastic container on my credentials holder that stores a set of spare foam earplugs just in case something happens to my bag or other earplugs.

There are three different types of earplugs. Each has advantages and disadvantages. It makes no difference which ones you use. Just make sure you use them.

DISPOSABLE FOAM EARPLUGS

These are foam earplugs that can be tapered, cylindrical, or shaped to fit into the ear. They usually come in a wide variety of colors and individually wrapped in plastic bags. I really like the North Decidamp II brand that comes in boxes of two hundred individually wrapped sets for about $35. These are pretty comfortable and do a great job with blocking the sound. I always carry extra pairs of these to hand out to anyone who might not have some with them.

REUSABLE/MUSICIAN EARPLUGS

Musician earplugs are of a much higher quality and price than the disposable foam variety, but they are designed to block music (especially very loud amplified music). They do it in a way that preserves sound quality though. This is important if you like the music of the band you're shooting.

These earplugs can range in price … from a few dollars per pair to more than $20 for a pair. I really like the MusicSafe Classic Natural Sound Musicians Ear Plugs ($20/pair). The nice thing about this product is that the earplugs can be adjusted by changing the filter.

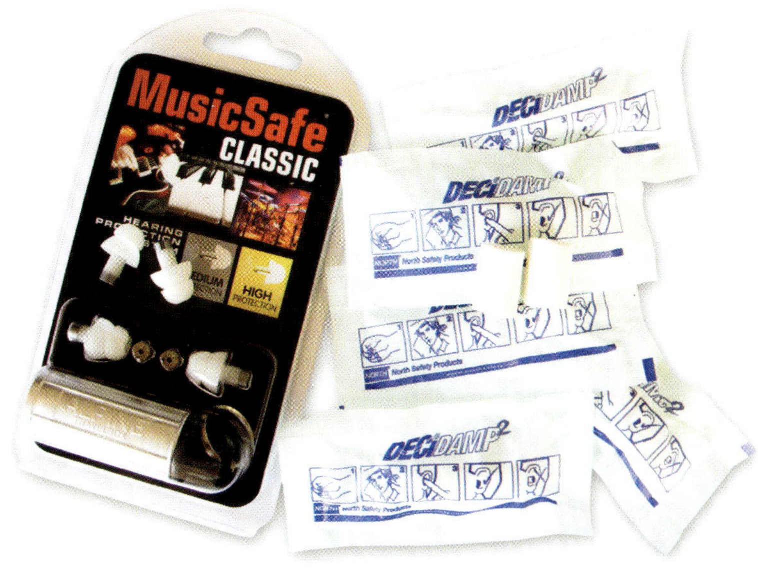

I make sure that I have my main earplugs with me at every concert, and I also carry spares. I offer inexpensive earplugs to security staff and fans in the front rows who might not have them. It's a great way to make friends.

CUSTOM EARPLUGS

The best option for both comfort and protection is a set of custom earplugs. But this option costs the most money. For example, if you go for the Ultimate Ears earplugs by Logitech, then you can expect to pay $170 for the earplugs alone. The only problem I have with this option is the cost … and the fact that I drop things. I would hate to take a great pair of earplugs to a shoot and drop them in the photo pit. Of course, this isn't to say *you'd* drop them; I'm sure you're more coordinated than I am!

As for my own preferences: I use a pair of the reusable musician earplugs and keep a handful of the disposable foam earplugs in my bag at all times. I do plan on investing in a set of custom earplugs soon though ... and being very careful not to lose them.

BUSINESS CARDS

Always have at least a small stock of your business cards on hand when you're out shooting concerts … even if you're just shooting in a bar. I give my card to anyone who asks and also to a lot of people who don't.

Your business card needs to have information about you and how to access your photographs. And it should say something about your photography work. The best business card for a concert photographer that I've ever seen belongs to Allen Ross Thomas. He created a card that not only looks like a laminate but can be carried like one. Plus, it just screams Rock 'n Roll and won't be forgotten by anyone who sees it.

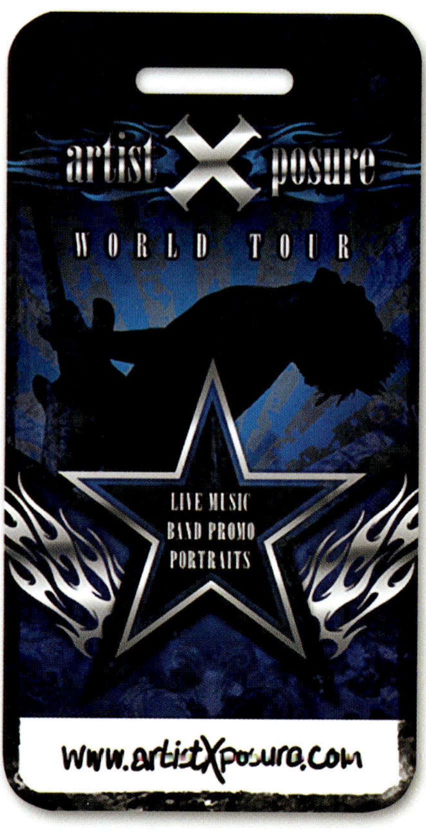

These are the business cards of concert photographer Allen Ross Thomas, and they rock.

MONOPOD

There are times when you'll have to shoot from the soundboard using long lenses. For these types of shoots, I carry a monopod to help manage with the long lens.

Using a monopod for this type of shooting situation allows me to use shutter speeds that are slower than I would be able to use if I was hand holding the lens from a spot closer to the stage. A good monopod will be sturdy enough to hold the lens steady and light enough for easy transport into and out of the venue.

When I shoot from the soundboard, I usually use the ThinkTankPhoto Shape Shifter backpack, because this bag has straps that attach the monopod to its front.

CREDENTIAL HOLDER

I love photo passes and treasure all that I've received over the years. Early in my concert photography career, I'd stick the photo passes on my shirt, right in the middle, so that everyone could see it. Then, one night while photographing at a club, the pass fell off during the opening band. I have no idea if it was a faulty pass or if I was sweating a little too much that night or if my camera strap dislodged the pass. But it disappeared and caused me a lot of trouble. I had to go to the venue office to plead my case and try to get another pass.

From that time on, I've used a different method to hold my credentials. I now use a plastic sleeve that's attached to a ring and a small carabineer. The plastic sleeve was purchased at Office Depot, and the edges are reinforced with some black duct tape. I also have a small flashlight (discussed later) and lens cloth (also discussed later) and a earplug holder (which we covered earlier) attached to the ring. And I can clip the whole thing onto my belt or camera bag so the credentials can be seen easily but not get in my way.

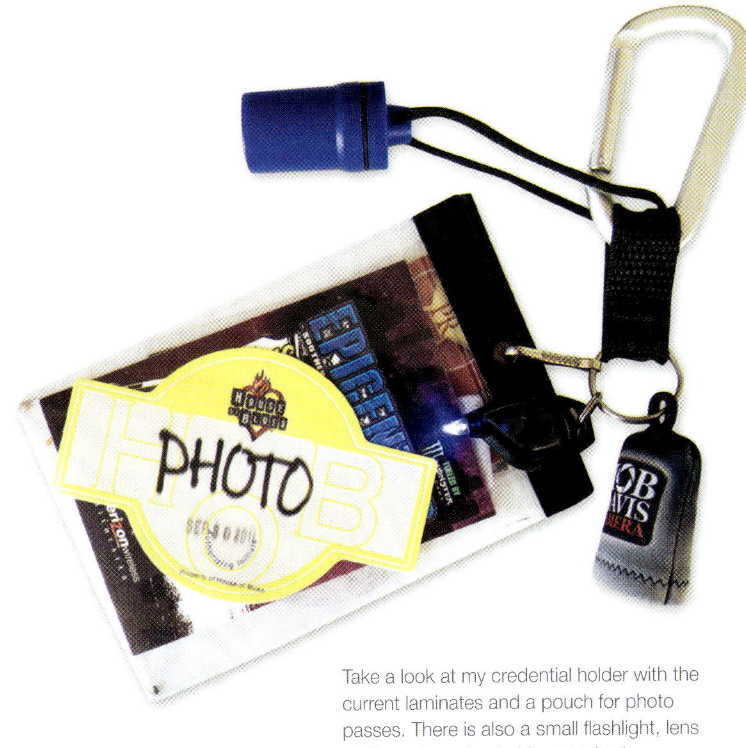

Take a look at my credential holder with the current laminates and a pouch for photo passes. There is also a small flashlight, lens cloth, and earplug holder attached.

Sometimes a venue will ask me to actually stick the pass on. When this happens, I usually put it on the front right leg of my pants or shorts so it won't be in the way or get rubbed off.

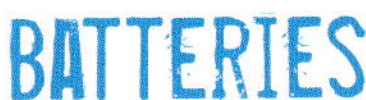

BATTERIES

Your camera came with a battery. Now go out and get a second battery—right away. Yes, there was a time when cameras took off-the-shelf batteries, but digital cameras need more power than those older models (so they can run those LCD screens on the back). The good thing about this is that today's camera batteries are more powerful and allow you to take more photos. The problem is that when they run down, they can only be replaced by another special battery. So make sure you have a second battery for your camera and that both batteries are charged at all times.

BATTERY GRIP

Pro-level cameras, like the Nikon D3, have a larger battery than consumer cameras, like the Nikon D700. But it's possible to add more power and a longer battery life to the consumer-level cameras. You just need to buy an external battery grip that holds a second battery. This extra battery can increase the frame rate of the camera, but the real bonus is the longer battery life. This means there's less of a chance that you'll run out of power at a critical time during a shoot.

Another great feature of a battery grip is that it can make your camera easier to hold and use when in portrait orientation. Many battery grips add a second shutter release button

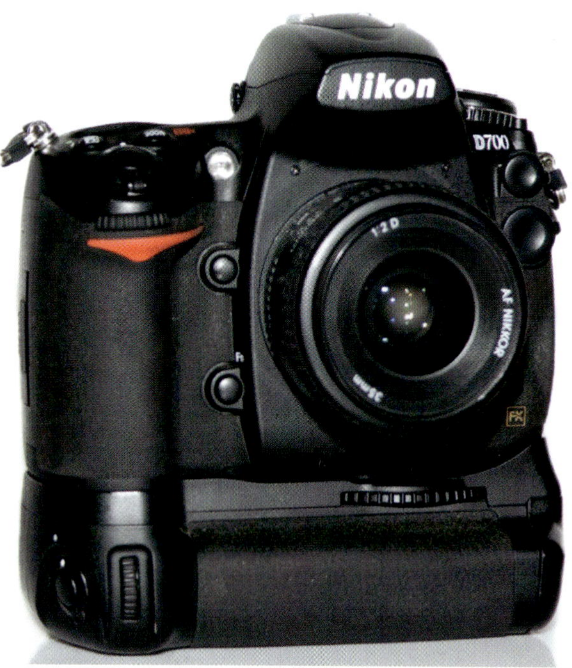

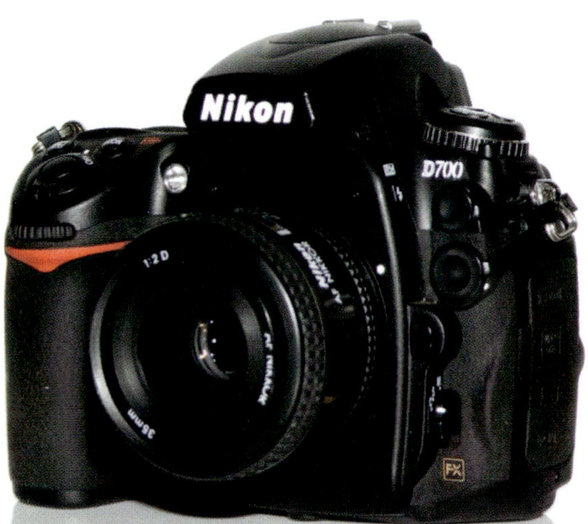

Notice the size difference when using the battery grip on the Nikon D700 and not using it.

that's set up for portrait-orientation shooting. This is especially useful if you have big hands.

The one downside of the battery grip is the extra weight. This weight can make it easier to steady the camera, but it can make the camera much heavier. This matters a lot when you're on a job that requires you to carry the camera for an extended period of time. Just remember that the battery grip can be removed if needed.

CAMERA STRAP

When it comes to camera straps, the ones that come with a camera are usually pretty uncomfortable. I have a huge collection of different straps, and I feel like I've tried them all. Right now I have two different straps on my two camera bodies, and I'm pretty sure I will be trying other straps soon. Some of the brands I've used and liked are described below:

The Black Rapid Straps

www.blackrapid.com

These are different from traditional straps, because they attach to the tripod-mounting screw hole on the bottom of the camera and not to the traditional strap-mounting spots. This means the camera hangs upside down, which works really well because the camera is carried across your body instead of over your shoulder or around your neck. There is also a Rapid Strap that holds two camera bodies at the same time—one on each side of your body—comfortably and securely.

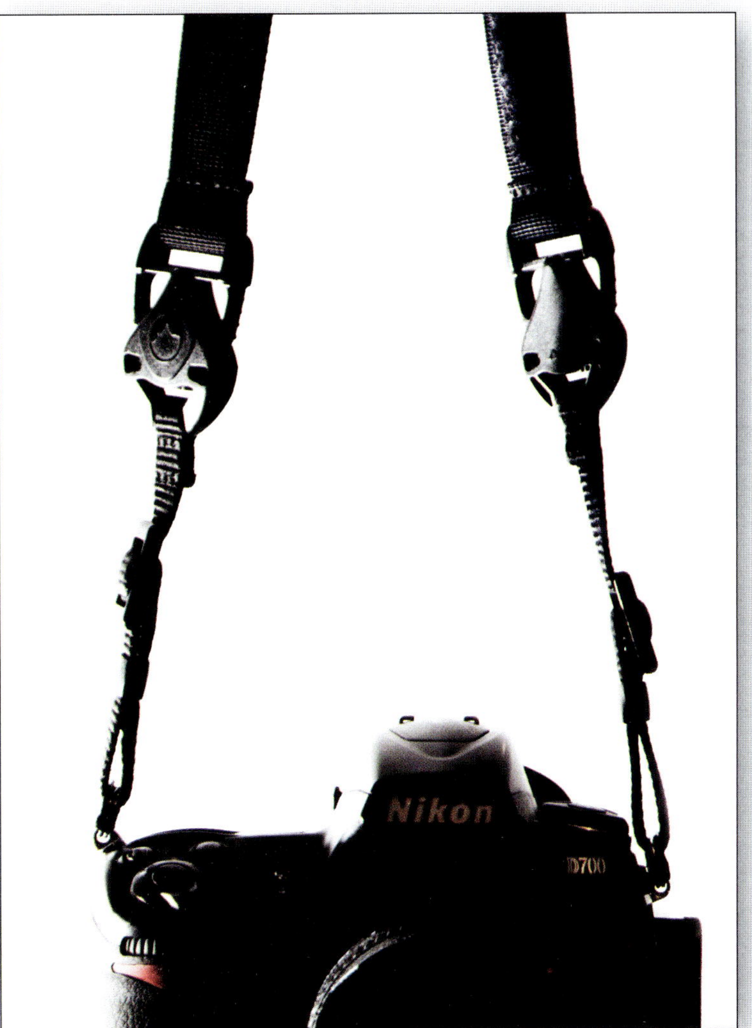

My D700 with the Domke strap attached is shown here. Notice the quick-release snaps that allow the strap to be quickly removed.

ThinkTank Photo Camera Strap V.20

www.thinktankphoto.com

The ThinkTankPhoto strap is like all the ThinkTankPhoto products: well-made and well-considered design-wise. The strap is thin and doesn't get in the way, and it has grip material on both sides, so no matter which shoulder you put it over, the strap stays there.

Domke Gripper Utility Strap

www.tiffen.com

The Domke strap is built really well and has a non-slip side and a regular side, but the non-slip side is not as grippy as the ThinkTankPhoto strap. The real plus of this strap is that it is quickly detachable, which allows users to hook it through other bags or remove it all together.

UPstrap

www.upstrap-pro.com

This strap is amazing when it comes to staying on your shoulder when walking around. I find it most useful for all-day shows, when I'm walking miles between stages.

The greatest gift you can give yourself is a good camera strap, especially if you are going to be carrying two cameras and walking a lot.

LENS CLEANING CLOTH/KIT

Lenses get dirty, so it's a good idea to have a lens cloth handy, especially when shooting outdoors, where the chance of dust and debris getting on your lens is high. And you've got to remember that there are bands that like to throw water or other fluids out at the crowd. Photographers can get wet at these shows. So I carry a small microfiber lens cleaning cloth on my credentials and a bigger cloth in my bag if shooting all-day festivals or a show of one of those bands that might cause my camera to get wet. If my camera gets really dirty, then I send it to the manufacturer for a real cleaning.

FLASHLIGHT

Most of the time, concert photographers work in the dark. Having a small flashlight is really important. I actually have two flashlights that I use all the time. The first one is a very small light that is attached to my credential holder. The light is a small keychain light with a blue bulb that I find works well without destroying my night vision. The flashlight can be purchased for about $12 at Amazon.com:
http://www.amazon.com/LRI-PBK-Photon-Keychain-Micro-Light/dp/B0001FT28U/.

The second flashlight is much more powerful. It's small but powerful. It lives in my camera bag and is mainly there for emergencies. It allows me to check the area where I'm working, especially in press areas. It also allows me to see where I'm going when walking back to my car in dark parking lots. A small LED flashlight like this one works great:
http://www.amazon.com/Nu-Flare-Ultra-Compact-78R91AA-Flashlight/dp/B001LYYOS8/.

APPENDIX B: COPYRIGHT

I am not a lawyer … even though my parents said I argued like one when I got in trouble as a child. So I'm not giving legal advice here. This appendix just provides a step-by-step walkthrough of how to register your images with the U.S. Copyright Office. And it includes some of the reasons it's a good idea to do so. If you feel like you need real legal advice though, contact a lawyer.

Copyright law can be very confusing. Ask five photographers about their copyrights, and you'll probably get five different answers. And I'm writing this section, because I never used to register my images with the Copyright Office. Instead, I thought my ownership of the images was covered under general copyright law, and that the watermark I placed on my images would protect me.

Well, when a website took a slew of my images from a photo-sharing site and used them on pages that sold advertising, I found out differently. The website used my images even though they were watermarked and labeled All Rights Reserved.

I thought I'd be able to take the website to court and get compensation for the unlawful use of my images … until I spoke with a lawyer whose first question to me was, "Did you register the images?" Since I had not, the firm didn't take the case.

I had the images removed from the website by filing a Digital Millennium Copyright Act (or DMCA) takedown notice (more on that a little later on), but I have still not received any compensation. So now I register my images, and it's really very easy.

REGISTER YOUR IMAGES

The Internet has made it easy for anyone to register images. And while there are ways to register your work by mail, this section covers only the electronic Copyright Office (eCO) system.

There are three steps to registering your work. The first time you do this, it might seem long and complicated, but you'll catch on. It really is easy.

1. Fill out the application on the eCO website.
2. Pay for the registration (currently $35).
3. Upload the images.

To make the process smoother, before you begin the eCO process, I recommend getting your images in upload-ready condition. The images files that are uploaded do not need to be the full size, high-resolution version. And really, they shouldn't be due to the large file size that would require. Remember that you have to upload these images to the eCO website, and the bigger the files, the longer it will take.

I tend to upload entire shoots at a time, because if images are related, they can be registered together for the one $35 fee. So I created an export preset in Lightroom that will export selected images—at 800px on the longest side at 72 dpi and JPEG format—into a folder called BandName_Date_copyright. Then I compress (or zip) the folder. Refer back to Chapter 14 for directions on how to set up export presets.

With the folder of images ready to be uploaded, it's time to begin registering your work.

THE APPLICATION

Go to the U.S Copyright Office website. Two important things here:

- The correct url is www.copyright.gov. It is NOT www.copyright.com; that is the Copyright Clearance Center site, which is not part of the U.S. Copyright Office.
- If you're using an Apple computer, then you'll need to use a browser that is not Safari. This browser doesn't work right with the site, so it causes trouble later in this process.

To begin registration, click on the Electronic Copyright Office button on the right side of the page under "How to Register a Work." If this is your first time

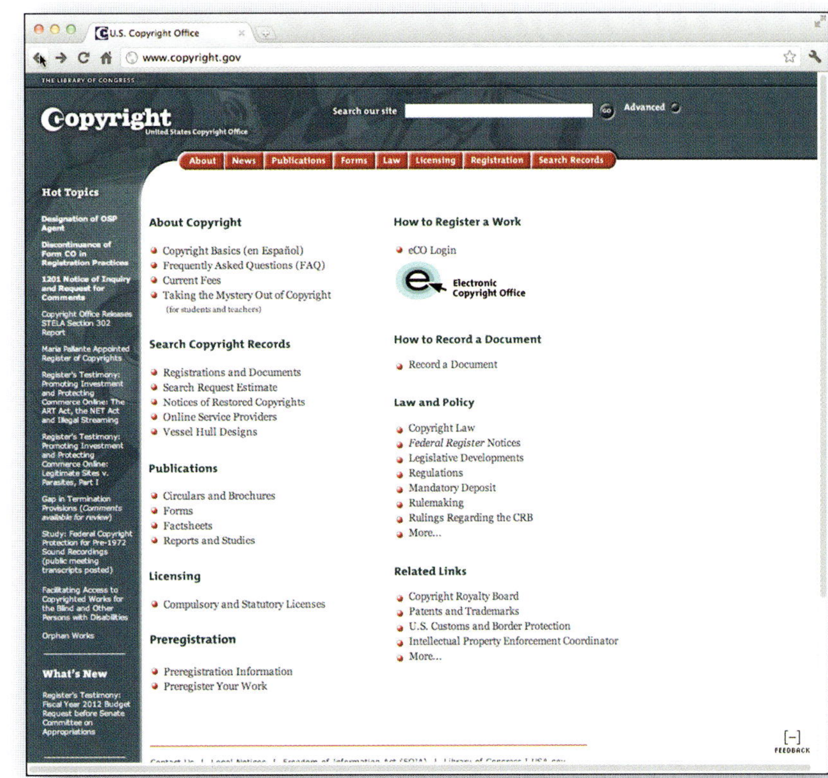

This is the home page of the United States Copyright Office. To start the registration process, click on the Electronic Copyright Office button.

Once you start the registration process, you need to use the website's Next and Back buttons (not the browser's forward and back buttons).

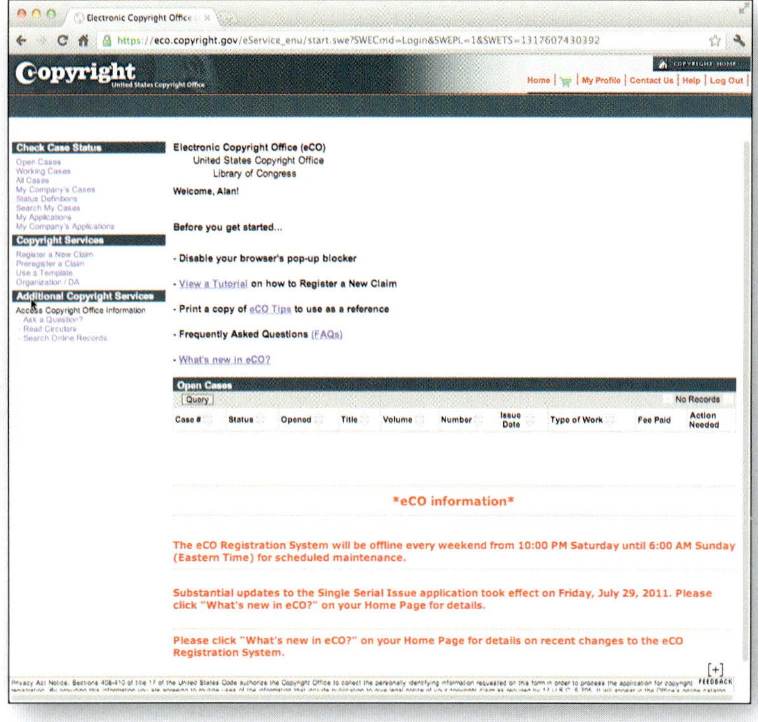

This is the Start page of the registration process. Click on Register a New Claim to begin.

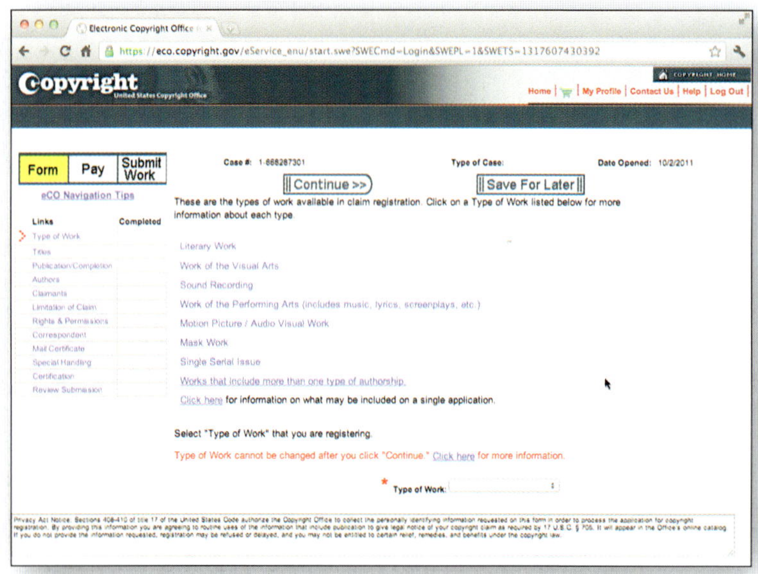

Pick the type of work you are registering.

registering an image, you'll have to create a username and password. Once you've entered this information, you can log in to the system and start registering your images.

On the left side of the page is a link to Register a New Claim. Click this to begin. It is possible to create a template to use the next time you need to register images. Do it, because this will make the whole process a lot faster … the next time. Your first time through the process requires you to complete all the steps.

When you click on Register a New Claim, the Start Registration page appears. This shows the three steps needed to complete your registration. The important thing on this page is to click on Start Registration at the top and not the three big links in the middle of the page. These just take you to Help pages about each step.

Now let's take a peek at each of the fields on the application:

- **Type of Work**
  Since we're talking about photographs in this book, pick *Work of the Visual Arts* from the choices in the drop-down menu on the bottom of the page. If you click on the link in the middle of the page, it will take you to a page that explains that the Visual Arts category includes photographs. Click Continue at the top of the page.

- **Title**
  Click the New button and enter the Title Type as Title of Work being registered from the drop-down menu. Then enter the title of the work. For example, I would enter *Bruce Hornsby in Concert - Belly Up Tavern - 9/11/2011* to register the photos I shot at that concert. Click Save. And click Continue to move on.

- **Publication/Completion**
  When you get to this page, you have to tell the Copyright Office if the work has been published or not. It is easier—less information is needed—if the answer to this question is No. In that case, all you need to answer is the year of completion, which is probably the current year if you're up to date on your image registrations.

  If, however, you answer Yes—your images have been published—then you need to enter the following additional information:

  - Year of Completion
  - Date of First Publication
  - Nation of First Publication
  - International Standard Number Type (Optional)
    If you have a Preregistration Number, you can enter it here. I never have completed this field and can't see any reason to provide this information.

  Click Continue.

- **Authors**
  The Author's page allows you to enter information on the author of the work. There are two options: *New* and *Add Me*. The first time you do this, you'll need to enter the information by clicking the New button. But the next time, you can just click the Add Me button.

  Enter your information in the fields. Keep in mind that only fields with the red asterisk are mandatory. Click on Save to open the Author Created page. Check the box next to Photograph(s) and click Save. Then click Continue.

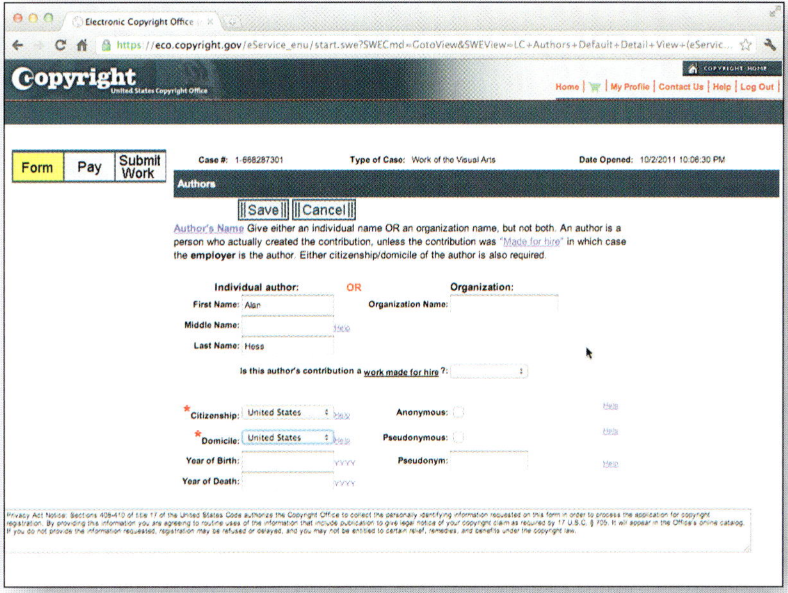

The fields with a red asterisk must to be completed to continue.

- **Claimants**
  Unless you've given away or sold the copyright to your image(s), then you are the claimant and need to add your info here. Click New and add all the information needed. When you're finished, click Save. Click Continue to move on.

- **Limitation of Claim**
  I have never limited the claim and I've never heard a good reason to do so. Click Continue here.

- **Rights & Permissions**
  This is where you can add information for people looking to use your work. If you have an agent, you might want to list them, but I like to manage my own images. Enter the information and click Continue.

- **Correspondents**
  You need to fill out this field so if anyone at the Copyright Office has a question about your registration, (s)he can contact you. Remember that the red asterisk means that you must enter the information requested. When this is completed, click Continue.

- **Mail Certificate**
  Enter the address of the location at which you want to receive the copyright certificate. Press Continue when done.

- **Special Handling**
  This is the expensive page. Here, the registration can jump from $35 to $760, but the additional costs are really only for people in the middle of litigation. If that's you, then ask your lawyer for advice on what to do here, because I think $760 is a lot of money. Click Continue.

- **Certification**
  The government reminds you here that it is against the law to furnish false information. When duly reminded, check the box and type in your name. When done, click Continue.

- **Review Submission**
  Check over all the information you've entered before paying the registration fee. Make sure everything is correct. When you've done that, click *Save Template* or *Add to Cart.*

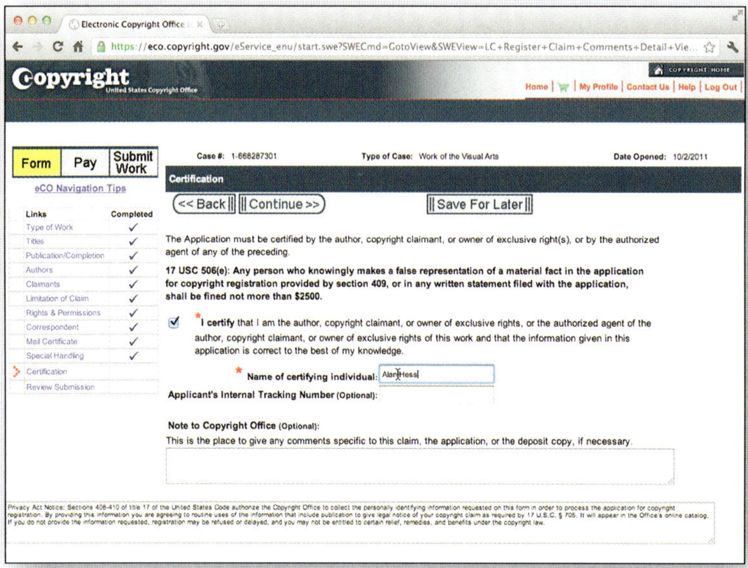

You have to make sure you don't lie to the government. They take that stuff very seriously.

If you save this as a template, you can use it the next time you want to register a set of images. Just remember to change the Title information the next time around, or there will be problems.

If you need to change anything on your forms, you can use the menu on the right side of the screen. Just click on the page you need to update and make your changes. Then click on the Review Submission page. Once you click Add to Cart, this information is locked.

PAY

When you've added your registration to your cart, you can pay for it. Just click on the Checkout button. This will take you to the pay site of the U.S. Treasury department.

You have two options here. You can pay using an account at the Treasury Department or with a credit card. I recommend using a credit card, because setting up an Treasury Department account is a long and boring process, while using a credit card is quick and easy. A credit card purchase also gives you a nice record of the fees paid when tax time comes around.

When you get to the payment page, you will see that it wants all your information ... just like any e-commerce site. Enter your credit card information and sign up for the email confirmation.

Note that the site warns that there might be a delay in the eCO site getting confirmation of your payment and that you can't proceed until eCO gets it. But I have never had to wait more than a few seconds.

UPLOAD IMAGES

After you pay your registration fee, you can begin uploading your images to the eCO site. Remember that folder of images you created at the beginning of this process? Well now is the time to upload it!

Start at the Home screen. Here, you'll see the case number of the current registration. Click on it to open the case. You'll see two options: you can choose to upload your images or mail them in. I upload, because it's easier and there's less of a chance that the images will get lost. If you want to send the images in by disk, then the mailing address is:

Library of Congress
Copyright Office
101 Independence Ave SE
Washington, DC 20559-6211

When you check the upload delivery option, you'll get a screen that asks you to navigate to the file that contains the images you want to upload. Pick the zipped file you created earlier and click on the *Submit Files to the Copyright Office* button. When the files are done uploading, you will receive a confirmation along with a service request number that can be useful if something goes wrong.

That's it. In a few weeks you'll receive a certificate from the U.S. Copyright Office. Ahhh ... feel that peace of mind?

WHY REGISTER?

It is true that when you press the shutter release button, you automatically create and own the copyright to the image you just created. But to really protect your ownership of the image, you need to register it. And when you file your registration with the Copyright Office, you get some other benefits that you otherwise don't have. For instance, with a registered image, you get:

- **Legal Backing**
  If your image is not registered with the Copyright Office and someone uses it without your permission, you cannot file a lawsuit. Your image has to be registered with the Copyright Office to enable you to file a Federal lawsuit against the thieves. Remember, copyright infringement is a Federal offense.
- **Infringement Compensation**
  If you register your image(s) and someone uses them without your permission, you can receive compensation at the value that you would have licensed or sold the image. The idea here is that you'll be paid the amount of money you would have received if the image had been sold instead of stolen.
- **Statutory Damages**
  You can choose not to sue for compensatory damages and instead sue for statutory damages, which can be greater. If you don't register, then you can't get either of these damages.
- **Reimbursement for Lawyer Fees**
  If you sue and win a copyright infringement case, then the defendant will be required to pay your lawyer fees as well as any award you receive through the verdict. This makes it pretty easy to get a lawyer, especially if your image is inappropriately used by a company with deep pockets.

DIGITAL MILLENNIUM COPYRIGHT ACT

The Digital Millennium Copyright Act (or DMCA) is a United States law that's meant to protect copyright holders from people who bypass digital rights management protection and use copyrighted works without permission. A key part of this law is that it limits the liability of online providers when their users infringe on a copyright.

So if I upload someone else's image to my website, for example, the company that hosts my website is not responsible. Now, this protection only stays in place if, when told about the copyright infringement, the online provider does something about it. This is where the DMCA takedown notice comes into play. It's the leverage you need to tell an online provider that your image has been used without permission ... and ensure it's removed.

If you find a website that's using one of your images and you want it removed, you have to contact the hosting ISP (Internet Service Provider) and report the unauthorized use. This works even if you haven't registered your work with the copyright office. The steps are pretty simple:

1. Find the website owners and hosting company by doing a free "who is " search at Whois.net
2. Notify the ISP by sending a letter/email that meets certain requirements. You must:
   - Put the notice in writing.
   - Sign the notice as the copyright holder (electronic signature is fine).
   - Identify the work(s) that were used without permission.
   - State that your complaint of unauthorized use is in "good faith."
   - State that the information in the letter/email is " under penalty of perjury, that the information contained in the notification is accurate."
   - State that you are the copyright owner and have the right to proceed.
   - Include your contact information.

I take screen captures of the infringing website and attach those to the email to make it perfectly clear what I'm talking about.

Be aware that I've had to send a notice like this more than once to address a single issue. And while a notice should be acted upon when it is received, it sometimes goes ignored the first time.

Sample Takedown Notice

TO: [Hosting company of infringing website]

SUBJECT: DMCA Takedown Notice

I am the copyright owner of photographs being infringed at:

[Infringing Web site URL]

I have included screen captures of the images that are being used without permission.

This is official notification under the provisions of Section 512(c) of the Digital Millennium Copyright Act ("DMCA") to effect removal of the above-reported infringements. I request takedown of the identified web pages or removal of the images from the pages. Please be advised that law requires you, as a service provider, to remove the infringing photographs upon receipt of this notice.

I have a good faith belief that this use of the attached image(s) is not authorized by me, the copyright holder, cut this. I swear under penalty of perjury, that the information contained in the notification is accurate and that I am the copyright holder.

[Your Name]

[Contact Information]

APPENDIX C: RESOURCES

Before sending you out into the wild world of concert photography, I want to provide a list of Internet resources for you to reference for additional information on the topics we've covered. These links are current as I write this in late 2011. But if they've changed or are no longer valid, I apologize. Use Google.com or your favorite search engine to find the current websites.

CAMERAS

NIKON

Nikon Imaging: http://imaging.nikon.com/index.htm
Nikon DSLR: http://imaging.nikon.com/lineup/dslr/index.htm
Nikon USA: http://www.nikonusa.com/index.page
Nikon Europe: http://www.europe-nikon.com/
Nikon Professional Services: http://www.nikonpro.com/

CANON

Canon Global: http://www.canon.com/
Canon DSLR: http://www.usa.canon.com/cusa/consumer/products/cameras/slr_cameras
Canon USA: http://www.usa.canon.com/cusa/home
Canon Professional Services: http://www.cps.usa.canon.com/

LENSES

Nikon: http://imaging.nikon.com/lineup/lens/
Canon: http://usa.canon.com/cusa/consumer/standard_display/Lens_Advantage_Select
Tamron: http://www.tamron.com/en/photolens/
Sigma: http://www.sigmaphoto.com/shop/lenses

MEMORY CARDS

Hoodman USA: http://www.hoodmanusa.com/
Lexar: http://www.lexar.com/
SanDisk: http://www.sandisk.com/

CAMERA BAGS

ThinkTankPhoto: http://www.thinktankphoto.com/
LowePro: http://www.lowepro.com/
Boda: http://www.goboda.com/main.html
Domke: http://www.tiffen.com/products.html?tablename=domke
Crumpler: http://www.crumpler.com

TRAINING

Kelby Training: http://kelbytraining.com/
National Association of Photoshop Professionals: http://www.photoshopuser.com/
Photoshop World: http://photoshopworld.com/

FLICKR GROUPS

Concert Photography: http://www.flickr.com/groups/concertshots/
Band Photography: http://www.flickr.com/groups/bandphotography/
Live Music: http://www.flickr.com/groups/live-music/
Rock and Roll: Live Shows Only: http://www.flickr.com/groups/rockandroll/
Concert Photographer: http://www.flickr.com/groups/concertphotographer/
Rock Photography: http://www.flickr.com/groups/rockphotography/
Music Makers: http://www.flickr.com/groups/musicmakers/

SOFTWARE

Adobe: http://www.adobe.com/
Adobe Photoshop: http://www.adobe.com/products/photoshopfamily.html
Adobe Lightroom: http://www.adobe.com/products/photoshoplightroom/
Nik Software: http://www.niksoftware.com
OnOne: http://www.ononesoftware.com/

PHOTOGRAPHERS

Jay Blakesburg: http://www.blakesberg.com/
Scott Diussa: http://www.scottdiussa.com
Herbie Greene: www.herbgreenefoto.com/
Drew Gurian: http://www.drewgurian.com/
Alan Hess: www.alanhessphotography.com
Charles Jischke: www.cfjphoto.com/cfjphoto/Home.html
Chelsea Lauren: http://www.chelsealauren.com/
Jim Marshall: www.jimmarshallphotographyllc.com/
Susana Millman: http://www.mamarazi.com/
Bob Minkin: http://www.minkindesign.com/photo/
Brad Moore: http://bmoorevisuals.com/
Todd Owyoung: http://ishootshows.com/
Allen Ross Thomas: http://www.artistxposure.com/

ONE LAST THING

Earplugs: http://www.earplugstore.com/

INDEX

A

B

D

E

F

J

K

L

M

R

S